From Perception to Meaning

Cognitive Linguistics Research
29

Editors
René Dirven
Ronald W. Langacker
John R. Taylor

Mouton de Gruyter
Berlin · New York

From Perception to Meaning

Image Schemas in Cognitive Linguistics

Edited by
Beate Hampe

In cooperation with
Joseph E. Grady

Mouton de Gruyter
Berlin · New York

Mouton de Gruyter (formerly Mouton, The Hague)
is a Division of Walter de Gruyter GmbH & Co. KG, Berlin

Library of Congress Cataloging-in-Publication Data

From perception to meaning : image schemas in cognitive linguistics /
edited by Beate Hampe in cooperation with Joseph E. Grady.
   p. cm. − (Cognitive linguistics research ; 29)
Includes bibliographical references and index.
ISBN-13: 978-3-11-018311-5 (cloth : alk. paper)
ISBN-10: 3-11-018311-0 (cloth : alk. paper)
   1. Cognitive grammar.   2. Imagery (Psychology)   3. Perception.
I. Hampe, Beate, 1968−   II. Grady, Joseph E.   III. Series.
P165.F76   2005
415−dc22
                                               2005031038

ISBN-13: 978-3-11-018311-5
ISBN-10: 3-11-018311-0
ISSN 1861-4132

Bibliographic information published by Die Deutsche Bibliothek

Die Deutsche Bibliothek lists this publication in the Deutsche Nationalbibliografie;
detailed bibliographic data is available in the Internet at <http://dnb.ddb.de>.

Preface and acknowledgements

In June 2004, an image schema workshop – unrelated to the project of this edition, but accidentally coinciding with its first deadline for chapter submission – was announced on the "CogLing" mailing list as a satellite event to "Language, Culture and Mind" (Portsmouth, July 2004). This announcement immediately kindled an intense, even fiery, debate, which made it plain that the notion of image schema is so central to the Cognitive-Linguistics enterprise that the possibility of an *embodied* and *experiential* view of linguistic meaning may to a considerable extent hinge on an adequate and generally accepted understanding of this notion. Less conveniently, this internet exchange also reflected that the latter is exactly what Cognitive Linguistics had so far not achieved.

In order to give a broader audience in Cognitive Linguistics and its neighbouring disciplines in the social and cognitive sciences access to the current state-of-the-art in image schema theory, "*From Perception to Meaning*" unites a comprehensive range of original papers by renowned scholars – many of whom have shaped image schema theory from the very beginning. Rather than trying to resolve all currently existing tensions into a completely unified notion, however, this collection is intended to document the innovations as well as inconsistencies that have accumulated over the past two decades, to take stock of both the question marks that accompany them, and the great promise they hold for advancing the entire field.

As Part I of this edition surveys image schema theory in great detail from a range of different angles, and as most authors in the other sections individually do so, too, the editor's introductory chapter will be restricted to a slim outline of the original conception as well as some of the major issues that have driven image schema research to date, and also shaped the contributions to this volume. In addition, all authors have provided summary abstracts of their chapters.

"*From Perception to Meaning*" is the result of the sustained commitment and joint hard work of a whole group of scholars. Without their outstanding sense of community and cooperation, this interdisciplinary edition could never have been assembled. The collection – for the most part made up of original papers elicited for the sole purpose of creating this book – brings together a range of divergent perspectives from Cognitive Linguistics and such neighbouring disciplines as anthropology, psychology, and the neurosciences. Two chapters are continuations of pertinent earlier research on spatial cognition and language (Talmy, *this volume*; Deane, *this volume*); the four chapters that originate in pertinent conference talks delivered at, e.g., the "7th International Cognitive Linguistics Conference", Santa Barbara 2001 (Grady, *this volume*; Popova, *this volume*), or the "Portsmouth Image Schema Workshop" (Zlatev, *this volume*; Beningfield et al., *this volume*), present much elaborated and updated versions of the respective earlier presentations. I thus wish to thank the contributors to this CLR volume for all of their patience and the efforts they have invested, which have ultimately turned their individual essays into the tightly connected chapters of a book project belonging to all of us.

I am also deeply grateful to the following colleagues from a range of disciplines, all of whom agreed to act as anonymous reviewers of the chapter drafts and thus provided the authors and myself with their invaluable feedback and support: *Benjamin Bergen, Geert Brône, Alan Cienki, Timothy Clausner, Herbert Colston, Seana Coulson, William Croft, Robert Dewell, René Dirven, Kurt Feyarts, Vittorio Galese, Dirk Geeraerts, Raymond Gibbs, Stefan Th. Gries, Ronald Langacker, Cornelia Müller, Gary Palmer, Naomi Quinn, Doris Schönefeld, Augusto Soares da Silva, Chris Sinha, Sarah Taub, Michael Tomasello,* and *Claude Vandeloise.*

I would further like to thank the series editors of *CLR*, especially *René Dirven*, for their generous and unwavering support from the very beginning. Many thanks for a very fruitful period of cooperation also go to *Birgit Sieverts* and *Monika Wendland* at Mouton, as well as to *Antje Lahne*, my student assistant in the final editing phase.

Lastly, but by no means least of all, I wish to thank *Joseph Grady* for joining me on this arduous journey. Without his initial encouragement, this project would probably never have got off the ground in the first place. Nor would I, without his continuous enthusiasm and feedback, have found the stamina to see this book all the way through to its final completion.

Beate Hampe,   Friedrich-Schiller-Universität Jena, September 2005

Table of contents

List of contributors

Alan J. Cienki
The Graduate Institute of the Liberal Arts and the Program in Linguistics, Emory University, Atlanta, GA
e-mail: anac@LearnLink.Emory.Edu

Timothy C. Clausner
HRL Laboratories, LLC, Malibu, CA
e-mail: clausner@hrl.com

Margarita Correa-Beningfield
Departamento de Filología Inglesa I,
Universidad Complutense de Madrid, Spain
e-mail: mcorrea@filol.ucm.es

Paul D. Deane
Educational Testing Service. Princeton, NJ
e-mail: pdeane@ets.org

Robert B. Dewell
Department of Modern Foreign Languages and Literatures,
Loyola University New Orleans, Alexandria, LA
e-mail: dewell@loyno.edu

Ellen Dodge
Linguistics Department, University of California, Berkeley, CA
e-mail: edodge@berkeley.edu

Raymond W. Gibbs, Jr.
Department of Psychology, University of California, Santa Cruz, CA
e-mail: gibbs@ucsc.edu

Joseph E. Grady
Cultural Logics, Providence, RI
e-mail: joegrady@cox.net

Beate Hampe
Institute of English and American Studies,
Friedrich-Schiller-Universität, Jena, Germany
e-mail: beate.hampe@uni-jena.de

Mark Johnson
Department of Philosophy, University of Oregon, Eugene, OR
e-mail: markj@uoregon.edu

Michael Kimmel
Institut für Europäische Integrationsforschung (EIF)
Österreichische Akademie der Wissenschaften (ÖAW), Wien, Österreich
e-mail: michael.kimmel@gmx.at

Gitte Kristiansen
Department of English Language and Linguistics,
Universidad Complutense de Madrid, Madrid, Spain
e-mail: gkristia@filol.ucm.es

George Lakoff
Departments of Linguistics and Cognitive Sciences,
University of California, Berkeley
e-mail: lakoff@berkeley.edu

Jean M. Mandler
Department of Cognitive Science, University of California, San Diego, CA,
and University College London
e-mail: jmandler@ucsd.edu

Ignasi Navarro-Ferrando
Departament d'Estudis Anglesos, Universitat Jaume I, Spain
e-mail: ignasi.navarro@ang.uji.es

Todd Oakley
Departments of English and Cognitive Science
Case Western Reserve University, Cleveland, OH
Email: todd.oakley@case.edu

Yanna Popova
University of Oxford, Hertford College, Oxford, U.K.
e-mail: yanna.popova@hertford.oxford.ac.uk

Tim Rohrer
Colorado Advanced Research Institute, Boulder, CO
e-mail: rohrer@cogsci.ucsd.edu

Leonard Talmy
    Department of Linguistics and Center for Cognitive Science,
    University at Buffalo, State University of New York, Buffalo, NY
    e-mail: talmy@buffalo.edu

Claude Vandeloise
    Department of French Studies, 205 Prescott Hall
    Louisiana State University, 70803, Baton Rouge, LA
    e-mail: vdllsu@aol.com

Jordan Zlatev
    Department of Linguistics, Center for Languages and Literature,
    Lund University, Lund, Sweden
    e-mail: jordan.zlatev@ling.lu.se

Image schemas in Cognitive Linguistics: Introduction

Beate Hampe[*]

> An image schema is a recurring dynamic pattern of our perceptual interactions and motor programs that gives coherence and structure to our experience. ... 'Experience' ... is to be understood in a very rich, broad sense as including basic perceptual, motor-program, emotional, historical, social and linguistic dimensions. (Johnson 1987: xiv, xvi)

1. The original notion in a nutshell

Advancing a non-objectivist, "experiential" approach to language and thought in their pathbreaking 1987 publications, George Lakoff and Mark Johnson jointly introduced the notion of "image schema" as one of experientialism's major foundational pillars, though with the linguist's and philosopher's different sources of inspiration and foci of interest (cf. Lakoff 1987: 459-461; Dodge and Lakoff, *this volume*; Johnson 1987: 19-21, *this volume*). My own cross-reading of their 1987 monographs for definitional criteria has yielded the following condensed characterization of their original conception:

- Image schemas are *directly meaningful* ("experiential"/ "embodied"), *preconceptual* structures, which arise from, or are grounded in, human recurrent bodily movements through space, perceptual interactions, and ways of manipulating objects.

- Image schemas are highly *schematic* gestalts which capture the structural *contours* of sensory-motor experience, integrating information from multiple modalities.

- Image schemas exist as *continuous* and *analogue* patterns *beneath* conscious awareness, prior to and independently of other concepts.

---

* I wish to thank Joe Grady for his very helpful comments on an earlier draft.

- As gestalts, image schemas are both *internally structured*, i.e., made up of very few related parts, and highly *flexible*. This flexibility becomes manifest in the numerous transformations they undergo in various experiential contexts, all of which are closely related to perceptual (gestalt) principles.

In conjunction with the capacity for conceptual metaphor, which allows human beings to map experiential structure from the "imagistic" realms of sensory-motor experience to non-imagistic ("abstract") ones, image schemas were hypothesized to provide one of the "embodied" anchors of the entire conceptual system (for a survey, cf. Johnson, *this volume*).

The initial identification of image schemas was mainly achieved through the cross-linguistic analysis of concepts of motion and spatial relations (cf. the survey in Dodge and Lakoff, *this volume*; Talmy, *this volume*), and the "informal analysis" of the phenomenological contours of every-day experience (cf. Johnson 1987, *this volume*). The image schemas in (1) appear in both Johnson (1987) and Lakoff (1987) and constitute the core of the standard inventory (cf. Johnson 1987: 126; Lakoff 1987: 267; Lakoff and Turner 1989: 97-98; Cienki 1997: 3, 12; Clausner and Croft 1999: 15); the more diverse items in (2a) occur only in Johnson's list,[1] and the orientational schemas in (2b) only in Lakoff's discussion. The image schema list has never constituted a closed set, and by far not all of the numerous subsequent additions were in such relatively close keeping with its original spirit, as the few additional examples given in (3).

(1) a. CONTAINMENT/CONTAINER, PATH/SOURCE-PATH-GOAL, LINK, PART-WHOLE, CENTER-PERIPHERY, BALANCE

     b. the FORCE schemas: ENABLEMENT, BLOCKAGE, COUNTERFORCE, ATTRACTION, COMPULSION, RESTRAINT, REMOVAL, DIVERSION

(2) a. CONTACT, SCALE, NEAR-FAR, SURFACE, FULL-EMPTY, PROCESS, CYCLE, ITERATION, MERGING, MATCHING, SPLITTING, OBJECT, COLLECTION, [MASS-COUNT], [SUPERIMPOSITION]

     b. UP-DOWN, FRONT-BACK

(3) a. INANIMATE MOTION, ANIMATE MOTION, SELF MOTION, CAUSED MOTION (Mandler 1992: 593-596), LOCOMOTION (Dodge and Lakoff, *this volume*)

---

1. MASS-COUNT and SUPERIMPOSITION, though included in Johnson's image-schema list, appeared as "image-schema transformations" in Lakoff (1987; cf. also Johnson 1987: 26).

b. EXPANSION (Turner 1991: 171), STRAIGHT (Cienki 1998), RESISTANCE (Gibbs et al. 1994: 235), LEFT-RIGHT (Clausner and Croft 1999: 15), ...

2. Divergent definitions, expanding lists, multiple perspectives

Much discussion of virtually all of the crucial dimensions of the initial definition was inspired by the fact that the original proposal and image schema lists were partly suggestive and not entirely consistent themselves. Various subsequent interpretations were based on divergent specifications of selected criteria, pertaining to, e.g., the relational character of image schemas, their level of specificity, or the role of perceptual information (for an in-depth discussion of these, cf. Grady, *this volume*). Turner's (1991: 57, 177) relatively loose conception of image schemas as "extremely skeletal images", to quote only one highly illustrative example here, did not only suggest a very close affinity to visual images, but was also much more inclusive than the original notion, allowing in even various geometrical configurations, such as "vertical lines ... ordered by relative size" (cf. Turner 1991: 177), as well as images normally regarded as basic-level ones, like that of a 'cup' or 'plate' (Turner 1991: 177), which contrast with the most closely related items on the standard image schema list, CONTAINER and SURFACE, along various of the aforementioned aspects. Other dimensions of the original proposal, such as the postulated preconceptual and unconscious nature of image schemas, or their assumed status as universal cognitive primitives have even caused considerable theoretical debate (cf. Zlatev 1997: 40-43, *this volume*).

Neither the original characterization, nor the entire subsequent research to date can thus be said to have provided the Cognitive-Linguistics community with a set of clear-cut criteria to set image-schematic representations apart from other basic or schematic concepts. It has thus been suggested that the failure to predict a complete image-schema inventory on the basis of any set of definitional criteria may not just stem from any disagreements over specific points, but be misguided in principle (cf. Clausner and Croft 1999: 21-22; Clausner, *this volume*). Clausner and Croft's (1999) suggestions to redefine image schemas as image-schematic domains on the basis of the *distributional* criterion of occurrence in a large number of domain matrices can thus also be understood as the rejection of any definitional attempts via necessary and sufficient criteria.

Apart from the various existing disagreements as to how inclusive or restrictive definitions of "image schema" should be, the notion has invited treatment from a variety of viewpoints and at multiple levels of analysis, which by necessity cut across established academic compartmentalizations and methods of investigation. Accordingly, attempts to elaborate and utilize the notion of image schema have been made within a range of different disciplines simultaneously. Traditionally, image schema theory has been driven by (neuro-)psychologically plausible linguistic analyses (e.g., Brugman [1981] 1988; Lindner 1983; Lakoff 1987: 440-444; Deane 1992, 1993, 1995; Dewell 1994, 1997; Kreitzer 1997) as well as philosophical considerations (Johnson 1987). While this is still the case (*this volume*: Johnson; Deane; Popova), studies along the lines of classic Cognitive Linguistics have for some time been amended by evidence from cognitive and developmental psychology (e.g., Gibbs and Colston 1995; Gibbs and Berg 2002; Gibbs, *this volume*; Mandler 1992, 1996, 2000, 2004, *this volume*), as well as from computer science (for surveys, cf. Lakoff and Johnson 1999: 569-583; Feldman and Narayanan, in press) and the neurosciences (e.g., Deane 1991, 1995; Gallese and Lakoff 2005; *this volume*: Lakoff and Dodge; Rohrer). To these, findings from cognitive anthropology (e.g., Quinn 1991; Shore 1996; Sinha and Jensen de López 2000; Kimmel, *this volume*) have been added for some time, which are now accompanied by work from such newly established smaller fields of enquiry as gesture studies (Cienki, *this volume*) or cognitive rhetoric (e.g., Turner 1991: 99-120; Oakley, *this volume*). While each of these areas of investigation naturally foregrounds distinct facets of the phenomenon, the resulting elaborations of the original conception of image schema should ideally be mutually compatible, or even re-inforcing. We might hope that such accounts would ultimately amount to a set of "converging evidence". Unfortunately, this collection also testifies to the fact that, in practice, this ideal has not been attained to date.

3.   Two long-standing dualisms and the embodiment hypothesis

Some of the more recent disagreements in image schema research may be of a more fundamental kind in that they stem from two broadly contrasting developments of the overarching notion of "embodiment" itself, one located in the broad context of cognitive psychology and the neurosciences, the other in cognitive anthropology and cognitive-cultural linguistics. Originally, the embodiment hypothesis was intended to overcome the *mind-body dualism* inherent in much of Cartesian scientific and philosophical thinking up to and including "first-generation" cognitive science, by grounding (universal) aspects of the human mind in (universal) aspects of the human body (Johnson 1987; Lakoff and Johnson 1999, 2002; Johnson, *this volume*). In order to back up and explain cognitive-linguistic findings, research in psycholinguistics, experimental and developmental psychology as well as cognitive neuro-science has sought to spell out earlier embodiment postulations in psychological terms (Gibbs et al. 1994; Gibbs and Colston 1995; Gibbs and Berg 2002; Gibbs, *this volume*; Mandler 1992, 1996, 2000, 2004, *this volume*) or in neuro-biological and neuro-computational terms (Gallese and Lakoff 2005; Dodge and Lakoff, *this volume*; Feldman and Narayanan, in press) – focussing on the human brain and the kind of processing/computing it affords. Accordingly, research in this direction has concentrated on general properties of human cognition, among them the "primitive" image schemas listed in the standard inventories (*this volume*: Grady; Lakoff and Dodge; Gibbs; Mandler; Rohrer; Dewell; Cienki; Popova).

It has been critically noted that this line of research – especially if relying on "strong neural embodiment" (Sinha 2002: 274) – has maintained a "universalistic" conception of the mind and tended to obscure the socio-cultural dimensions of human cognition. Another long-standing *dualism*, namely that *between individual and social/cultural cognition*, has thus been left intact (cf. Sinha and Jensen de López 2000; Kimmel, *this volume*). To make up for this, proponents of the "cultural-cognition" approach to the embodiment hypothesis have striven to understand language and cognition as part of the *triad body-mind-culture*, and "extended" the notion of embodiment – with its original focus on bodily (as opposed to social) experience – by "situating" cognition in socio-culturally determined contexts. They have thus naturally come to stress culture-specificity and linguistic relativity (cf., e.g., Zlatev 1997; Sinha 2002). Research in this framework has consequently focussed on "situated" instantiations of image schemas and image-schematic "compounds" in real settings (e.g., Shore 1996; Kimmel, *this volume*), as well as on the divergent strategies employed by specific languages to refer to image-schematic dimensions of experience and their consequences for the acquisition of concepts and language (e.g., Bowerman 1996a,b; Sinha and Jensen de López 2000; Beningfield et al., *this volume*).

Though the two strands of embodiment research have so far not been integrated in a unified theory of image schema, proponents of both approaches to the embodiment hypothesis have also stressed that cognitive models and schemas – including image schemas – can be seen both as expressions of universal principles at work in individual cognition *and* as properties of an underlying, "institutionalized" cultural "world view" (cf., e.g., Shore 1996; Palmer 1996). Consequently, a "naturalistic, biologically informed approach to human cognition" does not necessarily preclude "the recognition of the constitutive role in it of culture" (Sinha 2002: 273), for the general constraints created by shared biology and basic environmental dimensions leave enough room for "extensive cultural variation" (Lakoff and Johnson 2002: 251). It is thus worth noting that some of the more intensely debated cross-linguistic evidence, such as the Zapotec concept corresponding to what is split up into 'in' and 'under' in languages like Danish and English (Sinha and Jensen de López 2000), or the distinction between 'tight' and 'loose' fit made by the Korean verb system is revisited by various authors in this edition – both of a "universalistic" and more "relativistic" orientation (*this volume*: Dodge and Lakoff; Mandler; Kimmel; Zlatev; Beningfield et al., Dewell).

4. Preview of this edition

In the following, I will very briefly remark on the five sections of this edition in order to complement the separate chapter abstracts and cross-references provided by the authors themselves with a general survey of the edition.

The chapters in PART 1 (ISSUES IN IMAGE SCHEMA THEORY) deal with major theoretical issues concerning philosophical and linguistic significance of ("primitive") image schemas as "structures of perceiving and doing" which "can be recruited to structure abstract concepts and to carry out inferences about abstract domains" (Johnson, *this volume*). In particular, the main issues discussed relate to the identification and resolution of definitional inconsistencies (Grady, *this volume*), the relevance of neurobiological information to a truly cognitive approach to language and thought (Dodge and Lakoff, *this volume*), as well as – from a more general meta-theoretical perspective – to image-schema theory as an important part of the experiential framework developed by Cognitive Semantics as a whole (Clausner, *this volume*). A theme reverberating throughout the entire volume (*this volume*: Gibbs; Kimmel) is set up by Mark Johnson's concerns that image schemas should not be conceived of as "fleshless skeletons" cut off from "the felt qualities of our experience, understanding and thought".

The chapters in PART 2 (IMAGE SCHEMAS IN MIND AND BRAIN) bring together much of the psychological and neurological evidence currently available for image schemas as structures between perception and conception. In accordance with growing consensus in the cognitive sciences about the "embodied" roots of conception in perception, several chapters are guided by the assumption that both imagination and (language) understanding are based to some extent on the "mental simulation" of sensory-motor experiences, the outlines of which are captured by image schemas (*this volume*: Gibbs; Rohrer; Dodge and Lakoff). These simulations are hypothesized to underlie many aspects of on-line cognition and language processing (Gibbs: *this volume*), and even to share brain circuitry with the sensory-motor system (Galese and Lakoff 2005; *this volume*: Rohrer; Dodge and Lakoff), though there is some disagreement about the (in parts still highly speculative) specifics of this. Another major theme of this section pertains to image-schema formation itself, which Jean Mandler (*this volume*) discusses in great detail in terms of the attention-driven, innately given process she calls "perceptual meaning analysis", but for which other authors offer competing explanations in terms of self-organizing dynamic systems (Gibbs, *this volume*) or in terms of the properties of the brain circuitry involved (Dodge and Lakoff, *this volume*).

As research on spatial cognition and language has constituted one of the sources of image schema theory as well as one of its most productive areas of application, PART 3 (IMAGE SCHEMAS IN SPATIAL COGNITION AND LANGUAGE) of this edition offers two extensive papers on the conceptualization and linguistic expression of spatial relations. Leonard Talmy's (1983) work is generally acknowledged to be one of the main inspirations of image-schema theory (cf. Lakoff 1987: 459-461; Dodge and Lakoff, *this volume*), the section thus includes a chapter in which he continues to investigate the distinctions in the conceptualization of space that can generally be made by the closed-class elements of the spoken (vs. signed) languages around the world. Paul Deane's chapter in this section revisits the long-standing and still unresolved issue of the semantic unity of highly polysemous spatial-relations terms and presents a detailed, neuro-psychologically informed, image-based analysis of *over* – the one spatial-relations term that has, together with some of its equivalents in other Indo-European languages, enjoyed the vastest amount of attention since the first application of the notion of image schema to the analysis of prepositional polysemy (cf., e.g., Brugman [1981] 1988; Lakoff 1987: 416-461; Geeraerts 1992; Dewell 1994; Kreitzer 1997; Tyler and Evans 2001).

PART 4 (IMAGE SCHEMAS AND BEYOND) collects papers that expand or even reject the notion of image schema as currently conceived, whereby it is noteworthy that all authors in this section share a commitment to "extended", or "situated" embodiment (cf. Zlatev 1997; Sinha 2002). Michael Kimmel's contribution reviews a large range of evidence from cognitive anthropology supporting "extended" notions of embodiment in general and of image schema in particular. He suggests that image schema theory has hitherto neglected the study of "situated" as well as "compound" image schemas, both of which are tied to culture-specific, affect-laden experience defined by body practices, artefact use and specific languages. The remaining two chapters in PART IV (*this volume*: Zlatev; Beningfield et al.) comment on image schema theory via comparisons with two alternative conceptions, namely Jordan Zlatev's "mimetic schema", and Claude Vandeloise's notion of "Complex Primitive" (Beningfield et al., *this volume*). Hopefully, these may help to sharpen the awareness and discussion of a potential blind spot within image schema theory itself which might stem from the "universalist bias" in the standard account (cf. Kimmel, *this volume*) and which relates to the way in which specific languages force universal preconceptual structures into culturally determined, consciously accessible, public and conventional concepts.

The chapters in PART 5 (NEW CASE STUDIES ON IMAGE SCHEMAS), finally, present four highly diverse and detailed case studies (*this volume*: Dewell, Popova, Cienki, Oakley), all to some extent explorative, rather than merely applicative, and all with theoretical implications that reach well beyond their immediate subjects of investigation. Robert Dewell performs an in-depth "informal phenomenological analysis" (Johnson, *this volume*) of developmentally early CONTAINMENT patterns from which he concludes that image schemas are highly dynamic conceptual patterns that exist only in the multitude of their transformations. Yanna Popova's case study on synaesthetic adjective-noun combination in present-day British English addresses the cross-modal character of image schemas from a new angle, and especially deals with the role of non-visual perceptual information in image schemas. Utilizing existing knowledge about the lower perceptual modalities, touch and taste, and about the cross-modal mappings in verbal synaesthesia, it aims to establish the perceptual origin of the SCALE schema in the lower modalities, which are argued to contrast with higher ones, sound and vision, in being inherently graded and normative. Alan Cienki's chapter reports on experiments which constitute the first attempt to bring together image schema research and gesture studies, both in order to understand the role of gestures in "thinking for speaking" and to exploit gestures as a new source of empirical evidence for image schemas. Todd Oakley, finally, presents a fine-grained force-dynamic analysis of two very different, but highly influential political speeches from the history and present of the United States. In the spirit of Mark Turner's (1991: 99-120) work on the force-dynamic image schemas motivating many metaphors of everyday as well as rhetoricians' conceptions of argumentation, he intends to advance the (re-) establishment of rhetoric as one of the cognitive sciences.

5. Resumé

My preceding remarks may have underemphasized that, despite of all theoretical and practical complications, the concept of image schema has without doubt proved extremely fruitful in the past two decades and inspired research in a broad variety of fields both inside and outside linguistics. Still, the highly diverse positions to be found in current image-schema theory, many of which are documented in this edition, also indicate strongly that renewed discussion within Cognitive Linguistics is necessary to ensure the theoretical unity of the notion and to maintain its value as a central and foundational concept of Cognitive Semantics, as the field is progressing towards a deeper understanding of the embodied roots of cognition and language.

References

Bowerman, Melissa
    1996a   The origins of children's spatial semantic categories: Cognitive versus linguistic determinants. In *Rethinking Linguistic Relativity*. John J. Gumperz and Stephen C. Levinson (eds.), 145-176. Cambridge/New York: Cambridge University Press.
    1996b   Learning how to structure space for language: A cross-linguistic perspective. In *Language and Space*. Paul Bloom, Mary A. Peterson, Lynn Nadel, and Merill F. Garrett (eds.), 385-436. Cambridge, MA, and London: The MIT Press.

Brugman, Claudia
    1988   *The Story of over. Polysemy, Semantics and the Structure of the Lexicon.* New York: Garland [originally: M.A. thesis at the University of California, Berkeley, 1981].

Cienki, Alan
    1997   Some properties and groupings of image schemas. In *Lexical and Syntactical Constructions and the Construction of Meaning,* Marjolijn Verspoor, Kee Dong Lee, & Eve Sweetser (eds.), 3-15. Amsterdam/Philadelphia: John Benjamins.

Clausner, Timothy, and William Croft
    1999   Domains and image schemas. *Cognitive Linguistics* 10: 1-31.

Deane, Paul D.
    1991   Syntax and the brain: Neurological Evidence for the Spatialization of Form Hypothesis. *Cognitive Linguistics* 2: 361-367.
    1992   *Grammar in Mind and Brain. Explorations in Cognitive Syntax.* Berlin/New York: Mouton de Gruyter.
    1993   *At, by, to,* and *past*: An essay in multimodal image theory. *Berkeley Linguistics Society* 19: 112-124.
    1995   Neurological evidence for a cognitive theory of syntax: Agrammatic aphasia and the Spatialization of Form hypothesis. In *Cognitive Linguistics in the Redwoods: The Expansion of a New Paradigm in Linguistics*, Eugene H. Casad (ed.), 55-115. Berlin/New York: Mouton de Gruyter.

Dewell, Robert B.
    1994   *Over* again: Image-schema transformations in semantic analysis. *Cognitive Linguistics* 5: 351-380.
    1997   Construal Transformations: Internal and External Viewpoints in Interpreting Containment. In *Lexical and Syntactical Constructions and the Construction of Meaning*, Marjolijn Verspoor, Kee Dong Lee and Eve Sweetser (eds), 17-32. Amsterdam/Philadephia: Benjamins.

Feldman, Jerome, and Srinivas Narayanan
   in press   Embodied meaning in a neural theory of language. *Brain and Language*

Gallese, Vittorio, and George Lakoff
    2005   The Brain's concepts: The role of the sensory-motor system in conceptual knowledge. *Cognitive Neuropsychology* 22: 455-479.

Geeraerts, Dirk
    1992   The semantic structure of Dutch *over*. *Leuvense Bijdragen* 81: 205-230.

Gibbs, Raymond W., Jr., and Eric A. Berg
    2002   Mental Imagery and Embodied Activity. *Journal of Mental Imagery* 26: 1-30.
Gibbs, Raymond W., Jr., and Herbert L. Colston
    1995   The cognitive psychological reality of image schemas and their transformations. *Cognitive Linguistics* 6: 347-378.
Gibbs, Raymond W., Jr., Dinara A. Beitel, Michael Harrington, and Paul E. Sanders
    1994   Taking a stand on the meanings of stand: Bodily experience as motivation for Polysemy. *Journal of Semantics* 11: 231-251.
Johnson, Mark
    1987   *The Body in the Mind. The Bodily Basis of Meaning, Imagination, and Reason.* Chicago: Chicago University Press.
Kreitzer, Anatol
    1997   Multiple levels of schematization: A study in the conceptualization of space. *Cognitive Linguistics* 8: 291-325.
Lakoff, George
    1987   *Women, Fire and Dangerous Things. What Categories reveal about the Mind.* Chicago: The University of Chicago Press.
Lakoff, George, and Mark Johnson
    1999   *Philosophy in the Flesh. The Embodied Mind and its Challenge to Western Thought.* New York: Basic Books.
    2002   Why cognitive linguistics requires embodied realism. *Cognitive Linguistics* 13: 245-263.
Lakoff, George, and Mark Turner
    1989   *More than Cool Reason. A field Guide to Poetic Metaphor.* Chicago: The University of Chicago Press.
Lindner, Susan
    1983   *A Lexico-Semantic Analysis of English Verb-Particle Constructions.* Trier: L.A.U.T. (series A: 101).
Mandler, Jean M.
    1992   How to build a baby: II. Conceptual Primitives. *Psychological Review* 99: 587-604.
    1996   Preverbal Representation and Language. In *Language and Space*, Paul Bloom, Mary A. Peterson, Lynn Nadel and Merrill F. Garrett (eds.), 365-384. Cambridge, MA, and London: The MIT Press.
    2000   Perceptual and conceptual processes in infancy. *Journal of Cognition and Development* 1: 3-36.
    2004   *The Foundations of Mind: Origins of Conceptual Thought.* Oxford: Oxford University Press.

Palmer, Gary
    1996   *Towards a Theory of Cultural Linguistics*. Austin: University of Texas Press.

Quinn, Naomi
    1991   The cultural basis of metaphor. In *Beyond Tropes: The Theory of Tropes in Anthropology*, J.W. Fernandez (ed.), 56-93. Stanford: Stanford University Press.

Sinha, Chris
    2002   The cost of renovating the property: A reply to Marina Rakova. *Cognitive Linguistics* 13: 271-276.

Sinha, Chris, and Kristine Jensen de Lopez
    2000   Language, Culture and the Embodiment of Spatial Cognition. *Cognitive Linguistics* 11: 17-41.

Shore, Bradd
    1996   *Culture in Mind. Cognition, Culture, and the Problem of Meaning*. New York/Oxford: Oxford University Press.

Talmy, Leonard
    1983   How Language structures Space. In *Spatial Orientation: Theory, Research and Application*, Herbert Pick and Linda Acredolo (eds.), 225-282. New York: Plenum Press.

Turner, Mark
    1991   *Reading Minds. The Study of English in the Age of Cognitive Sciences*. Princeton, NJ: Princeton University Press.

Tyler, Andrea, and Vyvyan Evans
    2001   Reconsidering prepositional polysemy networks: The case of *over. Language* 77: 724-765.

Zlatev, Jordan
    1997   *Situated Embodiment. Studies in the Emergence of Spatial Meaning*. Stockholm: Gotab.

Part 1: Issues in image schema theory

The philosophical significance of image schemas

Mark Johnson

Abstract

From a philosophical perspective image schemas are important primarily because they help to explain how our intrinsically embodied mind can at the same time be capable of abstract thought. As patterns of sensory-motor experience, image schemas play a crucial role in the emergence of meaning and in our ability to engage in abstract conceptualization and reasoning that is grounded in our bodily engagement with our environment. However, our current accounts of the workings of image-schematic structure do not adequately capture the felt, qualitative aspects of embodied human understanding. To the extent that these accounts remain exclusively structural, they are bound to leave out significant dimensions of human meaning.

Keywords: embodied mind, meaning, metaphor, imagination, reasoning

1.   The problem solved by image schemas

The term "image schema" first appeared simultaneously in 1987 in my book *The Body in the Mind* and in George Lakoff's *Women, Fire, and Dangerous Things.*[1] Our conception of an image schema was a key part of our explanation of the embodied origins of human meaning and thought. At that time, we were grappling (and still are) with a profound philosophical, psychological, and linguistic problem: What makes meaning and reason possible for creatures like us, whose cognitive operations are embodied? If the human mind is embodied – that is, if there is no fundamental ontological separation of "mind" and "body" – then how are we capable of abstract conceptualization and reasoning? In other words, how do meaning, imagination, and reason – the marks of human intelligence – emerge from our organic, bodily interactions with our environment?

---

1. Although the term itself was new, the basic idea had been partially anticipated at least in the works of Immanuel Kant, Maurice Merleau-Ponty, William James, and John Dewey.

If, as I do, you reject (on scientific, philosophical and moral grounds) the notion of disembodied mind, then it is incumbent on you to explain how all of our marvelous feats of abstract thought are possible. Scientifically, there is a growing mountain of empirical evidence from the cognitive sciences that there can be no thought without a brain in a body in an environment. Moreover, the nature of our brains, bodies, and environments constrains and shapes what and how we understand and reason. Philosophically, thinkers as diverse in their orientation as John Dewey ([1925] 1958), Maurice Merleau-Ponty ([1945] 1962), and Patricia Churchland (2002) have lambasted all of the ontological and epistemological dualisms (such as mind/body, subject/object, cognition/emotion, and knowledge/imagination) that characterize large parts of Western philosophy of mind and language. Finally, from a moral perspective, the legacy of disembodied mind has generated ethical theories that are incompatible with what psychology tells us about mind, motivation, value, and reason. We thus need to replace disembodied accounts of meaning, thought and reason with an alternative general theory of embodied cognition capable of explaining where our concepts come from, and capable of explaining the syntax, semantics, and pragmatics of natural languages. Obviously, this is not just a question about language. It is a question about the possibility of human cognition, and it applies to all forms of symbolic human interaction and expression. It is a question about where meaning comes from and how thought is possible.

The basic form of the answer to this embodiment problem appears to be this: Structures of *perceiving* and *doing* must be appropriated to shape our acts of *understanding* and *knowing*. Our sensory-motor capacities must be recruited for abstract thinking. If you approach this problem at the level of concepts, then you want to know where conceptual structure comes from for both concrete (e.g., 'tree', 'house', 'on', 'in front of') and abstract concepts (e.g., 'mind', 'ideas', 'knowledge', 'justice') and how relations of concepts support inferences. Answering this question leads you to focus on *structure.* That is, you must identify structures of sensory-motor experience – image schemas – which can be used to understand abstract concepts and to perform abstract reasoning.

Historically, Immanuel Kant was one of the first to deal extensively with a similar problem, the problem of how concepts, which he thought of as formal structures, could ever be applied to the "matter" of sensory perception. In his *Critique of Pure Reason* ([1781] 1968), in the famous chapter on "The Schematism of the Pure Concepts of Understanding," Kant tried to find a connecting link, a "third thing," that would bind the concept, which he thought of as *formal,* to the *matter* of sensation. That necessary connecting link, he claimed, was the "schema" of a concept, by which he meant a procedure of imagination for structuring images in accordance with concepts. Consider Kant's example of the schema for the concept *dog.* The schema is neither the *concept* dog, nor a particular *image* of a dog, nor the actual furry creature that wags its tail and looks cheerfully up at you. Instead, Kant asserted that the schema for *dog* is a procedure of imagination for constructing an image of a certain kind of four-footed furry animal, so that the image manifests all of the features that are specified by the concept one has of a dog. To cite another of Kant's examples, the schema for the concept *triangle* would be a specific "rule of synthesis of the imagination, in respect to pure figures in space" (Kant 1968: A141/B180), in this case, it would be a rule of imagination for constructing an image of a three-sided closed plane figure.

The chief problem with Kant's account is that it is based on an absolute dichotomy between form and matter. He thought there could be "pure" form – form without empirical content – and his problem was to explain how this form could get connected to the material aspects of experience. But if you define form as radically distinguished from matter, then it is hard to see how there could be some "third thing", something that is *both* formal *and* material, that could bridge the alleged gap between the formal and the material aspects of cognition. Kant's candidate for this bridging function was imagination, which he thought of as a formal, structure-giving capacity to order material sensations into unified wholes of experience.

I have no interest in defending Kant's general metaphysical system, which seems to me to be too laden with a disastrous set of fundamental ontological and epistemological dichotomies, such as form vs. matter, mental vs. physical, pure vs. empirical, and cognition vs. emotion. Once such dichotomies are assumed, they create absolute unbridgeable gaps that cannot capture the continuous and multi-dimensional character of our experience and understanding. However, what *is* worth salvaging from Kant's account is his recognition of imagination as the locus of human meaning, thought, and judgment. Kant correctly recognized the schematizing, form-giving function of human imagination. Imagination is not an activity of alleged pure understanding or reason, but rather is an embodied process of human meaning-making that is responsible for the order, quality, and significance in terms of which we are able to make sense of our experience. What Kant called the "faculty of imagination" is not a discrete *faculty,* but rather multiple processes for discerning and utilizing structure within our experience.

Moreover, we must not think of imagination as merely a subjective, idio-syncratic private "mental" operation to be contrasted with objective thought and reason. Imaginative activity occurs, instead, in the ongoing flow of our everyday experience that is neither merely mental nor merely bodily, neither merely cognitive nor emotional, and neither thought alone nor feeling alone. All of these dimensions are inextricably tied up together in the perceptual and motor patterns of organism-environment interaction, which provide the basis for our patterns of understanding and thought. What we identify as the "mental" and then contrast with the "bodily" dimensions of our experience are really just abstractions from the embodied patterns and activities that make up that experience. What we call "mind" and "body" are not separate things. Rather, we use these terms to make sense of various aspects of the flow of our experience. *Image schemas are some of the basic patterns of that flow.*

2. Where do image schemas come from?

The correct part of Kant's view is his understanding of the pervasive imagi-native structuring of all experience. Unfortunately, because Kant believed in the existence of pure (non-empirical) autonomous reason, he did not recog-nize the crucial role of imagination in *all thought*. Subsequently, it took the non-dualistic philosophies of people such as William James (1890), John Dewey (1958), and Maurice Merleau-Ponty (1962) – and, later, the bur-geoning work of neonate cognitive neuroscience – to articulate a richer em-bodied view of imagination, meaning, and thought. James, Dewey, and Mer-leau-Ponty all shared the fundamental insight that mind and body are not two things or substances somehow yoked together, but rather that what we *call* "mind" and "body" are aspects of an ongoing sequence of organism-environment interactions that are at once both physical *and* mental. They recognized that the human mind is embodied – that all of our meaning, thought, and symbolic expressions are grounded in patterns of perception and bodily movement. George Lakoff and I (Johnson 1987; Lakoff 1987) coined the term "*image* schema" primarily to emphasize the bodily, sensory-motor nature of various structures of our conceptualization and reasoning. We wanted to stress that image schemas are not archetypes of some alleg-edly pure form-making capacity (as Kant had held), nor are they merely abstract knowledge structures (such as Schank and Abelson's (1977) notion of a "script"). Instead, image schemas are the recurring patterns of our sensory-motor experience by means of which we can make sense of that experience and reason about it, and that can also be recruited to structure abstract concepts and to carry out inferences about abstract domains of thought.

In the terms of contemporary cognitive neuroscience, we would say that image schemas are not the products of some (non-existent) autonomous neural modules for producing form, but rather are patterns characterizing invariant structures within topological neural maps for various sensory and motor areas of the brain. In his book *The Human Semantic Potential* (1996) Terry Regier has developed what he calls "constrained connectionist" models that are able to compute the image-schematic structures of a range of selected spatial terms. The built-in constraints of such connectionist networks are intended to represent known neural architectures, such as motion detectors, spreading activation, orientation-sensitive cells, and center-surround structures. These networks can learn to correctly apply terms for spatial relations and motions (such as *on, above, below, outside, to the right (left) of, across,* and *into*) to movies of static and moving objects.

In speaking of image schemas as invariant topological structures in various perceptual and motor maps, however, we must not think of image schemas as existing merely in the brain apart from the bodily perceptions, feelings, and actions in which that brain plays a central role. We must always remember that image schemas exist only for organisms that have certain kinds of brain architecture, operating within bodies of a particular physiological makeup, interacting with environments that offer very specific "affordances" (Gibson 1979) for creatures like us.[2]

3.   Identifying image schemas

Since an image schema is a dynamic recurring pattern of organism-environment interactions, it will often reveal itself in the contours of our basic sensory-motor experience. Consequently, one way to begin to survey the range of image schemas is via a phenomenological description of the most basic structural features of all human bodily experience. When I speak

---

2. A Gibsonian "affordance" is a pattern of potential engagement and interaction with parts of our environment. A chair "affords" sit-on-ability for human beings, but not for elephants. A cup "affords" grasp-ability for human beings, but not for a sea slug. An affordance is thus relative to the makeup of the organism, and yet it is an objective feature of the environment *for that organism with its particular embodiment and perceptual and motor capacities.*

of a phenomenological survey of image schemas, I do not mean the use of anything like a formal Husserlian method of "transcendental reduction,"[3] but rather only a reflective interrogation of recurring patterns of our embodied experience. Ask yourself what the most fundamental structures of your perception, object manipulation, and bodily movement are, given that human bodies share several quite specific sensory-motor capacities keyed to the size and constitution of our bodies and to the common characteristics of the different environments we inhabit. Certain obvious patterns immediately jump out at you. For example, given the relative bilateral symmetry of our bodies, we have an intimate acquaintance with right-left symmetry. As Mark Turner (1991) observes, if we were non-symmetric creatures floating in a liquid medium with no up or down, no right or left, no front or back, the meaning of our bodily experience would be quite different from the ways we *actually* do make sense of things. Because of our particular embodiment, we project RIGHT and LEFT, FRONT and BACK, NEAR and FAR, throughout the horizon of our perceptual interactions. In fact, the very concept HORIZON is image-schematic. Our perceptual fields have focal areas that fade off into a vague horizon of possible experiences that are not currently at the center of our conscious awareness. Hence, it comes as no surprise that we have a CENTER-PERIPHERY image schema. Because of our ongoing bodily encounter with physical forces that push and pull us, we experience the image-schematic structures of COMPULSION, ATTRACTION, and BLOCKAGE OF MOVEMENT, to name but a few aspects of what Leonard Talmy (1983) calls "force dynamics." The bodily logic of such force schemas will involve inferences about speed of movement, the rhythmic flow of movement, whether a moving object starts and stops, and so on.

There are quite distinctive patterns and logics to these dimensions of our perception of moving objects and of our kinesthetic sense of our own motion. Because we exist within a gravitational field at the earth's surface, and due to our ability to stand erect, we give great significance to standing up, rising, and falling down. Our understanding of these bodily experiences is organized by a VERTICALITY schema. We experience and draw inferences about RECTILINEAR MOTION (Cienki 1998) and draw different inferences about curved motions or deviating motions that have no obvious goal (relative to a SOURCE-PATH-GOAL schema). Because we must continually monitor our

---

3. Husserl ([1913] 1931) proposed a method of "suspending" one's practical engagement with everyday experience in order to supposedly allow the fundamental structures of experience to reveal themselves.

own changing bodily states, we are exquisitely attuned to changes in degree, intensity, and quality of feelings, which is the basis for our sense of scales of intensity of a quality (the SCALARITY schema). Because we must constantly interact with containers of all shapes and sizes, we naturally learn the "logic" of containment (for the CONTAINER schema).

Through this type of informal phenomenological analysis of the structural dimensions of our sensory-motor experience, most of the basic image schemas will show themselves. However, we must keep in mind that phenomenological analysis alone is never enough, because image schemas typically operate beneath the level of conscious awareness. That is why we must go beyond phenomenology to employ standard explanatory methods of linguistics, psychology, and neuroscience that allow us to probe structures within our unconscious thought processes. A great deal of our current knowledge of image schemas comes from linguistic analyses of their role in the semantics of spatial terms and bodily operations and of their role in conceptualizing and reasoning about abstract domains. Originally, Lakoff and I hypothesized the existence of various image schemas, in order to frame explanatory generalizations concerning syntactic, semantic, and pragmatic aspects of language and other forms of symbolic interaction. Over the past two decades a burgeoning body of empirical linguistic research has explored the role of image-schematic structures in a vast array of syntactic and semantic phenomena in languages around the world. Raymond Gibbs and Herbert Colston (1995) have described the main types of empirical evidence currently available for image schemas (see also Gibbs, *this volume*). And there is considerable evidence concerning the role of image schemas in inference (Lakoff 1987; Lakoff and Johnson 1999; Lakoff and Nunez 2000).

Alan Cienki (1997) has compiled a list of basic image schemas, although he recognizes that it is probably not exhaustive. Many complex image schemas are built up from the basic ones through processes of combination, superimposition, and further elaboration or specification. Lakoff and Nunez (2000), for instance, have shown how the meanings of *into* and *out of* involve the superimposition of a SOURCE-PATH-GOAL image schema onto a CONTAINER schema. For example, *into* is based on a CONTAINER schema with the interior profiled and with the goal of the SOURCE-PATH-GOAL schema located within the interior of the container, thus capturing the motion of an object from a starting location outside the container to an endpoint within the container.

Three important aspects of image schemas can now be emphasized. First, image schemas are an important part of what makes it possible for our bodily experiences to have meaning for us. The meaning is that of the recurring structures and patterns of our sensory-motor experience. As such, it typically operates beneath the level of our conscious awareness, although it also plays a role in our discrimination of the contours of our bodily orientation and experience. Meaning structures of this sort are part of what Lakoff and I (1999) call the "Cognitive Unconscious". For example, humans will share certain general understandings of what it means for something to be located within a container, and will understand at least part of this without having to reflect upon it or think about it. Seeing a container, or hearing or reading the word *in* will activate a CONTAINER image schema as crucial to our understanding of a particular scene. Certain types and sizes of containers will offer different specific affordances for a being with our type of body, brain, and environments.

Second, there is a *logic* of image-schematic structure. Consider a case in which you are moving along a linear path toward a destination and at time T1 you are halfway to the destination. If you then travel farther along the path at time T2, you will be closer to your destination at T2 than you were at T1. This is part of the spatial logic of the SOURCE-PATH-GOAL schema. Or, consider what follows if your car keys are *in* your hand and you then place your hand *in* your pocket. Via the transitive logic of CONTAINMENT, the car keys end up *in* your pocket. Such apparently trivial spatial logic is *not* trivial. On the contrary, it is just such spatial and bodily logic that makes it possible for us to make sense of, and to act intelligently within, our ordinary experience.

The third moral is that image schemas are not to be understood either as merely "mental" or merely "bodily", but rather as contours of what Dewey (1958) called the "body-mind." Dewey recognized the underlying continuity that connects our physical interactions in the world with our activities of imagining and thinking. He summarized the body-mind continuity as follows:

> But body-mind simply designates what actually takes place when a living body is implicated in situations of discourse, communication, and participation. In the hyphenated phrase body-mind, "body" designates the continued and conserved, the registered and cumulative operation of factors continuous with the rest of nature, inanimate as well as animate; while "mind" designates the characters and consequences which are differential, indicative of features which emerge when "body" is engaged in a wider, more complex and interdependent situation. (Dewey 1958: 285).

If we could only disabuse ourselves of the mistaken idea that "thought" must somehow be a type of activity metaphysically different in nature from our other bodily engagements (like seeing, hearing, holding things, and walking), then our entire understanding of the so-called "mind-body problem" would be transformed. Instead of interpreting the problem as how two completely different kinds of things (body and mind) can be united in interaction, we would re-phrase the problem as being about the conditions of experience that make it possible for us to engage in inquiry, reason about things, and coordinate our social interactions with others through communication.

I am suggesting that the very possibility of abstract conceptualization and reasoning depends directly on the fact that "body" and "mind" are not two separate things, but only abstractions from our ongoing continuous interactive experience. Although Dewey did not have the benefit of the elaborate analyses from today's cognitive science showing how meaning and thought are based on patterns of sensory-motor experience, he understood that what we think of as "higher" cognitive activities are grounded in, and shaped by, activities of bodily perception and movement:

> Just as when men start to talk they must use sounds and gestures antecedent to speech, and as when they begin to hunt animals, catch fish or make baskets, they must employ materials and processes that exist antecedently to these operations, so when men begin to observe and think they must use the nervous system and other organic structures which existed independently and antecedently. That the use reshapes the prior materials so as to adapt them more efficiently and freely to the uses to which they are put, is not a problem to be solved: it is an expression of the common fact that anything changes according to the interacting field it enters. (Dewey 1958: 285).

If you treat an image schema as merely an abstract formal cognitive structure, then you leave out its embodied origin and its arena of operation. On the other hand, if you treat the image schema as nothing but a structure of a bodily (sensory-motor) process, you cannot explain abstract conceptualization and thought. Only when image schemas are seen as structures of sensory-motor experience that can be recruited for abstract conceptualization and reasoning does it become possible to answer the key question: How can meaning emerge from embodied experience to play a crucial role in abstract concepts and in our reasoning with them, without calling upon disembodied mind, autonomous language modules, or pure reason? Failure to recognize the non-dualistic mental-bodily reality of image schemas would cause the collapse of the whole project of utilizing image-schematic logic to explain abstract thought.

4.   How image schemas help to solve the embodied meaning problem

We are now in a position to address this problem of the bodily grounding of meaning and the nature of abstract thought. The principal philosophical reason why image schemas are important is that they make it possible for us to use the structure of sensory and motor operations to understand abstract concepts and to draw inferences about them. The central idea is that image schemas, which arise recurrently in our perception and bodily movement, have their own logic, which can be applied to abstract conceptual domains. Image-schematic logic then serves as the basis for inferences about abstract entities and operations.[4] From a neural perspective, this means that certain connections to sensory-motor areas are inhibited, while the image-schematic structure remains activated and is appropriated for abstract thinking. According to this view, we do not have two kinds of logic, one for spatial-bodily concepts and a wholly different one for abstract concepts. There is no disembodied logic at all. Instead, we recruit body-based image-schematic logic to perform abstract reasoning.[5]

Excellent examples of this use of image-schematic structure in abstract reasoning come from mathematics. In *Where Mathematics Comes From: How the Embodied Mind Brings Mathematics Into Being*, George Lakoff and Rafael Nunez (2000) provide detailed analyses of scores of image schemas operating within conceptual metaphors that define the basic concepts and operations across a broad range of mathematical fields. To cite just a couple of elementary examples, consider two of the basic metaphors by which we understand the operations of arithmetic, such as addition, subtraction, multiplication, and division. Let's begin with the COLLECTION image schema, which involves the pattern of adding objects to a group or pile, or taking them away. We experience correlations between addition and the

---

4. I am not claiming that an image schema analysis is sufficient to tell the whole story of human reasoning. A complete account would include the role of emotions, qualities, social interaction, speech-act conditions, and patterns of inquiry. However, the structural aspects of concepts and inference would appear to be primarily a matter of image schema logic.
5. See Dodge and Lakoff (*this volume*) for a theory of the neural basis of image schemas.

action of adding objects to a collection and between subtraction and taking objects away from a collection. Such correlations are the basis for a "conceptual metaphor" (Lakoff and Johnson 1980; Lakoff and Johnson 1999), in this case, a conceptual metaphor whose source domain is object collection and whose target domain is arithmetic. The metaphor ARITHMETIC IS OBJECT COLLECTION is a mapping of entities and operations from the source domain (object collection) onto the target domain (mathematical addition).

ARITHMETIC IS OBJECT COLLECTION

Source Domain (OBJECT COLLECTION)		*Target Domain* (ARITHMETIC)
Collections of objects of the same size	>>>>	Numbers
The size of the collection	>>>>	The size of the number
Bigger	>>>>	Greater
Smaller	>>>>	Less
The smallest collection	>>>>	The unit (One)
Putting collections together	>>>>	Addition
Taking a smaller collection from a larger collection	>>>>	Subtraction

Lakoff and Nunez show how several key entailments of this metaphor, which involves the COLLECTION schema, generate various laws of arithmetic:

> Take the basic truths about collections of physical objects. Map them onto statements about numbers, using the metaphorical mapping. The result is a set of "truths" about natural numbers under the operations of addition and subtraction.
>
> For example, suppose we have two collections, A and B, of physical objects with A bigger than B. Now suppose we add the same collection C to each. Then A plus C will be a bigger collection of physical objects than B plus C. This is a fact about collections of physical objects of the same size. Using the mapping Numbers Are Collections of Objects, this physical truth that we experience in grouping objects becomes a mathematical truth about numbers: If A is greater than B, then $A+C$ is greater than $B+C$. (Lakoff and Nunez 2000: 56).

This simple analysis may seem pedestrian, but Lakoff and Nunez go on to show how the analysis explains many important properties of natural numbers, such as magnitude, stability results for addition and subtraction, inverse operations, uniform ontology, closure for addition, unlimited iteration for addition, limited iteration for subtraction, sequential operations, equality of result, preservation of equality, commutativity, associativity, and on and on.

A second fundamental metaphor for arithmetic is based on a SOURCE-PATH-GOAL schema. The SOURCE-PATH-GOAL schema underlies our understanding of bodily motion along a path, where there is a starting point (Source), a continuous set of steps (Path), taken toward the destination (Goal). The SOURCE-PATH-GOAL schema is the foundation for our common understanding of arithmetical operations as motions along a linear path, according to the following mapping:

ARITHMETIC IS MOTION ALONG A PATH

Source Domain (MOTION ALONG A PATH)		*Target Domain* (ARITHMETIC OPERATIONS)
Motions along the path	>>>>	Arithmetic operations
Point-location on the path	>>>>	Result of an arithmetic operation
Origin point	>>>>	Zero
A point-location	>>>>	One
Further from the origin than	>>>>	Greater than
Closer to the origin than	>>>>	Less than
Moving from a point-location *A* away from the origin, a distance that is the same as the distance from the origin to the point-location *B*	>>>>	Addition of *B* to *A*
Moving toward the origin from *A*, a distance that is the same as the distance from the origin to *B*	>>>>	Subtraction of *B* from A

Based on this important metaphor mapping, we thus utilize the structure of the SOURCE-PATH-GOAL schema plus our knowledge of the "logic" of motion along a path, in order to understand and to reason about arithmetical operations in abstract domains and fields. Lakoff and Nunez explore the pervasive use of this foundational metaphor to conceptualize iterative processes like multiplication and the calculation of fractions. They also provide an extensive analysis of the mathematics and geometry of the number line and of the Cartesian coordinate system, as it employs the SOURCE-PATH-GOAL schema.

In short, image schemas (operating within conceptual metaphors) make it possible for us to employ the logic of our sensory-motor experience to perform high-level cognitive operations for abstract entities and domains. The resources of our bodily experience are appropriated for abstract thinking.

This process of image-schematic and metaphor-based understanding has been demonstrated for concepts in mathematics (Lakoff and Nunez 2000), law (Winter 2001), morality (Johnson 1993), analogical problem-solving (Craig, Nersessian and Catrambone 2002), scientific causality (Lakoff and Johnson 1999), psychology (Gibbs and Colston 1995; Fernandez-Duque and Johnson 1999), and other areas of abstract reasoning and theorizing.

5. Putting flesh on image-schematic skeletons

However, there is a "down side" to our standard way of describing image schemas. The character of image-schematic analysis that has always worried me since its inception is its exclusive focus on recurring *structures or patterns* of organism-environment sensory-motor interactions. In short, if you attend only to *structure*, you necessarily ignore the nonstructural, more qualitative aspects of meaning and thought. You are left with a skeletal structure without the flesh and blood of embodied understanding. You lose, or at least overlook, the very thing that gives image schemas their life, motivating force, and relevance to human meaning, namely, their embeddedness within affect-laden and value-laden experience. There may be no way around this problem, but we can at least recognize what is left out of our theory, without which image schemas could not play their crucial role in conceptualization and reasoning.

Before I address the depth of this problem, let me say unequivocally that the great value of image schema analysis, as mentioned above, is its contribution to a developing theory of the bodily basis of conceptualization and reasoning. The most striking and significant successes so far have come in the areas of lexical semantics and the theory of inference structure. Over the past seventeen years a growing number of outstanding studies have revealed the crucial role of image-schematic structure in a broad range of concepts extending from spatial relations and motion concepts all the way up to our most abstract conceptualizations of reason, mind, knowledge, justice, rights, and values. These latter concepts draw on image-schematic structure in the source domains of conceptual metaphors. Image schema analysis gives us some of the most important *precise details* of the semantics of terms and expressions in natural languages. And, when coupled with metaphor analysis, it takes us a long way toward understanding abstract inferential structure.

This being granted, I still cannot shake off the nagging sense that the limitations of our exclusively structural analysis of image schemas leave out something of great importance. Conscious life is very much an affair of felt qualities of situations. The human experience of meaning concerns *both* structure *and* quality. However, beyond phenomenological description, there appear to be no philosophical or scientific ways to talk adequately about the fundamental role of quality in *what* is meaningful and *how* things are meaningful. We can name the qualities, but we cannot even describe them adequately. When we describe the image-schematic structure alone, we never capture fully the qualities that are the flesh and blood of our experience.

This problem can be illustrated with an example of a SOURCE-PATH-GOAL image schema. When we experience motion along a path there are always qualitative differences for different types of motion. There is a quality of rapid acceleration that differs markedly from gradual starting up. There is a particular quality of motion of the pulses one feels in a movement that consists of repeatedly starting and stopping a particular movement. There is a felt sense of completion as you gradually roll to a stop. Another example comes from numerous instantiations of the CONTAINER schema. There are felt qualities that you experience if you are held tightly in someone's arms, or are constrained within the confines of a small room. There are various ways it feels to leave a closed area and to enter an open expanse. Not only are there distinctive *qualities* for each of these experiences, but there are also possibly several layers of *values* and *norms* that characterize our interest and depth of engagement in these experiences. These values cannot be reduced to image-schematic structure. As a third example, consider any of the various manifestations of the SCALARITY schema that populate our daily lives. There is the distinctive crescendo of a rush of adrenaline, of rapidly turning up the lights with a rheostat, or feeling a hotflash wash over your body. There is much felt meaning here, but it cannot be reduced to discrete structural relations alone.

We are easily seduced into the habit of thinking only about the structural aspects of meaning and thought. This is not at all surprising, since it is principally the identification of discrete structures that allows us to discriminate features, to find meaningful gestalts, and to trace out relations among elements. But we must not mislead ourselves into thinking that this is the total content of meaning. Meaning is a matter concerning how we understand situations, people, things, and events, and this is as much a matter of values, felt qualities, and motivations as it is about structures of experience. Eugene Gendlin has made a life-long project of reminding us of the fundamental importance of this fact that there is much more to meaning than that which can be articulated via forms, patterns, and plans. He argues that

> We can develop a new mode of language and thinking which enters, and speaks from, what is *more than* conceptual patterns (distinctions, differences, comparisons, similarities, generalities, schemes, figures, categories, cognitions, cultural and social forms), although these are always inseparably at work as well. For example, "more than" is a pattern, but here it says more than the pattern. (Gendlin 1997: 3).

Gendlin's central point is that what we can formulate as articulate structure is always part of, and is interdependent with, *something more* – the felt experience of meaning that constitutes a dynamic process of organism-environment interaction. There are not two independent paths, one of symbolic structure and form and the other of felt qualities and tendencies of a situation. The structural cannot fully "represent" the non-formal, but the felt experience is never completely divorced from our structural understanding of it. As Gendlin says, that which exceeds the conceptual is precisely that which carries meaning and thought forward within a situation.

Some psychologists, linguists, and philosophers might wish to restrict the term "meaning" only to that which can be structurally articulated. However useful this might be as a strategy for formalizing aspects of our thought and language, it is far too restrictive to capture the fully embodied expanse of human meaning. To consider only the image schema skeletons of understanding and thought is to miss the flesh and blood meaning and value that makes the skeleton into a living organism.

I cannot imagine a method of linguistic or conceptual analysis that could ever adequately capture such qualitative aspects of meaning. I do not envision a different way of speaking about image schemas that would someday successfully incorporate qualities of experience. And yet, if image schemas are a principal key to the way all meaning grows from bodily experience, then the qualitative dimension is surely a crucial part of the process. The least we can do is to keep in mind that image schemas are not abstract imagistic skeletons. Rather, they are patterned, embodied interactions that are at once structural, qualitative, and dynamic.

William James and John Dewey famously tried to remedy this defect in our methods for explaining meaning, imagination, and thinking, but both were unsuccessful in convincing people to follow their lead. Neither of them could offer anything methodologically useful to linguists or psychologists. In his famous account of the "stream of thought" in *The Principles of Psychology* (1890), James reminded us that our inferences depend on the felt connections among our thoughts. These felt connections and transitions among thoughts are not merely formal structures, but are, instead, the contours of the flow of consciousness from one thought to another.

> If there be such things as feelings at all, then so surely as relations between objects exist in rerum natura, so surely, and more surely, do feelings exist to which these relations are known. There is not a conjunction or a preposition, and hardly an adverbial phrase, syntactic form, or inflection of voice, in human speech, that does not express some shading or other of relation which we at some moment actually feel to exist between the larger objects of our thought. If we speak objectively, it is the real relations that appear revealed; if we speak subjectively, it is the stream of consciousness that matches each of them by an inward coloring of its own. In either case the relations are numberless, and no existing language is capable of doing justice to all their relations. (James 1890, vol. I: 245).

James offered no explicit account of anything like an image schema, but he did understand that thinking involves patterns of relation and connection, and he argued that we *feel* these patterns as transitions in our thinking:

> The truth is that large tracts of human speech are nothing but *signs of direction* in thought, of which direction we nevertheless have an acutely discriminative sense, though no definite sensorial image plays any part in it whatsoever. (James 1890, vol. I: 252-53).

James even went so far as to claim that we "feel" logical relations, such as those indicated by *if...then, and, but,* and *or* (James 1890, vol. I: 245). In spite of James's remarkably rich account of the range of felt relations and qualities that populate our sentient experience, he never succeeded in convincing people to take seriously the role of feeling in thought. Only now, a century or more later, are cognitive neuroscientists returning to some of James's insights about the quality of thought and the role of emotion in reasoning (Damasio 1994, 1999, 2003).

The principal problem with this way of thinking about the nature of thinking is that it doesn't really seem to feed into syntactic or semantic explanations of the sort in which image schemas play a key role. I do not know how to account for the role of feeling in, and the qualitative dimensions of, image-schematic understanding. The chief issue is to determine whether feeling merely *accompanies* image-schematic structures, or whether it plays a more constitutive and constructive role in meaning. No one, as far as I know, has succeeded in making a strong case for the constitutive role, but I cannot ignore my intuition that image schemas have qualitative dimensions that are crucial to how they work in our conceptualization and reasoning.

One might protest that I seem to be asking too much of image schema analysis – trying to make it responsible for all dimensions of meaning. Perhaps image schemas only play a role in some of the most basic structural aspects of meaning, and we then need to analyze various additional strata of meaning, such as the social and affective dimensions, to flesh out the full story of meaning and thought. I wouldn't deny that this might be one possible strategy for at least identifying the full range of relevant phenomena for a theory of meaning and thought. However, I have suggested that the image schemas themselves have qualitative and normative dimensions. It strikes me that abstracting out these dimensions is, at best, an artificial after-the-fact reflective move that fails to do justice to the ways we construct and experience meaning.

Perhaps there is no way to return this important qualitative flesh and blood to our image-schematic skeletons. But let us not forget that the truly significant philosophical work done by image schemas is tied to the fact that they are not merely skeletons or abstractions. They are recurring patterns of organism-environment interactions that exist *in* the felt qualities of our experience, understanding, and thought. Image schemas are the sort of structures that demarcate the basic contours of our experience as embodied creatures. They depend on how our brains work, what our physiology is like, and the kinds of environments we inhabit. They are one of the most basic means we have for discrimination, differentiation, and determination within our experience. Their philosophical significance, in other words, lies in the way they bind together body and mind, inner and outer, and thought and feeling. They are an essential part of embodied meaning and provide the basis for much of our abstract inference.

References

Churchland, Patricia
    2002   *Brain-Wise: Studies in Neurophilosophy.* Cambridge, MA: MIT Press.
Cienki, Alan
    1997   Some properties and groupings of image schemas. In *Lexical and Syntactical Constructions and the Construction of Meaning*, Marjolijn Verspoor, Kee Dong Lee and Eve Sweetser (eds.), 3-15. Amsterdam/Philadephia: Benjamins.

1998   STRAIGHT: an image schema and its metaphorical extensions. *Cognitive Linguistics* 9: 107-149.

Craig, David, Nancy Nersessian, and Richard Catrambone
2002   Perceptual simulation in analogical problem solving. In *Model-Based Reasoning: Science, Technology, Values*, Lorenzo Magnani and Nancy Nersessian (eds.), 167-190. New York: Kluwer.

Damasio, Antonio
1994   *Descartes' Error: Emotion, Reason, and the Human Brain*. New York: G. P. Putnam's Sons.
1999   *The Feeling of What Happens: Body and Emotion in the Making of Consciousness*. New York: Harcourt, Brace & Co.
2003   *Looking for Spinoza: Joy, Sorrow, and the Feeling Brain*. New York: Basic Books.

Dewey, John
1958   Reprint. *Experience and Nature*. New York: Dover Publications. [Original edition: Chicago/London: Open Court, 1925].

Fernandez-Duque, Diego, and Mark Johnson
1999   Attention metaphors: How metaphor guide the cognitive psychology of attention. *Cognitive Science* 23: 83-116.

Gendlin, Eugene
1997   How philosophy cannot appeal to experience, and how it can. In *Language beyond Postmodernism: Saying and Thinking in Gendlin's Philosophy*, David M. Levin (ed.), 3-41. Evanston: Northwestern University Press.

Gibbs, Raymond W., Jr., and Herbert Colston
1995   The psychological reality of image schemas and their transformations. *Cognitive Linguistics* 6: 347-378.

Gibson, James J.
1979   *The Ecological Approach to Visual Perception*. Boston: Houghton-Mifflin.

Husserl, Edmund
1931   *Ideas: General Introduction to Pure Phenomenology*. Translated by W.R.B. Gibson. London: Collier-Macmillan [German original 1913].

James, William
1890   *The Principles of Psychology*. New York: Dover.

Johnson, Mark
1987   *The Body in the Mind: The Bodily Basis of Meaning, Imagination, and Reason*. Chicago: University of Chicago Press.
1993   *Moral Imagination: Implications of Cognitive Science for Ethics*. Chicago: University of Chicago Press.

Kant, Immanuel
  1968   Reprint. *Critique of Pure Reason*. Translated by N.K. Smith. New York: St. Martin's Press [German original 1781].
Lakoff, George
  1987   *Women, Fire, and Dangerous Things: What Our Categories Reveal About the Mind*. Chicago: University of Chicago Press.
Lakoff, George, and Mark Johnson
  1999   *Philosophy in the Flesh: The Embodied Mind and its Challenge to Western Thought*. New York: Basic Books.
  1980   *Metaphors we live by*. Chicago: University of Chicago Press.
Lakoff, George, and Rafael Nunez
  2000   *Where Mathematics Comes From: How the Embodied Mind Brings Mathematics into Being*. New York: Basic Books.
Merleau-Ponty, Maurice
  1962   *Phenomenology of Perception*. Translated by Colin Smith. London: Routledge [French original 1945].
Regier, Terry
  1996   *The Human Semantic Potential*. Cambridge, MA: MIT Press.
Schank, Roger, and Robert Abelson
  1977   *Scripts, Plans, Goals, and Understanding: An Inquiry into Human Knowledge Structures*. Hillsdale, NJ: Erlbaum.
Talmy, Leonard
  1983   How language structures space. In *Spatial Orientation: Theory, Research, and Application*, Herbert L. Pick and Linda P. Acredolo (eds.), 225-282. New York: Plenum Press.
Turner, Mark
  1991   *Reading Minds: The Study of English in the Age of Cognitive Science*. Princeton: Princeton University Press.
Winter, Steven
  2001   *A Clearing in the Forest: Law, Life, and Mind*. Chicago: University of Chicago Press.

Image schemas and perception:
Refining a definition

Joseph E. Grady[*]

Abstract

Though they have been among the central conceptual pillars of cognitive linguistics and have served as points of reference in related fields as well, image schemas have never been defined precisely or consistently. I propose first that the definition of image schemas should specify that they are representations (in a broad sense) of perceptual, including kinetic, experience. This specification is in the spirit of the earliest discussions of the concept, which nevertheless were not explicit or consistent on this point. It also reflects the "anchoring" function of perception in cognitive experience, and in conceptual structure. Additionally, I propose that the definition of image schemas should rule out certain schemas that are too general to be associated with any particular type of perceptual experience, or too rich to count as fundamental dimensions of perceptual representation.

Keywords: sensory-motor experience, perception, primary metaphor, image schema, response schema, superschema

1. Introduction

Image schemas are among the central conceptual pillars of cognitive linguistics (and have served as points of reference in related fields as well) because so many scholars have been drawn to them as intuitive and powerful instruments for analyzing the nature of thought and language. Since Lakoff and Johnson introduced the term in 1987, researchers have repeatedly found the idea of image schemas useful in developing their own accounts of how concepts are structured in the mind, and of the relationship between bodily experience and thought (Lakoff 1987; Johnson 1987; Lakoff and Turner 1989;

---

[*] An earlier version of this article was delivered at the 7th *International Cognitive Linguistics Conference* (Santa Barbara, July 2001). The author wishes to thank two anonymous reviewers and the editor of this volume for very insightful comments that helped in the preparation of the chapter.

Gibbs and Colston 1995; Cienki 1997; Clausner and Croft 1999; etc.). More particularly, researchers have emphasized the important role of image schemas in structuring metaphor,[1] children's acquisition of concepts (Mandler 1992, 2004); historical language change (Sweetser 1990); and the conceptual system in general. And yet there is still disagreement, and even confusion, about what image-schemas are, and what exactly the term refers to.

> It is difficult if not impossible to define image schematic domains in terms of some necessary and sufficient condition. Instead, it appears that one can define image schematic domains only by enumeration (Clausner and Croft 1999: 21).

The contributors to this volume, in fact, hold a divergent set of understandings of the concept, and a chief contribution of the collection is that it gathers these perspectives together in one place, offering any scholar interested in image schemas a chance to deeply consider the range of questions associated with the topic.

It is self-evident that if researchers can agree on a more precise definition of image schemas – or at least acknowledge the parameters that distinguish the variants – we stand to make real progress towards understanding important issues. After all, the differences arise not simply because everyone recognizes the term's possible range of referents and chooses a favorite – rather, there are important questions about the nature of cognition which make it difficult to define image schemas precisely. In this chapter I consider two particular parameters that separate one definition from another, in the hope that the discussion helps move our collective understanding forward – even if the resulting proposals bring the term back towards its earliest intended meaning.

2.   How schematic are image schemas?

It is universally agreed that image schemas are mental patterns associated with broad classes of concepts or experiences. A mental image of a particular beach would not fit anyone's understanding of image schemas, since it is both too specific and too rich in detail to be considered a schema. Ideas like 'Contact' (two objects touching) or 'Edge' are much more along the lines that most scholars intend when they use the term. Still, there is a wide range

---

1. See discussions of "Invariance" in, e.g., Brugman 1990; Lakoff 1990, 1993; Turner 1991; Gibbs 1994.

of degrees of schematicity that different researchers would accept into the category. Mark Turner (Turner 1991: 176-177), for example, has referred to image schemas of the following:

(1) a. two circles of the same size
     b. a circle with a marked point at its center
     c. a cup
     d. a particular phoneme

The complexity and particularity of these images would exclude them from many researchers' conception of what "should" count as an image schema. We surely have a schematic mental representation of cups, which helps define that class of objects, but the original spirit of the notion of image schemas, as presented in Lakoff (1987) and Johnson (1987) suggested a set of much more general representations.[2] However, since there is no agreed-upon definition of image schemas, degree of specificity remains a parameter that distinguishes one scholar's understanding from another.

3. What type of content are image schemas representations of?

An even more fundamental question, and one I will devote more attention to in this article, concerns the sort of content image schemas may represent.

3.1. Perceptual prototype

Across many of the discussions of image schemas in the cognitive linguistics literature, a clear prototype emerges, in which they refer to aspects of bodily, perceptual experience. In fact, Lakoff and Johnson's original presentations of the term each emphasized this bodily aspect explicitly:

> Image schemas are relatively simple structures that constantly recur in our everyday *bodily* experience: CONTAINERS, PATHS, LINKS, FORCES, BALANCE, and in various orientations and relations: UP-DOWN, FRONT-BACK, PART-WHOLE, CENTER-PERIPHERY, etc. (Lakoff 1987: 267, emphasis added)

---

2. I use the term "representation" here in a very broad sense that allows, e.g., for the conception of image schemas as dynamic patterns of activation in particular (combinations of) brain regions, or as the phenomenological experiences associated with such patterns of activation (see also Mandler, *this volume*).

In what follows I shall use the terms "schema," "embodied schema," and "image schema" interchangeably. The last two terms remind us that we are dealing with schematic structures that are constantly operating in our *perception, bodily movement through space, and physical manipulation of objects*. (Johnson 1987: 23, emphasis added)

Some of the schemas proposed by Johnson, illustrating this clear link with physical experience, are PART-WHOLE, CENTER-PERIPHERY, LINK, CONTACT, ADJACENCY, SUPPORT, BALANCE, and CONTAINER (cf. Johnson 1987: 126).

3.2. Nonperceptual image schemas

On the other hand, despite frequent emphasis on the perceptual basis of image schemas, even these earliest discussions in the literature proposed candidate schemas which are not tied to any particular aspect of sensory experience. Johnson (1987), for example, includes the following:

CYCLE: This schema refers not to any specific type of cycle which we perceive – such as a circle, or circular motion – nor in fact to any particular type of perceptual experience, but to the more general pattern of recurring states of whatever sort:

Most fundamentally, a cycle is a temporal circle. The cycle begins with some initial state, proceeds through a sequence of connected events, and ends where it began, to start anew the recurring cyclic pattern. (Johnson 1987: 119)

PROCESS: This schema is self-evidently not tied to any particular perceptual experience. It presumably structures our understanding of a variety of straighforwardly physical processes (chewing, walking, washing, etc.) as well as more "abstract" ones (thinking, evolving and so forth).

SCALE: Like CYCLE and PROCESS, this schema refers to a dimension which crosscuts many different types of perceptual and nonperceptual experiences:

Our world is experienced partly in terms of *more, less,* and *the same*. We can have more, less, or the same *number* of objects, *amount* of substance, *degree* of force, or *intensity* of sensation. This "more" or "less" aspect of human experience is the basis of the SCALE schema. (Johnson 1987: 122, emphasis in the original)

In their subsequent discussion of the SCALE schema, Clausner and Croft (1999) make it even more explicit that this image schema does not refer to any sort of physical scale, or to anything bodily or perceptual at all.[3] They propose that SCALE is an abstract parameter of degree, which combines with other concepts – some perceptual (e.g., sharpness), others not (e.g., goodness) – to yield scalar conceptual complexes. The SCALE schema is specifically *not* the perceptual (and "qualitative") element of this complex.[4]

The domain matrix for each of these concepts (i.e., 'tall', 'short', 'sharp', 'dull', 'good', 'bad') includes a qualitative dimension – spatial property, sensation, and judgment, respectively – and the domain of SCALE. The SCALE domain contributes the 'linear' ordering of the property, sensation, or judgment that is part of the meaning of the adjective (and that is what makes the adjective gradable). A word such as *sharp* profiles a location beyond the norm in the scale domain in its matrix; the word *sharp* also profiles a qualitative dimension of SHARPNESS. (Clausner and Croft 1999: 17)

For his part, Mark Turner suggests that CEASING TO EXIST is an image schema. The understanding of death Turner refers to does not involve an event or process that can be directly perceived with the senses – the scenario is not perceptual:

> We can invent new metaphors by figuring out *the image-schematic structure of the target* and finding a source that matches it. For example, if we observe that in death *something goes out of existence with no return*, then we can hunt about for some other event that fits this structure … (Turner 1991: 174, emphasis added)

In the same passage, Turner discusses another metaphor in which we can "see image-schematic structure existing in the target prior to the invention of the unconventional metaphor." In this case, the preexisting image-schematic structure is: "states of less complexity precede in time states of more complexity." As an example of this quite abstract schema, Turner cites Western society's evolving notion of justice. Of course, there could hardly be a conceptualization further removed from the concrete and physical. Nonetheless, Turner's discussion implies that the process, which we could call "complexification," is represented as image-schematic structure. And in a discussion of

3. The central (and interesting) proposal of Clausner and Croft's (1999) article is that image schemas should properly be considered image-schematic domains, but for my purposes here it is not necessary to take a position on this issue.
4. Popova (*this volume*), however, attempts to establish touch and taste as the perceptual modalities determining the SCALE schema.

the PATH schema – which is metaphorically mapped onto any number of other domains – Turner states that "it is part of the image-schematic structure of the path to be fixed, to be independent of our traversal of it. Traversing the path neither creates nor destroys it" (Turner 1991: 274). Again, this aspect of what Turner considers image-schematic structure, i.e., 'Permanence', is not directly perceptual or bodily in nature.

Sweetser (1990: 60), too, suggests image schemas which are not tied to bodily experience. In an influential discussion of modals, she offers the following description of the image-schematic structure shared between physical, social and epistemic senses of *may*:

1. In both the sociophysical and the epistemic worlds, nothing prevents the occurrence of whatever is modally marked with *may*; the chain of events is not obstructed.
2. In both the sociophysical and epistemic worlds, there is some background understanding that if things were different, something could obstruct the chain of events.

Sweetser goes on to point out that once we begin constructing a metaphorical mapping between the sociophysical realm and the domain of cognitive processes, it is

> ... clearly natural to map the meaning of *may* onto epistemic possibility ... because there is some very general topological structure shared by the two senses of *may*. (Sweetser 1990: 60)

This discussion, in other words, makes it explicit that the image schema in question is not tied specifically to bodily experience, but is a "topological" schema neutral between the epistemic and sociophysical realms.

While each of the schemas proposed by these scholars certainly *can* relate to bodily, perceptual experiences – and the discussions all refer to physical scenarios associated with the schemas – none of them is *defined* by any particular sort of perceptual experience. It is by means of our senses that we notice the cyclic nature of our own breathing, of day and night, or of the rotation of a wheel, for example; but these disparate cases depend on very different perceptual and cognitive systems. The level on which they share structure is not bodily in the same way that visual or tactile images are, but instead is a domain of greater abstractness, related to temporal structure and the recognition of familiar states. While a concept like cyclicity can be associated with any sort of perception, it does not in itself specify anything about perception.

3.3. Image schemas as the broadest sort of schema

Discussions like those cited above suggest that <u>image schemas may represent</u> <u>any recurring experience type</u> – whether perceptual or not – which crosscuts, or intersects with, many different domains. Clausner and Croft (1999: 22) take this position explicitly, and follow it to its logical conclusion. Their "natural definition of image schematicity" is the following: "domains which are image schematic are those found in the largest number of domain matrices (for the concepts used in human experience)." This view of image schemas as <u>a set of the very most ubiquitous mental representations</u> leads them to conclude that a schema is *less* image-schematic if it is "concrete," i.e., perceptual. On their account the concept CONTAINER, for instance, would not be especially image-schematic, due to its association with spatial arrangements and "material substance," which *a priori* narrows the range of concepts for which it can serve as a direct basis. Likewise, since temperature is a domain that is not central to our understanding of a wide range of more elaborated concepts, the authors conclude that while "the temperature domain is a basic, embodied domain, grounded in our physiological bodily experience … [it] is not image schematic." (Clausner and Croft 1999: 22)

In short, the range of views on this central question about the nature of 🔆 image schemas could hardly be greater.

4.   Basic, nonperceptual dimensions of mental structure

Some discussions in the cognitive linguistics literature suggest that there are few if any concepts that can be adequately defined without reference to perception or bodily experience. According to this view, which I will refer to as the "Constitutive Position", <u>the metaphors that gather around an "abstract"</u> <u>concept</u> like 'Process' or 'Love' <u>actually constitute that concept</u>, in an important sense.

One of the important assumptions of the discussion in this article is that, to the contrary, many very basic concepts are not based directly on perceptual experience. While schemas like CYCLE and SCALE may be strongly *associated* with perceptual concepts such as CIRCLE, PATH, etc., the schemas are also recognizable as free-standing concepts in their own right, referring to basic (nonsensory) dimensions of phenomenological experience, independent of the sensory associations. Clausner and Croft's discussion of the SCALE schema illustrates this view: they recognize scalarity as a fundamental, nonperceptual dimension of mental structure, which is independent of any of the myriad, more specific properties (such as goodness, warmth, redness, etc.) with which it interacts. A brief discussion of 'Causation', a concept which has received substantial attention from various scholarly perspectives, and which is associated with a rich network of metaphors, will help further illustrate the view that perceptual content may be connected with, yet not be constitutive of, a concept.

The nature of causation has offered fertile ground for philosophical speculation and analysis – like *image schema*, causation is a concept which proves useful even in the absence of a clear, shared definition of the term.[5] In fact, it is famously difficult to define the nature of causation, for a variety of reasons. One of these is that, on close examination, the relationship between events thought of as cause and effect are so different in various cases. For example, the mechanism by which one billiard ball imparts energy to another is very different in kind from the means by which a command leads a subordinate to perform an action. Many philosophers have taken up the challenge of explaining how it is that such different phenomena may belong to the same category.

Cognitive linguists have observed that causation is regularly conceptualized and talked about in metaphorical terms. Talmy's (1988) analysis of force-dynamic understandings of causation has been very influential, and more recently, Lakoff and Johnson (1999: 224) have offered a comprehensive treatment of metaphors for causation, taking the (Constitutive) position that "metaphor is central to our concept of causation. Most of our notions of causation use metaphor in an ineliminable way ...". Several of the common metaphorical patterns associated with causation are illustrated below with examples taken from Lakoff and Johnson:

(2)   a.   *Source*:   The chaos in Eastern Europe *emerged from* the end of the Cold War.
       b.   *Progenitor*:   Necessity is the *mother* of invention.
       c.   *Compelling Force*: FDR's leadership *brought* the country out of the Depression.

These patterns are often crosslinguistic, demonstrating even more strongly the basic associations in conceptual structure between causation and more concrete notions such as Source:

5. See Sosa and Tooley (1993) for a collection of articles from a variety of philosophical perspectives.

(3)	a.	French:	*L'argent est* la source de *tous nos maux.*
			'Money is *the source of* all our ills.'
	b.	Irish:	Tiocfaidh *an chointinn* as.
			'Contention will *come out of* it.'
	c.	Arabic:	*min* 'from, out of; due to'
	d.	German:	*aus* 'out of; as a result of'
	e.	Russian:	*iz* 'out of; because of'
			iz-za 'out from behind; because of'
	f.	Indonesian:	*asal* 'source, origin; cause'
			dari 'from; due to'

On the other hand, despite the richness of this radial conceptual category, we can also identify a sense in which causation is a basic dimension of understanding and mental experience, which develops from infancy on. Psychological experimenters interested in "causal attribution" have explored infants' expectations that one event will lead to another – removing an obstacle will make a hidden object visible (the basis of peek-a-boo); pushing on a stack of blocks will make it fall over; etc.[6] Even if the idea of "one true causation" in the real world is untenable, as Lakoff and Johnson (1999: 170-178, 206-234) argue compellingly, this still allows for a phenomenologically basic notion of causation, perhaps associated with a state of expectation, on which adults' rich conceptual complex is built. Causal attribution, in this sense, is analogous to the judgment that two entities are "similar" – it is a subjective interpretation (sometimes automatic and unconscious), which may or may not be traceable to any objective "truth" about a situation. Such a basic building block of mental experience (which might be called "Causal Belief") need not be metaphorical, nor tied to any particular type of sensory experience. (Peek-a-boo is about the causal logic of vision and occlusion, for instance, whereas many other games are about the causal logic of objects and force dynamics.) Lakoff and Johnson (1999: 176-177) suggest in the course of their discussion of "Skeletal literal causation" that there is something like a core definition of causation which is independent of particular concrete associations – according to which "a cause is a determining factor for a situation" – but argue that this notion is so impoverished that actual

---

6. See work on the phenomenology of explanation and causal maps (Gopnik 2000, following Campbell 1994); on infant perception (e.g., Schlottmann and Surian 1999); and on parameters of causal attribution such as Contiguity, Covariation, Antecedence, Simultaneity, Contingency, Probabilistic Contrast, etc. by psychological researchers such as Cheng (2000), Hilton (1998), Morris, Nisbett, and Peng (1995), Yanchar (2000).

understandings of the term cannot adequately be explained without reference to the metaphors. But if instead of starting with objective phenomena we focus on a phenomenological perspective,[7] and consider the mental *experience* of causal scenarios, then there does seem to be a very simple and important dimension (i.e., 'Causal Belief') which unites all such experiences. Importantly, we can distinguish this nonperceptual dimension of our mental representations of the world from the sensory experiences with which it is associated.

5.   A refined definition and its implications

If we recognize the distinctions drawn so far, then there are several logical possibilities for refining the definition of image schemas, differentiated by the degree of specificity they allow, and by the extent to which the schemas must be tied to perception. I propose that of these, the most useful way of understanding image schemas is to see them as mental representations of *fundamental units of sensory experience*.

5.1. Fundamental units

The sensory experiences associated with image schemas can be seen as minimal gestalts – self-contained dimensions of our richer perceptual experience. For example, when we walk downhill, our mental experience presumably includes, among other elements, patterns corresponding to motion forward and motion downward. While the idea of forward motion can be analyzed to include such elements as a trajector and a path, these parts form a whole that strikes us as coherent and experientially basic – one makes no sense without the other. It may even be possible at some later date to tie individual image schemas to elements of human cognitive and neural "programming" relating to perception of the physical world – a possibility suggested in Turner (1991: 182) and elsewhere. We have built-in detectors of

---

7. See Mark Johnson's (*this volume*) discussion of "informal phenomenological analysis."

up and down, based on gravity, for example, and of relative brightness, and relative heaviness.[8]

Defining image schemas in this way allows us to refer to a set of mental representations with a special and fundamental status, distinct from the infinite variety of "schematic" images which we can form over the course of a lifetime, including schemas of cups and other objects. In fact, if we take this definition seriously, we may need to exclude some of the spatial meanings encoded by prepositions and other such markers, even though it has been common in the literature to offer such meanings automatic membership in the image schema club. Talmy (2003: 216) mentions an Atsugewi spatial particle (the verb satellite *-ik's*) which denotes "motion horizontally into solid matter, as chopping an ax into a tree trunk." Since this meaning elaborates other, more basic schemas such as PENETRATION, it does not seem to be a candidate for the set of basic meanings. Whatever our choice of terminology, it is useful to make such distinctions between the more basic and more complex (or derived) varieties of schematic image.

5.2. Sensory experience

According to the proposed definition, image schemas are related to recurring patterns of particular bodily experience, including perceptions via sight, hearing, touch, kinesthetic perception, smell and possibly also internal sensations such as hunger, pain, etc. A minor reason to delimit image schemas in this way is that failing to make the distinction between sensory and non-sensory schemas obscures a chief characteristic of metaphor: many of the most common metaphorical patterns, i.e., primary metaphors (see below), project sensory concepts which can often be identified with image schemas onto nonsensory concepts.

More generally, by sorting out the dimensions of cognitive experience that are and are not based on sensory perception, we preserve a distinction that yields important insights into the nature and development of conceptual structure. Sensory/perceptual concepts have a special status in human thought, and by defining image schemas as schematic representations of physical experience per se, we clarify their role as organizing "anchors" of

---

8. See Rohrer (*this volume*) as well as Dodge and Lakoff (*this volume*) for further discussions of neural correlates of image schemas.

cognition.[9] This emphasis on bodily, perceptual experience locates image schemas within the growing body of research in psychology and other fields demonstrating that mental representations of perceptual experience are central to cognition (e.g., Damasio 1994; Edelman 1990; Finke, Pinker, and Farah 1989; Kosslyn 1976, 1980).

5.3. Response schemas

If image schemas are representations of fundamental units of sensory experience, then we need other ways of referring to kinds of schemas excluded by this definition. I have already referred above to complex "schematic images," such as representations of a cup and of horizontal motion into solid matter. How may we characterize the kinds of schemas referred to in the literature which do not refer to sensory experience – SCALE, CYCLE, PROCESS, and so forth? I have proposed elsewhere (Grady 1997, 1999, 2005, in prep.) that the source concepts of primary metaphors have "image content" while the corresponding target concepts have "response content." If we consider the metaphors below, we can recognize the sensory nature of the source and the nonsensory nature of the target in each case:

(4) a.   *heavy/light* tax *burden*/work*load*
          source: 'heaviness'   target: 'difficulty'
     b.   *rising/soaring/plummeting* unemployment
          source: 'height'   target: 'quantity'
     c.   *close to/far from* what I had in mind
          source: 'proximity'   target: 'similarity'
     d.   We're not *where we want to be* yet on the project./
          We have *a long way to go.*
          source: 'arriving at a destination'
          target: 'achieving a goal'
     e.   weak *from* hunger/ No good *came out of* his attempts to talk to her.
          source: 'source'   target: 'cause'

---

9. Metaphors may in fact serve to provide perceptual anchors, or handles, to concepts which are quite fundamental (e.g., 'Causation', 'Anger', 'Similarity', 'Achieving a Purpose'), but not ideally suited to direct, intersubjective reference. They may also provide a bridge between these concepts and the selective attention mechanisms associated with sensory systems (discussed, e.g., in Goldstone and Barsalou 1998).

f.   *red-hot* anger, *hothead*
    source: 'heat'   target: 'anger'

The target concepts refer to elements of mental experience which are just as fundamental to our experience as the corresponding source concepts, but are of a different sort. They relate to our interpretations of and responses to the world, our assessments of the physical situations we encounter, their nature and their meaning. Just as elements of sensory experience may be associated with particular cognitive systems (and even brain regions) dedicated to the processing of perceptual stimuli, these dimensions of experience might plausibly be associated with other cognitive and neural systems, such as those associated with motivation, for example. Some might correspond instead to different levels of processing within the cognitive system as a whole. A judgment of similarity, for example, must obviously require two logically antecedent representations as input. Whatever the exact nature of response schemas and the elements of experience which they are based on, it is helpful to have a way of referring to these nonperceptual analogs of image schemas.

5.4. Superschemas

One of the important roles ascribed to image schemas in the cognitive linguistics literature is that they license and constrain the mapping of one concept onto another. The discussions by Turner and Sweetser cited above, concerning metaphors for complexification and epistemic possibility, respectively, illustrate the view that the source and target concepts of a metaphor must share image-schematic structure. The principle of "Invariance," (cf., e.g., Brugman 1990; Lakoff 1990, 1993; Turner 1991; Gibbs 1994) has been defined in ways that vary subtly, but always refer to the preservation of image-schematic structure present within the target domain. If we adopt the notions of image content and response content above, and the proposed definition of image schemas as representations of sensory experience, then the invariance constraint cannot apply to primary metaphors, though it may apply to other types of metaphors (see below). Since the target concepts of these pervasive metaphors have no perceptual content, and therefore no image-schematic structure, there is none to preserve.

Does this mean that the source and target concepts of a primary metaphor share nothing at all? I believe that they do share structure, but on a level more abstract than the one at which sensory images are represented. I will refer to this level as the "superschematic" level of conceptual organization, since it transcends the distinction between sensory and response content. It includes information like the following:[10] *Ontological category* (e.g., Event, Process, Thing; Nominal, Relational); *Scalarity* and *Dimensionality*; *Aspect* (e.g., Punctual, Durative, fast/slow, etc.); *Boundedness*; *Arity* (i.e., the number of arguments in a relation); *Trajector-Landmark structure* (i.e., figure-ground organization); *Causal structure*; *Profile-Base structure*; *Simplex vs. Complex* (i.e., internal configuration).

That is, if the target of a primary metaphor is a scalar property (e.g., 'Happiness'), then the source must be as well (e.g., 'Brightness'). If the target is a punctual event (e.g., 'Death'), then the source must be as well (e.g., 'Departure'). If the target is a relation or process involving two participants (e.g., 'Group' and 'Member'; 'Knower' and 'Information known'), then the source must also have these features (e.g., 'Container' and 'Contained'; 'Seer' and 'Object seen'). The table below illustrates a number of image schemas, response schemas and superschemas – corresponding to metaphoric source concepts, target concepts and structure shared by these.

Table 1. Image-, Response- and Superschemas

Image Schema	Response Schema	Superschema
Heaviness	Difficulty	Scalar property
Up	More	Scalar property
Proximity	Similarity	Scalar binary relation
Arriving at a Destination/Goal	Achieving success	Bounded (punctual) event involving an actor (TR) and a LM
(Emerging from) Source	(Resulting from) Cause	Binary temporal relation involving TR and LM
Heat	Anger	Unbounded entity (or scalar property)

Note that while shared superschematic structure is a necessary condition for primary metaphor, it is not a sufficient condition. Superschemas are not "grounds" in the usual philosophical sense of this term, and shared superschematic structure does not constitute the "similarity" on which metaphors

---

10. For further discussion of superschemas, including parallels with the elements of semantics most relevant to grammar, such as those identified by Langacker (e.g., 1987), see Grady (in prep.).

are based. We equate soaring with increasing not simply because both are intransitive processes, but because of the correlation in experience between height and quantity. A metaphoric association does not arise between just any two scalar properties, intransitive processes, etc.[11]

Naturally, superschemas, as constraints on metaphoric mappings, always apply at the level of construal. They do not refer to literal, objective properties of the world, but to our ways of understanding the world. To illustrate this point, let us consider the expression *Unemployment soared last quarter*. The metaphorical conceptualization underlying the usage of *soar* maps rapid upward motion onto change that is also *conceived* as rapid, although the standards for making this judgment are less obvious than in the case of a moving object. Furthermore, the idea that unemployment is *an entity* which is capable of undergoing change (and which is conceptualized as a flying object) is a fact about our natural patterns of thought, rather than a fact about the world. Lakoff and Johnson (1980: 25) in *Metaphors We Live By*, referred to this pattern, the reification of abstractions such as events, activities, emotions, ideas, etc., as "ontological metaphor." Whether we wish to think of this ubiquitous pattern of construal as metaphor is perhaps a terminological question.[12] In any case, we must construe unemployment as an entity in order for the mapping to be realized.

A distinctive feature of the conceptual elements that make up superschematic structure is that they are typically neither sources nor targets of meta-phor. 'Two-ness' is not a metaphor for anything, nor a concept we have metaphors for, but a feature *shared* by source and target. We can say the same for rapidity and for the property of being an event. Likewise, relative positions on the thematic-role hierarchy are shared by sources and targets – an agent maps to an agent (or an experiencer, etc.) while a patient maps onto a patient (or a stimulus), etc.

---

11. Zlatev's (*this volume*) contention that "the metaphorical 'mapping' between image schemas and 'response schemas' ... can be most naturally explained as deriving from conscious processes of *analogy*... constrained by the shared structure (the 'superschemas') in the source and target domains induced in part by language" thus misses my major point.
12. I have argued (Grady 1997) that the patterns that can clearly be identified as metaphoric involve a more specific mapping – we think of, e.g., ideas as things we can *grasp* or *see*, or in terms of properties like *fuzziness* or *slipperiness*. We don't simply conceptualize them as objects, full stop, without further context.

In sum, superschematic features of a scene have some of the properties that have been ascribed to image schemas, but allow us to draw a distinction between the level of sensory representation, with all its special status in cognition, and a more general level that truly crosscuts the broadest range of conceptual domains.

6.   Conclusion

The vagueness of a central term within cognitive linguistics should not be surprising. In other areas of research, too (as well as in everyday life), certain terms are so useful that they are often treated as though their definition were clearly understood.[13] Understandings of the concept are accepted as good enough to serve whatever important purposes of the moment. Nonetheless, pursuing this path long enough ultimately involves risks. Elaborate theories are erected on foundations that are known to be unstable – like the landfill on which certain irresistibly attractive San Francisco neighborhoods are built. Such has been the situation with image schemas, but by focusing critical attention on them, we can solidify the grounds for future research and theory.

The distinctions outlined in this article – between image schemas, response schemas and superschemas – help clarify a number of issues, but many other important and fundamental questions still await adequate exploration. Among these are:

How can the perceptual experience-types represented by image-schemas be distinguished from other basic perceptions? For example, it does not seem plausible that there is an image schema corresponding to "pressure on the bottom of the left foot" – yet it could be argued that this is a fundamental element of (a small subset of) physical experience. It is interesting to note that there is no *concept* corresponding to "pressure on the bottom of the left foot," but this cannot be taken as the reason why there is no such image schema – the question is, why is there no entrenched conceptual representation, image-schematic or not, of this basic type of perceptual experience? Previous researchers, especially Talmy, have explored ways in which meaning can be organized by "topological" rather than absolute properties. The English spatial concept 'Enter', for example, refers to crossing a boundary into a defined region, but is neutral with respect to the size and shape of the

---

13. *Species* is an example from the hard sciences.

region, the thickness of the boundary, and so forth; likewise, the past tense marker *-ed* indicates that an event occurred in the past, without suggesting whether it happened ten seconds or ten million years ago. This notion of topology may be helpful for appropriately characterizing the kinds of representations that act like image schemas (see Johnson, *this volume*). Other promising approaches might ultimately be based on the nature of the neurological activity associated with a given category of perceptual experience. For instance, we know that pressure on a given portion of the body's surface causes activity in a corresponding region of the brain's sensory region; if there is a single, characteristic pattern of neurological activity prompted by touching sharp objects with different parts of the skin, it is presumably different in kind from the location-based pattern.[14]

Are there patterns of neurological activation associated with response content (as opposed to image content)? There is an increasing amount of evidence that concepts referring to physical objects and properties are stored in neural representations that extend to sensory and motor regions of the brain (e.g., Simmons et al., 2003). When we read words like *marble* and *cool*, tactile regions of the brain show signs of activity, when we read *soap* and *perfumed*, the regions subserving olfaction are active, and so forth. If "sensory concepts" are, by definition, stored in neural networks that include the brain regions associated with sensory perception, are there corresponding neural signatures of concepts which have "response content" rather than image content? For some of the concepts I have associated with response content – those referring to emotion and affect – the potential connections with particular types of brain activity are self-evident. For others, such as 'Similar', 'Achieving-a-Purpose', and 'Causal Belief', it may be much more difficult to find characteristic patterns of brain activity.

And finally, *Is it always possible to draw neat distinctions between image schemas?* Many likely image schemas, including ones widely discussed in previous studies, represent spatial concepts which may correspond with visual or kinesthetic (or tactile) experience – e.g., UP, SHARP, LARGE,[15] Do

---

14. Also see Mark Johnson's suggestion (*this volume*) regarding an operational distinction that sets image schemas apart from other perceptual patterns: Image schemas are "structures of sensory-motor experience *that can be recruited for abstract conceptualization and reasoning*" [emphasis added].
15. Mandler (*this volume*), for example, maintains that, in image schemas, information becomes "spatialized": "Although derived from perceptual information, this form of representation no longer has visual, auditory, or kinesthetic properties."

we need to distinguish an image schema like SHARP$_{visual}$ (which refers to acute angles) from one like SHARP$_{tactile}$ (which refers to the sensation of touching something pointy), acknowledging that these are two schemas which happen to be closely correlated in (cross-modal) experience? Many other proposed image schemas represent experience types which, though they can be distinguished, are clearly related – e.g., the many different types of experiences associated with motion along a PATH (making progress, reaching a goal, changing directions, etc.) or with interactions with CONTAINERS (constraints on one's own motion, the impossibility of seeing one object inside another, etc.). Do PATH and CONTAINER each refer to a single image schema, or to a family of schemas, or to an even more loosely connected set?

Both these types of uncertainty ultimately revolve around another basic parameter that can distinguish understandings of image schemas. Do we focus more on a phenomenological perspective, i.e., on image schemas as elements of subjective experience, or on image schemas as building blocks of our mental representation of the physical world? Seeing an acute angle is very different from feeling the touch of a pointy stick, though they may both be ways of experiencing the same physical stimulus. Likewise, the experience of being contained – e.g., within a room, or our mother's arms – is very different from not being able to see an object hidden inside a box. If image schemas are understood primarily as dimensions of subjective experience, then we should probably draw more distinctions rather than fewer – e.g., between schemas in different modalities – while also recognizing that some schemas are so tightly correlated that it is difficult to evoke one without evoking the other.

In the end, like other questions in this article, the question of whether we have two schemas for, e.g., sharpness depends on our most basic beliefs about the relationship between perception and understanding.

References

Brugman, Claudia
    1990   What is the Invariance Hypothesis? *Cognitive Linguistics* 1: 257-266.
Campbell, John
    1994   *Past, Space and Self.* Cambridge, Mass.: MIT Press.

Cheng, Patricia W.
    2000   Causality in the mind: Estimating contextual and conjunctive power. In *Explanation and Cognition*, Frank C. Keil, and Robert A. Wilson (eds.), 227-253. Cambridge, Mass.: MIT Press.
Cienki, Alan
    1997   Some Properties and groupings of image schemas. In *Lexical and Syntactical Constructions and the Construction of Meaning*, Marjolijn Verspoor, Kee Dong Lee, and Eve Sweetser (eds.), 3-15. Amsterdam/Philadelphia: Benjamins.
Clausner, Timothy C., and William Croft
    1999   Domains and image schemas. *Cognitive Linguistics* 10: 1-31.
Damasio, Antonio
    1994   *Descartes' Error*. New York: Grosset-Putnam.
Das Gupta, Prajna, and Peter E. Bryant
    1989   Young children's causal inferences. *Child Development* 60: 1138-1146.
Edelman, Gerard M.
    1990   *Remembered Present: A Biological Theory of Consciousness*. New York: Basic Books.
Finke, Ronald A., Steven Pinker and Martha Farah
    1989   Reinterpreting visual patterns in mental imagery. *Cognitive Science* 13: 51-78.
Gentner, Deidre
    1988   Metaphors as structure mapping: The relational shift. *Journal of Child Development* 59: 47-59.
Gibbs, Raymond W.
    1994   *The Poetics of Mind: Figurative Thought, Language, and Understanding*. Cambridge: Cambridge University Press.
Gibbs, Raymond W., and Herbert L. Colston
    1995   The cognitive psychological reality of image schemas and their transformations. *Cognitive Linguistics* 6: 93-125.
Goldstone, Robert L., and Lawrence Barsalou
    1998   Reuniting perception and conception. *Cognition* 65: 231-262.
Gopnik, Alison
    2000   Explanation as orgasm and the drive for causal knowledge. In *Explanation and Cognition*, Frank C. Keil, and Robert A. Wilson (eds.), 299-324. Cambridge, Mass.: MIT Press.
Grady, Joseph E.
    1997   Foundations of meaning: Primary metaphors and primary scenes. Ph.D. dissertation at the University of Berkeley.

1999   Heaviness and difficulty: "image content" vs. "response content" in conceptual metaphors. Talk at the 6th *International Cognitive Linguistics Conference* (Stockholm, July 1999).

2005   Primary metaphors as inputs to conceptual integration. *Journal of Pragmatics* 37 (10: Special Issue: Conceptual Blending Theory): 1595-1614.

In prep. 'Superschemas' and the grammar of metaphorical mappings. In *Proceedings of the 2004 Georgetown University Round Table*, Andrea Tyler (ed.). Berlin/New York: Mouton de Gruyter.

Hilton, Denis J.

1998   Causal judgment and explanation. *Educational and Child Psychology* 15: 22-34.

Johnson, Mark

1987   *The Body In the Mind: The Bodily Basis of Meaning, Imagination, and Reason.* Chicago: University of Chicago Press.

Kosslyn, Stephen M.

1976   Can imagery be distinguished from other forms of conceptual representation? Evidence from studies of information retrieval times. *Memory and Cognition* 4: 291-297.

1980   *Image and Mind.* Cambridge, Mass.: Harvard University Press.

Lakoff, George

1990   The Invariance Hypothesis: Is abstract reason based on image schemas?. *Cognitive Linguistics* 1: 39-74.

1993   The contemporary theory of metaphor, In *Metaphor and Thought*, Andrew Ortony (ed.), 202-251. 2nd ed. Cambridge: Cambridge University Press.

Lakoff, George, and Mark Johnson

1999   *Philosophy in the Flesh.* New York: Basic Books.

Lakoff, George, and Mark Turner

1989   *More than Cool Reason: A Field Guide to Poetic Metaphor.* Chicago: University of Chicago Press.

Langacker, Ronald W.

1987   *Foundations of Cognitive Grammar.* Vol. 1. *Theoretical Prerequisites.* Stanford: Stanford University Press.

Mandler, Jean M.

1992   How to build a baby, 2: Conceptual Primitives. *Psychological Review* 99: 587-604.

2004   *The Foundations of Mind: The Origins of Conceptual Thought.* Oxford: Oxford University Press.

Morris, Michael W., Richard E. Nisbett, and Kaipeng Peng

1995   Causal attribution across domains and cultures. In *Causal Cognition: A Multidisciplinary Debate*, Dan Sperber, David Premack and

Ann James-Premack (eds.), 577-614. Oxford/New York: Oxford University Press.

Schlottmann, Anne, and Luca Surian
1999   Do 9-month-olds perceive causation-at-a-distance? *Perception* 28: 1105-1113.

Simmons, W. Kyle, Diane Pecher, Stephan B. Hamann, Rene Zeelenberg, and Lawrence Barsalou
2003   FMRI evidence for modality-specific processing of conceptual knowledge on six modalities. Poster presented at the "Annual meeting of the Cognitive Neuroscience Society", New York, NY: March 29-April 1 2003.

Sosa, Ernest, and Michael Tooley (eds.)
1993   *Causation.* (Oxford Readings in Philosophy) Oxford/New York: Oxford University Press.

Sweetser, Eve
1990   *From Etymology to Pragmatics: Metaphorical and Cultural Aspects of Semantic Structure.* Cambridge: Cambridge University Press.

Talmy, Leonard
1985   Lexicalization patterns: semantic structure in lexical forms. In *Language Typology and the Lexicon.* Vol. 3. *Grammatical Categories and the Lexicon,* Timothy Shopen (ed.), 57-149. Cambridge: Cambridge University Press.
1988   Force dynamics in language and cognition. *Cognitive Science* 12: 49-100.
2000   *Toward A Cognitive Semantics.* Vol. 1. *Concept Structuring Systems.* Cambridge, Mass.: MIT Press.
2003   The representation of spatial structure in spoken and signed language: A neural model. *Language and Linguistics* 4: 207-250.

Turner, Mark
1991   *Reading Minds: The Study of English in the Age of Cognitive Science.* Princeton: Princeton University Press.

Yanchar, Stephen C.
2000   Some problems with Humean causality. *American Psychologist* 55: 767-768.

Image schemas:
From linguistic analysis to neural grounding

Ellen Dodge and George Lakoff

Abstract

What are image schemas? Why should the same primitive image schemas occur in the world's languages, even though spatial relations differ widely? What methodologies should we use to study them? How is linguistic theory affected by the answers to these questions? We argue that common primitive image-schemas arise from common brain structures, and that linguistic theory must be based on, and consistent with, what we know about the brain and experience. Focusing on motion-related experiences, we show how linguistics and neuroscience, when taken together, increase our understanding of image schemas. First, we look at how image schemas are expressed in language. Then, working from the assumption that linguistic structure is an expression of neural structure, we shift our attention to the brain, showing how recent findings in neuroscience can support an analysis of image schemas that relates the structure of experience, thought, and language to neural structure. This analysis not only enhances our current understanding of image schemas, but also suggests future avenues for image schema research.

Keywords: primitive image schema, LOCOMOTION schema, Cog theory, secondary sensory-motor areas

1. Introduction

The idea of image schemas emerged from the empirical research on spatial-relations terms by Len Talmy (1972, 1975, 1978, 1983) and Ron Langacker (1976, 1987) in the mid-1970's. They found, independently, that (1) even closely related languages vary widely in the meanings of their spatial-relations terms, and that (2) despite this variation, the cross-linguistic differences could be analyzed in terms of combinations of universal schemas: paths, bounded regions, contact, forces of various kinds, and so on – together with metaphorical versions of these. Research since then has confirmed and extended their findings, with analyses done of languages around the world.

The methodology behind these discoveries is commonplace within linguistics. (1) A cross-linguistic search within some natural domain (e.g., spatial relations) is conducted, uncovering diverse and complex systems. (2) A hypothesis is made that the complexity and diversity can be explained in terms of combinations of simple universal primitives. (3) Language-by-language analysis is performed, showing that the same universal primitives combine differently in different languages to yield the observed complexity and diversity.

Not all linguists work with this explicit methodology. The Nijmegen group, for instance, starts with the same first step of performing a cross-linguistic search in a particular domain. In the domain of spatial relations, for example, the group uses a methodology based on line drawings (Bowerman 1996; Bowerman and Choi 2001; Levinson et al. 2003). Each drawing represents a spatial relation between two objects. The native consultant is to supply the term most appropriate for describing that relation. They find the first result that Talmy and Langacker found: there is a lot of diversity across languages regarding which words name which collection of pictures.

Assuming that universal primitives would be relatively unitary concepts associated with individual words, they consequently argue against the presence of universal primitive and innate concepts. It is important to note, however, that these conclusions are based on a different notion of "universal primitive" than the one used by Talmy and Langacker, who assume that words may express concepts which are themselves complex combinations of primitives. Different assumptions about the nature of universal primitives may thus lead to different choices of methodology and to different conclusions. Since we take the Talmy-Langacker analyses as deep and insightful, and since we are interested in maximizing explanations from neuroscience, our results are, not surprisingly, very different from those of the Nijmegen group.

By the early 1980's, image schema research had led to a deep question: Where do the universal primitive image schemas come from? Since then two answers have been proposed: (1) Johnson (1987) saw them as arising from recurrent everyday bodily experiences, such as the early childhood experience of putting things into containers and taking them out again. (2) Regier (1995, 1996) argued that the human brain is structured naturally so as to compute the primitive universal image schemas, and to combine them. These are, of course, not mutually exclusive. Regier's hypothesis explains the *types* of experiences that Johnson observes. That is where things stand today. To get a better idea of the details, let us begin with Johnson's ideas.

1.1. Motion experience

Consider motion-related experiences. From the time you first learn to crawl, moving yourself around in the world is a significant part of your daily routine. On a typical morning you might get out of bed, leave the bedroom, and walk to the kitchen to get something to eat. Going outside, you may then jog around the block, run away from an angry dog, bicycle to work, or drive to the store. What types of image-schematic structures are associated with such basic experiences as these? To answer this, we first have to have some idea of what an image schema is. Johnson (1987), using an experiential approach, proposed the following defining elements: (1) recurrence across many different experiences; (2) a relatively small number of parts or components; and (3) an internal structure that supports inferences. Considering the motion experiences just mentioned, we can see that while they clearly differ in some respects (e.g., what time of day it is, how far we move, whether food is involved in the experience), all of them have at least one very schematic commonality: they involve a change in the mover's location. These locational changes have the structure of the very basic SOURCE-PATH-GOAL image schema (Johnson 1987; Lakoff 1987): we are one place when we start to move (a Source location); over time we change location (a series of Path locations); and when we stop moving, we are usually somewhere different than where we started (a Goal location). This very basic schema has few parts (Mover, Source, Path, Goal), applies over a very wide range of motion situations, and supports inferences (e.g., if you are at the goal location you have already been at the source and path locations). Thus, we see that recurrent, everyday motion experiences display at least one kind of image-schematic structure.

1.2. Moving beyond experience

To gain a fuller understanding of image schemas, though, we need more than an experience-based analysis. Our next step will be to examine the image schemas associated with descriptions of motion events, using the linguistic methodology described in the introduction. We will start with an analysis of some English sentence examples, and will then look at work done on cross-linguistic variation and universality. An examination of motion descriptions indicates that, in addition to containing a variety of spatial image schemas, they contain other kinds of image schemas as well. Linguistic analysis thus helps us identify the existence of primitive image schemas. Moreover, linguistic analysis can lead to a better understanding of how different languages may use and combine these primitive image schemas.

However, linguistic analysis does not, by itself, explain the origins of image schemas. And, even though image schemas may be associated with recurrent regularities in experience, an experiential analysis by itself does not explain how languages may make use of these schemas, nor does it explain why we perceive the particular schematic structures we do. In order to provide more complete explanations, we believe it is necessary to consider the role of the human brain. In the second half of the paper we will therefore pursue Regier's line of argument that the brain computes image schemas. First, we review some of the work that supports the link between image schemas and neural structure. Then, we will once again focus on motion experiences and descriptions, exploring a hypothesis about the relation between image schemas and particular neural structures. Through such an analysis, we will show how the study of the brain not only can lead to a fuller understanding of image schemas, but also can provide insight into the relations between image schemas, experience, language, and the brain.

2.   Image-schematic structure in language

2.1.   Image schemas, experience, and language

Image schemas structure our experience independently of language. For example, we experience many things as containers – boxes, cups, baskets, our mouths, rooms, and so on. Prior to learning language, children go through a stage of exploration in which they repeatedly put things in and take them out of many different kinds of objects, thus treating these objects as containers. Starting at an even earlier age, they observe actions such as these being performed by others. As Mandler (*this volume*) describes, infants show some understanding of containment well before their first birthday.

Image schemas play a vital role in fitting language to experience. Image schemas define classes of experiences that are characterized by the same word (e.g., *in* or *out* or *up*). This fact raises two questions: How is it possible for different experiences to have the same image-schematic structure? And how are image schemas expressed in language? We will start with the second question and get to the first later in this essay. What is of note is that the way image schemas are expressed in language is a central feature of linguistic structure. They may be expressed by prepositions, postpositions, verbs, cases, body-part metaphors, or morphemes (e.g., in Cora, cf. Casad and Langacker 1975). The way that image schemas are expressed in a language is a typological feature of the language.

2.2. English examples

When we describe a person's motion, what sorts of image-schematic structure do we express? Consider the following two sentences:

(1)   a.   He walked *to* the kitchen.
       b.   He walked *into* the kitchen.

Both of these sentences indicate that a mover (*he*) is changing location with respect to a "landmark" (*the kitchen*). But this change is only schematically specified; all we can really infer from these sentences is that initially the mover was not at the kitchen, then he moved, and after moving the mover was at or in the kitchen. Both of these motion descriptions thus seem to express SOURCE-PATH-GOAL schematic structure.

The second sentence expresses additional schematic structure, which serves to further specify the spatial relation between the mover and the landmark. The first sentence only indicates, roughly, that at the end of motion the mover is somehow co-located with the kitchen. This may mean that the mover is inside the kitchen, but could also mean that he is directly outside it, or that he is standing in the doorway. The second sentence, however, using the preposition *into,* indicates that that the goal location is actually inside the kitchen and the source location is somewhere outside the kitchen. In this case, schematic structural elements of the landmark are used to indicate the mover's location; that is, the kitchen is understood as a container. The kitchen walls effectively divide space into an interior (the space enclosed by the walls) and an exterior (the space "surrounding" the kitchen). In addition, these walls have some opening, such as a doorway, which allows the mover to go from the exterior to the interior of the kitchen. Thus, the following schematic elements seem relevant:

- Boundary (in this case, the walls, which define the shape of the room)
- Interior (a space enclosed by the Boundary)
- Exterior (the surrounding area – space not enclosed by the Boundary)
- Portal (an opening in the Boundary that allows motion between the Interior and Exterior)

Taken together, these schematic elements define what is often referred to as the CONTAINER schema. These same structural elements are unconsciously and automatically used to conceptualize a variety of objects of various sizes: cups, boxes, bags, rooms, tents, buildings, valleys, etc. Not surprisingly, then, in addition to descriptions of people moving around in the world, this schema may also be used in descriptions of other types of experiences, such as putting food in your mouth or apples into a basket.

Some motion descriptions specify location by making use of these same schematic structural elements of a landmark, but specify a different temporal order of spatial relations. For example, in (2a), Harry is initially inside the room then moves to the exterior, the opposite of the sequence specified by (2b):

(2)   a.   Harry sauntered *out of* the room
      b.   Harry sauntered *into* the room.

These changes in location can be analyzed in terms of SOURCE-PATH-GOAL schematic structure: *out of* indicates that the exterior is the Goal location, and *into* indicates that the interior is the Goal. Each of these sentences thus expresses both CONTAINER and SOURCE-PATH-GOAL schematic structure, but combines these schemas in different ways.

These facts are so obvious that the theoretical implications of them could easily be missed: the same image-schematic elements can appear in reversed order in a language with a minimal shift in linguistic form (*in* → *out*) indicating the reversal. That is, *in* and *out* are not utterly different. They are inverses. But this can be seen only via an image-schematic analysis of language.

Similarly, the experiences of moving in and moving out are also understood as inverses – but only because the experiences themselves are structured by image schemas. Because image-schematic structuring of experience is done automatically and unconsciously, it escapes notice.

Our experience of a room may be structured image-schematically in many ways, though a given sentence may only focus on one of these ways. For example, a room is experienced as a container, but it is also experienced as having different sides. This second experience is focused on in (3a).

(3)   a.   Harry sauntered across the room.
     b.   The shadow moved across his face.

The use of *across* in (3a) indicates that the mover (*Harry*) is moving from one side of a landmark (*the room*) to the opposite side. These sides may be determined based on the geometry of the landmark, in particular its axial structure. For the example here, the relative lengths of the room's walls may serve to define a main axis that effectively divides the room into two sides. In example (3a), then, as Harry moves from one side to the other side of the room, he crosses this main axis.[1] Sometimes, sides may be considered inherent to a landmark, as in (3b), where a face has inherent sides.

Motion descriptions vary not only with respect to which schemas they express, but also with respect to which grammatical forms are used to express this schematic information. In the examples we have examined thus far, the verb (*walk, saunter*) indicated that the mover was moving, the preposition (*to, into, out, across*) gave information about the schematic spatial relation between the mover and a landmark, and the prepositional object (*the kitchen, the room*) specified which landmark was being used. However, in other sentences, the schematic spatial relation may be indicated by the verb rather than by a preposition. For example, in (4a), the verb *enter* not only indicates that the mover is moving, but also indicates that the mover is moving into the room. (4b) indicates motion out of or across the room. In such sentences, no preposition appears, and the landmark entity is indicated by the direct object of the verb.

(4)   a.   He entered the room
     b.   He exited/crossed the room

While both of these ways of encoding locational information use similar schematic structure to specify location, they differ in other important respects, as we will see later in this paper.

By analyzing sentences that describe a person's motion, we have found a variety of schematic structures. The basic temporal sequence of the mover's change in location is expressed using SOURCE-PATH-GOAL schematic structure. Different types of schematic structural elements of the landmark can be used to further specify (albeit schematically) the mover's locations. Fur-

---

1. Commonly, *across* is used with long, thin landmarks. In such cases, the entire landmark may be considered an axis. This axis may serve to the divide the space surrounding the landmark into two areas, each of which might be called a side.

thermore, we have seen that schematic spatial relations information can be encoded in at least two different grammatical forms – prepositions and verbs.

If all this seems simple and obvious, it is only because we are taking for granted the image-schematic structuring of experience and taking for granted the fact that image schemas exist independently of the linguistic forms used to express them. In a theory without image schemas, none of this would even make sense, much less be obvious.

Thus far, however, we have looked at only one language. If we are to investigate whether image schemas such as those described above are universal primitives, we need to consider a much wider range of languages. Therefore, we next turn our attention to cross-linguistic studies of spatial descriptions.

2.3. Cross-linguistic variation and universality

The image-schematic structuring of experience means that primitive image schemas are *available* to be expressed *somehow* in a given language. But, as Talmy's and Langacker's initial cross-linguistic studies showed, there is significant diversity in the ways languages describe space and location. Consider just a few examples:

– Importance of landmark's shape and/or orientation.

For many spatial-relations terms, the shape and orientation of the landmark does not play a role. For example, *above* (and many other English prepositions, such as *in*, *on*, *to*, and *under*) can be applied to landmarks of different shapes and orientations, as in *The bird is above the birdhouse/tree/table*. Compare this with Mixtec, which uses body part terms as a primary means of expressing location. For vertically extended landmarks, locations are described using body part terms of upright bipeds. For instance, an object described in English as being *above* a tree would be considered in Mixtec to be located at the tree's "head". If the landmark were horizontally extended, body part terms for a quadruped on all fours would be used; something *above* a landmark such as a table would be at the landmark's "back" (Brugman 1983). Thus, Mixtec uses two different spatial words to describe scenes that in English would be labeled the same.

– Presence or absence of contact.

Some spatial-relations terms distinguish between the presence and absence of contact. For example, English terms *on* and *above* make this distinction for vertical object-landmark relations. In the Mixtec examples discussed above, however, the same spatial term would be used regardless of whether or not the object was in contact with the landmark.

– Tight versus loose fit.

When expressing directed motion, Korean verbs distinguish between relations involving "tight" fit and "loose" fit rather than distinguishing between CONTAINMENT and surface SUPPORT. (Choi and Bowerman 1991; Bowerman 1996; see also Mandler, *this volume*).

  However, despite this cross-linguistic diversity, the number of primitive image schemas used by spatial terms seems to be fairly limited. Talmy (1983, 1988, 2000, *this volume*) has conducted an extensive cross-linguistic analysis of the grammatical forms used in the linguistic description of space. Based on his analysis he surmises that there is a limited inventory of basic spatial distinctions that languages will make in their closed class systems.[2] This inventory of basic distinctions includes:

– Focal distinctions within a scene – figure (focal object) and ground (sec-
 ondary focus, serves as reference object to locate figure)
– Figure and ground geometries, relative orientations
– Presence/absence of contact of the figure with the ground
– Force-dynamics – reflects non-visual modalities, and is largely independent of other spatial distinctions

Lakoff (1987) has used the term "primitive image schema" for such primitives. Within a Talmy-Langacker style theory, then, there are a limited number of primitive image schemas present in spatial descriptions of different languages, at least in their closed-class forms.

  If this inventory is universally available, why do languages exhibit such diversity? Talmy proposed that the spatial-relations terms used in language are actually complex concepts composed of primitives selected from this inventory. Thus, the spatial relation encoded by a given form (say, *into*) may actually evoke a complex of schemas (CONTAINER, SOURCE-PATH-GOAL) rather than being related to only a single primitive schema. In support of this idea, Langacker and Casad (1985), Lindner (1982, 1983), Vandeloise (1984,

---

2. A closed class is one whose membership is fixed and relatively small (cf. Talmy 2000, Vol. 1: 22).

1991) and Brugman ([1981] 1988) have provided detailed image-schematic analyses of spatial terms showing how their meanings may be decomposed into such primitives (though there is some controversy about which decompositions are cognitively correct). Additionally, as indicated earlier, the spatial-relations terms of a given language may not necessarily make use of all of these schematic spatial distinctions. For example, although the tight-loose distinction structures the experience of English as well as Korean speakers, Korean makes use of this distinction but English does not. Thus, while spatial relation terms utilize primitive image schemas, there is by no means a one-to-one correspondence between the spatial-relations terms of a given language and the primitives in this presumably universally-available inventory.

Additional cross-linguistic variation in locational descriptions may arise for a somewhat different reason: languages may vary in terms of which frame(s) of spatial reference they use to specify spatial relations. Based on the study of a broad range of languages, Levinson (2003) and others (Talmy 2000) concluded that these languages grammaticalized or lexicalized three different frames of reference.

The first type is an intrinsic frame of reference, where spatial coordinates are determined using "inherent" features of the landmark object. For example, in *He ran into the room*, the spatial relation *into* makes use of the inherent image-schematic structure of the room to specify the mover's location.

A second type is a relative frame of reference, where the determination of spatial coordinates is made relative to a particular viewpoint. This frame of reference may also involve the use of a landmark and schematic structure. However, the schematic structure in this case is not inherent to the landmark. So, for example, in *He ran in front of the tree*, "in front of " makes use of the front/back elements of a body schema. But, rather than being inherent schematic structural elements of the tree, they are associated with a viewer of the scene (typically the speaker). Thus, while a landmark object is present, the viewer serves as the schematic "anchor" for this frame of reference.

The third frame of reference that they found is an absolute frame of reference. As an example, *He ran north* does not include reference to a particular spatial landmark. Instead, location is specified with respect to fixed bearings. In this case the language user has to conceive of the environment itself as having pervasive schematic structure of a kind similar to the pervasive up/down structure supplied by gravity. Languages vary in terms of which of these frames they use. For example, some use both the relative and the absolute frames, while others use one but not the other (Pedersen et al. 1998). So, different elements – landmark, viewer, environment as a whole – may serve to anchor the frame of reference for locational descriptions and spatial-relations terms in different languages. Spatial descriptions may thus include specifications of both spatial schematic structure and spatial frame of reference. In this way, they may indicate which element of the spatial environment the evoked schematic structure is linked to.

In sum, we have seen that there is great cross-linguistic diversity in spatial-relations terms and their use of schematic structure. Languages differ as to the basic spatial distinctions they make, the combinations of distinctions they "package" together in their spatial-relations terms, and the grammatical class membership of these spatial terms. Use of different frames of reference for spatial descriptions is an additional source of variation. Given this linguistic diversity, we can see that if we were to call each spatial relation term in a language an "image schema", then we could rightly say that languages differ widely in their inventory of spatial image schemas. However, we have also seen that these spatial-relations terms can instead be analyzed as complex combinations of more primitive image-schematic structures. Consequently, if we restrict application of the term "image schema" to these primitives, cross-linguistic analysis indicates that there is a limited inventory of image schemas used by the world's languages (see also Talmy, *this volume*).

2.4. Other types of schematic structure in language: manner of motion

Thus far in our analysis of motion descriptions, we have concentrated on the image schemas used to convey information about the mover's change in location. However, motion descriptions can include other types of motion-related information. Consider the following sentences:

(5)   a.   She *sprinted*.
      b.   He *trudged* many miles.
      c.   We *strolled* arm in arm.

These sentences do not specify anything about where any of these movers are or where they are going. However, the verb in each of these sentences specifies something about the *manner* in which the mover is moving. *Stroll*, for example, indicates that the mover is walking slowly and leisurely, while *sprint* indicates a fast running motion. In English there are a large number of verbs that can be used to describe different manners of self-generated, animate motion, including *walk, march, stroll, amble, pace, saunter, limp, skip, jog, run,* and *sprint,* to name just a few.

Are there image schemas associated with these "manner" verbs? While the schemas used in spatial relations descriptions don't seem applicable, an examination of these verbs indicates the presence of other types of schematic structure. Many of these verbs describe variants of a basic walking gait (*walk, march, saunter, amble, pace, tramp*), some describe types of running (*run, jog, sprint, trot*), while others involve jumping of some form (*jump, hop, skip, gambol, leap*). So one schematic element in manner-related information may be the basic gait or general rhythm of muscular activity that the mover is using to bring about his motion. Within any one of these basic gaits (*walk, run, jump*), different verbs indicate different speeds of motion. For example, *saunter* is a low speed walk, while *striding* is a higher speed walk. Manner of motion verbs may also give a schematic indication of how much effort is required on the part of the mover to actually move. *Trudge,* for instance indicates greater effort than *walk,* while *stroll* implies less effort. However these verbs don't specify the mover's exact speed of motion or the absolute amount of effort expended. Speed and effort are only schematically specified, not quantified. Manner verbs may also schematically specify the part(s) of the body used in motion; while most predominantly involve the use of our feet and legs, some may involve the use of hands and arms (*crawling, climbing*). Taken together, these different types of manner-related information suggest that manner verbs may make use of the following schematic structural elements: Mover, Gait (e.g., *walk, run, jump*), Speed, Effort, and BodyPart. If we consider these elements to be different roles in a single schema, we can say that they collectively constitute what might be called a "Locomotion" schema for self-motion. This schema meets Johnson's criteria for image schemas, described at the beginning of this paper: in addition to applying across a wide range of situations and containing a limited number of structural elements, this schema supports some types of inference. For instance, we can infer that if a person is sprinting she isn't walking, but is running. Also, if a person is trudging we can infer both that she is moving more slowly than she would be if she were running and that her motion is more effortful than it would be if she were strolling. So, while this LOCO-MOTION schema is not one commonly described in the literature on image schemas (but see Mandler 1992, *this volume*), it does seem to meet the criteria for being an image schema. Consequently, manner verbs such as these do seem to express image-schematic structure.[3]

So, motion descriptions that convey manner-related information, as well as those which convey locational information, both express image-schematic structure, albeit of different kinds. Some sentences include both kinds of information. For example, manner verbs often appear in sentences that also contain locational information, as in *I strolled across the garden* or *I trudged over the hill.* As discussed previously, the locational information in such sentences is schematically specified using a spatial relations preposition (*across, over*); manner verbs themselves do not themselves specify anything about the path of motion. Recall too that verbs can also encode locational information. "Path" verbs such as *enter, exit,* and *cross* supply information about the mover's path of motion, but not about the mover's manner of motion. So, a sentence like *He entered the room* can be used felicitously regardless of whether the mover walked, sprinted, hopped, or even crawled into the room. Manner-related information can be included in such sentences through the addition of adverbs (*slowly, effortlessly*) or phrases (*on foot, at a run*). We see, then, that English verbs can supply either manner or path of motion information, though a given verb does not seem to include both. Sentences may convey path, manner, or both types of information. Because each type of information is associated with different kinds of image-schematic structure, these verbs and sentences will vary as to which kind(s) of image schemas they express.

Looking across languages, there appear to be two predominant lexicalization patterns associated with motion descriptions. One pattern is to encode path information in verbs, and (optionally) encode manner information in other grammatical elements, such as adverbs. The other pattern is to encode manner information in verbs and (optionally) encode path information in other grammatical elements, such as prepositions. Within a given language, there is a tendency for one of these lexicalization patterns to predominate (Slobin 1996, 2003; Talmy 1985, 2000). As we have seen in English, both patterns are present, but manner encoding predominates. Many other lan-

---

3. Mandler's motion schemas distinguish biological from non-biological motion based mostly on the path of motion. For ANIMATE-MOTION, the entity's motion does not follow a straight line and may have some rhythmic characteristics. Unlike the LOCOMOTION schema (described more fully later in this paper), the ANIMATE-MOTION schema is not explicitly related to the locomotor action performed by the animate entity, and consequently does not include roles for gait or effort.

guages, such as Russian, Chinese and Ojibwe also predominantly encode manner. In other languages, such as Spanish, Japanese, and Turkish, path encoding in the verb predominates. Languages thus differ in terms of which type of motion information they tend to encode in the verb. Furthermore, since each type of motion information is associated with a distinctly different type of schematic structure, we can also conclude that languages differ in terms of what kind of schematic information they tend to encode in the verb.

What are the possible implications of these encoding differences? Slobin has proposed that lexicalization patterns may affect how we think about motion events. In particular, he suggests that different mental imagery may be associated with each lexicalization pattern. Supporting evidence for this idea comes from an experiment in which speakers read passages in their native language, either Spanish (where path is encoded in the verb) or English. In neither language did the passage include any manner information, but it did include information about the terrain and the mover's internal state. Speakers of Spanish reported images related to the physical surroundings of a scene, but not imagery related to the manner in which a mover is moving. Speakers of English tended to have mental imagery related to the manner in which the mover is moving. Bilinguals of both languages reported more manner imagery and less imagery related to surroundings when reading in English compared to reading in Spanish (Slobin 2003). Thus, there seems to be a correlation between the type of information that is typically encoded in the verb of a language (i.e., the type of information the language user typically has to attend to while using that language), and the type of imagery the reader has while reading in that language. Moreover, it may well be that these differences in imagery correspond to the different types of image-schematic structure associated with these two types of information. We will pursue this possibility later in this paper, as well as considering how the different types of imagery may correspond to the activation of different neural structures.

2.5. Language Section: summary

As we saw in this section, linguistic analysis provides a methodology to study image schemas. An examination of motion descriptions shows that they commonly include two types of information – path and manner – and that different types of image schemas are associated with each of these types of information. For the spatial schemas used in path descriptions, we briefly reviewed some significant cross-linguistic work that explored issues of linguistic diversity and primitives. From this we saw that although the spatial-relations terms and locational descriptions used by different languages may differ in many respects, they may nonetheless all may make use of the same relatively limited inventory of basic primitive image schemas and frames of reference. From this work we can also see that it is important to clarify what we mean when we use the term "image schema". We need to make a clear distinction between the complex schematic structures of individual spatial-relations terms and the primitive, simpler image schemas which are combined to form such complex structures. We also saw that manner-of-movement information seems to have schematic structure, albeit of a different kind than spatial image schemas. Additionally, languages vary in terms of which type of motion-related information their verbs tend to encode. Because different types of schemas are associated with these two different types of motion information, this variation implies that different types of schematic structure may be associated with the verbal systems of different languages.

However, while cognitive linguistic analysis in the Talmy-Langacker tradition helps us determine what the inventory of primitive image schemas may be, it does not provide us with an answer to the deep question mentioned earlier in this paper: Where do universal primitive image schemas come from? *Why* do the primitives that Talmy and Langacker have found exist? While Johnson's experiential approach goes some way towards addressing this question, we believe that to answer it more fully it is essential to further pursue Regier's arguments, looking at how the structure of the human brain may compute primitive image schemas as well as how it may combine them to form the more complex schematic structures found in different languages. The brain is thus the seat of *explanation* for cognitive linguistic results.

But there is an even deeper reason for looking to Regier-style brain-based characterizations of primitive image schemas. By looking to the brain, we see why there *should* be primitive image schemas, and why they *should* structure experience independently of the language that expresses them. In short, what we know about the brain leads us to choose among linguistic theories. That knowledge leads us to choose Talmy-Langacker style theories with combinations of universally available primitives over Nijmegen-style theories, where each language has spatial relation terms that are not decomposable into primitives, but are just different – and may differ arbitrarily. In short, neuroscience matters for linguistics.

Therefore, we will now shift our attention to the question of what the study of the brain can tell us about image schemas.

3.   Neural structure and image schemas

Regier (1996) expanded on Talmy's previously discussed work on spatial relations. Regier proposed that spatial relations primitives were the consequence of brain structure – specifically, human perceptual mechanisms. Further, he proposed that spatial-relations terms could be learned as different complex combinations of these primitives. He demonstrated the plausibility of his proposals by creating a computer program that could, from a set of labeled scenes, learn spatial relations words from a wide variety of languages (e.g., English, Mixtec, German, Russian, Japanese). Within this program, perceptual mechanisms were modeled using two classes of visual features: orientation features such as verticality, and topological features such as contact and inclusion. These features form the basis of much of the image-schematic structure expressed in spatial relations words. For example, given the shape of a landmark object, topological maps are used to compute CONTAINER schema roles – *boundary, interior, exterior* – in part by using a spreading activation procedure. Comparison of trajector and landmark maps determines the trajector's relation to the landmark in terms of these schematic roles. Other features support other schemas. The program uses this model in conjunction with a neurally-inspired connectionist network to learn different spatial relations words. Significantly, this learning process does not simply involve matching a word to a single pre-existing, pre-packaged concept; instead, it requires the combination of evidence from several perceptual structures. Thus, Regier demonstrated that the meaning of a given spatial-relations term involves complex combinations of primitive, neurally-plausible image schemas.

   Regier's work is significant in two respects. It supports the idea that primitive image schemas are based on specific types of neural structure. In addition it supports Talmy's analysis that cross-linguistic diversity in spatial-relations terms may reflect different ways of using an "inventory" of such primitive schemas. However, his model was an oversimplification in many respects. While his model was motivated by brain structure and processing, it was not based on a detailed analysis or modeling of actual neuroanatomy. Additionally, while many properties of image-schematic structure are included in this model, it was not designed to support inferences.

Narayanan (1997) looked at the neural basis of a different kind of schematic structure. He proposed that aspectual structure in language could be modeled as aspectual schemas, that these schemas are neural structures in the premotor cortex of the brain, and that aspectual inferences are arrived at by neural computation over these neural structures. In addition, he showed how metaphorical inference might utilize this same set of structures. The computer program he created demonstrates how neurally-based schematic structure can support inferences.

Importantly, Narayanan's model fits with the theory of neural simulation which proposes that imagining and talking about an action utilizes some of the same brain structures as are used to actually execute that action (Lakoff and Johnson 1999). This theory is supported by recent neuroscientific research, which has found evidence that neural networks active when performing an action are also active in other circumstances. There are three key findings. (1) Imagining an action or perception activates much of the same neural network as is active when actually performing that action or experiencing that perception. (for review, cf. Kosslyn et al. 2001). (2) Observation of an action activates much of the same neural substrate as actual execution; certain visuomotor neurons in the motor system, known as mirror neurons, discharge both when an individual performs an action and when he observes someone else performing that action (di Pellegrino et al. 1992; Gallese et al. 1996; Rizzolati et al. 1996; review in Rizzolati and Craighero 2004). (3) Particularly significant are recent studies which indicate that language (verbs and sentences) denoting actions performed by different body parts (mouth, arms, feet) activates some of the same regions as are active when each type of action is actually performed (Hauk et al. 2004; Hauk and Pulvermüller 2004; Tettamanti et al. 2005). In addition to supporting simulation theory, these findings also suggest an avenue of research; in order to discover the brain structures that are used when we talk about a type of event, we should investigate the brain structures that are used when we imagine, observe, or physically experience that event.

During actual experience, many different parts of the brain will typically be active. But which of these areas compute the image schemas we find in language? Lakoff's *Cog theory* proposes some answers to this question. Firstly, Lakoff noted that Narayanan's aspectual schemas are located in "secondary" rather than "primary" motor areas of the brain (cf. Gallese and Lakoff 2005).[4] Secondly, he noted that Narayanan's aspectual schemas not

---

4. This proposal was first presented in a plenary talk at the 7th ICLC (July 2003).

only structure motor-control experiences, they also compute the semantics of grammatical elements of language. Moreover, he realized that this same set of properties applies to many additional cases, including Regier's spatial image schemas. In all of these cases, there is a structure that seems consistent with that of secondary sensory-motor areas, and this structure applies not only to experience, but to grammatical elements of language as well. Lakoff termed each of these cases a "cog".

What are the differences between primary and secondary brain areas, and why are they significant? Primary sensory-motor areas are concerned with processing information related to a particular modality (visual, auditory, tactile, motor-control), and are fairly directly connected to the receptors or effectors related to that particular modality (eyes, ears, skin, muscles). Secondary sensory-motor areas are connected to primary areas and, of particular importance, some neurons within these secondary areas are sensitive to more than one modality of information. For example, secondary motor areas integrate motor, visual, and somato-sensory modalities for the purpose of performing motor functions. The neural structures found within secondary areas, then, apply not to just one modality of experience, but to multiple modalities.

As with other cogs, then, we would expect image schemas to be computed by neural circuits used in multi-modal sensory-motor operations (Gallese and Lakoff 2005). It should not be surprising that these neural circuits are multi-modal since the image schemas they compute are multi-modal as well. As an example, consider the CONTAINER schema. Experientially, containers may be perceived visually, through touch and/or through motor activity (putting objects into and taking them out of containers). In language, CONTAINER schemas can appear in descriptions of many kinds of physical events, experienced through different modalities (*I saw a cat in the box, I felt a coin in my pocket*), as well as being used metaphorically (people in different states of mind, objects in a category). Accordingly, we would not expect the neural circuitry that computes image schemas to be restricted to a particular modality.

We would, however, expect a variety of neural circuits to be involved in the computation of image schemas. Different parts of the brain perform different functions, and make use of different types of information to perform these functions. As a consequence, the neural circuitry of different brain areas will presumably impose different types of structure on experience and compute different image schemas. However, we would not expect these neural circuits to be unrelated to one another. The brain is necessarily highly interconnected; to function in a coordinated fashion, different parts of the brain must be able to "talk to" and "work with" one another. Additionally, there will be some degree of overlap between the information used by different brain areas since, for instance, information originating in a particular primary area may be used by several secondary areas. Thus, while different brain areas may impose different types of image-schematic structures on experience, brain structure also relates these structures to one another.

Brain structure also affects linguistic structure. In particular, we presume that the neural circuits that compute image-schematic structure also provide the neural substrate for image schema-related language, such as closed-class spatial-relations terms. As we saw earlier in this paper, spatial relations words are not, however, linked one-to-one with individual primitive image schemas. Instead, they are linked to complex schematic structures, which may often exhibit radial category structure (Lindner 1983, Brugman 1988). This is natural, considering the way the brain is structured. The neural circuitry computing a primitive image schema does not operate as a completely independent or isolated module. Instead, it is interconnected with other brain areas, including neural circuits that compute other image schemas. Consequently, it is not surprising that spatial relations words are frequently linked with different complex combinations of related image-schematic structures.

3.1. Neural basis of schemas in path and manner-of-motion descriptions

Where can we go from here? How can we use these findings and theories about the neural basis of image schemas to further explore the relation between image schemas, experience, language and the brain? In this section we will address these questions by exploring a hypothesis about the neural structure supporting path- and manner-related schemas.

Briefly, here is the hypothesis and the reasoning behind it. Based on the theory of neural simulation, we would expect that some of the same neural structures that are active during motion experiences such as walking and running would also be active when we imagine or talk about such experiences. While many areas of the brain are active during actual experience of motion, we would expect only a subset of these areas to serve as neural substrates for language. Furthermore, we would expect this subset of active areas to include the neural circuitry that computes motion-related schemas. And, in accordance with *Cog theory*, we would expect such neural circuitry to be found in multi-modal secondary brain areas rather than in more primary sensory-motor areas. Since the experience of path of motion (e.g., moving in a direction, changing location) is different than that of manner (e.g., moving legs quickly), we would expect different neural substrates for each. Consequently, we would expect the schemas associated with each of these types of experience to be computed by different neural circuits. Based on these expectations, we more specifically propose that: (1) path schemas may be computed by the neural circuitry of multi-modal secondary areas concerned with keeping track of where we are in the world, and (2) manner schemas may be computed by the neural circuitry of multi-modal secondary areas concerned with moving the body.

If this hypothesis is correct, we might further expect to find that processing these different types of motion information is correlated with activity in different regions of the brain. This possibility could be tested by, for example, measuring the brain activation patterns of a person who is listening to or reading different types of motion descriptions. If different brain areas are active for each type of motion information, this may suggest a neural basis for the differences in imagery reportedly associated with path and manner languages.

Before proceeding with an investigation of the claims put forth in this hypothesis, some caveats are in order. First, some of the information about neural structures that is presented here is a simplification, quite possibly an oversimplification, of current neurocognitive research. Moreover, although more is being learned about the brain all the time, much about the brain still remains a mystery. While intriguing, current research on the brain doesn't necessarily give us a full and accurate picture of what is actually going on. Secondly, while we can talk about the function of particular brain areas, we shouldn't think of these areas as independent modules with a single function. Each area is interconnected with many other different areas of the brain, and may participate in more than one functional network. Thirdly, the same or similar information may be used by many parts of the brain. Additionally, general neuronal processes will presumably be similar throughout the brain. For these reasons, the presence of image-schematic structure in a given area of the brain does not necessarily mean that this is the only area that computes this image schema. In fact, it seems reasonable to suppose that the more generally applicable a schema is, the more areas it is likely to "appear" in. Keeping all of these things in mind, we now return to our hypothesis.

How can we go about investigating this hypothesis? Following the line of reasoning presented above, we can start by using existing brain research to try to answer the following questions: (1) Which areas of the brain are active when we walk, run, enter buildings, etc.? (2) What sorts of neural circuitry are present in these areas? (3) How might this circuitry support the sorts of schematic structure we saw in motion descriptions? Further brain research will also be needed; we will suggest ways that such research might test (and likely lead to modifications of) this hypothesis.

Let us start by considering the types of brain activity which occur during self-motion experiences. Although we may not pay conscious attention to what we are doing when we move around, several different functions need to be performed by our brain. We have to execute and monitor motor control routines to make our body move, monitor our immediate environment so we don't run into things while we're moving, and we also need to keep track of where we are so we don't get lost. In order to perform these and other necessary functions, many different parts of the brain will be simultaneously active. Of these active areas, we will want to focus on multi-modal secondary brain areas rather than more primary areas, since, as discussed above, we believe that they have the right sort of circuitry to compute image schemas.

From this set of active areas, we have chosen to focus on two functional networks. First we will look at a network concerned with location and navigational functions, and then at a network related to motor-control functions. We will examine the structure and function of selected brain areas within these networks in order to determine what sorts of structure they may impose on motion experiences. Further, we will consider what sorts of schematic structures might be computed by their neural circuitry, and how such structures may be similar to the path- and manner-related image schemas that appear in motion descriptions.

3.2. Navigational functions – the hippocampus

While several brain areas are involved in processing spatial information for navigational purposes, we will focus on one area, the hippocampus. As well as being involved in episodic memory, the hippocampus is thought to play a particularly important role in navigation, helping to keep track of current location and to find novel routes within an environment. It has been theorized to function as an allocentric cognitive map, determining an organism's location with respect to objects in the environment rather than with respect to the organism itself. (O'Keefe and Nadel 1978).[5] Notice that this use of a self-to-environment relation to determine location is similar to what is used in motion descriptions containing path information. As we saw, path-related locations are commonly specified via the spatial relation between the mover and some object in the environment (*He ran to/into the house*).

Contained within the hippocampus are "place cells". A given place cell is active only when an organism is in a particular relatively small region of its current environment (the cell's "place field"). Although much of what is known about place cells and the hippocampus' role in navigation is the result of animal studies, similar findings have been made in humans. (Maguire et al. 1998; Ekstrom et al. 2003; Hartley et al. 2003; Hartley et al. 2004).

Place cell activity is related to the presence of certain kinds of environmental information. Significantly for our current endeavor, the informational sensitivities that seem to be exhibited by place cells are similar in many ways to the schematic elements commonly found in path descriptions. Some of the key similarities are as follows:

–   The most influential type of information for place cells seems to be that provided by distal sensory cues, particularly stable visual cues. Place cell firing fields do *not* generally seem to be affected by the movement of small objects within the environment, though Rivard et al. (2004) found that some the firing of some cells seemed to be related to barriers within an environment. In language, the landmarks used to describe the mover's location are usually objects with a fixed location, quite commonly ones that are visible from a distance (e.g., *He walked to the mail-box/tree/store*, but not usually *He walked to the cat.*).

–   Distortions of place fields that result from changing the shape and size of the environment suggest that place fields are sensitive to distance and angular relations to boundaries, such as walls. (cf. Hartley et al. 2004: 5). Recall that in language, boundaries and walls were seen to be important schematic structural elements of the landmarks used in motion descriptions. For example, in both *He entered the building* and *He ran out of the kitchen,* the landmark's boundaries, in conjunction with other elements of the CONTAINER schema, were used to specify the changing locations of the mover. Additionally, we saw that spatial-relations terms such as *cross* and *across* utilized schematic structure that involved the geome-

---

5. In this respect it differs from path integration (originally called "dead reckoning") in which, it is theorized, a mover keeps track of location by relying on cues derived from self-motion (cf. Etienne and Jeffrey 2004).

try of the landmark. In such cases, the geometry of the landmark may be used to differentiate its boundaries, and a mover's current location could be coded with respect to relative distance (and angular relation) to different landmark boundaries. Recall also that Talmy noted that ground (landmark) geometry was one of the basic distinctions made by spatial-relations terms.

— Significantly, while place cell activity is related to an entity's location within the environment, it is independent of the entity's orientation (cf. Hartley et al. 2004: 4). In other words, an organism isn't sensitive to which direction it is facing while at that location. In language, the schematic structure of these landmarks seems to be the same regardless of the mover's orientation to them; a building has the schematic structure of a container whether someone is *entering* it or is *exiting* it.

To summarize, the hippocampus seems to rely on place cell activity to keep track of the organism's location. Place cell activity correlates with certain limited types of information. Place cells seem to be particularly sensitive to distal landmarks and schematic elements of local landmarks (boundaries, in particular). Place cells do not seem to be sensitive to the organism's current orientation in relation to the environment. And, the types of information to which place cells are sensitive seems to be very similar to many of the types of schematic information that commonly occur in path descriptions of motion.

The neural circuitry within the hippocampus effectively imposes a particular kind of schematic structure on motion experiences. This is not to say that the hippocampus is the origin of each of the individual schematic structural elements described above. Object boundaries, for example, may be computed by basic perceptual systems of the kind modeled by Regier. What is significant is that the hippocampus is "selective" about which information it uses to perform its navigational functions. In addition to boundary information, perceptual systems detect many other object properties, such as shape and texture. Other brain areas, such as the parahippocampus (Epstein et al. 2003), are sensitive to a person's orientation relative to the environment. But place cells in the hippocampus do not seem to be sensitive to the entire range of information that is present as we move about. Instead, the hippocampus relies on only certain limited elements of motion experiences in order to perform its navigational functions. Within the hippocampus, then, experiences of moving about in the world are schematically structured. Path of motion descriptions evidence similar structure, suggesting that the hippocampus may provide a neural substrate for many of the schemas found in such descriptions.

3.3. Motor-control elements of locomotion

When we walk or run, in addition to knowing where we are and where we're going, we also have make our body move from one place to another. To do this, we need to execute and monitor motor-control routines. Since locomotor actions such as walking and running are kinds of motor actions, the neural circuitry associated with locomotion will presumably be similar in many respects to the circuitry involved in other types of motor actions. Indeed, imagining locomotor actions has been found to activate cortical regions which are part of "a well-documented neural network associated with the mental representation of motor actions" (Malouin et al. 2003: 56). Descriptions of locomotor actions may therefore express some of the same image-schematic structure as appears in descriptions of other types of motor control actions. However, recall that the proposed LOCOMOTION schema included some schematic elements, such as gait, which would distinguish locomotion from other types of motor actions. In this section we will focus on these distinctive elements, and the neural circuitry that might compute them. In order to determine which brain areas might contain such circuitry, we will explore some of the ways that brain activation during locomotion may differ from activation during other types of motor actions.

One difference between locomotion and other motor actions may relate to the somatotopic organization of motor control regions. Within these regions, which group of neighboring neurons is active during a motor-control action depends on which part of the body (feet/legs, hands/arms, teeth/ mouth) is used to perform that action. Walking involves foot and leg actions, and these actions have been found to show activation consistent with this somatotopic organization (Sayhoun et al. 2004). The execution, observation, or imagination of actions involving other parts of the body, such as hands (grabbing) or teeth (biting), will each activate other areas (Buccino 2001; Ehrsson 2003). Significantly, recent studies show that reading or hearing language about actions performed by different body parts (mouth, fingers, feet) also produced a pattern of activation that is consistent with such somatotopic organization (Hauk et al. 2004; Hauk and Pulvermüller 2004; Tettamanti et al. 2005). Thus, the neural circuitry of somatotopically-organized motor-control regions seems to support schematic specification of the body part used in a motor action. For locomotion and manner of motion verbs, the relevant body part will usually be feet and legs, though some manner verbs (*climb, crawl*) may also indicate the use of hands and arms.

Walking and running differ from many other motor actions in that they involve sequential rhythmic behavior. Selection of a particular gait and/or speed of locomotion may be related to the level of activation in the cerebellar locomotor region. Increased activation within this area leads, in cats, to a change in gait, such as a change from walking to running (see Jahn et al. 2004). In humans, Jahn and colleagues found greater cerebellar activation for running than for walking or standing imagery. They suggest that in-creased activation within this region "might reflect the correlation between neuronal activity and speed reported in animal experiments" (Jahn et al. 2004: 1729). Thus the cerebellar region seems to have neural circuitry that relates to speed and gait elements of locomotion. These same schematic ele-ments appear in motion descriptions; as we saw earlier, different manner verbs schematically specify different gaits and/or speeds. We might, for example, differentiate between *walk, stride, jog* and *run* on this basis.

As we perform the locomotor routines involved in walking or running, we need to monitor and react to our immediate surroundings; if there's a hole in the road we want to step over it, not into it. Performance of this function may in part depend on the parietal cortex. Activity in some areas in the pa-rietal cortex seems to be related to the presence in the immediate environ-ment of obstacles that require modification of the current motion pattern (Beloozerova and Sirota 2003; Malouin et al. 2003). The parietal cortex is thought to be involved in multimodal representations of local space used for the control of limb movements (Andersen et al. 1997; Colby and Goldberg 1999; Rizzolatti et al. 1997).[6] For locomotor actions like walking, where control of the feet and legs is important, the area immediately in front of the feet would presumably be particularly relevant. When the walking surface is smooth and no obstacles are present, relatively little attention needs to be paid to the immediate surroundings and, consequently, neural activity in these areas would be expected to be relatively low. But for adverse condi-tions, such as the presence of obstacles or rough path surfaces, motion may

---

6. The spatial sensitivities of parietal areas are different than those exhibited by the hippocampus. While hippocampal place cells process information about landmarks some distance away from the body (walls, distal landmarks), parie-tal areas seem to only process information about more proximal landmarks (cf. Save and Poucet 2000).

need to be modified, and the level of activation in this area would consequently be higher. In language, manner verbs can also distinguish between situations where no hindrances are present, as in verbs like *stroll, glide,* and *amble,* and ones where gait has been modified, possibly in response to adverse conditions, as in verbs like *trudge, slog, leap, duck, stumble* and *crawl.* The particular conditions are not specified, though a "schematic" value may be inferable (e.g., *slog* may indicate some sort of wet or marshy surface). In the proposed LOCOMOTION schema, the structural element we called "Effort" may to some extent reflect the presence of such adversity, since the amount of effort needed for locomotion is often correlated with the nature of the surroundings. Avoiding obstacles, for example, will presumably require more effort. Neural circuitry within the parietal cortex may be at least partly responsible for computing image-schematic elements such as the presence of obstacles and related modifications of gait.

In sum, motor-control-related brain areas that are active while we are walking or running are responsive to many of the same sorts of information as are schematically specified by manner verbs. Within somatotopically-organized motor-control regions, different groups of neurons will be active when different body parts (head, hands, feet) are used to perform an action. Activation in the cerebellar locomotor region seems to be related to the gait and/or speed of locomotion. Activity levels in some parts of the parietal cortex seem to be related to the presence or absence of adverse surface conditions or obstacles. Working together, these areas effectively impose a different sort of structure on motion experiences than does the hippocampus. Moreover, many of these same areas have also been found to be active when we are imagining, observing or even talking about such actions. Significantly, the particular types of information associated with the neural circuitry of these areas – body part, gait, speed, and effort or difficulty of motion – are very similar to the schematic parameters specified by manner of motion verbs. This leads us to propose that these motor control regions may serve as the neural substrate for the image schemas found in manner of motion descriptions.

3.4. Neural section: summary

Now let us put all this together to tell what we think is a plausible story about motion experiences, neural structure, and the image-schematic structures used in motion descriptions. As we walk or run from one place to another, many different parts of our brain will be concurrently active. Some sub-set of these active areas will have the sort of neural circuitry that computes image-schematic structure. There may well be some degree of "overlap" in terms of what sort of schematic structures are computed by these neural circuits. Many different brain areas, for instance, include object boundaries as part of their computations. However, the schematic structures computed within a given area will differ in at least some respects from those computed in other areas. These differences will presumably be related to what functions an area performs, and what types of information it needs to perform those functions. Working together, these active areas will compute a wide range of schematic structures. We might therefore consider these active brain areas as somehow supplying an "inventory" of different image schemas that structure experiences of walking and running. Notice that such schematic structuring of motion experience occurs independently of the language which expresses these image schemas.

When we talk about motion experiences like walking and running, we activate some of the same neural circuitry as is active during actual experience. These active areas will presumably include the neural circuitry used to compute the above-mentioned "inventory" of image schemas. However, not all motion descriptions will make equal use of this inventory. While the speaker has some discretion as to which schematic elements he chooses to express, the choice will also be guided by the language he is using; languages differ in terms of which schematic elements tend to be or are obligatorily expressed. Of particular relevance to this section, motion verbs in some languages tend to include manner of motion information, while motion verbs in other languages tend to include path of motion information. These two types of information are each associated with the use of a different set of image schemas. And, as we've shown in this paper, these path- and manner-related schemas may each be computed by the neural circuitry of different functional brain networks. Consequently, "manner-predominant" and "path-predominant" languages may differ not only in their utilization of the basic image schema inventory, but also in terms of their underlying neural substrates. In sum, for either type of language we may be using some of the same brain circuitry as is active during actual motion experiences. However, when verbs include path information, we may activate different neural circuitry than when they include manner information. More specifically, we have hypothesized that the use of path information may correlate with activation in the hippocampus, while use of manner information may correlate with activation of motor-control areas concerned with locomotion. To the extent that these different brain areas also support different types of imagery, it would not be surprising to find that manner verbs are associated with different imagery than path verbs.

While this story seems plausible, it is by no means proven. However, it suggests several directions for future research. The specific hypothesis made here can be tested by conducting research on the patterns of brain activation associated with the use and comprehension of path and manner verbs. We might also investigate the question of what happens when we use more than one kind of image-schematic structure in a sentence. For example, what happens when sentences with a manner verb also include path information? Additionally, image-schematic structures in other domains of experience might be fruitfully analyzed using an approach similar to that shown in this paper.

4.   Concluding remarks

Image schemas are sometimes viewed as abstractions over experiences. However, this is misleading, in that it implies that we start with full, rich representations of experiences and then somehow "abstract out" or extract certain schematic structural elements that are common to all of these experiences. This view doesn't explain how or why we perceive the particular schematic structural elements that we do, nor does it explain how this abstraction process is performed.

Viewing image schemas as neural circuits, however, we see the relation between experience, language and image-schematic structure very differently. If a given brain area or circuit is sensitive only to a few types of information relating to an experience, and is not sensitive to a vast range of other information about the experience, then that area or circuit in effect provides a schematic representation of that experience. If we anthropomorphize this circuit, we might say that all it can perceive about the experience are these few schematic elements. This doesn't necessarily mean that each neural circuit supports a different primitive image schema (if it did, it would mean that there were a huge number of primitive image schemas!). The brain is massively interconnected, and the same or similar information may be used for different functions in many different parts of the brain. Consequently, related image-schematic structures may be distributed across several brain areas. Whenever the neural circuits within these brain areas are active, they may serve to impose schematic structure on the current experience. There are two very important consequences to this. Firstly, because the same neural circuit may be active for many different experiences, it is possible for the same image-schematic structure(s) to be imposed upon a large variety of experiences. This explains why we can "find" the same image schema in many different experiences. Secondly, for a given experience, many different brain areas and neural circuits will be active. Thus, more than one type of image-schematic structure may be imposed upon that experience. This explains why we can "find" more than one type of image-schematic structure in a given experience. Importantly, the image-schematic structure imposed upon experience exists independently from the language that expresses it. Consequently, languages may vary in terms of which elements of schematic structure they tend to express. Additionally, words may link with different complex combinations of related image-schematic structures. Thus, the image-schematic structure that we observe both in experiences and in language about those experiences are both natural results of the way the brain is structured.

Extensive cross-linguistic variation in spatial-relations terms and motion descriptions has sometimes been taken as an indication that it is misguided to spend time looking for neural structures associated with primitive image schemas. We believe this attitude is itself misguided. To a large extent this position seems to be based on a notion that image schemas are concepts associated with individual words. Since such concepts do not seem to be universal, there seems to be no point in looking for universally available structures, neural or otherwise. However, while individual spatial-relations terms, for example, may evidence different types of complex schematic structures, we've seen that they appear to use only a limited set of basic distinctions or primitive image schemas. It is this limited, presumably universally-available set of image schemas which we believe to be associated with language-independent neural structures. Furthermore, many linguistic theories do not attempt to link linguistic structure to neural structure. Sometimes this is because neither image schemas nor a detailed understanding of the brain are considered critical to an understanding of language or linguistic diversity. Other times it is justified by saying that we just don't know enough about the brain, its structure, and how it may affect language to seriously take neuroscience into consideration when making linguistic theories. It is true that much remains to be learned about the brain. However, as we have shown in this paper, neuroscience matters. It guides us in our choice of theories and approaches to linguistic diversity. Moreover, it leads us to a deeper understanding of image schemas and their relation to experience, language, and the brain.

Coda

- Linguistic structure reflects brain structure.
- Linguistic structure is schematic (image schemas, force-dynamic schemas, aspectual schemas, and so on) because the corresponding brain regions each perform limited, small-scale computations.
- Linguistic schemas can form complex superpositions because the corresponding brain structures can be active simultaneously.
- Complex linguistic structures that vary widely are each made up of the same ultimate universal primitives because we all have the same brain structures that perform the same computations.
- Linguistic structure is below the level of consciousness because the brain structures that compute them are unconscious.
- Abstract schematic structures are not learned by a process of abstraction over many instances, but rather are imposed by brain structure.
- Image schemas are created by our brain structures; they have been discovered, not just imposed on language by analysts.
- Cognitive linguistics isn't cognitive linguistics if it ignores relevant knowledge about the brain.

References

Andersen, Richard A.; Lawrence H. Snyder, David C. Bradley and Jing Xing
    1997   Multimodal representation of space in the posterior parietal cortex and its use in planning movements. *Annual Review of Neuroscience* 20: 303-30.
Beloozerova, Irina N. and Mikhail G. Sirota
    2003   Integration of motor and visual information in the parietal area 5 during locomotion. *Journal of Neurophysiology* 90: 961-971.
Bowerman, Melissa
    1996   Learning how to structure space for language: A cross-linguistic perspective. In *Language and Space*, P. Bloom, M. Peterson, L. Nadel and M. Garrett (eds.), 385-436. Cambridge, MA: MIT Press.

Bowerman, Melissa and Soonja Choi
   2001   Shaping meanings for language: universal and language-specific in
             the acquisition of spatial semantic categories. In *Language Acquisi-
             tion and Conceptual Development*, Melissa Bowerman and Stephen
             C. Levinson (eds.), 475-511. Cambridge: Cambridge University
             Press.
Brugman, Claudia
   1983   The use of body-part terms as locatives in Chalcatongo Mixtec.
             Report 4 of the Survey of California and Other Indian Languages,
             University of California: 235-90.
   1988   *The Story of 'Over'. Polysemy, Semantics and the Structure of the
             Lexicon*. New York and London: Garland. [M.A. thesis, The Uni-
             versity of California, Berkeley, 1981]
Buccino, Giovanni, Ferdinand Binkofski, Gereon R. Fink, Luciano Fadiga,
             Leonardo Fogassi, Vittorio Gallese, Rüdiger J. Seitz, Karl Zilles,
             Giacomo Rizzolatti and Hans-Joachim Freund
   2001   Action observation activates premotor and parietal areas in a
             somatotopic manner: an fMRI study. *European Journal of Neu-
             roscience* 13: 400-404.
Choi, Soonja and Melissa Bowerman
   1991   Learning to express motion events in English and Korean: The
             influence of language-specific lexicalization patterns. *Cognitive
             Development* 41: 83-121.
Colby, Carol and Michael Goldberg
   1999   Space and attention in parietal cortex. *Annual Review of Neurosci-
             ence* 22: 319-49.
Di Pellegrino, Giacomo, Luciano Fadiga, Leonardo Fogassi, Vittorio Gallese
             and Giacomo Rizzolati
   1992   Understanding motor events: A neurophysiological study. *Ex-
             perimental Brain Research* 91: 176-180.
Ehrsson, H. Henrik, Stefan Geyer and Eiichi Naito
   2003   Imagery of voluntary movement of fingers, toes and tongue acti-
             vates corresponding body-part-specific motor representations. *Jour-
             nal of Neurophysiology* 90: 3304-3316.
Ekstrom, Arne D. and Michael J. Kahana, Jeremy B. Caplan, Tony A. Fields,
             Eve A. Isham, Ehren L. Newman and Itzhak Fried
   2003   Cellular networks underlying human spatial navigation. *Nature*
             425: 184-188.
Epstein, Russel, Kim S. Graham and Paul E. Downing
   2003   Viewpoint-specific scene representations in human parahippocam-
             pal cortex. *Neuron* 37: 865-76.

Etienne, Adriane S. and Kathryn J. Jeffery
  2004   Path integration in mammals. *Hippocampus* 14: 180-192.
Gallese, Vittorio, Luciano Fadiga, Leonardo Fogassi and Giacomo Rizzolatti
  1996   Action recognition in the premotor cortex. *Brain* 119: 593-609.
Gallese, Vittorio and George Lakoff
  2005   The brain's concepts: The role of the sensory-motor system in
            conceptual knowledge. *Cognitive Neuropsychology* 22: 455-479.
Hartley, Tom, Eleanor Maguire, Hugo Spiers and Neil Burgess
  2003   The well-worn route and the path less traveled: Distinct neural
            bases of route following and wayfinding in humans. *Neuron* 37:
            877-888.
Hartley, Tom, Iris Trinkler and Neil Burgess
  2004   Geometric determinants of human spatial memory. *Cognition* 94:
            39-75.
Hauk, Olaf, Ingrid Johnsrude and Friedman Pulvermüller
  2004   Somatotopic representation of action words in human motor and
            premotor cortex. *Neuron* 41: 301-307.
Hauk, Olaf and Friedman Pulvermüller
  2004   Neurophysiological distinction of action words in the fronto-central
            cortex. *Human Brain Mapping* 21: 191-201.
Jahn, Klaus, Angela Deutschländer, Stephan Thomas, Michael Strupp, Martin
            Wiesmann and Thomas Brandt
  2004   Brain activation patterns during imagined stance and locomotion
            in functional magnetic resonance imaging. *NeuroImage* 22:
            1722-1731.
Johnson, Mark
  1987   *The Body in the Mind. The Bodily Basis of Meaning, Imagination
            and Reason*. Chicago: The University of Chicago Press.
Kosslyn, Stephen M., Giorgio Ganis and William Thompson
  2001   Neural foundations of imagery. *Nature Reviews Neuroscience* 2:
            635-642.
Lakoff, George
  1987   *Women, Fire and Dangerous Things. What Categories Reveal
            about the Mind*. Chicago: The University of Chicago Press.
Lakoff, George and Mark Johnson
  1999   *Philosophy in the Flesh: The Embodied Mind and its Challenge to
            Western Thought*. New York: Basic Books.
Langacker, Ronald W.
  1976   Semantic Representations and the linguistic relativity hypothe-
            sis. *Foundations of Language* 14: 307-357.
  1987   *Foundations of Cognitive Grammar*, Vol. 1: *Theoretical Pre-
            requisites*. Stanford: Stanford University Press.

Langacker, Ronald, and Eugene H. Casad
   1985   'Inside' and 'Outside' in Cora Grammar. *International Journal of American Linguistics* 51: 247-281.
Levinson, Stephen C.
   2003   *Space in Language and Cognition: Explorations in Cognitive Diversity*. Cambridge: Cambridge University Press.
Levinson, Stephen, Sergio Meira and "The Language and Cognition Group"
   2003   'Natural concepts' in the spatial topological domain—adpositional meanings in crosslinguistic perspective: An exercise in semantic typology. *Language* 79: 485-516.
Lindner, Susan
   1982   What goes up doesn't necessarily come down: the ins and outs of opposites. *Chicago Linguistic Society* 18: 305-323.
   1983   *A Lexico-Semantic Analysis of English Verb-Particle Constructions*. Trier: L.A.U.T. (series A: 101).
Maguire, Eleanor, Neil Burgess, James G. Donnett, Richard S. J. Frackowiak, Christopher D. Frith and John O'Keefe
   1997   Knowing where and getting there: A human navigation network. *Science* 280: 921-924.
Malouin, Francine, Carol L. Richards, Philip L. Jackson, Francine Dumas and Julien Doyon
   2003   Brain activations during motor imagery of locomotor-related tasks: A PET study. *Human Brain Mapping* 19: 47-62.
Mandler, Jean M.
   1992   How to build a baby 2. *Psychological Review* 99-4: 587-604.
Narayanan, Srini
   1997   Karma: Knowledge-based active representations for metaphor and aspect. Ph.D. Dissertation, Computer Science Division of The University of California at Berkeley.
O'Keefe, John, and Lynn Nadel
   1978   *The Hippocampus as a Cognitive Map*. Oxford: Clarendon Press.
Pedersen, Eric, Eve Danziger, David Wilkins, Stephen Levinson, Sotaro Kita and Gunter Senft
   1998   Semantic typology and spatial conceptualization. *Language* 74: 557-589.
Regier, Terry
   1995   A model of the human capacity for categorizing spatial relations. *Cognitive Linguistics* 6: 63-88.
   1996   *The Human Semantic Potential: Spatial Language and Constrained Connectionism*. Cambridge, MA: The MIT Press

Rivard, Bruno, Yu Li, Pierre-Pascal Lenck-Santini, Bruno Poucet, Robert U. Muller
2004   Representation of objects in space by two classes of hippocampal pyramidal cells. *The Journal of General Physiology* 124: 9-25.
Rizzolatti, Giacomo, Luciano Fadiga, Vittorio Gallese and Leonardo Fogassi
1996   Premotor cortex and the recognition of motor actions. *Cognitive Brain Research* 3: 131-141.
Rizzolatti, Giacomo, Leonardo Fogassi and Vittorio Gallese
1997   Parietal cortex: from sight to action. *Current Opinion in Neurobiology* 7: 562-567.
Rizzolatti, Giacomo, and Laila Craighero
2004   The mirror-neuron system. *Annual Review of Neuroscience* 27: 169-192.
Sahyoun, C., Anna Floyer-Lea, Heidi Johansen-Berg and Paul M. Matthews
2004   Towards an understanding of gait control: brain activation during the anticipation, preparation and execution of foot movements. *NeuroImage* 21: 568-575.
Save, Etienne, and Bruno Poucet
2000   Involvement of the hippocampus and associative parietal cortex in the use of proximal and distal landmarks for navigation. Behavioural Brain Research 109 : 195-206.
Slobin, Dan I.
1996   From "Thought and Language" to "Thinking for Speaking". In *Rethinking Linguistic Relativity,* John J. Gumperz and Stephen C. Levinson (eds), 70-96. Cambridge: Cambridge University Press.
2003   Language and thought online. In *Language in Mind; Advances in the Study of Language and Thought*, Dedre Gentner and Susan Goldin-Meadow (eds.), 157-191. Cambridge, Mass: The MIT Press.
Talmy, Leonard
1972   Semantic structures in English and Atsugewi. Ph.D. Dissertation, The University of California, Berkeley.
1975   Semantics and syntax of motion. In *Syntax and Semantics*, Vol. 4. John P. Kimball (ed.), 181-238. New York: Academic Press.
1978   Relation of grammar to cognition. In *Syntax and Semantics*. Vol. 6: *The Grammar of Causative Constructions*, Masayoshi Shibatani (ed.), 43-116. New York: Academic Press.
1983   How languages structure space. In *Spatial Orientation: Theory, Research and Application,* Herbert Pick and Linda Acredolo (eds.), 225-282. New York: Plenum Press.

1985   Lexicalization patterns: Semantic structure in lexical forms. In *Language Typology and Syntactic Description*. Vol. 3: *Grammatical categories and the lexicon*, Timothy Shopen (ed.), 57-149. Cambridge: Cambridge University Press.
1988   Force dynamics in language and cognition. *Cognitive Science* 12: 49-100.
2000   *Toward a Cognitive Semantics I: Concept Structuring Systems.* Cambridge and London: MIT Press.
Tettamanti, Marco, Giovanni Buccino, Maria Cristina Saccuman, Vittorio Gallese, Massimo Danna, Paola Scifo, Ferruccio Fazio, Giacomo Rizzolatti, Stefano F. Cappa, and Daniela Perani
2005   Listening to action-related sentences activates fronto-parietal motor circuits. *Journal of Cognitive Neuroscience* 17: 273-281.
Vandeloise, Claude
1984   Description of space in French. Ph.D. Dissertation, University of California, San Diego.
1991   *Spatial Prepositions: A Case Study from French.* Chicago and London: The University of Chicago Press.

Image schema paradoxes:
Implications for cognitive semantics

Timothy C. Clausner

Abstract

Two paradoxes arise from questions regarding image schemas. How do image schemas relate experience, brain/body, and objective reality? How do image schemas come to be in relation to cognitive structure/systems, and what is that dynamic organization? Just as paradox resolution in physics and debate in philosophy advance those fields, investigation of image schema paradoxes aims to advance cognitive semantics. Implications for cognitive semantic theory are discussed, as are the methodological roles of experiments, computational modeling, and introspective analyses for improving theory.

Keywords: image schemas, schematic systems, paradox, phenomenology, embodiment, experience, objective reality, methodology, theory, model

1. What is an image schema?

The theory of image schemas initiated by Johnson (1987), Lakoff (1987), Talmy (1983), and Turner (1991) inspired me to ask at "The Second Annual Cognitive Linguistics Conference" held at Santa Cruz in 1991, "What is an image schema?" Responses indicated that it is an apt, but difficult question about a fundamental concept in cognitive semantics. As the theory advances, image schemas have become a subject of investigation and application in various disciplines including computer science, cognitive science, linguistics, neuroscience, philosophy, and psychology.

This chapter pursues advancement of our understanding of image schemas in the theory and application of cognitive semantics. Paradoxes arise when considering image schemas and their relations. The standard theory of image schemas does not solve the paradoxes, which serve as points of discussion about the nature and status of image schemas as a fundamental element in cognitive semantics. Two image schema paradoxes are presented: Paradox 1 is about the relation of image schemas to experience and reality.

Paradox 2 is about the relation of image schemas to cognitive semantic structure. Implications of these paradoxes for cognitive semantics and its methodologies are discussed in turn.

2. The relation of image schemas to reality

Before we introduce the first image schema paradox, we describe one bearing on our understanding of reality, mentioned in Einstein's (1905) paper on special relativity. The relativistic "clock paradox", also called the "twin paradox", became the center of debate about the validity of special relativity. Critics of the theory argued that paradoxical predictions about space and time either invalidate the theory or call into question an objective reality.[1] The clock paradox arises from a thought experiment in which twins each have a clock, and one twin remains on earth while the other twin rockets away at relativistic velocity later returning to earth. Special relativity predicts time dilation for moving clocks. The paradox is that since the twins are moving relative to one another, each should measure their respective twin's clock as running slower than their own. The argument was, if both clocks run slow then special relativity is inconsistent, otherwise, if the theory is correct then there is no objective reality. That argument wrongly assumed that the two twins and their respective clocks are in symmetric inertial reference frames. However, the reference frame of the twin on earth is asymmetric relative to the rocket's reference frame. Specifically, the rocket's turnaround as it begins the return journey would be experienced on board as forces betraying its motion. Only one clock slows down. The clock in the rocket will have advanced less than the one that remained on earth, and the rocket passenger will age less than the twin who remained on earth. What special relativity reveals is that time dilation does not contradict the existence of objective reality, only that it is less uniform and stranger than expected. The clock paradox has implications for how we regard reality in cognitive semantics.

---

1. Miller's ([1981] 1998: 248) definitive history quotes debates between Einstein and critics Henri Bergson and Herbert Dingle. The term "objective reality" is used by Einstein in his epistemological discussions of special relativity (Miller 1998: 257, note 34). Similarly, the term is used in this chapter to mean the raw material of the world existing independent of human experience.

Paradox 1: The relation of image schemas to experience and reality
Image schemas structure our experience, and our experience is about reality. Reality exists independent of our experience, yet image schemas structure experiences about objective reality.

The CONTAINER image schema can serve as an example for illustrating the paradox. A cup is a concrete thing in the world, that we interact with and experience as a container by means of the CONTAINER image schema. At some stage of cognitive development, we experience cups. We learn to drink from cups, and we learn they can be filled and spilled. We learn to categorize cups and distinguish them from other things.[2] We learn the word *cup* and relate that to our experience of cups. Development and learning changes our brain resulting in our ability to use and talk about cups, experiencing them as containers. Throughout cognitive development, and our entire life, there is a gap between real cups and what is in our head. This gap is never bridged. Never does a real cup go into our head. (That experience would be of a cerebral missile, not of a cup.) Despite the gap between what is in our head and real cups, our experience of cups is paradoxically real.

In the extreme case this paradox implies that real cups exist in objective reality, but we can never learn about them or experience them as containers because of a gap between real cups and our brain. This reasoning applied to everything leads to the conclusion that we cannot learn about anything in the real world, yet we know these things as real.[3] In another extreme case, the paradox implies that the brain changes in ways we call learning about cups, causing us to think we experience them and their container properties. But due to the gap, this has nothing to do with real cups. In this case what we experience as a cup is only in our head (and that is not the real cup). This reasoning applied to everything implies that what is in our head is all there is, that our experiences are illusory, and there is no objective reality. Both conclusions are unsatisfactory. How can any consistent theory of meaning – and, specifically, the theory of image schemas – both accept objective reality and account for our experiences?

---

2. The CONTAINER image schema is not categorial knowledge of cups. Clausner and Croft (1999) identify the fundamental elements of cognitive semantics as image schemas, categories, concepts, domains, and construals. Grady (*this volume*) also distinguishes image schemas from categories.
3. This case is the learner's paradox found in Plato's *Meno*.

Merleau-Ponty ([1964] 1968) confronts the quandary in terms of the body as a "thickness" which both distances experience from the world and connects it to the world.

> We understand then why we see the things themselves, in their places, where they are, according to their being which is indeed more than their being-perceived – and why at the same time we are separated from them by all the thickness of the look and of the body; it is that this distance is not the contrary of this proximity, it is deeply consonant with it, it is synonymous with it. It is that the thickness of the flesh between the seer and the thing is constitutive for the thing of its visibility as for the seer of his corporeity; it is not an obstacle between them, it is their means of communication. (Merleau-Ponty 1968: 135)

He later suggests that the gap of self-world dualism is addressable by correspondence of experience, body and world.

> One can say that we perceive the things themselves, that we are the world that thinks itself – or that the world is at the heart of our flesh. In any case, once a body-world relationship is recognized, there is a ramification of my body and a ramification of the world and a correspondence between its inside and my outside, between my inside and its outside. (Merleau-Ponty 1968: 136, note 2)

Correspondence between perceiver and world aims to bridge the gap. Interaction serves a similar function in ecological theories of perception, most notably Gibson's (1979) approach to visual perception. But, interaction does not solve the paradox.[4] Investigations of consciousness confront the paradox in qualia, i.e., qualitative aspects of what it is like to experience green or a pain). A central theme of research on consciousness is its reduction to neuroscience, with positions ranging from irreducibility to eliminative. Chalmers (1996: 177) argues that "consciousness cannot be reductively explained" – if it can, then judgements about consciousness should be explainable in terms independent of consciousness, but paradoxically "it seems that consciousness is *explanatorily irrelevant* to our claims and judgements about consciousness". Greenspan and Baars (2005) argue a moderate view that historical success of explanatory reductionism in biology is near the limit for

---

4. Bermúdez (1998: 164) relates self-world dualism to "the paradox of self-consciousness": first person pronoun self-reference is interdependent on our experience of self. His proposed solution is that pre-linguistic boundaries between self and world emerge in somatic proprioception. This is similar to some accounts of image schemas, e.g., mimetic schemas (Zlatev, *this volume*).

explaining consciousness, which will be explained but will require more than simple reductionism to do so. Even the most eliminative treatments of qualia remain a hypothesis. Crick (1993) acknowledges an, albeit illusory, gap in that experience of the world "seems so like 'the real thing'." Then he remarks, "But in fact we have no direct knowledge of objects in the world." (Crick 1993: 33). Presently, neuroscience can only hypothesize elimination of the paradox. The gap is not fully bridged by self-world interactions in ecological psychology or correspondences between experiencer and reality in phenomenology. It is no slight to cognitive semantics, as I will argue, that image schemas also do not close the gap.

Johnson (1987) introduces image schemas with a description of two gaps created by the Cartesian account of experience, "a basic ontological gulf between mind and body, reason and sensation," and "the epistemological gap between ideas and aspects of external reality that they are 'about'." (Johnson 1987: xxvi-xxvii). The epistemological status of image schemas in relation to experience and reality is our chief concern. The theory of image schemas from its introduction by Johnson (1987) and Lakoff (1987), has held that image schemas are patterns of our interactions with reality. That reality is objective, "the reality of a world that exists independent of human beings" (Lakoff 1987: 266). A central principle of the theory of image schemas is that they are embodied in reality, that is,

> ... experience is the result of embodied sensorimotor and cognitive structures that generate meaning in and through our ongoing interactions with our changing environments. ... Meaning comes, not just from 'internal' structures of the organism (the 'subject'), nor solely from 'external' inputs (the 'objects'), but rather from recurring patterns of engagement between organism and environment. (Johnson and Lakoff 2002: 248)

This view situates image schemas in the brain, embodied, in reality, functioning as a connection between experience and the world. We can apply embodied realism to the cup example to illustrate the CONTAINTER image schema. The brain and body are in reality; they interact with a real cup. It's all in reality. This is an ecological approach to meaning because it treats experience of a cup as a container in terms of dynamic interaction between the brain/body and cups in the world by means of the CONTAINTER image schema. This is the embodied approach to meaning. Johnson and Lakoff offer the following characterization (see also Johnson, *this volume*; Dodge and Lakoff, *this volume*):

> An image schema is a neural structure residing in the sensorimotor system that allows us to make sense of what we experience. (Johnson and Lakoff 2002: 248)

Key elements of this view are the neurological locus of image schemas (see also Rohrer, *this volume*) and their dynamic nature (see also Dewell, *this volume*). This implies that image schemas are dynamic, reside in the brain, and emerge from interaction of brain/body with the real world. They are not static and are not exclusive of the brain or objects in world. The CONTAINER image schema, which structures our experience of the cup, resides in the brain, not in the raw material of the cup. The cup is external to the brain/body, and our experience of it is not. Regardless of how dynamic the CONTAINER image schema is, it does not reach beyond the brain/body. A CONTAINER construal is distinct from and may combine with domain content, such as categorial knowledge of cups, but it cannot structure the real cup or explain our experience of the cup as being a container. Therefore, the paradox of how image schemas bridge experience and reality remains.

Image schemas function to structure experience. One aim of cognitive semantics is to characterize that function (in terms that include structure, construal, and interaction). Talmy (2000) uses the term *schematic systems* in his account of the structuring of experience. Part of his system is the *system of spatial schemas* (see also Talmy, *this volume*). His phenomenological view of experience, brain and world is developed in a parametric account of the conscious experience of entities:

> The parameter of *objectivity* is a gradient the high end of which is experienced as being "out there" – that is, as external to oneself, specifically, to one's mind if not one's body. At the low end of the gradient, the entity is experienced as being subjective, a cognitive construct, a product of one's own mental activity. (Talmy 2000: 142)

He offers a possible neural-processing account of internal versus external experience.

> Once stimuli from the entity impinge on the body's sensory receptors, the neural processing of the stimulus, including the portion that leads to conscious experiencing of the entity, never again leaves the body. Despite this fact, we experience the entity as external. Our processing is specifically organized to generate the experience of the entity's situatedness at a particular external location. We lack any direct conscious experience that our processing of the entity is itself internal. In physiological terms, we apparently lack brain internal sense organs or other neural mechanisms that reg-

ister the interior location of the processing and that transmit that information to the neural consciousness system. (Talmy 2000: 174, note 14)

This view traces a *fictive* course from external to internal terminating outside of conscious qualitative experience. Objects external to the brain/body,
are experienced as a result of processes internal to the brain/body, yet objects are paradoxically experienced as being external. The paradoxical gap
remains for schema systems and image schemas.

2.1. Implications for cognitive semantics

The paradox of image schemas in relation to experience and reality has three
distinct implications for cognitive semantics. First, the paradox may be un-
resolvable, for example if qualia in conscious experience is fundamentally
irreducible and unexplainable, then no theory of meaning will overcome the
paradox. Second, if the paradox implies an invalid theory, then there may be
no superior cognitive theory of semantics that eliminates the paradox. A
third possibility is that some assumptions in the theory of image schemas are
invalid, or require revision. The clock paradox in special relativity does not
invalidate that theory, because it arises from wrongly assuming that all reference frames are symmetric, or falsely implies there is no objective reality.
Likewise, Paradox 1 may imply that the theory of image schemas contains
assumptions that require refinement.

The theory of embodied image schemas (Johnson 1987, *this volume*;
Johnson and Lakoff 2002) and schematic systems (Talmy 2000, *this volume*) are partly based on a phenomenological analysis of human experience.
The debate in philosophy between phenomenology and its critics covers a
vast literature, which space permits only mention of a characteristic debate
between Dreyfus (1999) and Searle (2005). Dreyfus advocates embodied
consciousness, siding with existential phenomenologists like Heidegger and
Merleau-Ponty.[5] He holds no strict separation between subjective experience
and objective reality by invoking a "third alternative". Searle (2005: 327)
criticizes Dreyfus' view, and phenomenology in general, for being based on
an illusion: "we do not consciously think of ourselves as embodied con-
sciousnesses in interaction with the world; rather it seems like you and the

---

5. I am indebted to the anonymous reviewer who points out that Geeraerts (1985)
   argues that embodiment in cognitive linguistics has its basis in Heidegger's
   type of phenomenology.

world form a single unity". Searle rejects the "third alternative". For Searle perception, memory, and voluntary action, which require logical analysis to determine their structure, are beyond the reach of phenomenology. On Dreyfus' account, when I drink from a cup without skillful concentration, there is no representation of self-world interaction and there is no subject-object structure. Searle takes this account as self-contradictory and an example of what he calls the phenomenological illusion. In some respects the theory of image schemas spans parts of both views. It is principally a phenomenological theory of experience, meaning, and reality, but also describes logical, albeit non-representational and non-propositional, structure. The theory requires a reconciliation of theses views.

A clearly evident shortcoming is that the theory presently adopts new image schemas – e.g., STRAIGHT (Cienki 1998), AGENCY, CAUSE (Mandler 2004) – but that this process is accretive not predictive. It is dissatisfying that we cannot predict new image schemas, or criteria for a complete inventory (Johnson, *this volume*). Clausner and Croft (1999: 22) argue that the failure to find necessary and sufficient criteria for being image-schematic suggests this may be the wrong approach; a natural definition of this property is distributional: its occurrence in the largest number of domains of human experience. For example, CONTAINER is image-schematic because boundedness is a property found in a large number of experiential domains. Similarly, SCALE is nearly ubiquitous in experience in that nearly every domain involves gradable properties.

If we could predict images schemas, it might lead to a complete inventory. Moreover, if we could characterize image schemas in terms of specific cognitive systems, it might lead to a superior theory of meaning, perhaps obviating Paradox 1.

3.   The relation of image schemas to cognitive semantic structure

Having discussed the paradoxical status of image schemas in relation to experiences about reality, a second paradox arises with respect to image schemas in relation to semantic structures or structuring systems, which includes relations among image schemas.

> *Paradox 2: The relation of image schemas to cognitive semantic structure*
> Image schemas are schematic or topological structure, the primitives that
> organize experience and ground meaning. On the other hand, image sche
> mas are emergent from patterns of interaction or derived from perceptual

experience. Image schemas cannot be both derived from perceptual experience and prerequisite structure for organizing experience.

This paradox pertains to image schemas in two ways, how they come to be in relation to cognitive structure, and what that structural organization is. The first aspect of Paradox 2 is related to the *learner's paradox*, which is about how we can learn what we do not know.[6] Paradox 1, is about how we can know a world we cannot directly experience, and in this way is linked to Paradox 2.

Johnson and Lakoff (2002: 248) argue based on evidence from brain imaging studies, experimental and computational studies in cognitive science, and linguistic analysis that image schemas are both "derived from experience" and "composites of universal, and possibly innate, primitives" – moreover, they

> … reject the rationalist-empiricist dichotomy in favor of the evidence indicating a third alternative that allows both inborn and learned aspects of our conceptual systems, as well as many that cannot clearly be called either inborn or learned. (Johnson and Lakoff 2002: 248)

It is widely agreed that image schemas are not abstracted from or formed by generalization over detailed images in the mind (Dodge and Lakoff, *this volume*; Johnson, *this volume*). However, they are also widely described as derived from perception or sensorimotor processes, e.g., in the context of cognitive development (Mandler, *this volume*) and with regard to their psychological reality (Gibbs, *this volume*). Grady (*this volume*) proposes that some image schemas are more perceptually basic in their bodily physical experience (e.g., PART-WHOLE, CENTER-PERIPHERY, LINK, CONTACT, ADJACENCY, SUPPORT, BALANCE, CONTACT), while others he calls more "complex" (or: "derived"), e.g., CYCLE, PROCESS, SCALE; but he questions whether it is always possible to make such a clear distinction, particularly for PATH and CONTAINER.

An example of bodily CONTAINER illustrates the paradox. Image schemas are basic structures such that experience of our body as a CONTAINER is a given, due to our body's form and function (Lakoff 1987: 271; Johnson

---

6. Chomsky applied the learner's paradox to language spawning innate universal grammar, which Jackendoff (1999: 275) recasts with "the paradox of language acquisition" by arguing that children require only partly innate cognitive constraints to learn a language (which cognitive linguistics and other theories cannot explain, and that may require a new model of language learning and use).

1987: 267). But if image schemas are also derived from our sensorimotor experience, then recurring patterns of bodily perception (e.g., ingesting, drinking from a cup) are a basis for the CONTAINER image schema. It is paradoxical for image schemas to be both basic and derived.

Another sense of this paradox regards levels of image schemas. Image schemas are low-level, a ground for meaning, spatially concrete, and perceptually based. The bodily container is concrete, it is physical, the basis for being a prerequisite CONTAINER image schema. But image schemas are also high-level, derived, or emergent. Paradoxically, image schemas are both high-level *and* low-level, derived *and* basic.

3.1. Implications for cognitive semantics

A paradox does not necessarily invalidate a theory. Just as we argued above regarding Paradox 1, the theory of image schemas can be enhanced as a result of investigating Paradox 2. We discuss relations between and within image schemas in this section principally with the aim of furthering the development of cognitive semantics.

Relations between image schemas were independently investigated by Cienki (1997) and Clausner and Croft (1999) using an inventory of image schemas, and both concluded they are organized into groups. The resulting groups differed, but agreed that FORCE is a group which includes COUNTER-FORCE, COMPULSION, RESTRAINT, ENABLEMENT, and BLOCKAGE; Clausner and Croft additionally included BALANCE and DIVERSION.

Other analyses propose levels of image schemas. Grady (*this volume*) distinguishes between perceptual image schemas based on sensory experience (e.g., UP/HEIGHT) and derived image schemas (e.g., MORE/QUANTITY). The later are derived in two different senses of his analysis: (i) they are not immediately perceptual, and (ii) they are the target domains of primary metaphors.[7] Grady also argues for superschemas (e.g., SCALE) that operate over perceptual and derived image schemas. Zlatev (*this volume*) proposes mimetic schemas (e.g., CLIMB, JUMP) that are derived from and closer to sensory experience, and are hierarchically lower than image schemas. Zlatev further claims that image schemas cannot ground meaning, in contrast to mimetic schemas which are concrete and not based on language. I argue, just

---

7. See also Clausner and Croft (1997) for an analysis of metaphors as derivational relations between domains.

as images schemas do not bridge the gap between experience and reality, neither can schema hierarchies, because the ground limit is bodily proprioception. Whether image schemas can be distinguished from other kinds of schemas based on immediacy to proprioception is an empirical question requiring further study. It is also paradoxical to explain these hierarchies in terms of closeness to perceptual experience, because the meaningful structure of experience is what image schemas are supposed to explain.

Next we consider relations within image schemas, for which Johnson (1987: 61) argues, "it is the [internal] organization of their structure that makes them experientially basic meaningful patterns in our experience and understanding." Mandler (2004: 84, *this volume*) applies this view to cognitive development seeking evidence for preverbal meaning.

A detailed example of the internal parts of CONTAINER is provided by Clausner (1994).[8] The three major parts of CONTAINER are containment, container object, and content, which each presuppose subparts, described with a pertinent container concept (e.g., *cup*) in italics: Containment presupposes the spatial properties of location (*in/out*), direction (*into/out of*), and closure (*open/close*). Containment is a relation between container object and content. Container object presupposes the properties surface (*smooth*), barrier (*opaque*), and material closure (*lid, the opening*). Lastly, there is content (*full/empty*). This analysis illustrates how CONTAINER is highest in a hierarchy of cognitive structures, because it is derived from presupposed bodily experience in real space and material interaction. Alternatively, CONTAINER can be analyzed as presupposed structure that organizes our experience – thus it is low in a hierarchy of cognitive structure. If the theory of image schemas maintains *both* positions, the paradox remains. A third position that *is both* does not solve the paradox either. This implies that the theory requires more specific elaboration to reveal as yet undiscovered asymmetries, akin to obviating the relativistic clock paradox discussed above. The challenge for cognitive semantics is to achieve an empirically testable theory of meaning that avoids Paradoxes 1 and 2. Recent research on image schemas offers a variety of specific elaborations.

The current theory of image schemas includes at least the following principal elements: experience (Johnson, *this volume*), the brain (Dodge and Lakoff, *this volume*; Rohrer, *this volume*), dynamic structure (Dewell, *this volume*), learning (Mandler, *this volume*), interaction in the world (Gibbs,

---

8. This part-whole analysis does not exclude dynamic properties of image schemas, e.g., motion into/out of, closing/opening. (cf. Dewell, *this volume*).

this volume), and cultural settings (Kimmel, *this volume*). We must also account for relations among image schemas (Grady; *this volume*; Zlatev, *this volume*) and for the relation of image schemas to cognitive domains (Clausner and Croft 1999). The dynamic nature of image schemas is emphasized in proposals to subsume them under construal operations (Croft and Cruse 2004: 63-69; Dewell, *this volume*).

Clausner and Croft (1999) argue that the relations found among image schemas are the same kind found among basic experiential domains that support both configurational and locational construals. For example, the cardinal number *three* is a configurational construal because three units of a scale mean *three* regardless of their location on the scale. The ordinal number *third* is a specific location of scale, the third unit from the scale's reference point.

> Thus, two very fundamental image-schematic concepts, gradability and quantity, can be analyzed as locational and configurational concepts respectively, profiled in a single image-schematic domain of SCALE. (Clausner and Croft 1999: 19).

If we apply this analysis of image schemas and construal to Paradox 2, the result is two alternate construals of the entire system of image schemas. One construal is that image schemas are derived from experience, and the other is they are a presupposed structuring system of experience. However, alternate construals of a theory do not constitute a distinct new theory that resolves the paradox. Something more is required, specific structure, akin to asymmetric reference frames in special relativity.

Experimental evidence for the relation of cognitive domains to image schemas is reported in Clausner (2002). Participants labeled a vertical map legend of storm severity. Despite the absence of biasing cues, 91% of responses labeled higher verticality as greater severity (e.g., *high/low, most/least, stormy/fair*). The qualitative domain of severity was construed relative to a vertical scale, consistent with the metaphor MORE IS UP. One interpretation follows Clausner and Croft's (1999) argument that SCALE is a basic *image-schematic domain* that can combine with both spatial verticality and quantity. Alternatively, Grady (*this volume*) proposes that SCALE is a *superschema* that abstracts over perceptual UP/HEIGHT and the quality MORE/QUANTITY. These interpretations are not necessarily contradictory, but do exemplify Paradox 2, because image schemas cannot be both basic and derived. The structural relation between the qualitative domains and image schemas must be explained in a more detailed theory, possibly by investigating metaphors (see Clausner and Croft 1997; Grady, *this volume*; Zlatev, *this volume*).

Talmy's (2000) theory of schematic systems offers specific structure in terms of parameters, for example: "The parameter of palpability is a gradient parameter that pertains to the degree of palpability which some entity is experienced in consciousness, from the fully concrete to the fully abstract." (Talmy 2000: 141). Palpability is characterized by thirteen other parameters, one is the objectivity parameter. A range from subjective to objective construals obtains because parameters can apply to one another.

If parameters applied system-wide, this might result in more than co-experience or combination among multiple schemas, as Johnson's (1987) SUPERIMPOSITION image schema is intended to apply. I propose an image schema (or schematic-system parameter) of RELATIVITY that applies to the entire system of image schemas such that it constitutes distinct construals of the system. Each construal serves as its own frame, such that the frames are relativistically coordinated with the others, symmetrically or asymmetrically in a single reality. We can illustrate how this parameter might be applied, by first noting Talmy's (2000: 130) analysis of "frame relative motion," which is fictive motion and reference applied to whole frames. This is not relativistic in the sense intended here, which is the sense of Einstein's special relativity pertaining to asymmetric reference frames in physical space and time. The latter case will be taken as image-schematic RELATIVITY applied to the domains of space and time.

The application of image-schematic RELATIVITY to more abstract domains may account for technical concepts found in grammatical systems. Subjectivity in Langacker's (1987: 129) cognitive grammar is a continuum of construals relating subject and object grounded in the world. Subjectivity in terms of image-schematic RELATIVITY is the gradability of the subject/object relation while maintaining subject/object asymmetry. Still more abstract and general is the domain of *semantic relativity* (e.g., Boroditsky 2003; Lakoff 1987: 304-337). In my proposal, RELATIVITY applies to the entire system of image schemas, thus constituting experiential construals expressed in one language, that are asymmetric with a second construal for another language, e.g., the English *in/on* distinction is asymmetrically relative to Korean TIGHT/LOOSE FIT (see Mandler, *this volume*; Talmy, *this volume*).

This proposal implies that image schemas can be *trans-schematic* in that they operate over the entire schematic system. Extending the theory of image schemas in this fashion hints toward resolving paradoxes in terms of multiple construals of one image-schematic system, not merely alternate construals of the same theory. Just as alternate construals of Newtonian physics cannot resolve the clock paradox, a transformative theory is required that obviates the paradox. Until such a transformation is found for cognitive semantics, we must apply all available methodologies for strengthening the theory.

4. Theories and models

Methodologies for investigating image schemas include experiments, computational modeling, and introspective analyses. Evidence for image schemas is indicated both from experiments (Gibbs and Colston 1995; Mandler 2004; Richardson, Spivey, Barsalou and McRae 2003), and from computational modeling (Narayanan 1999; Regier 1996).

If Paradoxes 1 and 2 are to yield to cognitive semantic investigations, then we must understand how distinct methods bear on our field of investigation. Both theory building and modeling are key to our understanding of image schemas.

McCloskey (1991) distinguishes between models and theories, arguing that computational models are not themselves cognitive theories or simulations of theories, but can contribute to building and testing theories.

> Although the ability of a connectionist network (or other computational device) to reproduce certain aspects of human performance is interesting and impressive, this ability alone does not qualify as a theory, and does not amount to explaining the performance. (McCloskey 1991: 388)

Human performance data can be used to build a model that simulates or reproduces the data. Alternately we can make a theory that accounts for or explains the data. He argues that simulations and theories in principle can never be the same, but the simulation's coding of representations should be consistent with theoretical principles. A theory serves as a prediction generator. If the theory is very complex, then a simulation of the theory may reveal specific predictions not clearly evident from the theory.

The distinction between models (or simulations) and theories also bears on conclusions allowable from introspection and experiments.

> … introspective evidence alone cannot determine the proper model of mental representation of linguistic forms and meanings. Introspective linguistic evidence can limit the range of alternative mental representations to a set

of possibilities. However, only evidence beyond introspection, such as usage data or psycholinguistic experimentation, might be able to narrow this set of possibilities to a single plausible model. (Croft 1998: 154).

Given the scientific goal of developing the best explanation of the phenomena under investigation, the theory of image schemas/systems addresses the need to bridge the gap between experience, brain/body, and reality. Gibbs and Matlock (1999: 267) add to Croft's argument that evidence from experimental methods greatly underdetermines theories about mental representation, but "theories of cognition should stop maintaining the idea that cognitive structures are necessarily 'in the head', and acknowledge that they are dynamic systems of 'structural couplings' which model how people interact with the world and in different linguistic environments". Gibbs (*this volume*) specifically argues from experimental evidence that image schemas are models of that kind. Rohrer (*this volume*) argues from neuropsychological evidence for "image-schematic simulations" in the brain, which support mental simulations of sensorimotor experience (see also Dodge and Lakoff, *this volume*). All of these methods are required to advance cognitive semantics. As we apply experimental results to build new theories of image schemas/systems, test them with computational models and select among competing theories using introspective analyses, we seek an as yet undiscovered theory without paradoxes.

5. Conclusion

Regarding Paradox 1, the theory of image schemas approaches but does not bridge the gap between experience and objective reality. A cup construed as container seems to be a contiguity between the objectively real cup and the body/brain's experience – the real cup is experienced as a real container. However, the structuring operation of the CONTAINER image schema, together with categorial knowledge about cups, and other cognitive structure/systems, do not explain that qualitative experience. Cognitive semantics must account for this gap, but as yet no semantic theory can. Regarding Paradox 2, the theory rightly eschews dualities, to explain the origin of and relations among image schemas, but paradoxically treats image schemas as *both* presupposed and acquired, and *both* basic and derived. We can conclude the paradoxes remain, but highlight requisite elements of image schema theory: experience, brain/body, dynamic cognitive structure, construal, and culture. A superior cognitive semantics must discard as yet unidentified wrong assumptions, and confront challenges to phenomenology. Both models and theories are required for achieving an empirically testable theory of image schemas absent Paradoxes 1 and 2.

This investigation of image schema paradoxes discussed a number of outstanding empirical problems. What is an image schema? How can we characterize and predict as yet unidentified image schemas? Can a complete inventory be determined? How do image schemas relate experience, brain/body, and reality? What are the relations among image schemas and other cognitive structures/systems? Advances in cognitive semantics resulting from this kind of investigation look toward a theory that solves or obviates these problems.

References

Bermúdez, José Luis
    1998   *The Paradox of Self Consciousness*. Cambridge, Mass.: MIT Press.
Boroditsky, Lera
    2003   Linguistic Relativity. In *The Encyclopedia of Cognitive Science*. Vol. 2, Lynn Nadel (ed), 917-921. London: MacMillan Press.
Chalmers, David J.
    1996   *The Conscious Mind*. New York: Oxford University Press
Cienki, Alan
    1997   Some properties and groupings of image schemas. In *Lexical and Syntactical Constructions and the Construction of Meaning*, Marjolijn Verspoor, Kee Dong Lee, and Eve Sweetser (eds.), 3-15. Amsterdam/Philadelphia: Benjamins.
    1998   STRAIGHT: an image schema and its metaphorical extensions. *Cognitive Linguistics* 9: 107-149.
Clausner, Timothy C.
    1994   Commonsense knowledge and conceptual structure in container metaphors. In *Proceedings of the Sixteenth Annual Conference of the Cognitive Science Society*, Ashwin Ram, and Kurt Eiselt (eds.), 189-194. Hillsdale, NJ: Lawrence Erlbaum Associates.
    2002   How conceptual metaphors are productive of spatial-graphical expressions. In *Proceedings of the 24th Annual Conference of the Cognitive Science Society*, Wayne D. Gray, and Christian D. Shunn (eds.), 208-213. Mahwaw, NJ: Lawrence Erlbaum Associates.
Clausner, Timothy C., and William Croft
    1997   Productivity and schematicity in metaphors. *Cognitive Science* 21: 247-282.

1999   Domains and image schemas. *Cognitive Linguistics* 10: 1-31.

Crick, Francis
1993   *The Astonishing Hypothesis: The Scientific Search for the Soul.* New York: Charles Scribner's Sons.

Croft, William
1998   Linguistic evidence and mental representations. *Cognitive Linguistics* 9: 151-173.

Croft, William, and Alan Cruse
2004   *Cognitive Linguistics.* Cambridge: Cambridge University Press.

Dreyfus, Hubert L.
1999   The primacy of phenomenology over logical analysis. *Philosophical Topics* 27: 3-24.

Einstein, Albert
1905   Zur Elektrodynamik bewegter Körper. *Annalen der Physik, Leipzig* 17: 891-921.

Gibbs, Raymond W., and Herbert L. Colston
1995   The cognitive psychological reality of image-schemas and their transformations. *Cognitive Linguistics* 6: 347-378.

Gibson, James J.
1979   *The Ecological Approach to Visual Perception.* Boston: Houghton-Mifflin.

Geeraerts, Dirk
1985   *Paradigm and Paradox: Explorations into a Paradigmatic Theory of Meaning and its Epistemological Background.* Leuven: Leuven University Press.

Greenspan, Ralph J., and Bernard J. Baars
2005   Consciousness eclipsed: Jacques Loaeb, Ivan P. Pavlov, and the rise of reductionistic biology after 1900. *Consciousness and Cognition* 14: 219-230.

Jackendoff, Ray
1999   Paradox regained. *Cognitive Linguistics* 10: 271-277.

Johnson, Mark
1987   *The Body in the Mind: The Bodily Basis of Meaning, Imagination, and Reason.* Chicago: University of Chicago Press.

Johnson, Mark, and George Lakoff
2002   Why cognitive linguistics requires embodied realism. *Cognitive Linguistics* 13: 245-263.

Lakoff, George
1987   *Women, Fire, and Dangerous Things: What Our Categories Reveal About the Mind.* Chicago: University of Chicago Press.

Lakoff, George, and Mark Johnson
  1999   *Philosophy in the Flesh: The Embodied Mind and its Challenge to Western Thought.* New York: Basic Books.
Merleau-Ponty, Maurice
  1968   *The Visible and the Invisible.* Translated by Alphonso Lingis. Evanston: Northwestern University Press [French original 1964].
Miller, Arthur I.
  1998   Reprint. *Albert Einstein's Special Theory of Relativity: Emergence (1905) and Early Interpretation (1905-1911).* New York: Springer [original 1981].
Mandler, Jean M.
  2004   *The Foundations of Mind: Origins of Conceptual Thought.* Oxford University Press.
McCloskey, Michael
  1991   Networks and theories: The place of connectionism in cognitive science. *Psychological Science* 2: 387-395.
Narayanan, Srinivas
  1999   Moving right along: A computational model of metaphoric reasoning about events. In *Proceedings of the Sixteenth National Conference on Artificial Intelligence and Eleventh Conference on Innovative Applications of Artificial Intelligence*, James Hendler and Devika Subramanian (eds.), 121-127. Menlo Park, California: AAAI Press.
Regier, Terry
  1996   *The Human Semantic Potential: Spatial Language and Constrained Connectionism.* Cambridge, Mass.: MIT Press.
Richardson, Daniel C., Michael J. Spivey, Lawrence W. Barsalou, and Ken McRae
  2003   Spatial representations activated during real-time comprehension of verbs. *Cognitive Science* 27: 767-780.
Searle, John R.
  2005   The phenomenological illusion. In *Experience and Analysis. Erfahrung und Analyse*, Maria E. Reicher, and Johann C. Marek (eds.), 317-336. Wien: öbv&hpt.
Talmy, Leonard
  1983   How language structures space. In *Spatial Orientation: Theory, research, and application*, Herbert L. Pick, Jr., and Linda P. Acredolo (eds.), 225-282. New York: Plenum Press.
  2000   *Toward a Cognitive Semantics.* Vol. 1: *Concept Structuring Systems.* Cambridge, Mass.: MIT Press.
Turner, Mark
  1991   *Reading Minds: The Study of English in the Age of Cognitive Science.* Princeton, NJ: Princeton University Press.

Part 2: Image schemas in mind and brain

The psychological status of image schemas

Raymond W. Gibbs, Jr.

Abstract

Cognitive linguists have proposed that image schemas underlie significant aspects of language and thought. Image schemas are generally understood as "experiential gestalts" that arise from recurring patterns of embodied experience (e.g., BALANCE, CONTAINMENT, SOURCE-PATH-GOAL). In earlier work I argued that there is significant empirical evidence from cognitive and developmental psychology to suggest that image schemas are "psychologically real" (Gibbs and Colston 1995). My aim in this chapter is to consider in greater detail the issue of whether image schemas are enduring mental representations, or better understood as temporary linkages between sensory experience and short-lived conceptualizations of both concrete events and abstract ideas. Under the later view, image schemas are not "representational structures" that provide the causal basis for thought and language, but are emergent, fleeting entities that are part of the embodied simulations used in online thought, including abstract reasoning. Research from cognitive psychology, developmental psychology, psycholinguistics, and cognitive neuroscience will be discussed in relation to cognitive linguistic observations about image schemas and image-schematic processing.

Keywords: image schemas, image-schematic processing, mental representations, embodied simulations in on-line thought

1. Introduction

Image schemas represent the essential glue that binds embodied experience, thought, and language. Since the 1980s, cognitive linguists, most prominently, have demonstrated through different case studies how image schemas play a critical role in describing a wide variety of linguistic structure and behavior. The impetus for cognitive linguists' discovery of image schemas is their discipline's commitment to study the formal structures of language

> ... not as if they were autonomous, but as reflections of general conceptual
> organization, categorization principles, processing mechanisms, and expe-
> riential and environmental influences. (Geeraerts 1990: 1).

But what are image schemas? There is a large range of responses cognitive
linguists give in reply to this question. I recently attended a conference on
empirical methods in cognitive linguistics at Cornell University where the
closing session was devoted to the issue of defining image schemas, and
there was little consensus as to what these things were and how they func-
tioned in linguistic structure and behavior. Moreover, there was much disagreement over the best methods that might be employed to uncover the
structure and functions of image schemas. The present volume should provide an important forum for open discussion of these matters. As I now
write, before seeing all of the other chapters to be included in this volume,
my guess is that there will still be a fair amount of disparity over the nature
and functions of image schemas in cognitive linguistic theory.

My general aim in this chapter is to update some of the relevant findings
from psychology, and cognitive science more generally, on the psychological
status of image schemas. Cognitive linguistic research surely provides evidence on the cognitive nature of image schemas. But I wish to defend the
possibility that image schemas are also psychologically real, in the sense of
playing a critical role in people's real-time thought and linguistic processes.
Beyond this, I have a more specific goal of trying to recapture the experiential nature of image schemas, and to provide an important corrective to the
trend in cognitive linguistics to conceive of image schemas as explicit kinds
of abstract mental representations.

Ten years ago, Herbert Colston and I published a lengthy paper in the
journal "Cognitive Linguistics" that offered a range of empirical evidence
from cognitive psychology, psycholinguistics, and developmental psychology
that appeared, in our view, to be entirely consistent with the possibility that
image schemas underlie significant aspects of language and thought, enough
so as to strongly argue that image schemas were indeed psychological entities and not just mere linguistic fictions (Gibbs and Colston 1995). We concluded the article with a note of warning that serves as the starting point for
my argument in this chapter. We suggested

> ... that linguists and psychologists be cautious in making concrete claims
> about how and where image schemas might be mentally represented. It is
> even possible that image schemas are not specific properties of the mind
> but reflect experiential gestalts that never get encoded as explicit mental
> representations. A different possibility is that image schemas might be

characterized as emergent properties of our ordinary conceptual systems and therefore are not explicitly represented in any specific part of the mind. (Gibbs and Colston 1995: 370)

Despite this warning, most of the literature on image schemas implicitly assumes that these entities are encoded as explicit abstract mental representations in long-term memory, and serve as the enduring foundation for abstract concepts and different aspects of linguistic meaning. I strongly agree with the claim that image schemas are essential aspects of thought and language, but believe that image schemas are best understood as experiential gestalts which momentarily emerge from ongoing brain, body, and world interactions. Image-schematic reasoning, such as that seen in linguistic understanding, involves the embodied simulation of events, and is not simply a matter of activating pre-existing representational entities. Image-schematic reasoning does not simply mean doing something with one's mind, but constructing a simulation of experience using one's body.

2. Body schemas and image schemas

Image-schemas have traditionally been defined as dynamic analog mental representations of spatial relations and movements in space. Even though image schemas are derived from perceptual and motor processes, they are not themselves sensorimotor processes (Johnson 1987). The abstract nature of image schemas, given their emergence from recurring aspects of bodily experience, has unfortunately led cognitive linguists to talk of image schemas in a too static and disembodied way.

For example, image schemas are frequently employed in the analysis of spatial meanings of prepositions by demonstrating how topographic relationships are used to conceptualize more abstract domains (e.g., how SOURCE-PATH-GOAL provides a concrete topographic representation for an abstract expression such as *The premier wants his industrial relations minister to hack his way through the state bureaucracy* (Lee 2001: 41). In this manner, the basic "schema is strongly activated in producing the relevant meaning" and is represented as part of the "semantic network" associated with a preposition like *through* (Lee 2001: 48-49). Even if our understanding grows from basic sensorimotor knowledge and experience, the ultimate representation of image-schematic meaning is characterized as activation within some network that is abstracted away from experience.

My argument is that image-schematic reasoning is always being recreated by the body as people continue to engage in sensorimotor behaviors related to BALANCE, RESISTENCE, SOURCE-PATH-GOAL, CONTAINMENT, and so on. Understanding this point requires paying greater attention to the phenomenology of the human body in action. A key point here is that bodily schemas do not just give rise to image schemas, but that image schemas – including more static schemas such as OBJECT, or COMPLEXITY and COMPACTNESS – are continually tied to embodied action and simulations of experience.

Consider, for a moment, the idea of "body schema." Body schemas underlie how the body actively integrates its posture and position in the environment (Gallagher 1995). We do not ordinarily sense our bodies making postural adjustments as we perceive objects, events, and move about in the world. Body schemas allow us to adroitly walk without bumping into or tripping over things, to follow and locate objects, to perceive shape, distance, duration, and to catch a ball with accuracy. These mundane events all take place independently of our conscious thoughts of the body.

The ongoing operation of body schemas is significantly regulated by our proprioceptive system. Proprioception, often referred to as the "sixth sense," is neglected as an important embodied system, because it is not traditionally seen as an input system for presenting the world to the mind. The information proprioception provides comes from the nerve endings in muscles and joints, and partly also from those in the skin. The balance organ in the ear also contributes to the information about one's posture and position in space. Nerve endings in the muscles give information about the amount and fluctuation of muscle tone and the length and tension of the muscles and in doing so also gives information about movement and the amount of force used. Nerve endings in the joints give information about movement and position of the joints, and thus about movement and posture. Stretch receptors in the skin, especially in the face, give information about facial expressions and movement in speech and eating. The balance organ, together with information from the neck muscles, gives information about the body's global posture and position with respect to the horizontal plane.

Proprioception functions automatically, unconsciously, and may even operate when the brain is disconnected from the nervous system. All our movements and also the maintenance of a posture require a subtle coordination of countless muscles and joints that make up our body schema. Without immediate feedback from the sensory nerves about what the muscles and joints are doing, all of our movements and even the maintenance of our posture would go totally awry. The body schema provides the continually updated, non-conceptual, non-conscious information about the body necessary for the execution of both our gross motor programs and their fine tuning.

Take, for example, a simple bodily action like standing up straight. We have known how to stand up since late infancy, and we no longer have to bother consciously with the appropriate motor programs we have at our disposal to perform this action. Also, the fine tuning of this posture is provided for by the body schema. If our arms are slightly in front of the body, we have to lean back somewhat to compensate for the extra weight in front. If we carry something in front of us, we have to compensate more. The compensating just happens; we don't have to think about it. We don't even notice these small corrections, not in others and not in our own case. It is only when we see people with very large beer-bellies or pregnant women that we notice that we are leaning backwards. All that information from the nerve endings in muscles and joints together with the information from the balance organ is needed. The body schema has to feed it in time to the motor program, otherwise we would fall over. But we don't have to be bothered with it. It all happens automatically, so that we have our hands literally free for other things.

Standing up straight is a recurring body experience, regulated by various body schemas, that is fundamental to a variety of image schemas, such as VERTICALITY, STRAIGHT, and BALANCE. However, the fact that image schemas may arise, or emerge, from recurring patterns of bodily experience does not mean that once they have emerged, they are then divorced from the ongoing functioning of body schemas. Different body schemas, such as those involved in standing up straight, continue to invigorate, and sustain, image schemas, like BALANCE, over the course of one's lifetime. Image-schematic reasoning continually recruits sensorimotor processes that are critical to how we understand ourselves, other people, and the world around us. In this way, image schemas are as much created in the moment, even in the absence of bodily movement, as they are retrieved from long-term memory. This perspective on image-schematic reasoning suggests that many aspects of perception, cognition, and language use are intimately tied to both real and imagined bodily action. There are several lines of evidence from cognitive science that are consistent with this idea (Gibbs 2005).

For example, one of the most important developments in cognitive science over the last 10 years is the discovery of "mirror neurons" in the frontal lobes of humans, and other primates. Mirror neurons are specialized brain cells that show activity both when a person performs an action and when it observes the same action performed by another (possibly cospecific) individual. Research has demonstrated that mirror neurons are activated when individuals watch others perform bodily movement, observe others feeling pain and different emotions, hear voices and music, and see gestures (Stamenov and Gallese 2002). Other studies show that visual perception is rooted in both real and anticipated bodily movement, called "sensorimotor contingencies" (O'Regan and Noe 2001), and that speech perception is accomplished partly through the activation of the motor programs involved in speech production (Liberman and Mattingly 1985). Although cognitive scientists continue to debate these findings and their implications, there is an important trend in the literature to view many aspects of perception as being fundamentally coupled with action. A significant part of how we understand the behaviors of others is accomplished through real and simulated body actions, sometimes described in terms of "as-if body" loops (Damasio 1999, 2003).

3.   Image schemas as embodied simulations

The processes by which we understand other's actions through concurrently activated "as-if body" loops is consistent with the idea that we understand others' thoughts by pretending to be in their "mental shoes" and by using our own mind/body as a model for the minds of others (Davis and Stone 1995).

Image-schematic reasoning may also depend on the embodied simulations created in different circumstances, such as listening to speech, that are part of "as-if body" loops. A critical part of this argument depends on a very specific view of what constitutes a simulation. Most scientists engaged in creating simulations of physical and behavioral processes do so by modeling the formal characteristics of those behaviors. Consider a meteorologist creating a computer simulation of the path of a hurricane along the eastern seaboard of the United States. This simulation nicely maps various topological relationships of this weather system and may even be used to predict the behavior of real hurricanes. To some extent, computer simulations of cognitive processes are similar to the meteorologist's simulations of the behavior of hurricanes – they capture relevant information about the formal characteristics of a set of operations that are carried out on particular representations.

But my claim that image schemas are embodied simulations is based on the idea of an actual "simulator" (Berthoz 2000). Unlike a computer simulation of behavior (e.g., neural networks or any symbolic computing device), a simulator provides something close to what it actually feels like in a full-bodied manner to, say, fly an aircraft in a flight simulator where one feels all the movements associated with flying a real airplane. Image schemas, under this view, are simulators of action that are based on real-life actions and potential actions that a person may engage in. As a simulator, image schemas provide a kinesthetic feel that is not simply the output of some abstract computational machine, but the results of full-bodied experiences that have textures and a felt-sense of three-dimensional depth.[1] For example, when Hamlet says "To be or not to be, that is the question", he describes his suffering as an unbearable symmetry, a stasis. This remark is understood metaphorically in terms of BALANCE and how symmetrically opposed forces can sometimes lead to one feeling almost paralyzed. We do not simply understand Hamlet's comments in an abstract way, but implicitly interpret it by imagining what it feels like to be in this kind of situation, perhaps by recalling personal circumstances in which we have felt similarly. In this way, the embodied simulations involved in understanding language evoke bodily sensations that are directly related to the meanings we give to what people say or write.

The traditional focus in cognitive linguistics on image schemas as emergent from bodily experience sometimes fools people into thinking that image schemas function without much engagement from the rest of the body. But as Damasio (1994, 1999, 2003) has long argued, we have an ongoing awareness of our somatasensory system. Noting that the brain continually receives feedback signals from the body's autonomic processes, Damasio suggests that this feedback provides us with a constant background awareness of our own body's somatasensory systems. This low level of awareness is akin to mood that colors our ordinary consciousness:

> The background body sense is continuous, although one may hardly notice it, since it represents not a specific part of anything in the body but an overall state of most everything in it. (Damasio 1994: 152)

Adopting this perspective of image schemas as "simulations of bodily action" properly acknowledges how image schemas are "experiential gestalts" or "as-if body" loops that are actively created on-the-fly during different cognitive activity, and not as encoded structures in the head that are passively activated as part of unconscious linguistic understanding processes. Once more, this view of image schemas as simulations of bodily actions encompasses schemas that are traditionally seen as being more static, such

---

1. This can be read as a reply to Johnson's (*this volume*) concerns about image schemas as "fleshless skeletons".

as OBJECT. People continually simulate "static" schemas in a more dynamic manner than is mostly assumed in cognitive linguistics (see also Dewell, *this volume*).

4.   Image schemas in language understanding

The claim that image schemas underlie linguistic meaning partly suggests that understanding sentences like *John stood at attention* requires listeners to engage in simulation processes which recreate an embodied model of what is meant. In fact, there is psycholinguistic research that is consistent with this idea. Although most of this work does not specifically mention "image schemas," the findings reported here are, at the very least, consistent with the idea that people are creating embodied construals of meaning as part of their imaginative understanding of linguistic expressions.

For instance, participants in one set of studies were presented with sentences such as *He hammered the nail into the wall* and *He hammered the nail into the floor* (Stanfield and Zwaan 2001). After reading a specific sentence, participants saw a picture depicting the object mentioned in the sentence (e.g., *the nail*). This picture either presented the object in a horizontal or vertical orientation, thus creating a match or mismatch with the orientation of the object implied by the sentence. In fact, comprehension responses were significantly quicker when there was a match between the implied orientation and the picture than when these were mismatched. These results support the idea that people create an image-schematic understanding of the verticality or horizontal nature of an event, even if these inferences are not explicitly mentioned in the linguistic statements.

A follow-up set of studies extended the previous findings to the representation of an object's shape in sentence comprehension (Zwaan et al. 2002). Participants saw sentences like *The ranger saw the eagle in the sky* followed by a picture of an eagle with either folded or outstretched wings. Not surprisingly, people gave faster recognition judgments to the eagle when the picture matched the shape implied by the sentence. A second study showed the same findings using a naming task that did not involve people matching the picture with the previous sentence. Once more, the results support the hypothesis that people create image-schematic construal of events alluded to in each expression.

Other experiments also show that people create dynamic, image-schematic construals of events as part of their understanding of linguistic meaning. Zwaan, Magliano, and Graesser (1996) demonstrated that time shifts in narratives increase processing time. Thus, people reading the phrase *An hour later* after some event, take longer to process this phrase than when a minor time shift is implied, such as with the phrase *A moment later*. These findings are consistent with the "iconicity assumption" that events are assumed to occur in chronological order, but also occur contiguously. Other data indicate that continuing actions in sentences are more prominent in memory than are events not continuing. Thus, people are faster to say that *walked* is a word after reading the following pair of sentences *Teresa walked onto the stage. A moment later she collapsed.* than they did having first read the sentence *Teresa walked onto the stage. An hour later she collapsed.* Related studies show that embodied actions that continue remain more salient in mind than events that have been discontinued. Thus, people were slower to judge that *kicking* was a word after reading *Steve stopped kicking the soccer ball* than after reading *Steve was kicking the soccer ball* (Carreiras et al. 1997). These findings, again, show how people's construals of events, based on their embodied understandings, play an important role in the processing of linguistic expressions.

Very recent work indicates that image schemas are recruited during immediate processing of verbs (Richardson et al. 2003). A norming study first showed that participants were generally consistent in pairing four different pictures that reflect various image schemas (e.g., a circle, a square, an arrow looking up, down, left, or right) with different concrete and abstract verbs (e.g., *push*, *lift*, *argue*, *respect*). A second norming study had participants create their own image schemas for verbs in a simple computer-based drawing environment. Once more, there was good consistency in the spatial shapes people thought best described the meanings of the different verbs. These findings show that people have regular intuitions about the spatial representations underlying different verbs, even abstract ones.

Additional studies in this series showed that verbs activate underlying spatial representations during online language comprehension. For instance, in one study, participants heard a sentence (e.g., *The girl hopes for a pony.*) with two pictures presented sequentially in the center of the computer screen. The two pictures reflected different images of the main subject and object nouns in either vertical or horizontal position. Afterwards, participants were tested on their memory for the pictures in a speeded recognition task. As predicted, people recognized the pictures faster when they were oriented along the same axis as that of the associated verb (e.g., *hope* is associated with an arrow looking up). Verb comprehension appears to activate image schemas that act as scaffolds for visual memory of the pictures. The pictures encoded as oriented similarly to the verbs' meanings were identified faster during the memory tests. These results suggest that verb meanings are actively linked with perceptual mechanisms that influence online comprehension and memory. One possibility is that different perceptual and motor experiences become associated with verbs, which are recreated as part of people's perceptual-motor simulations of the sentence during understanding.

Finally, different experiments demonstrate that previous embodied actions influence immediate symbolic, or semantic, judgments for simple linguistic statements. In these studies, participants were first asked to make hand shapes corresponding to verbal descriptions such as *pinch* and *clench* (Klatsky et al. 1989). Following this, the participants made speeded judgments on the sensibility of phrases such as *aim a dart* (sensible) or *close a nail* (not sensible). Embodied action relevant to the phrases facilitated people's speeded verifications of these phrases. For instance, the hand shape for *pinch* speeded the sensibility judgments for *throw a dart* but not *throw a punch*. Interestingly, when participants were asked to make verbal responses (but not hand shapes) to the nonverbal prime (e.g., the word *pinch* when shown the nonverbal signal for pinch), the priming effect was eliminated. It appears, then, that sensibility judgments, like online comprehension, require a type of mental simulation using an embodied, motoric medium.

These studies represent just a small part of the growing literature showing how immediate processing of nonfigurative language may involve different kinds of "as-if" embodied simulations. There are, of course, other possible interpretations of several of these studies. But this work is consistent with the possibility that language processing is not accomplished through the activation of pre-stored abstract representations, but by embodied simulations that are created on-the-fly in the very moment of understanding. Most generally, these studies offer support for the idea in cognitive linguistics that understanding meaning includes both conceptual content and construal (Langacker 1987; Croft and Cruse 2004).

5.   Image schemas in metaphor understanding

Cognitive linguistics has long argued that image schemas have a critical role in structuring metaphorical concepts. Consider several examples of how image schemas shape people's metaphorical understanding of linguistic actions (Goossens et al. 1996). For instance, the image schema BALANCE (i.e., a symmetrical arrangement of forces around a point or axis) motivates various phrases referring to a person's attempt to restore equilibrium of the body (and mind). When people say *get something off my chest*, they describe a forceful action to remove an impediment that causes imbalance. Speakers who get something off their chests remove oppressive forces by merely talking to an appropriate person, often the person most responsible for placing the burden or impediment on the speaker. *Getting something off one's chest*, just like *blowing off steam* and *coughing something up* restore a sense of balance or well-being to an individual.

The image schema CONTAINMENT underlies many metaphorical concepts related to our understanding of linguistic action. For instance, our mouths, like our bodies, are experienced as containers, such that when the container is open, then linguistic action is possible, and when closed, there is only silence. To be *closed-lipped* reflects the silent, closed container, and when one *bites one's lip*, the closing of the mouth and lips is done quickly with great force. When someone *lies through their teeth*, the container is perceived as a hiding place where true information resides, but the container is somewhat defective and we can see through the speaker's shameless attempt to lie about something when the truth can partly be seen. Some metaphors talk of entering the mouth container, as when one *puts words in someone's mouth* or *forces/rams/thrusts something down someone's throat*, with the more forceful entering into the container reflecting greater intensity on the speaker's linguistic action. Embodied CONTAINMENT also refers to cases where objects, or (pieces of) information, are removed from the mouth or head of a speaker, as in *He took the words right out of my mouth* and *pick someone's brains*, both of which imply that they are persons possessing some valuable object(s) worth stealing.

The importance of the PATH image schema is seen in the metaphors based on walking, such as in *backtrack*, where the directionality of movement along some path must be reversed. PATH also is relevant to cases of reversed motion as in the eating metaphor of *eat one's words* and *eat crow*, which are specific instances of the general idea of *taking back one's words* (i.e., moving words back along the conduit path that a speaker first send them).

The image schema of FORCE is central to many of the metaphors based on violent bodily actions noted above. In most of these instances, the force is noticeable because of its extreme nature (e.g., *bite someone's head off* and *snap at someone*).

These selected examples illustrate how image schemas connect the domains of embodied action with the domain of linguistic action. Most generally, this examination of metaphor and linguistic action reveals how people use their intuitive phenomenological sense of their bodies to interpret, and better structure, more abstract conceptual domains. There is now a growing body of psycholinguistic research that supports the idea that image schemas play an important role in metaphorical language use. In previous articles, I have discussed in some detail the work showing how people's bodily experiences partly motivate their understanding of why the word *stand* has the various physical and nonphysical senses it has, e.g.: *The clock stands on the table.* and *He couldn't stand working for his boss.* (Gibbs et al. 1994).[2] An important methodological element of this research is the strategy to independently assess people's intuitions about their bodily experiences and use this information to make empirical predictions about other individuals' understanding of linguistic meaning. This strategy is important, in psychologists' view, because it helps eliminate some of the circular reasoning that cognitive linguists engage in when postulating the existence of image schemas from a systematic analysis of language only to test the theory by once more examining linguistic patterns.

Consider now two other sets of experiments that employed this methodological strategy to provide evidence in favor of the idea that image-schematic construal of experience shapes the understanding of metaphoric language. One set of psycholinguistic studies examined how people's intuitions of the bodily experience of CONTAINMENT, and several other image schemas, which partly structure the source domains for several important conceptual metaphors, underlie speakers' use and understanding of idioms. These studies were designed to show that the specific entailments of idioms reflect the source-to-target-domain mappings of their underlying conceptual metaphors (Gibbs 1992). Most importantly, these metaphorical mappings preserve the cognitive topology of these embodied, image-schematic source domains.

Participants in a first study were questioned about their understanding of events corresponding to particular bodily experiences that were viewed as motivating specific source domains in conceptual metaphors (e.g., the experience of one's body as a container filled with fluid). For instance, participants were asked to imagine the embodied experience of a sealed container filled with fluid, and then they were asked something about causation (e.g., "What would cause the container to explode?"), intentionality (e.g., "Does the container explode on purpose or does it explode through no volition of its

---

2. See also Beitel et al. (2000) for similar work related to understanding the various meanings of the preposition *on*.

own?"), and manner (e.g., "Does the explosion of the container occur in a gentle or a violent manner?").

Overall, the participants were remarkably consistent in their responses to the various questions. To give one example, people responded that the cause of a sealed container exploding its contents out is the internal pressure caused by the increase in the heat of the fluid inside the container. They also reported that this explosion is unintentional because containers and fluid have no intentional agency, and that the explosion occurs in a violent manner. These brief responses provide a rough, nonlinguistic profile of people's understanding of a particular source domain concept (i.e., heated fluid in the bodily container). These profiles are rough approximations of the image-schematic structures of the source domains.

These different image-schematic profiles about certain abstract concepts allowed me to predict something about people's understanding of idioms. Specifically, various source domains map onto their conceptualizations of different target domains in very predictable ways given the constraining influence of the underlying image schemas (i.e., the invariance hypothesis, Lakoff 1990). For instance, people's understanding of anger should partly be structured by their folk concept for heated fluid in the bodily container as described above. Several studies showed this to be true (Gibbs 1992). Not surprisingly, when people understand anger idioms, such as *blow your stack*, *flip your lid*, or *hit the ceiling*, they inferred that the cause of anger is internal pressure, that the expression of anger is unintentional, and is done in an abrupt violent manner. People do not draw these same inferences about causation, intentionality, and manner when comprehending literal paraphrases of idioms, such as *get very angry*. Moreover, people find it easy to process the idiomatic phrase *blow your stack* when this was read in a context that accurately described the cause of the person's anger as being due to internal pressure, where the expression of anger was unintentional and violent (all entailments are consistent with the entailments of the source-to-target-domain mappings of heated fluid in a container onto anger). But readers took significantly longer to read *blow your stack* when any of these source domain entailments were explicitly contradicted in the preceding story context.

These psycholinguistic findings demonstrate that people's intuitions about different image-schematic dimensions of experiences can be independently studied and then used to predict something about their use in understanding conventional metaphoric language. Of course, the image-schematic structuring of a concept, such as ANGER, does not imply that the concept is completely characterized by any single, or multiple, image schema (e.g.,

CONTAINMENT + FORCE). There are surely various concrete imagistic aspects of people's experiences of HEATED FLUID IN THE BODILY CONTAINER that are not image-schematic and this information may influence individual's answers to questions about the cause, intentionality, and manner of different events. Nonetheless, the high degree of consistency in people's answers to questions about the cause, intentionality, and manner of different source domain events is likely due to the constraining presence of underlying image schemas rather than to idiosyncratic mental images that people may have for these source domains (see Gibbs and O'Brien 1990).

A different line of research investigated the possible influence of bodily action on people's speeded processing of simple metaphoric phrases, as *stamp out a feeling, push an issue, sniff out the truth* and *cough up a secret,* each of which denote physical actions upon abstract items. Wilson and Gibbs (subm.) hypothesized that if abstract concepts are indeed understood as items that can be acted upon by the body, then performing a related action should facilitate sensibility judgments for a figurative phrase that mentions this action. For example, if participants first move their arms and hands as if to grasp something, and then read *grasp the concept,* they should verify that this phrase is meaningful faster than when they first performed an unrelated body action. Our hypothesis was that engaging in body movements associated with these phrases should enhance the simulations that people create to form a metaphorical understanding of abstract notions, such as "concept," even if "concepts" are not things that people can physically grasp. People's conceptual understandings of what a "concept" is, for example, need not be completely embodied and metaphorical. However, our suggestion is that some simulated construals of "concept" are rooted in embodied metaphor that may be highlighted by engaging in body actions relevant to what people mentally do with ideas.

Participants in this study first learned to perform various specific bodily actions (e.g., throw, stamp, push, swallow, cough, grasp) given different nonlinguistic cues. Following this, participants were individually seated in front of a computer screen. The experiment consisted of a series of trials where an icon flashed on the screen, prompting the participant to perform the appropriate bodily action. After doing this, a string of words appeared on the screen and participants had to judge as quickly as possible whether that word string was "sensible."

Analysis of the speeded sensibility judgments showed that participants responded more quickly to the metaphorical phrases that matched the preceding action (e.g., the motor action grasp was followed by *grasp the con-*

cept), than to the phrases that did not match the earlier movement (e.g., the motor action kick was followed by *grasp the concept*). People were also faster in responding to the metaphor phrases having performed a relevant body moment than when they did not move at all. In short, performing an action facilitates understanding of a figurative phrase containing that action word, just as it does for literal phrases. A second study showed that same pattern of bodily priming effects when participants were asked to imagine performing the actions before they made their speeded responses to word strings. This result reveals that real movement is not required to facilitate metaphor comprehension, only that people mentally simulate such action.

Most generally, people do not understand the nonliteral meanings of these figurative phrases as a matter of convention where their understandings of different phrases is arbitrarily given in a rote fashion. Instead, people actually understand *toss out a plan*, for instance, in terms of physically tossing something (i.e., the plan is viewed as a physical object). In this way, processing metaphoric meaning is not just a cognitive act, but involves some imaginative understanding of the body's role in structuring abstract concepts. People may create embodied simulations of speakers' messages that involve moment-by-moment "what must it be like" processes that make use of ongoing tactile-kinesthetic experiences. These simulations processes operate even when people encounter language that is abstract, or refers to actions that are physically impossible to perform. My claim that people engage in bodily simulations when understanding phrases like *grasp the concept* does not imply that they must access the literal meaning of the phrase before inferring its metaphorical interpretation. Instead, people's immediate construal of metaphoric meaning is shaped by bodily simulation processes which do not require that a literal meaning be examined and rejected.

6.   Image schemas as simulated actions: A case study

The research described above offers empirical findings that seem very compatible with the possibility that image schemas maintain their embodied roots and help create imaginative construals of linguistic meaning. I now describe in some detail an interesting new line of research that provides more direct evidence in favor of the idea that image schemas are different kinds of simulated action. This work focuses primarily on the conceptual metaphor RELATIONSHIPS ARE JOURNEYS, whose source domain is primarily structured by the image schema SOURCE-PATH-GOAL. In this work, college students listened to one of two kinds of stories about romantic relationships, as shown below (Gibbs, in prep.):

Smooth Journey
"Imagine that you are a single person. A friend sets you up on a blind date. You really like this person and start dating a lot. Your relationship was moving along in a good direction. But then it got even better. The relationship felt like it was the best you ever had. This continues to this day. No matter what happens, the two of you are quite happy together."

Interrupted Journey
"Imagine that you are a single person. A friend sets you up on a blind date. You really like this person and start dating a lot. Your relationship was moving along in a good direction. But then you encountered some difficulties. The relationship did not feel the same as before. This lasted for some time. No matter how hard you two tried, the two of you were not getting along."

These two stories describe relationships as being like a journey, as indicated solely by the statement *Your relationship was moving along in a good direction* in the fourth line of each story. Although no other part of the two stories refers to journeys in any way, the two stories differ in the kind of metaphorical journey (i.e., SOURCE-PATH-GOAL schema) that each relationship takes. The first story gives the impression of a smooth, uninterrupted journey, and the second of a more difficult, perhaps interrupted, journey. My basic hypothesis was that people understand these two stories not by merely activating a RELATIONSHIPS ARE JOURNEYS conceptual metaphor, in which the source domain is structured by the SOURCE-PATH-GOAL image schema. Instead, people imaginatively simulate themselves in the journey and actually experience some embodied sense of the SOURCE-PATH-GOAL schemas as part of their understanding of the stories. If this is the case, listening to these different renditions of the RELATIONSHIPS ARE JOURNEYS conceptual metaphor should have different embodied effects on the people who understand them.

To test this idea, I first asked a group of students to read the two stories and then answer as series of questions that were designed to tap into the students' intuitions about relationship journeys and the implicit image-schema of SOURCE-PATH-GOAL that underlies the source domain of this metaphor. The first question asked, "Which relationship progressed further?" to which 90% of the participants responded the smooth journey story (the stories were not actually labeled like this). The second question was "Which relationship was progressing faster at the beginning?" which provoked a split in the participants' responses with 45% saying the smooth journey story and 55% the interrupted journey story. The third question was "Which relationship is progressing faster at present?" to which 90% of the participants picked the smooth journey story. The fourth question asked, "Which relationship progressed more along a straight line?" to which 60% picked the smooth journey story. Finally, the participants were asked, "In which relationship were the individuals heading in the same direction?" to which 80% selected the smooth journey story.

It is important to note that there is nothing in the individual stories that directly assert anything about the distance, speed, extent, and direction of the journeys traveled. All of these inferences were drawn on the basis of people's metaphorical understandings of the stories as referring to RELATIONSHIPS ARE JOURNEYS. The data clearly suggest that the couple in the smooth story had progressed further overall, were doing so faster at the present time, were moving more along a straight path, and were headed in the same direction, compared to the couple depicted in the interrupted journey story. The question, then, was whether these detailed SOURCE-PATH-GOAL image-schematic understandings of the stories had any embodied influence on people as they imaginatively constructed their interpretations.

I examined this possibility in the following way. Groups of college students individually participated in an experiment on a large athletic field at the University of California, Santa Cruz. Each experiment began with a student standing on one spot looking out at a large yellow ball that was placed exactly 40 feet away. As the students stood and stared out at the yellow ball, they were read one of the two stories above. Immediately after hearing the story, the participants were blindfolded, and asked to walk out to the yellow ball while they were "thinking about the story" they had just heard. At that point, students began to walk out to where they thought the yellow ball was and then stopped when they thought they were right at the ball. Once they stopped, an experimenter nearby asked each participant to rate on a 7-point scale (from "bad" to "good") how they felt at the moment. After this, the blindfold was removed, and the experiment was over. The experimenters then measured how close the student actually was to the yellow ball, and how far away from a straight line each participant wandered from the starting point to the yellow ball.

Did students walk differently having heard the smooth journey as opposed to the interrupted journey story? In fact they did. According to the preliminary study, students hearing the smooth journey story assumed that the relationship progressed further than the one in the interrupted journey.

Indeed, in the walking study, blindfolded students who heard the smooth journey story walked past the yellow ball by almost 4 feet on average, while the students who heard the interrupted journey undershot the yellow ball by more than 1 foot, a statistically significant difference. This difference in walking distance was not due to participants being happier or in a better mood because they simply heard a more positive story as indicted by the fact that the students who heard the interrupted journey actually gave higher mood ratings than did those in the smooth journey condition. I am not sure how to explain this mood difference between the two story conditions. At the very least, though, these mood ratings eliminate the alternative explanation that longer walking distance was due to the participants being momentarily happier.

A different version of this experiment had college students listening to the same stories, again looking out at the yellow ball. This time, however, students were blindfolded, but instructed to only imagine themselves walking out to the yellow ball as they thought about the story, and to press a stop watch as soon as they imagined themselves arriving at the ball. Interestingly, the identical pattern of effects was obtained as found during real walking. It appears, then, that thinking about the two stories differentially affected people's imagined walking, and it did this for both real and imagined motion.

This line of research is still in its infancy. But the findings observed in these experiments strongly suggest that image-schematic reasoning in narrative comprehension involves the construction of embodied simulations. These simulations are embodied because of the functioning of "as-if body" loops that are part of people's immediate understanding of other individuals' actions, including those associated with overt communication. One implication of this view is that people's aesthetic appreciation of language is itself embodied. Instead of people first understanding language, and then having emotional/aesthetic responses to it, people experience emotions as part of their immediate simulated construals of meaning. Thus, we feel something when reading or thinking about a successful or interrupted relationship journey because of the embodied "as-if" simulations that are being created during our image-schematic (e.g., SOURCE-PATH-GOAL) construals of each respective relationship.

7.   Image schemas as attractors within self-organizing systems

The emergent nature of image schemas as in-the-moment embodied simulations is best understood theoretically in terms of the complex interplay of brain, body, and world. Many cognitive scientists now argue that understanding this complex interaction requires the tools and methods of nonlinear dynamical systems theory (Freeman 2001; Kelso 1995; Port and Van Gelder 1995; Thompson and Varela 2001). Dynamic approaches to cognition emphasize that learning is a self-organized process that occurs only in systems that are environmentally embedded, corporeally embodied, and neurally entrained by feedback. Virtually all living organisms self-assemble, or are self-organizing systems, "as emergent consequences of nonlinear interaction among active components" (Kelso 1995: 67). The nervous system, the body, and the environment are highly structured dynamical systems, coupled to each other at multiple levels. Three kinds of cycles are most relevant to creating self-organization (Thompson and Varela 2001): cycles of organismic regulation of the entire body, cycles of sensorimotor coupling between organism and environment, and cycles of intersubjective interaction, involving the recognition of the intentional meaning of actions and linguistic communication.

For the present purpose, image schemas may be described as emergent properties that arise from different "cycles of operation" constituting a person's life and represent a kind of "structural coupling" between brain, body, and world. Image schemas reflect a form of stability within cognitive systems. According to self-organization theory, order in a system arises around what are called "attractors," which help create and hold stable patterns within the system. Attractors are preferred patterns, such that if the system is started from one state it will evolve until it arrives at the attractors and will stay there in the absence of other factors. An attractor can be a point (e.g., the center of a bowl containing a rolling ball), a regular path (e.g., a planetary orbit), a complex series of states (e.g., the metabolism of a cell), or an infinite sequence (called a "strange attractor"). A complex system will have many attractors and the study of self-organizing systems is focused on investigating the forms and dynamics of these attractors.

My suggestion is that image schemas are attractors within human self-organizing systems. Attractors, such as BALANCE, SOURCE-PATH-GOAL/PATH, RESISTENCE, VERTICALITY, etc., reflect emerging points of stability in a system as it engages in real-world interaction. New, surprising, patterns encountered in the environment throw a system into momentary chaos (e.g., the system goes out of BALANCE), until the system, through its self-assembling process, reorganizes and reaches a new stability (e.g., reaches a new state of equilibrium or BALANCE). The important point here is attractors are not localized representations, but emerging patterns of entire systems in action (i.e., the interplay of brain, body, and world). In this way, the stable properties of image schemas (e.g., the topographic structure of something like SOURCE-PATH-GOAL) are not separate from sensorimotor activity. Image schemas should not be reduced to sensorimotor activity, and it is also a mistake to view image schemas as mental representations that are abstracted away from experience. One implication of this dynamical view is that each construal of an image schema will have a different profile depending on the overall state of the organism involved in some activity, and past basins of attractions created within the system (i.e., past simulations of particular behavioral modes such as BALANCE).

8. Conclusion

My argument has been that image schemas are created on-the-fly as part of people's ongoing simulations of actions when they engage in cognitive tasks, such as understanding language. Image schemas are not divorced from their bodily origins, despite their emergence from recurring patterns of bodily experience, nor are they structured as pre-stored entities in long-term memory. Instead, image schemas are emergent properties of human self-organizing systems that are continually recreated and re-experienced during cognitive and perceptual activity. This perspective helps restore image schemas to their rightful status as "experiential gestalts" that are psychologically real, not because they are part of the mind, but because they are meaningful, stable states of embodied experience.

References

Beitel, Dinara, Raymond Gibbs, and Paul Sanders
    2001   Psycholinguistic perspectives on polysemy. In *Polysemy in Cognitive Linguistics,* Hubert Cuykens, and Britta E. Zawada (eds.), 213-239. Amsterdam: Benjamins.
Berthoz, Anthony
    2000   *The Brain's Sense of Movement.* Cambridge, Mass.: Harvard University Press.

Carreiras, Manuel, Nuria Carriedo, Maria Alonso, and Angel Fernandez
    1997   The role of verb tense and verb aspect in the foregrounding of information during reading. *Memory and Cognition* 25: 438-446.

Croft, William, and Alan Cruse
    2004   *Cognitive Linguistics*. Cambridge: Cambride University Press.

Damasio, Antonio
    1994   *Descartes' Error*. New York: Harcourt Brace and Co.
    1999   *The Feeling of What Happens: Body and Emotion In the Making of Consciousness*. New York: Harcourt Brace and Co.
    2003   *Looking for Spinoza: Joy, Sorrow, and the Feeling Brain*. New York: Harcourt Brace and Co.

Davis, Martin, and Thomas Stone (eds.)
    1995   *Mental Simulation: Evaluations and Applications*. Oxford: Blackwell.

Freeman, Walter
    2001   *How Brains Make Up their Minds*. New York: Columbia University Press.

Gallagher, Shaun
    1995   Body schema and intentionality. In *The Body and Self*, Jose Luis Bermudez, and Anthony Marcel (eds.), 225-244. Cambridge, Mass.: MIT Press.

Geeraerts, Dirk
    1990   Editorial statement. *Cognitive Linguistics* 1: 1-3

Gibbs, Raymond
    1992   What do idioms really mean? *Journal of Memory and Language* 31: 485-506.
    1994   *The Poetics of Mind: Figurative Thought, Language, and Understanding*. New York: Cambridge University Press.
    2005   *Embodiment and Cognitive Science*. New York: Cambridge University Press.
    in prep.   Walking with Metaphor: Understanding as Embodied Simulation.

Gibbs, Raymond, and Jennifer O'Brien
    1990   Idioms and mental imagery: The metaphorical motivation for Idiomatic meaning. *Cognition* 36: 35-68.

Gibbs, Raymond, Dinara Beitel, Michael Harrington, and Paul Sanders
    1994   Taking a stand on the meanings of "stand": Embodied experience as motivation for polysemy. *Journal of Semantics* 11: 31-251.

Gibbs, Raymond, and Herbert Colston
    1995   The cognitive psychological reality of image schemas and their transformations. *Cognitive Linguistics* 6: 347-378.

Goosens, Louis, Paul Pauwels, Brygida Rudzka-Ostyn, Anne-Marie Simon-Vanderbergen, and Johan Varpays.
  1996   *Word of mouth: Metaphor, metonymy, and linguistic action in a cognitive perspective*. Amsterdam: Benjamins.
Johnson, Mark
  1987   *The Body in the Mind. The Bodily Basis of Meaning, Imagination, and Reason*. Chicago: University of Chicago Press.
Kelso, Scott
  1995   *Dynamic Patterns: The Self-organization of Brain and Behavior*. Cambridge, MA: MIT Press.
Klatzky, Roberta, James Pellegrino, Brian McCloskey, and Susan Doherty
  1989   Can you squeeze a tomato? The role of motor representations in semantic sensibility judgments. *Journal of Memory and Language* 28: 56-77.
Lakoff, George
  1987   *Women, Fire and Dangerous Things. What Categories reveal about the Mind*. Chicago: University of Chicago Press
  1990   The invariance hypothesis: Is abstract reason based on image schemas? *Cognitive Linguistics* 1: 39-74.
Langacker, Ronald
  1987   *Foundations of Cognitive Linguistics*. Vol. 1. *Theoretical Prerequisites*. Stanford, Ca.: Stanford University Press
Lee, David
  2001   *Cognitive Linguistics: An Introduction*. New York: Oxford University Press.
Liberman, Alivin, and Ignatius Mattingly
  1985   The motor theory of speech perception revised. *Cognition* 21: 1-36.
O'Regan, Kevin, and Alva Noe
  2001   A sensorimotor account of vision and visual consciousness. *Behavioral and Brain Sciences* 24: 939-1031.
Port, Robert, and Timothy van Gelder
  1995   *Mind as Motion: Explorations in the Dynamics of Cognition*. Cambridge, Mass: MIT Press.
Richardson, Daniel, Michael Spivey, Lawrence Barsalou, and Ken McRae
  2003   Spatial representations activated during real-time comprehension of verbs. *Cognitive Science* 27: 767-780.
Stamenov, Maxim, and Vittorio Gallese (eds.)
  2002   *Mirror Neurons and the Evolution of Brain and Language*. Amsterdam: Benjamins.
Stanfield, Robert, and Rolf Zwaan
  2001   The effect of implied orientation derived from verbal context on picture recognition. *Psychological Science* 12: 153-156.

Thompson, Evan, and Francisco Varela
   2001   Radical embodiment: Neural dynamics and consciousness. *Trends in Cognitive Science* 5: 418-425.
Wilson, Nicole, and Raymond Gibbs
   subm.   Body movement primes metaphor comprehension.
Zwaan, Rolf, Joesph Magliano, and Arthur Graesser
   1995   Dimensions of situated model construction in narrative comprehension. *Journal of Experimental Psychology: Learning, Memory, and Cognition* 21: 386-397.
Zwaan, Rolf, Robert Stanfield, and Richard Yaxley
   2002   Language comprehenders mentally represent the shapes of objects. *Psychological Science* 13: 168-171.

How to build a baby: III.
Image schemas and the transition to verbal thought

Jean M. Mandler

Abstract

Language, however it is characterized, must be learnable by children. Therefore, to understand why language takes the forms it does it is useful to know the kinds of preverbal concepts that infants bring to the language learning task. My research program was not designed to study language per se, but it uncovered a number of fundamental concepts in infancy that also underlie linguistic understanding. These concepts involve animate beings interacting with inanimate objects, and the various paths these interactions take, as well as a variety of spatial concepts. A mechanism of perceptual meaning analysis is described that outputs spatially-based image-schemas that represent these concepts. After summarizing some of the early concepts derived in this way, I describe how image-schema conceptualizations underlie simple grammatical learning. Using preverbal concepts of containment and support as examples, I summarize research showing that both Korean and American children begin with the same preverbal concepts, but as they begin to understand their native tongue their conceptualizations of spatial relations become concatenated in different ways. Further study of Korean and English-speaking adults suggests that extended experience with the different linguistic concatenations may result in characteristic differences in the way that scenes are interpreted.

Keywords: preverbal concepts, semantic primitives, perceptual meaning analysis, image-schema representations, language acquisition

1. Introduction

Language, however it is characterized, must be learnable by children. It is only possible to bypass this obvious fact by assuming that children come equipped with a specialized language acquisition device that can do whatever is necessary for language to be learned. The unfortunate result of such a stance is to ignore whatever the preverbal mind might tell us about why language is structured the way it is and what might be universal underpinnings of language understanding. Obviously there are many constraints that determine language form and content, and learnability is only one of them. Nevertheless it should be useful in understanding language structure to uncover the kinds of concepts preverbal children bring to the language learning task, and to see how these concepts influence what infants understand from the language they hear. I suggest that anyone interested in language universals will find preverbal conceptualizations a rich source of what have been called semantic primitives (e.g., Bierwisch 1967; Talmy 1983).

At the same time, we must honor the distinction made by Carey (1982) between meaning components that are definitionally primitive and those that are developmentally primitive. Semantic analyses of the adult lexicon often use sophisticated and theory-laden concepts unlikely to be in the new language learner's repertoire. The young child cannot have the same understanding of *brother* as an adult without knowing something about biological relations or understand the word *buy* without some appreciation of money. This means that there will be some semantic primitives that do not appear in analyses of preverbal concepts. Nevertheless, examination of preverbal concepts provides clues to what is primitive in the sense of being foundational to human thought. These are the concepts that are used as an entree into language understanding. Perhaps even more important, the preverbal mind begins to develop before the particularities of culture have much opportunity to bias conceptualization, and therefore are especially likely to represent universal conceptual proclivities.

My research program was not designed to study language per se, but it uncovered a number of preverbal concepts that also underlie linguistic understanding. The earliest concepts, whether object concepts or relational ones, tend to be abstract and global in nature. For example, an early division is made between animals and inanimate things. Similarly, early concepts about events consist of path notions such as self-motion and goal, as well as a variety of spatial relations such as containment and support. All of these preverbal concepts are well represented by image-schemas. In this chapter I lay out the evidence we have for the presence of these concepts in infancy and describe a mechanism of *perceptual meaning analysis* that extracts the spatial and movement structure of events in image-schematic form to represent them.

The other topic I discuss in this chapter is the readiness with which these preverbal concepts are used to understand simple grammatical forms, regardless of the details of the language being learned. Because many early conceptualizations involve schematic descriptions of events, such as an animate thing acting on an inanimate thing or an object moving into a container, they enable grammatical learning to take place. I illustrate this point with data comparing preverbal concepts of containment and support in infants from Korean-speaking and English-speaking homes. This comparison is of interest not only because different components of meaning are combined into the words expressing containment and support in the two languages, but also because English relies on prepositions to express these concepts and Korean typically uses verbs. Infants begin with the same preverbal image-schemas, but as they begin to understand their native tongue their conceptualizations of spatial relations become concatenated in different ways. Study of Korean and English-speaking adults suggests that extended experience with the different concatenations results in some characteristic differences in the way that scenes are interpreted.

2.   How image-schemas structure the preverbal conceptual system

Until recently we had almost no information on preverbal concepts. In part because of the influence of Piaget's view of infancy as a purely sensorimotor period, it was largely assumed that infants have no conceptual life, and so it went unstudied. This has changed dramatically in the last decade or so. We have learned that a number of high-order cognitive functions develop in the first year, such as recall, making inductive inferences, and mental problem solving. Studies of deferred imitation, in which infants are shown a novel event sequence using little models and then tested after a delay to see if they imitate what they have seen, show that infants can recall the past at least from 9 months of age (Carver and Bauer 1999) and by 11 months can remember event sequences over a span of months (Mandler and McDonough 1995). To study inductive inferences, we use a technique known as generalized imitation. We demonstrate an event for infants, such as giving a little model of a dog a drink from a cup, but instead of giving them the dog to use for their imitations, we give them different objects, for example, a different dog, or a cat, a bird, or a car, to see how far they will generalize what they have seen. This work has shown that 9- to 14-month-old infants make broad-ranging inferences about appropriate behavior for many classes of objects (Mandler and McDonough 1996; McDonough and Mandler 1998). Still other work has shown that by 9 months, infants are beginning to engage in multistep problem-solving (Willatts 1997).

Where does such high-order conceptual processing come from? I have theorized that in addition to the usual perceptual processes that categorize and schematize objects, infants come equipped with a concept-creating mechanism that analyzes perceptual information and redescribes it into simpler form (Mandler 1992, 2004). I originally called this mechanism *perceptual analysis*, but because the mechanism was sometimes interpreted as a purely perceptual process, I changed its designation to *perceptual meaning analysis*.[1] Perceptual meaning analysis is an attentive process that analyses perceptual displays and recodes them into a reduced form that makes conscious thought possible. A great deal of perceptual information is taken in parallel and is processed outside of awareness. The information must be reduced into a vastly simpler form if we are to use it in the limited system that is conscious awareness. However, this is not a selective process that picks out bits and pieces of perceptual information leaving them untouched. As a large literature testifies, conceptual information is not the same as perceptual information. For example, our conception of what faces look like is a highly biased version of what we actually perceive and is formatted differently as well (Mandler 2004).

Of course, it is not sufficient just to describe the concepts resulting from perceptual meaning analysis; we also need to consider how they are represented. I have proposed that the format of the redescriptions carried out by perceptual meaning analysis is the *image-schema*. Image-schemas are not themselves accessible (if they were, we wouldn't have to theorize about them), but they structure the concepts that can be brought to mind either in the form of images or words. The idea is that infants not only see but also can analyze what they see – that is, create primitive descriptions of what they have observed, such as "object starts itself" or "object goes into another object." It is worth noting that this kind of concept formation does not depend upon hypothesis formation and testing (as suggested by Fodor 1981). Infants don't come to the perceptual displays they analyze with preformed hypotheses; rather, they apply an analytic mechanism that extracts simple descriptions of what is being attended. These descriptions put spatial information into the representational forms we call image-schemas.

Although concept formation does not require hypothesis formation, it does require attention. However, attention only sets the stage for perceptual meaning analysis; it is possible to attend to something and not analyze it but

---

1. I use the term *meaning* to refer to any conceptual interpretation, not just the meaning of words.

merely activate an already compiled description. Nevertheless, given that attention is required if analysis is to take place, it is not surprising that a number of early concepts crucial for human thought stem from the information that most attracts infant's attention – namely, motion. From birth, infants attend to moving objects, an attentive bias that leads to differentiation of animate and inanimate object paths. For example, studies using point-light displays have shown that 3-month-olds differentiate biologically correct from incorrect motion of people and other animals and also moving animal displays from moving vehicles (Arterberry and Bornstein 2001; Bertenthal 1993).

Within a few months (and perhaps earlier), infants are responsive to the difference between an object beginning to move without anything else coming in contact with it and an object moving when touched by another. Attention to the beginnings and endings of paths leads to differentiation of caused and self-motion. For example, 6-month-olds notice the difference between a film of a ball hitting and launching another ball, and films in which a ball appears to launch another ball but with either a very small spatial or temporal gap (e.g., Leslie 1982). Infants also are sensitive to the character of the motion on a path. Infants also treat objects that act contingently differently from those that do not. For example, 3-month-olds will smile indiscriminately at anything that interacts with them in a contingent fashion (Frye et al. 1983).

Each of these discriminations – animate versus inanimate motion, self- versus caused motion, and contingent motion – is by itself a simple perceptual discrimination. None of them alone, or even a combination of them, constitutes a concept of animal or inanimate object. These pieces of perceptual data need to be redescribed into an accessible format in order to qualify as concepts; this is the process carried out by perceptual meaning analysis, a process that produces a different and simpler representation than the perceptual system provides. Other kinds of data suggest that this process of conceptualization has begun at least by the second 6 months of life. For example, 7-month-olds categorize little models of animals and vehicles as different, even though the models are not moving and differ greatly in perceptual appearance (Mandler and McDonough 1993). Even more impressive, 9-month-olds categorize models of birds with outstretched wings and airplanes as different, in spite of their great perceptual similarity. Because infants cannot use either motion or perceptual similarity of the exemplars for this categorization, they must be relying on some conceptualization of the differences.

Image-schemas provide an excellent description of the kinds of information that infants first attend to and conceptualize (Mandler 1992, 2004). In the first instance, it may only be PATH that is analyzed – that is, an image-schema of an object following any trajectory through space, without regard to the characteristics of the object or the details of the trajectory itself. A very young infant may not get detailed information about the appearance of an object even when attending to it, but can extract a primitive description of something going from one place to another. Further analysis will highlight different aspects of paths and different kinds of paths, for example, upward or downward paths or paths that go into or out of other objects.

This attention to path information – how objects move and interact with each other – leads to concepts of animal and inanimate thing. At first, animals seem to be merely objects that start themselves, move on rhythmic but somewhat unpredictable paths, and interact with other objects both directly and from a distance. In contrast, inanimate objects do not start themselves but only move due to another object, and when they do move do so along direct paths, and do not interact with other objects from a distance. Image-schemas, such as ANIMATE MOTION, INANIMATE MOTION, SELF-MOTION, CAUSED MOTION, and LINK describe these notions (Mandler 1992, 2004). By the second half of the first year, infants have begun to attend to the physical features of animals and vehicles that enable them to categorize stationary models. (Even when using a conceptual distinction to categorize objects, one must be able to identify something as a member of a category).

In the second half of the first year infants begin to interpret objects moving on paths as goal-directed. As early as 5 months infants attend more to the goal of a reach than the direction of the path itself (Woodward 1998). By 9 months they distinguish between someone grasping an object and apparently unintentionally resting their hand on it; that is, they differentiate a purposeful from a nonpurposeful action (Woodward 1999). Woodward and Sommerville (2000) showed that 11-month-olds distinguish a goal-path (opening a lid of a transparent box and grasping a toy inside it) from a similar action sequence without a goal (opening a lid of a transparent box and then grasping a toy that is sitting outside the box). This series of studies suggests growing sophistication in interpretation of goals in the second six months.

One might assume that on the basis of what they have observed infants would restrict goal-directed interpretations to paths followed by people or other animals. However, an interesting series of experiments suggests that the tendency to interpret paths as goal-directed may be broader than that.

Gergely et al. (1995) used a computer display showing two circles separated by a short vertical bar. The first circle moved to the bar, hesitated, then backed up and rapidly moved to the bar and jumped over it, finally making contact with the second circle. Adults interpret this sort of display as goal-directed: The first circle is trying to reach the second circle. Apparently so do 12-month-olds. When habituated to this display, and then shown the identical jumping trajectory in a display without a bar, infants dishabituated (i.e., they started looking longer again), whereas they did not increase attention if shown a direct path from the first to second circle (a possible path now because the bar is gone). Csibra et al. (1999) found that this worked with 9-month-olds too, but not with 6-month-olds.

In the first experiment there were some indications of animacy in the stimuli: The circle pulsated when it came next to the second circle, and the second circle pulsated in turn. In addition the trajector started motion by itself. However, these niceties aren't necessary to get the same result. Csibra et al. (1999) also included a study in which all indications of animacy were removed and the trajector began motion off-screen. The height of the bar was varied and the circle always just skimmed over the top, making the height of the trajectory contingent on the height of the bar. The same kind of result was obtained: When the bar was removed infants dishabituated to a display following one of the same trajectories as before, but not to a new display in which the trajector moved on a straight path to the other circle. In this kind of experiment infants are habituated to a variety of trajectories, each of which is the most direct path to an end point. It is apparently the direct nature of the path that matters, not its starting point or its shape.

In these experiments, as in the Woodward experiments, an end-of-path was repeatedly shown. It turns out that even that is not necessary to give the viewer the impression of an object following a direct path to an "end." Csibra et al. (2003) used scenes of a large circle "chasing" a small circle. The small circle headed for and went through a gap in a short horizontal bar in front of it. The gap was too small for the large circle to go through, and at the last minute the large circle veered around the end of the bar and continued to chase the small circle on the other side until they went off the screen. After being habituated to this display, infants were shown the same scene but with the gap now big enough to accommodate the large circle. Twelve-month-olds did not dishabituate if the large circle now followed the little circle through the gap, but did dishabituate if the large circle continued to go around the end of the bar. The effect was not obtained with 9-month-olds.

The authors suggested that these displays are more difficult for infants to interpret because a clear end-of-path is not shown.

There are a number of interesting implications of these experiments. First, an image-schema of GOAL-PATH can be activated in a number of ways: either by showing an object following a direct path to an end point, or by showing continuous linked paths. LINKED PATH is one of a family of LINK image-schemas (Mandler 1992). LINK image-schemas are activated by any kind of contingent behavior between one object or event and another, such as when we press a light switch and notice that a light goes on, or when we take turns in a game. Contingent paths, however, seem to be especially important in activating GOAL-PATH. A goal-path does not require either a source or an end-point to activate what Lakoff (1987) called the SOURCE-PATH-GOAL image-schema.

Second, the abstract conceptual nature of the understanding represented by this kind of image-schema is clearly illustrated by these experiments. No figural information at all is required to activate the impression of a goal-path being followed. Third, and also important, there is nothing in these displays that implicates animacy. The notion of goal-seeking appears to be activated for inanimate as well as for animate objects. I originally assumed that an image-schema of AGENCY or AGENT was a combination of image-schemas of SELF-MOTION, ANIMATE MOTION, and END-OF-PATH (involving contact with another object) and was part of understanding goal-directed behavior (Mandler 1992). The idea behind this assumption was that agents are animate creatures who do things to objects. However, it appears from this kind of experimental work that contingent interactions between objects lead to assuming a goal-path independently of information about animacy or agency. The Gergely and Csibra displays are merely moving circles and in some cases following mechanical paths, yet to the observer the contingencies they present give a powerful impression of goal-directedness.

It seems that infants assume that any object taking the most direct route to another object (or following another object in linked fashion) is following a goal-path, and reach this conclusion independently of whether the object is animate or inanimate. They may do this by generalizing across the many displays they see in which one object goes in the shortest way to another. The experiments described here suggest a considerable amount of learning about goal-paths taking place in the first year. Infants see people get up and take a direct route to the telephone when it rings and they see balls rolling and knocking over other balls. Experience with both animate and inanimate objects following direct paths may lead infants to powerful expectations that at first apply to both kinds of objects. It may take developmental time to begin to limit goal-directed interpretations to animate objects. Alternatively, it is possible that there is an innate proclivity to interpret paths in this fashion. At the least, there is a known innate responsivity to contingent events that is responsible for associative learning, and it may be that it is this innate responsivity that leads to a tendency to interpret all events in a goal-directed fashion. In either case, even as adults we still sometimes ascribe goal-directed behavior to machines and other inanimates, and in some societies this tendency remains pervasive.

In addition to these broad conceptualizations about objects and their interactions with each other, infants learn a great deal about spatial relations in the first year. Baillargeon and her colleagues have conducted extensive research on how infants learn to conceptualize containment and support (e.g., Baillargeon and Wang 2002). Their work shows that as young as 2 ½ months infants know that if something is to go inside a container it must have an opening, and that if something is in the container it will move where the container moves (Hespos and Baillargeon 2001a). By 6 months infants understand that a wide object won't fit into a narrower container (Hespos and Baillargeon 2001b). By 7 ½ months infants have learned that a tall object won't disappear completely when lowered into a shorter container. Interestingly, this is 3 months after they learn that a tall object won't completely disappear when lowered behind a screen. The implication from this kind of finding is that because learning is being organized by a concept, it will not necessarily generalize to similar perceptual displays that are governed by a different concept. A screen is not the same as a container, so what one has observed about an object going behind a chair, say, may not be considered relevant to disappearance of an object into a bowl or other container.

Baillargeon and her colleagues suggest that the first concept of containment that organizes further learning is an open-closed distinction. Such an initial concept, although similar in spirit, differs in emphasis from Lakoff's description of CONTAINMENT as consisting of an inside, a boundary, and an outside. The infant concept appears to emphasize going into and going out. Containers are places into which objects disappear and from which they emerge. It is a dynamic spatial conception (see Dewell, *this volume*) that comes from countless observations of being put in and taken out of cribs, of food going into and out of containers, and so forth.

Baillargeon and her colleagues have done similar research on the development of a concept of support in the first year (Baillargeon et al. 1995). Using the same methodology, they showed that at 3 months infants expect objects to be supported if they are in any contact with a surface. By 5 months they have learned that objects need to be on top of a surface to be supported, but they still have no quantitative appreciation of how much overlap is needed to keep an object from falling. By 6 ½ months they differentiate between partial but inadequate support and adequate support. Again, we see a learning progression organized by an initial concept, in this case support as surface-contact, that gradually becomes refined.

There has also been some research on concepts of up and down. Quinn (2003) showed that if 3-month-olds are habituated to an object in several positions above a line, they dishabituate if the object appears below the line (or vice versa). However, this behavior seems to reflect merely encoding an object in a given spatial relationship, because the effect is lost if multiple objects are used or a different object is used during test (Quinn et al. 2002). To respond to the relations of above and below themselves takes a few more months. I assume that perceptual meaning analysis takes place in the interim, producing image-schemas of UP and DOWN.

Most recently, we have shown that preverbal infants have also developed concepts of tight and loose fit (McDonough et al. 2003; Spelke and Hespos 2002), which I discuss later in this chapter. To my knowledge these are about all the spatial relations that have been investigated in the first year of life. Still, along with the path notions discussed earlier they represent many of the important concepts grammaticized by languages and are well represented by image-schemas. Of course, other forms of relational representation are possible, but this form is particularly suited to characterize what infants abstract from the events they observe. Every one of the concepts I have discussed is derived from spatial information and is most easily represented in an analog format.

To my knowledge, no one has proposed an image-schema of TIGHT FIT or LOOSE FIT. Clearly there are many important spatial relations that have not yet been given proper study, perhaps in part because of the hegemony of English and a few related European languages. Distinctions not emphasized in these languages seem to have received short shrift in the developmental literature. Yet tight versus loose fit, contact, separating versus joining, and quite possibly a number of other spatial distinctions, are notions that preverbal infants everywhere acquire and that influence not only how they conceptualize the world but how they are able to interpret their native tongue.

3. The format of image-schemas

Definitions of image-schemas vary; I have defined them as dynamic analog representations, consisting of schematic versions of spatial information and movements in space (Mandler 1992).[2] Even if one wants to include force information as a component of some image-schemas, this information has become spatialized. Although derived from perceptual information, this form of representation no longer has visual, auditory, or kinesthetic properties.[3] The failure to differentiate analog representational forms from images or perception bedeviled the arguments in the 1970's between psychologists who espoused a propositional format for meaning representations (e.g., Fodor 1975) and those who espoused imagistic forms (e.g., Paivio 1978). It was apparently not understood that analog representations do not have to be perceptual or consist of images. One of the main arguments against imagery as a representation of meaning was (and still is, as the following quote illustrates) that images cannot represent meaning directly because they must themselves be interpreted. As Carey and Markman (1999: 234) put it:

> ... no matter how abstract the image, more is encoded than abstractions such as *path, containment*, and *goal*. To take Mandler's example, suppose all that children represent from an event is *path* – that an object has moved from one place to another. Direction and speed are not represented. In a given dynamic iconic representation, however, the path must have some direction, speed, and so on. How does the child know to interpret that iconic image as representing *path* alone, ignoring speed, location, and local details for direction? Thus, even iconic representation of the sort Mandler proposes requires interpretation of symbols and thus is not, in that sense, an advantage over a propositional system ...

But image-schemas are not iconic in this sense. An image-schema of PATH does not contain information about speed or direction. Even to call it a spatial representation may be misleading, if that implies the kinds of information we may observe when watching things move through space. This point may

---

2. My definition, which Gibbs (*this volume*) calls the traditional one, precludes the notion of nonperceptually-based image-schemas (cf. Grady, *this volume*).
3. Although Lakoff (1987) emphasized this point, his (and Johnson's 1987) discussion rested heavily on comparisons of image-schemas with "rich" images, which may have perpetuated the notion of image-schemas as in some sense still visual (or kinesthetic), even though schematic in form. But image-schemas are not even impoverished images.

be clearer if we relate image-schemas to topological representations. An image of a container must have a specific shape, but a topological representation ignores this information, leaving only the relation of a bounded space with an inside or outside. Of course, image-schemas are not strictly topological representations; although similar in many ways they include relations not found in topology, such as up and down. The point is that image-schemas can be derived from perception and redescribed without retaining all types of information, just as topological representations can.

Different neural pathways handle different kinds of perceptual information and they can be represented separately. So a spatial relation of one object joining another can be represented without orientation or direction. A precise realization of this notion is exemplified by Terry Regier's (1995) connectionist model of learning spatial terms. The architecture of the model has several information-reducing characteristics. One of these is that it represents paths in terms of starting and ending points and a *nonsequential* static representation of what occurs on the path between these points. Although it seems odd to everyday thought to talk about a path without any sequential order, it is not that difficult to design a spatial representational system that ignores various sources of information (cf. also Barsalou 1999).

A point that is not always appreciated in discussions of image-schemas is that they underlie the explicit conceptual system, not the implicit perceptual system. Some years ago at a conference of psychologists, linguists, and philosophers, when I presented my views of the spatial nature of our understanding of time, a linguistically oriented philosopher complained that time couldn't be represented solely by spatial notions because we can tell the difference between time and space. To be sure, we can see a spatial path and not a temporal one and in this sense we can tell the difference between the two. But this is an intuitive distinction that rests on implicit (unconceptualized) experience and not on explicit (conceptualized) knowledge. We live in time and we sense time passing, but this is not conceptual knowledge that enables us to describe, think, or reason about time. That we can only do in a spatial manner. We know that time is not the same as space, but whenever we *think* about and try to *describe* time it becomes spatialized.

Similar comments can be made about bodily feelings, such as force and desire. I hypothesize that these bodily experiences become spatialized when they become conceptualized, leaving behind their forceful aspects. It also seems likely that image-schemas derived from bodily feelings are developmentally relatively late constructions. Of course, infants experience physical force and resistance to force; however these experiences may be less likely to be subjected to perceptual meaning analysis early in life.

Reading back through the previous section on the information that infants use in their early conceptualizations of the world, one can see that all of it is spatially derived. Furthermore, the spatial information most crucial to human concept formation is delivered primarily by the visual system. Although spatial information can be gleaned from touch and audition (see Popova, *this volume*), these modalities are much less effective in encoding motion, paths, containment, and the other spatial information crucial for identifying objects and understanding events. It is probably for this reason that blindness delays conceptual development before language is learned; the most efficient source of information needed for concept formation is missing. It is also worth noting that the main elements of the conceptual system are in place very early, many of them before infants even learn to manipulate objects. Of course, it is possible that the conclusion that the earliest image-schemas are spatially based comes from the limited nature of the experiments we have been able to devise to uncover infants' conceptual life. Nevertheless, bodily sensations are more diffuse and inexpressible than what we see, which would seem to make them less than ideal candidates for primitive conceptual meanings (either developmental or semantic). We are visual creatures first and foremost, which is one of the reasons we are most adept at spatial analyses.

Consider again our understanding of physical causality. Is there not an element of force or compulsion in this notion? There seems to be, but it may be secondary to the spatial aspects that structure the concept. As I have described elsewhere (Mandler 1998, 2004), there is evidence that the powerful sense of causality we experience when, for example, we see one ball hit another and launch it, comes from temporal integration of the information that reaches the eye. Visual information is held in an iconic store prior to attentive processing; this store is continuously refreshed and enables the integration of information across time that makes us see motion as continuous. White (1988) analyzed in detail the temporal parameters involved in Michotte's (1963) studies of causal perception, in which a variety of films of balls hitting other balls were used. These analyses strongly suggest that the parameters that obtain in causal launching of one object by another make us interpret the scene as a transfer of motion from the first ball to the second.

Force cannot be seen, but "transfer of motion" can. Perceptual meaning analysis of such displays provides the summary view that the motion of one object is transferred to a second. I suggest this is the main root of our concept of causal force. An object hit by another moves because the motion of the hitter gets transferred into the "hittee." Bodily experiences of force may merely be grafted onto this more foundational notion of transfer of motion. It is not just infants who appear to be sensitive only to kinetic, as opposed to dynamic, information about moving objects; even adults have only very simple intuitions about force in their understanding of physical interactions between objects (Proffitt and Bertenthal 1990). We don't yet know in detail the relative contributions of the perception of transfer of motion from one object to another and bodily feelings of force to our concept of physical causality. Nevertheless, the spatial aspects of causal motion are clear even to young infants. It seems dubious to me that feelings of force are as likely to be subject to perceptual meaning analysis, given the less detailed information available to us on bodily feelings. So I continue to assume that spatial information is foundational for representing causality and that physical feelings are secondary. The same considerations apply to the concept of agent. We have no reason to think that an infant watching agents acting need any understanding of force, for example when watching someone putting food on a plate or using a knife to cut bread.

I have emphasized representations here rather than processing. Dewell (*this volume*) suggests that image-schemas often seem to be dynamic only in their content, not their structure, or as Gibbs (*this volume*) would add, their use in processing. I agree this should not be the case. I have always assumed that image-schemas are structured patterns of activation of spatial notions that are used in thought, so (at least in my formulation) content is not separate from structure, and thinking with image-schemas recreates their structure. Consider the comments here (and also in Dewell, *this volume*) on CONTAINMENT. Although we can have static representations of CONTAINMENT, the basic notion is derived from babies watching things go in and out of other things, sometimes tightly and constraining further movement, at other times loosely. CONTAINMENT is a set of closely related patterns (cf. Vandeloise 1991), but its core is a trajector through space to a particular endpoint configuration. I assume active recreations of these patterns occur during thought.

4.   Image-schemas and the transition to verbal thought

One of the serendipitous aspects of an account of the first meanings in terms of image-schemas is that this kind of representation forms a common denominator for concept formation and language. What we have learned about early concept formation helps us understand how the young language learner can learn grammatical forms. Grammatical relations are abstract but, as we have seen, so are many of the concepts infants learn during the first year. The image-schemas that provide the meaning of animal or inanimate object also provide the relational notions that structure sentences. For example, because infants understand that animals are things that move themselves and cause other things to move, they already have a simple concept of an agent. Because they understand inanimate objects as things that don't move by themselves but are caused to move they have at their disposal a notion of a patient.

Analyses of early language show that children rely on concepts of agent and patient, ongoing and completed action, location, possession, spatial relations such as support and containment, and object disappearance and reappearance. All of these notions are describable in image-schema terms.[4] Notions such as agent, action, and receiver of action are apparent even in early two-word speech, before the onset of specifically grammatical markings. Brown (1973), Bowerman (1973) and others analyzed two-word utterances by young English learners into the following relational expressions: agent acts, action on a patient, agent in (unspecified) relation to a patient, possessor in relation to possessed, action at a location (or goal of an action), object at a location, and an attribution to an object. With the exception of attribution, these are all path notions, referring to animates acting on inanimates, or aspects of paths themselves, such as their end points.

The first explicit grammatical markings and prepositions in English also reflect the kind of image-schemas described in the previous sections. Brown (1973) studied the earliest grammatical particles that appear in children's speech in the second year. Of the ones he made note of, the order of acquisition for the first 6 was as follows: 1) the present progressive (*-ing*), expressing an ongoing path; 2) *in*, expressing containment; 3) *on*, expressing support; 4) the plural *-s*, expressing individuation of objects; 5) the irregular past, exemplified by verbs such as *broke* and *ran*.[5] The 6th was the possessive *-s*. Several authors (e.g., Slobin 1985; Smiley and Huttenlocher 1995)

---

4. See Tomasello (1992) for many examples and illustrative diagrams in early speech.
5. These irregulars are the most common past forms in English, the point being not that irregular morphemes are learned first but that marked completed action, or end-of-path, is early.

have suggested that the earliest sense of possession is END-OF-PATH, that is, where objects come to rest, and possessors are animate ends of path.[6]

Similar image-schema notions underlie simple sentence structure. Infants come to the language learning task with a thorough understanding of events in which an agent acts on an object, and of the differences between such events and self motion. Slobin (1985) noted that the linguistic transitivity that differentiates these two kinds of events is among the first grammatical markings learned by children across a variety of languages, whether expressed by accusative inflections, direct object markers, or ergative inflections. In a similar vein, Choi and Bowerman (1991) showed that Korean children, whose language (in contrast to English) distinguishes clearly between transitive and intransitive verbs, learn this distinction early and errorlessly. As long as children have a well-established concept of an agent acting on an object it should be equally easy to differentiate transitive from intransitive frames, whether marked by subject noun, verb, or object noun.

Typically the earliest verbs express paths of various sorts. In a prepositional language such as English, however, these paths do not appear as verbs but as prepositions. In the one-word stage, infants do not say *go in* and *put in,* or *go out* and *take out,* but make do with the prepositions alone, thus, producing paths pure and simple, leaving manner and deixis aside. *In, on, up, down, on,* and *off* are typically the first paths that English-speaking children express. This use of prepositions is not an option in languages such as Korean, in which the same paths are expressed by verbs rather than by prepositions. Consider paths involving containment and support. English-learning children hear phrases such as *put in* and *take out, set on,* and *fall off,* and use the prepositions alone to express these notions. In Korean the degree of fit must be specified when expressing containment and support. Korean commonly uses three verbs (although there are a number of other closely related verbs). One of this is *kkita,* which means to fit together tightly, and is used to express either a tight-fit containment relation, such as putting a cassette into a case, or a tight-fit support relation, such as putting one Lego block onto another. A second verb is *nehta,* which means to put in or around loosely, as in an apple in a bowl or a horseshoe around a peg. In both these cases containment and support are subordinated to fit. Thirdly, *nohta* means to put something loosely on a surface, such as a cup on a table.

---

6. The remaining grammatical particles Brown studied seem more like implicit pattern learning than expressing conceptualizations, such as various forms of the copula *be.*

Thus, there are two major differences for a child learning containment and support terms in English and Korean. First, English learners have "pure" path options available to them by means of the prepositional system, whereas Korean learners must manage a variety of verbs that combine manner and path. Second, English specifies two very global distinctions – containment or support – by the prepositions *in* and *on*, whereas Korean specifies degree of fit for both containment and support. Do these differences matter to children learning these languages? Children from both language groups must learn the terms of their own language, but both must build their semantic categories on the basis of the conceptual categories they bring to the language learning task. To study this process in more detail, Choi, McDonough, Bowerman, and I first studied early comprehension of containment and support terms in children learning Korean and English, and then McDonough, Choi, and I investigated the preverbal concepts that get the spatial language learning process started.

In our first experiment (Choi et al. 1999), we used a preferential-looking technique to see when children begin to comprehend these relational terms in the two languages. In this technique two videos are presented side by side with a single audio track between them. The audio matches one of the films but not the other. If children understand the language they will tend to look at the video that matches the sound track. So, for example, we might show a film of putting a book onto a stack of other books along with another film of putting a book into a tight-fitting slipcover. The English audio would say, "Look, where is she putting it in?" The Korean audio would say, "Look, where is she tight-fitting it?" In this case, if the children understand the terms, they all should look at the same film (the book going into the slipcover). If, however, the two films show tossing a ring into a basket and putting the ring tightly on a pole, and the same audios are used, the children from the two language groups should look at different films. The English learning children should look at the ring going into the basket and the Koreans at the ring going onto the pole.

We made several different examples of these relationships and tested English learners and Korean learners aged from 14 to 23 months. The data were not reliable until 18 months, but by that age and beyond both groups looked appropriately at the films that matched the spatial terms of their own language. So, both groups begin to acquire the common spatial morphemes of their language at the same age. To understand this result, we need to reconsider what it is that infants are learning about containment, support, and fit before 14 months. We have seen that notions of containment and support are well established before that time, but what about the notion of tight-fit?

We conducted two experiments to answer this question (McDonough et al. 2003). First we used a familiarization/preferential-looking technique with 9-, 11-, and 14-month-old infants from English-speaking homes. We made more examples of the kinds of relations used in the first study so we could see if infants can abstract a common relation across many and diverse scenes without benefit of language. In the first experiment with this younger sample we familiarized infants with a series of either "loose-in" relations or "tight-on" relations. Then we presented another example of the familiarized relation along with the new relation and measured whether they preferred to look at the new relation. We realized "loose in" versus "tight on" confound the two variables of interest, but to begin we had to insure that the technique would work, and because the relational contrast seemed subtle in comparison to the variety of objects that were used, we wanted to test the most obvious comparison. We varied the objects as much as possible, so that infants would have to generalize across markedly different scenes to the relation itself.

Our data showed that 9-month-olds significantly preferred to look at the familiar relation during the test trials, whether they had been familiarized with "tight in" or "loose on." Eleven-month-olds began to show a preference for the novel relation, and 14-month-olds showed a significant preference for the novel relation. These results told us that even 9-month-olds made the discrimination between the two kinds of relations, but their preference for the familiar suggested they might still be in the process of analyzing these notions and so it might take them longer to be sure of what was being displayed. We also tested English-speaking adults, and like the 14-month-olds, they showed a preference for the novel relation. We gave the adults an explicit test as well, in which we modeled three of the actions they had seen in familiarization and one of the actions from the other category they had seen during the test, and asked them to say which one did not belong with the others. Seventy-eight percent of the adults were correct in their choices and always justified their choices by mentioning containment or support, not tightness or looseness. So, the adults were not only responsive to the distinction being tested but could verbalize it as well. It appears the contrast was not so subtle after all (although I note that 22% of the adults did not make the correct choice).

Next we carried out a finer comparison – that between tight and loose containment. The films we used, all scenes in which a hand was shown putting things into containers, and varying only in the degree of fit between the container and the contained, seemed even more subtle than before (although not so subtle to Choi, a native Korean speaker). Still, none of us was sure that infants would be responsive to the distinction. In this experiment we tested 9, 11, and 14-month-olds from both Korean and English-speaking homes, and both Korean and English speaking adults as well. We familiarized the subjects either with a series of "tight in" or "loose in" actions, then tested them on a new example of the familiarized action versus an action showing the relation they had not yet seen.

In this experiment the infants at all 3 ages and from both language groups showed a significant preference for the action they were familiarized with during the test trials, whether that was tight-fitting or loose-fitting containment. Although this result showed that the infants categorized the two types of containment actions as distinct from each other, it was still surprising. It is relatively unusual in the familiarization-dishabituation literature to show a preference for the same stimuli that have been used in familiarization – most instances of this kind of result have occurred in younger infants (or when tested after a long delay) and have been speculated to be due to factors such as lack of familiarity with the stimuli and/or slower processing of them. Perhaps the contrast we used was indeed so subtle that infants tended to continue analysis of the familiarization category during the test trials.

The adult data, however, suggest that this is not an entirely satisfactory explanation. First, the English speakers showed no sensitivity to the distinction at all, either in the looking test trials or in the explicit test in which they were asked which scene was different from the others. Second, the Korean speakers were sensitive to the distinction on both tests. On the explicit test, not only were they correct, they typically used the verbs *kkita* and *nehta* to describe the distinction. However, on the looking test trials, the Korean adults, just like the infants from both language groups, also showed a preference for the relation they had been familiarized with, whether that was tight or loose fit. An explanation for the preference for the familiarized stimuli in terms of subtlety of the distinction being tested does not seem entirely plausible for adults who have honored this distinction in their vocabulary throughout their lives. Nevertheless, it just possibly might be correct. Perhaps tightness is not as important a relation as containment, and even with the distinction entrenched in the language, adults might want to confirm that all the scenes expressed tightness (or looseness). Bear in mind that we did not test the overall Korean distinction of tight fit versus loose fit, only the subset that concerns containment, so we were in effect calling attention to a particular kind of containment rather than tightness or looseness more generally.

In any case, the data suggest that daily use of a language that makes this distinction affects the interpretation of scenes that involve containment. In contrast, when a language ignores the distinction, adults tend not to notice it. How deep this language-induced sensitivity, or lack thereof, may be is still unknown. Clearly, the English speakers could have discriminated the tight from loose scenes if asked to do so. Nevertheless, the distinction was not at the forefront of their minds. They have a concept of tightness but it appears not be as closely related to containment as it is for Korean speakers. However, because we did not test a contrast between tight-fitting containment and tight-fitting support, a contrast that is honored in English but not in Korean, we do not know whether Korean speakers would be less sensitive to that contrast. Such a test might help answer the question of whether containment is a more important relation than tightness. If it is, Korean speakers might remain sensitive to the difference between tight support and tight containment even though their language does not specify the difference. If they do not make the distinction, then along with English speakers' insensitivity to the contrast between tight and loose containment, it would suggest a powerful effect of entrenched language on relational conceptualization.

This kind of study would also be useful in telling us something about interrelationships among semantic primitives. Are TIGHT FIT and LOOSE FIT more closely related to CONTAINMENT than to SUPPORT? For example, Soonja Choi has indicated to me that when asked to give a typical example of the verb *nehta,* Korean adults are more likely to use an example of loose containment than of loose encirclement. Recent studies suggest that containment may also be more salient than support for infants (Casasola and Cohen 2002; Choi, in press). Is support so ubiquitous a relation that it gets overlooked? Or is it that a concept of support involves gravity and weight, factors that cannot be seen nor discovered through spatial analyses? This is a promising field of investigation, because if we discover the relations that especially attract infants' attention this will provide clues to the particular kinds of information most likely to become transformed into concepts.

5. Conclusions

Testing the effects of language on thought was not the goal of these experiments. Rather our purpose was to explore the preverbal concepts that enable children to learn spatial relational language. It has been suggested (e.g., Bowerman 1996) that different languages encode too many spatial distinctions to make it plausible that children could learn them all preverbally, and so language itself must teach the distinctions. Choi and Bowerman (1991) suggested that the Korean spatial terms – so different from English – cast doubt on containment and support as privileged spatial primitives onto which language can be directly mapped. They proposed that language learners do not map spatial words onto nonlinguistic spatial concepts but instead that children are sensitive to the structure of their input language from the beginning. At the same time they noted that how children figure out language-specific spatial categories is a puzzle. Yes, this would be a puzzle – learning any language, relational or otherwise, without concepts onto which words can be mapped is highly implausible. Although I agree that young children are sensitive to the structure of their language from *the beginning of language learning*, the learning is only a puzzle if one assumes that *in* and *on* are the only kinds of spatial analyses that have been carried out prior to that. But, as this chapter has shown, a considerable amount of evidence has accumulated for the presence in infancy of many of the most fundamental relational concepts expressed by languages everywhere. Even if a tight-loose contrast may be more subtle than some others, it has already been conceptualized in the preverbal period. It certainly has not been a prominent candidate in discussions of the universal primitives that underlie language understanding, yet our data indicate it has every right to be there.

How many such relations will be found? We have hardly begun to explore this question. As discussed in this chapter, we know a moderate amount about concepts of containment and support. We have learned a little about concepts of up and down (or above and below) and about tight versus loose fit. The fact that infants can categorize tight versus loose containment suggests that they also have a concept of contact (as does Leslie's work on causality, discussed earlier). But not only do many relational concepts in infancy remain unexplored – for example, separating, joining, going across, going through – we do not even have an agenda to explore how many there might be.

In any case, I do not think we need worry about Bowerman's (1996) concern that too many relational concepts would be needed to explain acquisition of different languages via image-schema representations. It is true that languages vary considerably in the spatial distinctions they make. But the number in any given language is relatively small and the whole gamut of spatial distinctions across languages appears not to be unduly large (see also

Talmy, *this volume*). For example, in English there are only about 80 spatial prepositions altogether (Landau and Jackendoff 1993) and a great many of them are virtual synonyms of each other (such as *atop* and *on top of,* *in* and *inside, under* and *beneath*). This may be due to the historical roots of English, which leaves it with redundant and in some cases almost obsolete prepositions, such as *atop* and *betwixt* (as opposed to *between*). Furthermore, in daily speech a much smaller subset is used (in my reckoning, about 20 or so). Of these, about 6 or 7 are among the earliest relational words (*in, out, on, off, up, down,* along with *to)* used by infants.

The child's task differs somewhat in other languages. In Mixtec, body parts are used to specify various spatial relations, but this familiar schema should pose no problem for young learners. In Korean, a goodly number of distinct verbs must be learned to express the prepositions of English. But Korean children learn a small subset of these first (just as English-learning children learn a small set of prepositions) and overextend them. For example, the verb *kkita* (fit tightly together) is reserved for three-dimensional objects, another verb being used for flat objects. Korean infants tend to overlook this nicety in the early stages and use *kkita* to express such things as a flat magnet on a refrigerator door. This is a common occurrence across languages: children learn a few general distinctions and overextend them, gradually adding the finer points over time as their attention (and analysis) is brought to them. I would predict that this would also happen in Tzeltal, in which, somewhat like Korean, the shape of the container affects containment terms (Brown 1994).

One of the advantages of a mechanism of perceptual meaning analysis is that new distinctions can be discovered at any time that attention and analysis take place. This means that not all distinctions need be made at once. As long as children can conceptualize the overall meaning of a scene, they can discover the individualities of their particular language. They may conceptualize a scene as showing a tight-fit relation and only later notice that tight-fit is expressed differently for 2- and 3-dimensional objects. But they would already have these concepts. We should not be misled by the fact that spatial information can be perceived to think that language can be mapped onto perception itself; it cannot.[7] Learning spatial morphemes requires conceptual underpinning just as much as learning the difference between transitive and intransitive verbs, markers for ongoing action, or possessive pronouns, all of which clearly involve conceptual rather than perceptual knowledge.

---

7. See Mandler (2004) for extensive discussion of this point.

One of the things we have learned about infants in the past decade or so is just how much about the world they are learning. They have richer conceptual lives than has often been ascribed to them. When we consider that the most likely format for these preverbal concepts are the image-schemas that also structure language, the process of language acquisition becomes demystified, in the sense that going from image-schemas of paths and spatial relations to words is a smaller step than we once thought would be required for infants to learn language.

References

Arterberry, Martha E. and Marc H. Bornstein
2001   Three-month-old infants' categorization of animals and vehicles based on static and dynamic attributes. *Journal of Experimental Child Psychology* 80: 333-346.
Baillargeon, Renée, Laura Kotovsky, and Amy Needham
1995   The acquisition of physical knowledge in infancy. In *Causal Cognition*, Dan Sperber, David Premack, and Ann J. Premack (eds.), 79-116. Oxford: Oxford University Press.
Baillargeon, Renée and Su-hua Wang
2002   Event categorization in infancy. *Trends in Cognitive Science* 6: 85-93.
Barsalou, Larry W.
1999   Perceptual symbol systems. *Behavioral and Brain Sciences* 22: 577-660.
Bertenthal, Bennett
1993   Infants' perception of biomechanical motions: Intrinsic image and knowledge-based constraints. In *Visual Perception and Cognition in Infancy*, Carl Granrud (ed.), 175-214. Hillsdale, NJ: Erlbaum.
Bierwisch, Manfred
1967   Some semantic universals of German adjectivals. *Foundations of Language* 3: 1-36.
Bowerman, Melissa
1973   *Early Syntactic Development*. Cambridge: Cambridge University Press.
1996   Learning how to structure space for language: A crosslinguistic perspective. In *Language and Space*, Paul Bloom, Mary A. Peterson, Lynn Nadel, and Merrill F. Garrett (eds.), 385-436. Cambridge, MA: MIT Press.

160   *Jean M. Mandler*

Brown, Penelope
1994   The INS and ONS of Tzeltal locative expressions: The semantics of static descriptions of location. *Linguistics* 32: 743-790.
Brown, Roger
1973   *A First Language: The Early Stages.* Cambridge, MA: Harvard University Press.
Carey, Susan
1982   Semantic development: the state of the art. In *Language Acquisition: The State of the Art*, Eric Wanner, and Lila R. Gleitman (eds.), 347-389. Cambridge: Cambridge University Press.
Carey, Susan, and Ellen M. Markman
1999   Cognitive development. In *Cognitive Science*, Benjamin M. Bly, and David E. Rumelhart (eds.), 201-254. San Diego: Academic Press.
Carver, Leslie J., and Patricia J. Bauer
1999   When the event is more than the sum of its parts: Nine-month-olds' long-term ordered recall. *Memory* 7: 147-174.
Casasola, Marianella, and Leslie B. Cohen
2002   Infant spatial categorization of containment, support, or tight-fit spatial relations. *Developmental Science* 5: 247-264.
Choi, Soonja
in press   Preverbal spatial cognition and language-specific input: Categories of containment and support. In *Action meets word: How children learn verbs*, Kathy Hirsh-Pasek and Roberta M. Golinkoff (eds.), New York: Oxford University Press.
Choi, Soonja, and Melissa Bowerman
1991   Learning to express motion events in English and Korean: The influence of language-specific lexicalization patterns. *Cognition* 41: 83-121.
Choi, Soonja, Laraine McDonough, Melissa Bowerman, and Jean M. Mandler
1999   Early sensitivity to language-specific spatial categories in English and Korean. *Cognitive Development* 14: 241-268.
Csibra, Gergely, György Gergely, Szilvia Bíró, Orsolya Koós, and Margaret Brockbank
1999   Goal attribution without agency cues: The perception of 'pure reason' in infancy. *Cognition* 72: 237-267.
Csibra, Gergely, Szilvia Bíró, Orsolya Koós, and György Gergely
2003   One-year-old infants use teleological representation of actions productively. *Cognitive Science* 27: 111-133.
Fodor, Jerry A.
1975   *The Language of Thought.* New York: Crowell.

1981   The current status of the innateness controversy. In *Representations,* Jerry A. Fodor (ed.), 257-316. Cambridge, MA: MIT Press.

Frye, Douglas, Piers Rawling, Chris Moore, and Ilana Myers
1983   Object-person discrimination and communication at 3 and 10 months. *Developmental Psychology* 19: 303-309.

Gergely, György, Nádasdy, Zoltán, Gergely Csibra, and Szilvia Bíró
1995   Taking the intentional stance at 12 months of age. *Cognition* 56: 165-193.

Hespos, Susan J., and Renée Baillargeon
2001a   Reasoning about containment events in very young infants. *Cognition* 78: 207-245.
2001b   Infants' knowledge about occlusion and containment events: A surprising discrepancy. *Psychological Science* 12: 141-147.

Johnson, Mark
1987   *The Body in the Mind: The Bodily Basis of Meaning, Imagination, and Reason.* Chicago: University of Chicago Press.

Lakoff, George
1987   *Women, Fire, and Dangerous Things: What Categories Reveal About the Mind.* Chicago: University of Chicago Press.

Landau, Barbara, and Ray Jackendoff
1993   "What" and "where" in spatial language and spatial cognition. *Behavior and Brain Sciences* 16: 217-265.

Leslie, Alan M.
1982   The perception of causality in infants. *Perception* 11: 173-186.

Mandler, Jean M.
1992   How to build a baby: II. Conceptual primitives. *Psychological Review* 99: 587-604.
1996   Preverbal representation and language. In *Language and Space,* Paul Bloom, Mary A. Peterson, Lynn Nadel, and Merrill F. Garrett (eds.), 365-384. Cambridge, Mass.: MIT Press.
1998   Representation. In *Cognition, Perception, and Language,* Deanna Kuhn and Robert S. Siegler (eds.), 255-308. (Handbook of Child Psychology 2.) New York: Wiley.
2004   *The Foundations of Mind: Origins of Conceptual Thought.* Oxford: Oxford University Press.

Mandler, Jean M., and Laraine McDonough
1993   Concept formation in infancy. *Cognitive Development* 8: 291-318.
1995   Long-term recall in infancy. *Journal of Experimental Child Psychology* 59: 457-474.
1996   Drinking and driving don't mix: Inductive generalization in infancy. *Cognition* 59: 307-335.

1998   Studies in inductive inference in infancy. *Cognitive Psychology* 37: 60-96.

McDonough, Laraine, Soonja Choi, and Jean M. Mandler
2003   Understanding spatial relations: Flexible infants, lexical adults. *Cognitive Psychology* 46: 229-259.

McDonough, Laraine, and Jean M. Mandler
1998   Inductive generalization in 9- and 11-month olds. *Developmental Science* 1: 227-232.

Michotte, Albert E.
1963   *The Perception of Causality*. London: Methuen.

Paivio, Alan
1978   The relationship between verbal and perceptual codes. In *Perceptual Coding,* Edward C. Carterette and Morton P. Friedman (eds.), 375-397 (Handbook of Perception 8). New York: Academic Press.

Proffitt, Dennis R. and Bennett I. Bertenthal
1990   Converging operations revisited: Assessing what infants perceive using discrimination measures. *Perception and Psychophysics* 47: 1-11.

Quinn, Paul C.
2003   Concepts are not just for objects: Categorization of spatial relation information by infants. In *Categories and Concepts in Early Development*, David H. Rakison and Lisa M. Oakes (eds.), 50-76. Oxford: Oxford University Press.

Quinn, Paul C., Jennifer L. Polly, Michael J. Furer, Velma Dobson, and Dana B. Narter
2002   Young infants' performance in the object-variation version of the above-below categorization task: A result of perceptual distraction or conceptual limitation? *Infancy* 3: 323-348.

Regier, Terry
1995   A model of the human capacity for categorizing spatial relations. *Cognitive Linguistics* 6: 63-88.

Slobin, Dan I.
1985   Crosslinguistic evidence for the Language-Making Capacity. In *The Crosslinguistic Study of Language Acquisition*, Dan I. Slobin (ed.), Vol. 2, 1157-1256. Hillsdale, NJ: Erlbaum.

Smiley, Patricia, and Janellen Huttenlocher
1995   Conceptual development and the child's early words for events, objects, and persons. In *Beyond Names for Things*, Michael Tomasello and William E. Merriman (eds.), 21-61. Hillsdale, NJ: Erlbaum.

Spelke, Elizabeth S., and Susan J. Hespos
  2002   Conceptual development in infancy: The case of containment. In
            *Representation, Memory, and Development: Essays in Honor of
            Jean Mandler*, Nancy L. Stein, Patricia Bauer, and Mitchell Rabi-
            nowitz (eds.), 223-246. Mahway, NJ: Erlbaum.
Talmy, Leonard
  1983   How language structures space. In *Spatial Orientation: Theory,
            Research, and Application*, Herbert L. Pick, Jr. and Linda P.
            Acredolo (eds.), 225-282. New York: Plenum.
Tomasello, Michael
  1992   *First Verbs: A Case Study of Early Grammatical Development*.
            Cambridge: Cambridge University Press.
Vandeloise, Claude
  1991   *Spatial Prepositions: A Case Study From French*. Chicago: Chi-
            cago University Press.
Watson, John S.
  1972   Smiling, cooing, and "the game." *Merrill-Palmer Quarterly* 18:
            323-340.
White, Peter A.
  1988   Causal processing: Origins and development. *Psychological Bulle-
            tin* 104: 36-52.
Willatts, Peter
  1997   Beyond the "couch potato" infant: How infants use their knowledge
            to regulate action, solve problems, and achieve goals. In *Infant De-
            velopment: Recent Advances*, Gavin Bremner, Alan Slate, and
            George Butterworth (eds.), 109-135. Hove: Psychology Press.
Woodward, Amanda L.
  1998   Infants selectively encode the goal object of an actor's reach. *Cogni-
            tion* 69: 1-34.
  1999   Infants' ability to distinguish between purposeful and non-
            purposeful behaviors. *Infant Behavior and Development* 22: 145-
            160.
Woodward, Amanda L., and Jessica A. Sommerville
  2000   Twelve-month-old infants interpret action in context. *Psychological
            Science* 11: 73-77.

Image schemata in the brain

Tim Rohrer[*]

Abstract

A focus on the brain as an organic biological entity that grows and develops as the organism does is a prerequisite to a neurally-plausible theory of how image schemata structure language. Convergent evidence from the cognitive neurosciences has begun to establish the neural basis of image schemata as dynamic activation patterns that are shared across the neural maps of the sensorimotor cortex. First, I discuss the numerous experimental studies on normal subjects that, coupled with recent neurological studies of body-part language deficits in patients, can be taken to indicate that the sensorimotor cortices are crucial to the semantic comprehension of bodily action terms and sentences. Second, by tracing the cognitive and neural development of image schemata through both animal neuroanatomical studies and human neuroimaging studies, I review the neurobiologically plausible bases for image schemata. I propose that Edelman's theory of secondary neural repertoires is the likeliest process to account for how integrative areas of the sensorimotor cortex can develop both sensorimotor and image schematic functions. Third, I assess the evidence from recent fMRI and ERP experiments showing that literal and metaphoric language stimuli activate areas of sensorimotor cortex consonant with the image schemata hypothesis. I conclude that these emerging bodies of evidence show how the image schematic functions of the sensorimotor cortex structure linguistic expression and metaphor.

Keywords: image schema, cognitive neuroscience, semantic comprehension, metaphor, neural development

[*] The author would like to acknowledge the Sereno and Kutas laboratories at UCSD for their role in obtaining the evidence discussed here, as well as the constructive comments of two anonymous reviewers and the editor of this volume.

1. Introduction

1.1. Dynamic patterns: image schemata as shared activation contours across perceptual modalities

Let me begin with a bold and preposterous claim. *I want to hand you an idea that at first may seem hard to grasp, but if you turn it over and over again in your head until you finally get a firm handle on it, it will feel completely right to you.* Now, if I could make a movie of what your brain was doing as you read that last sentence, it would most likely look very similar to a brain movie of you turning an unfamiliar object over and over again in your hand until you found a way to grip it well. Your primary motor and somatosensory cortices would be active in the areas mapping the hand and the wrist, and the premotor and secondary somatosensory hand cortices would also be active.

Until recently, these suggestions would have seemed to be more the stuff of idle speculation and science fiction than of scientific fact. However, over the past few years we have been able to paint just that kind of picture, given recent advances in brain imaging technology coupled with research findings by, e.g., Hauk et al. (2004); Coslett et al. (2002); Moore et al. (2000); Rizzolatti et al. (2002; 2001) and Rohrer (2001b). There have been substantial obstacles on the way, not the least of which was a long-standing misbelief that the language functions occur exclusively in areas of the inferior frontal lobe and superior temporal lobe – primarily in Broca's and Wernicke's areas.[1]

However, a new picture of a distributed model of semantic comprehension is now emerging. In the new model, brain areas formerly thought to be purely sensorimotoric are turning out to have important roles in the so-called "higher" cognitive processes, e.g., language. In other words, language makes much more use of the brain's processes of spatial, visual and mental imagery than previously thought. Inspired by linguistic and philosophical evidence,[2]

---

1. Such theories were driven by historical evidence from linguistic disorders such as aphasia and anomia, which showed that lesions to those areas in the left hemisphere of the brain were correlated with these disorders.
2. The linguistic evidence mostly stems from the semantics of spatial-relation terms, which tend to be extremely polysemous (cf. Lakoff 1987: 416-61; Brugman 1983; Dodge and Lakoff, *this volume*; Talmy, *this volume*, 2000: 409-70, 1985: 293-337).

the philosopher Mark Johnson (1987),[3] and the linguist George Lakoff (1987) theorized that linguistic expressions evidenced dynamic patterns of recurrent bodily experience which they called *image schemata,* and later hypothesized that these image schemata were such frequent and deeply held patterns of experience for human organisms that they were likely to be instantiated in our nervous system (Lakoff and Johnson 1999). For example Lakoff (1987: 416-61) observes that there are many linguistic senses of the English word *over.* Consider two of them: *The fly is over my head,* and *I turned the log over.* In the first sentence *over* is being used in what Lakoff calls a fairly canonical sense of an ABOVE image schema, where a small trajector (*the fly*) passes over a large landmark (*my head*). However, *over* in the second sentence also utilizes a REFLEXIVE image-schema transformation, in which the trajector and landmark become the same object (*the log*). Furthermore, he notes that such schematizations can be used metaphorically, as in *turning an idea over and over again.*

Johnson (1987) first defined an image schema as a recurrent pattern, shape or regularity in, or of, our actions, perceptions and conceptions. He argued that

> … these patterns emerge primarily as meaningful structures for us chiefly at the level of our bodily movements through space, our manipulation of objects, and our perceptual interactions (Johnson 1987: 29).

His definition was illustrated by several examples of how linguistic and conceptual structure is underlain by image-schematic structure. For instance, the CONTAINMENT schema structures our regular recurring experiences of putting objects into and taking them out of a bounded area. We can experience this pattern in the tactile perceptual modality with physical containers, or we can experience this perceptual pattern visually as we track the movement of some object into or out of some bounded area or container. He argued that these patterns can then be metaphorically extended to structure non-tactile, non-physical, and non-visual experiences.

In a particularly striking sequence of examples, Johnson (1987: 30-32) traced many of the habitual notions of CONTAINMENT we might experience during the course of a typical morning routine: We wake up *out of* a deep sleep, drag ourselves *up out of* bed and *into* the bathroom, where we look *into* the mirror and pull a comb *out from inside* the cabinet. Later that same morning we might wander *into* the kitchen, sit *in* a chair at the breakfast

---

3. For extensive details on philosophical aspects, see Johnson (*this volume*, 1987: 18-193).

table and *open up* the newspaper and become lost *in* an article. Some of these experiences are spatial and physical but do not involve the prototypical CON-TAINMENT image schema (as in the example of sitting *in* a chair) while some of these experiences draw on purely metaphorical extensions of CONTAIN-MENT (as in the example of getting lost *in* the newspaper article). Johnson proposed that the CONTAINMENT image schema, or some portion or variation of it, structures all of these experiences.

However, Johnson (1987: 19-27) proposed image schemata not only as a link between the linguistic evidence and the philosophical phenomenology, but explicitly intended them to be consonant with other research in the cognitive, developmental and brain sciences. Experimental studies of infant cognition (Meltzoff and Borton 1977; Meltzoff 1993; Stern 1985: 47-53) suggest a cross-modal perceptual basis for a SMOOTH-ROUGH schema: A blindfolded baby is given one of two pacifiers. One has a smooth nipple, the other a nubbed one covered with little bumps. The infant is allowed to suck on the nipple long enough to habituate to it, and then the pacifier and the blindfold are removed. When one smooth and one nubbed pacifier are placed on either side of the infant's head, the infant turns its head to stare at the pacifier just sucked about 75% of the time, suggesting that there is a cross-modal transfer between the tactile and visual modalities within the infant brain. It is as if the bumpy physical contours of the nipple are translated by the infant's tongue into bumpy activation contours in a tactile neural map of the object surface, which is then shared as (or activates a parallel set of) activation contours in a visual neural map of the object surface. Adults may not stare at such surfaces, but the experience of rough and smooth surfaces occurs myriads of times each day, as when we walk from a hardwood bedroom floor through a carpeted hall and onto the bathroom tile. As we do so, our eyes anticipate the change in surface and pass this on to our feet so that we can maintain our balance. If we perform the same bed-to-bath journey at night, we can utilize the surface underfoot in order to help us anticipate where to turn, visualize where the doorway is and so on. Whenever we accomplish such feats, we are relying on *our ability to share activation contours across perceptual modalities*.

Although the kind of abstractions evidenced in image schemata are perhaps most clearly introduced using examples of shared activation contours in cross-modal perception, there is no reason for image schemata to be construed as being *necessarily* cross-modal in every instance. Rather than an abstraction crossing perceptual modalities, an image schema might pick out an abstraction "crossing" temporal boundaries. An image schema might be a particular pattern of neural activations in a neural map of pitch, say something corresponding to the musical scale in sequence (*do-re-mi-fa-so-la* ...). From such an example we can see that image-schematic patterns are not temporally static, but take place in and through time. The musical scale is a sequence of activity in time; hearing an ascending pitch scale causes us to anticipate its next step. Given those first six notes, we sense its next step – *ti* – and expect the pattern to continue. The temporal character of image schemata creates the possibility of a normal pattern completion, which in turn serves as the felt basis for their inferential capacity.[4] Image schemata are thus temporally dynamic in the sense that once they are triggered, we tend to complete the whole perceptual contour of the schema.

1.2. Image schemata and the body within the brain

In developing their notion of an *image schema*, both Johnson and Lakoff (Johnson 1987; Lakoff 1987; Lakoff and Johnson 1999) used the term "image" in its broad neurocognitive sense of mental imagery and not as exclusively indicating visual imagery.[5] Mental imagery can also be kinaesthetic, as in the felt sense of one's own body image. Take another thought experiment as an example. Imagine that I wish to sharpen my pencil. However, the pencil sharpener is located atop a tall four-drawer file cabinet next to my writing desk. Seated, I cannot reach the pencil sharpener by merely moving my arms. It is beyond my immediate grasp, and I will have to get up. What is more, if you were with me in my office, you would immediately grasp my predicament as well.

But how do we know such things as what is within our reach? We know them because we have a coherent body image in our heads – somatotopic neurocortical maps of where our arms and hands are and how they can move,

---

4. While all humans normally develop neural maps for pitch, the musical scales do vary across cultures. Thus pattern-completion sequences such as the musical scale are good examples of how social and cultural forces can shape parts of image-schematic structure. Other image-schematic pattern completions, such as those for motor actions like grasping, are shared with other primates (Umiltá et al. 2001) and are likely to be universal across cultures.

5. It is important to acknowledge, however, that the term *image schema* partly emerges from research on visual imagery and mental rotation (cf. Johnson and Rohrer, in press; Johnson 1987: 25). The sentence *The fly walked all over the ceiling*, for example, incurs a rotated covering schema (Lakoff 1987: 416-61).

as well as neurocortical maps marking the location of objects in our visual field. We plan motor movements thousands of times each day, constantly re-evaluating the extent of our graspable space given our current bodily position. With a few discontinuities, the body image in the primary sensorimotor cortex is somatotopic, with adjacent neurons mapping largely contiguous sections of the body:[6] the ankle is next to the lower leg, and that to the knee and upper leg and so on. Similarly, the premotor cortical maps are also fairly somatotopic; e.g., neural arrays mapping hand motions are adjacent to those mapping wrist and arm motions. This topology is highly sensible, given that we need to use our hands and wrists in close co-ordination for tasks such as turning the pencil in the pencil sharpener.

Furthermore, in a series of recent studies on both macaque monkeys and humans, Rizzolatti, Buccino, Gallese and their colleagues have discovered that the sensorimotor cortices not only map "peripersonal" space – i.e., what is within one's own grasp – but also contain "mirror neurons" with which the premotor cortex simulates the actions being taken by another monkey, or another human (Rizzolatti and Craighero 2004; Fogassi et al. 2001; Buccino et al. 2001; Umiltá et al. 2001; Ferrari et al. 2003). When one monkey observes another monkey perform a grasping task with the hands, the mirror neurons will activate the motor-planning regions in the monkey's own hand cortex. The mirror neuron experiments of the Rizzolatti group (Rizzolatti and Craighero 2004) are cross-modal by design – experience in one modality must cross over into another. In this example, the visual perception of grasping crosses into the somatomotor cortices, activating the same sensorimotor schemata that would be activated by the monkey grasping something on its own. Moreover, other experiments (Umiltá et al. 2001) have also shown that the monkey needs only experience a small portion of the motor movement to complete the entire plan. Thus, their experiments also illustrate how the principle of the preservation of the bodily topology in the sensorimotor cortices affords the possibility of image-schematic pattern completion. Similarly, recent findings (Kohler et al. 2002) even suggest that such patterns can serve to integrate sensory input across modalities; a monkey's grasping mirror neurons can fire, for instance, when the monkey hears a sound correlated

---

6. The neural basis for the human body image was mapped by Wilder Penfield and colleagues at the Montreal Neurological Institute (Penfield and Rasmussen 1950), where neurosurgeons reported that patients under light anaesthesia either made movements or verbally reported feeling in the regions of their body when the cerebral cortex along the central sulcus was stimulated by the neurosurgeon.

with the grasping motion, such as tearing open a package. This suggests that even when triggered from another modality, the brain tends to complete the entire perceptual contour of an image schema.

1.3. Image schemata and language comprehension

Experimental studies on humans provide the additional avenue of investigating whether image schemata might arise in response to linguistic stimuli as well as to visual (or other sensory) stimuli. For instance we can use language to describe motor actions to participants in neuroimaging experiments, or we can ask brain-injured patients to name their body parts or to make simple pattern-completing inferences concerning their body parts (e.g., *the wrist is connected to the ... hand*).

Recent research has begun to establish that the sensorimotor cortical regions play a much larger role in such semantic comprehension tasks than previously thought. In the patient-based neurological literature, Suzuki et al. (1997) have reported on a brain-damaged patient who has a selective category deficit in body-part knowledge, while Coslett et al. (2002) have reported on patients in whom the body-part knowledge has largely been spared. The locations of these lesions suggest that the involvement of premotor and secondary somatosensory regions is functionally critical to the semantic comprehension of body-part terms (cf. Schwoebel and Coslett 2005). Similarly, but within experimental cognitive neuroscience, Hauk et al. (2004) measured the brain's hemodynamic response to action words involving the face, arm, and leg (i.e., *smile*, *punch* and *kick*) using functional magnetic resonance imaging (fMRI) techniques. Their results show differential responses in the somatomotor cortices, i.e., leg terms primarily activate premotor leg cortex, whereas hand terms activate premotor hand cortex and so on. Their research[7]

---

7. In a related study by the same group, Pulvermüller et al. (2002) used excitatory transcranial magnetic stimulation (TMS), electromyography (EMG) and a lexical-decision task to examine the semantic contribution of the somatomotor cortices. After using EMG to determine exactly where to place the TMS electrode for optimal stimulation of the hand cortex and the optimal amplitude and duration of the TMS pulse, participants viewed linguistic stimuli which consisted of either arm and leg action words or nonsensical psuedowords. The results show that when the left hemispheric cortical region which matched the arm or leg word was excited by TMS, the response time was significantly quicker than in the control condition without TMS. Similar results were obtained using TMS

shows that it is possible to drive the somatomotor neural maps using linguistic – as opposed to perceptual – input. The notion of an image schema may have originated in linguistic and philosophical hypotheses about spatial language, but – given the recent evidence from cognitive neuroscience – is likely to have its neurobiological grounding in the neural maps performing somatomotor and multimodal imagery tasks.

Parallel experimental results on action sentences from cognitive psychology lend additional credence to the neurological and neuroimaging evidence showing that the mental imagery carried out in the premotor and multimodal somatosensory cortices is *functionally* critical to semantic comprehension. Numerous experiments assessing the relationship between embodied cognition and language have shown that that there is a facilitatory/inhibitory effect on accuracy and/or response speed that holds for a diverse set of language comprehension tasks.[8] Such experiments suggest that the sensorimotor and somatosensory neural regions implicated by the neuroimaging and the selective-deficits studies are functionally related to language comprehension. The perceptual and motor imagery performed by certain regions of the brain subserve at least some processes of language comprehension: we understand an action sentence because we are subconsciously imagining performing the action.[9] Moreover, cognitive psychologists have shown that the sentence stimuli do not even need to be about literal actions to show the facilitation effects of image-schematic simulations (cf. Gibbs, *this volume*).

---

on both hemispheres, but not in the right hemisphere-only condition—as would be expected for right-hand dominant participants. The facilitation in the cortical excitation condition suggests that these somatosensory regions are not only active but functionally implicated in semantic comprehension.

8. Zwaan et al. (2004) found facilitatory effects when the direction of an object's motion implied by a sentence matched a change in the size of the object in two successive visual depictions of a scene; mismatches produced inhibition. Glenberg and Kaschak (2002) found similar effects for participants who listened to sentences describing bodily motions either toward or away from the body (e.g., "pull/push") and then responded via a sequence of button presses in a congruent or incongruent direction of movement (toward or away from the body).

9. Matlock et al. (in press) compared the effect of metaphoric motion and no-motion sentences on participants' reasoning in response to an ambiguous temporal question. The motion-sentence group were more likely to choose the response which reflected reasoning using a spatial metaphor for time that was congruent with the spatial metaphor introduced in the motion sentences.

In sum, there are several converging strands of evidence which support the assumption that language comprehension relies on image schemata. Apart from the linguistic and philosophical evidence traditionally cited (cf. Dodge and Lakoff, *this volume*; Johnson, *this volume*), there are congruent findings not only from cognitive psychology, but also from comparative neurophysiology, neurological-deficits research, and cognitive neuroscience.

1.4. Summary: Goals of this article and preview of remaining sections

By now it should be clear how richly cross-disciplinary the concept of an image schema is. As image schemata have phenomenological, linguistic, developmental, and neural purchase in explicating the preconceptual and preverbal structures of human experience, they can only be defined precisely in terms of a cross-disciplinary set of factors (cf. Johnson and Rohrer, in press):

- Image schemata are recurrent patterns of bodily experience;
- Image schemata are "image"-like in that they preserve the topological structure of the whole perceptual experience;
- Image schemata operate dynamically in and across time;
- Image schemata are structures which link sensorimotor experience to conceptualization and language;
- Image schemata are likely instantiated as activation patterns (or "contours") in topologic and topographic neural maps;
- Image schemata afford normal pattern completions that can serve as a basis for inference.

Throughout the remainder of this chapter my major objective is to pursue how image schemata might be neurobiologically grounded.

To deepen our understanding of what image schemata are, I first consider some of the developmental evidence concerning whether image schemata are innate for humans. This leads into a brief discussion of the neural development of image schemata in non-humans, where I explain how current research on the plasticity of neural maps provides candidate neurobiological mechanisms for image schemata and offer an admittedly speculative account of how image schemata might work at the neuronal level. In section 3, I return to the recent neuroimaging and neurological evidence of image schemata in humans, discussing how these neural areas are recruited in the comprehension of both literal and metaphoric language in a number of experiments carried out by my colleagues and myself at the University of California in San Diego.

2.   The cognitive and neural development of image schemata

When considering the definition of image schemata from the vantage points of cognitive and neural development, two important sets of interrelated questions arise. First, are image schemata innate or learned (as in a Piagetian account) from the co-occurrence of sensorimotor experiences in different modalities? Are they genetically programmed or do they require appropriate environmental stimuli? Given that image schemata supposedly link species-specific behaviors like language to sensorimotor experience, to what extent are they unique to humans? Are there relevant analogues in animals? Second, exactly how might such image schemata be neurobiologically grounded? Does the fact that they often integrate perceptual imagery from multiple perceptual modalities imply that they are coordinated activation patterns linking small neural assemblies within two or more primary sensorimotor cortical maps, are they instead specialized cross-modal maps which integrate multiple perceptual images in the sensorimotor cortices, or are they some combination of these? Can animal research on neural development also help in answering this second set of questions?

2.1. The developmental course of image schemata in infancy

The evidence from developmental cognition offers some intriguing – if also ambiguous – insights into whether image schemata are innate or learned. Mandler (*this volume*) summarizes much of the infant development research supporting the idea that at least some image schemata are present from very early ages. She argues that "… infants come equipped with a concept-creating mechanism that analyzes perceptual information and redescribes it into simpler form," and furthermore that this simpler form is image-schematic in character. Infants show early tendencies to attend to events which lead to the formation of highly general preverbal concepts, such as making distinctions between animate/inanimate motion and self versus caused motion. For example, infants are likely to have an innate PATH image schema as from birth as they are particularly attentive to the path and manner of motion of objects in their visual field. At just 3 months infants can differentiate between a point-light display affixed at the joints of people or animals from a biologically incoherent point-light display; similarly they can differentiate point-light displays depicting animal motion from those depicting moving vehicles (Arterberry and Bornstein 2001; Bertenthal 1993).

However, while some of the most basic image schemata are present from an early age, it is equally certain that infants clearly learn increasingly complex versions of them throughout the first two years of infancy. For example, the SOURCE-PATH-GOAL image schema shows a developmental timeline of increasing complexity throughout the first year. At five months infants are able to attend to the goal of the path traced out by a human hand reaching toward an object (Woodward 1998); then, at nine months they can distinguish between a hand grasping an object and a hand resting upon it (Woodward 1999); while at twelve months infants are able to selectively attend to objects by following changes in the direction that a caregiver points or looks (Woodward and Guajardo 2002).

An infant's ability to perform cross-modal experimental tasks is thus both present in early infancy and increases with age. In the Meltzoff and Borton study (1979) mentioned above, infants appear to be able to perform the pacifier-selection task from a very early age (1 month). Although there is some doubt about whether this experiment is replicable at such an early age (Maurer et al. 1998), other studies have shown that infants clearly get better at the task with age (Rose et al. 1972; Rose 1987). Other cross-modal image schemata are also present in early infancy. For example, Lewcowitz and Turkewitz (1980) show that at about three weeks infants can determine what levels of light intensity correspond to what levels of sound intensity (i.e., volume of white noise), suggesting that there is a cross-modal INTENSITY image schema already present in early stages of infant development. Finally, infants can imitate facial expressions from just minutes after birth, suggesting that some capacity for cross-modal coordination from the visual to the propioceptive motor modality is innate (Meltzoff 1977, 1993).

2.2. The neural development of image schemata

2.2.1. Neural maps and image schemata as developmental processes

One might well pause to ask, however, why we continue to define "innateness" in terms of the moment of birth. In a traditional Piagetian account the sensorimotoric schemata would emerge first after birth, and only then would the co-occurrence of sensory experiences in multiple modalities (or the cross-temporal sensory experiences in a single modality) interact and produce the "reciprocal assimilation" necessary for more abstract schemata to form (Stern 1985: 45-68). From the perspective of neuroembryology however, sensory stimuli in general (with the obvious large exception of the visual) do not commence at birth. We know from recent prenatal studies that foetuses hear maternal speech while still in the womb, and this influences their postnatal linguistic development, presumably by influencing the initial development of their auditory neural maps (DeCasper et al. 1994). Birth simply is not a determinative point after which some image schemata are fixed, or before which they do not exist. Although image schemata may ultimately require the consolidation of postnatal sensorimotor experience, their origins stretch back into prenatal experience. Innate *and* learned is a more accurate way to characterize image schemata.

The innate/learned dichotomy is now often rephrased as a question about whether something is genetically determined or environmentally acquired. Once again, considering this version of the innateness question from the vantage of neuroembryology gives the insight that the question may be poorly formed, given that it is mathematically improbable that the mechanisms underlying such schemata are entirely genetically specified (Edelman 1987: 121-126). Assuming that image schemata do take place in and/or between the sensorimotor neural maps, the initial development of them would begin during the development of those maps late in the formation of the neural tube. While cell differentiation is clearly genetically instructed, the developmental forerunners of the neural maps are what Edelman calls neuronal groups. He argues that their number, shape, connectivity and final locations are too numerous to be genetically determined.

Instead, Edelman argues that neuroembryonic development is best understood as a competitive process known as "neural Darwinism." As organic living things, neurons in the embryo seek to flourish, find nourishment and reinforcement. As a result the developing neurons begin to form Hebbian associations between one cell's axons and another's dendrites, clustering together in neuronal groups. These neuronal groups act like organisms that seek out stimulation as nourishment, and the neuronal groups compete with each other as they migrate along the neural tube toward the emerging sense organs. Some unfortunate groups perish at all stages of the process, while others hang on in intermediate states of success, creating overlapping neural arbors exhibiting a specific kind of redundancy called "neural degeneracy" (Edelman 1987: 46-57).

Over time, the population-growth dynamics and migration of the neuronal groups creates yet another emergent property: neurons array themselves into physical patterns which "map" the sensory modalities. This use of physical space within the brain to re-represent environmental stimuli yields the incipient primary topographic spatial neural maps of the various sensory modalities. Auditory areas develop maps indicating increasing pitch and volume; later, tactile areas develop somatic maps for pain and touch along the limbs; still later yet, somatomotoric maps develop for muscles distributed across the limbs. These formative neural maps are probably enough to sustain some rudimentary cross-modal image-schematic patterns, particularly between the tactile and auditory modalities. But the competition between neuronal groups does not end there. As different neurally degenerate neuronal groups are crowded out by the more successful groups mapping primary "topographic" stimuli, the intermediately successful groups hang on by mapping different, more abstractly topological aspects of the sensory stimuli. Although all this activity begins before birth, much of the ongoing development and refinement of these maps awaits the much stronger reinforcement of the increase in environmental stimuli that comes with the infant's first movements, cries and sights.

From this brief consideration of innateness and the neuroembryological underpinnings of image schemata, we see that the neural maps are dynamic developmental processes that rely on these underlying principles of neural Darwinism and redundant neural degeneracy. To understand how such organismic forces shape the postnatal development of image schemata, we now turn to detailed neuroanatomical studies of how animals develop cross-modal spatial schemata in and between their neural maps. This will yield the candidate neurobiological mechanisms for image schemata.

2.2.2. The plasticity of the neural maps in juvenile and adult animals

A series of experiments by Knudsen and colleagues (Knudsen 2002, 1998) address the question whether a barn owl can still successfully hunt if it were given prismatic glasses with lenses that distort the owl's perception 23 degrees to the right or left. Normally, a circling barn owl hears a mouse stirring in the fields below and locates it using the tiny difference in time that it takes for the sound to travel from one ear to the other along a path defined by the angle of its head and the origin of the sound. However, during the final dive of a strike the owl normally uses its eyes to pinpoint the exact location of its prey. Would the optical distortion from the glasses cause the owl miss its prey? If so, would it eventually learn to compensate?

Their results show that it depends on exactly *when* the experimenters put the prismatic glasses on the owl. Adult barn owls will reliably miss the target, but juvenile owls (~60 days) were able to learn to hunt accurately. Furthermore, juvenile owls raised with the prisms were able to learn as adults to hunt accurately either with or without their prisms. However, the prism-reared owls were not able to adapt to new prisms which distorted the visual field in the opposite direction of the prisms they wore as juveniles.

The barn owl experiments are of central importance to giving a neurobiological account of image schemata for a number of reasons. First, the barn owl locates its prey in space using cross-modal coordination between the auditory and visual perceptual modalities, making it a good animal analogue of image schemata. Second, the work on cross-modal schemata in barn owls addresses "neural plasticity," or the biological mechanisms by which experience-dependent learning takes place at the neuronal level. By understanding how an unnatural intervention into the juvenile owl's visual experience results in the abnormal neuroanatomical development of the owl's neural maps for space, we can better understand the normal neuroanatomical mechanisms by which human infants learn to make the sort of spatial distinctions picked out by image schemata. Related research on learning and neural plasticity in other animals, including frogs and monkeys, will introduce other important insights into how spatial information is re-organized, re-learned and abstracted at the neuronal level. Finally, for obvious ethical reasons we cannot normally obtain analogous human data at the same neuroanatomical level of investigation using these methods. However, after seeing these principles at work in animals we can ask whether homologous areas of the human cortex are active using less invasive methodologies such as lesion studies and neuro-imaging.

From the owl research, we know that a series of at least three neural maps are involved in this cross-modal schemata within the owl brain: a primarily auditory map of space in the central nucleus of the inferior colliculus (ICC), a multimodal auditory spatial map in the external nucleus of the inferior colliculus (ICX), and a primarily visual yet still multimodal spatial map in the optic tectum (also called the superior colliculus). When Knudsen and colleagues injected the ICX of their owls with an anatomical tracing dye, they were able to see significant differences in both the patterns of axonal growth and of the synaptic "boutons" (clusters). In comparing prism-reared owls compared to normal owls, they found an increased density of bouton-laden axon branches within the colliculus *only in the direction predicted* given the direction of the prismatic distortion. This suggests that reentrant connections from the visual map in the optic tectum of prism-reared owls changes the developmental course of the spatial map in the ICX. Furthermore, the unidirectional shift in the neuroanatomy of the map explains why adult prism-reared owls were unable to adapt to prisms which distorted the visual field in the opposite direction of their juvenile prisms (Knudsen 2002; DeBello et al. 2001; Knudsen and Brainerd 1991; Knudsen and Konishi 1978). These experiments reveal that epigenetic developmental experience can shape axonal structure in cross-modal neural maps, "showing that alternative learned and normal circuits can coexist in this network" (Knudsen et al. 2002: 325).[10]

The retention of overlapping and branched neural arbors in neural maps is crucial to the adaptive learning behavior exhibited by higher primates. Working on adult squirrel and owl monkeys, Merzenich and colleagues (Buonomano and Merzenich 1998; Merzenich et al. 1984, 1987; Allard et al. 1991; Jenkins et al. 1990; Wall et al. 1986) have shown that adult primates are able to dynamically reorganize the somatosensory cortical maps within certain constraints. Similar to the dual neural arborizations found in owls, these monkeys exhibited a plasticity based on their ability to select which parts of their neural arbors to use given different kinds of sensory activity. In a series of studies, the experimenters altered the monkey's normal hand sensory activity by such interventions as (1) cutting a peripheral nerve such as the medial or radial nerve and (1a) allowing it to regenerate naturally or (1b) tying it off to prevent regeneration; (2) amputating a single digit; and (3) taping together two digits so that they could not be moved independently. The results show that the somatomotor cortical areas now lacking their previous sensory connections (or independent sensory activity in the third condition) were "colonized" in a couple of weeks by adjacent neural maps with active sensory

---

10. By comparison, these dual neural circuits do not persist in a visual map of the frog's optic tectum. Neuroembryological experiments on frogs with surgically-rotated eyes has shown that after five weeks, the visual map in frog's optic tectum has neural arbors that initially exhibit a pattern of axonal growth similar to the juvenile owls called the "two-headed axons." However, after ten weeks the older axonal connections are starting to decay and disappear, while after sixteen weeks no two-headed axons could be traced (Guo and Udin 2000). Apparently, the frog's unimodal tectal maps do not receive enough reentrant neural connections from other sensory modalities to retain the overlapping and highly-branched neural arbors found in the cross-modal map of the owl inferior colliculus.

connections. In other words, the degree of existing but somewhat dormant neural arbor overlap was large enough that the cortex was able to reorganize to meet the demands of the new experiences. And in the case of (1a), where the nerve was allowed to regenerate, the somatosensory map gradually re-turned to re-occupy a similar-sized stretch of cortex, albeit with slightly different boundaries. This research suggests that adaptive learning behaviors in adult animals is accomplished in part by neural switching between overlapping and degenerate neural arbors. The competition for stimulation between neuronal groups is severe enough that, when deprived of their normal sensory stimulation, neurons will fall back on lesser-used axon branches to reorganize. Edelman (1987: 43-47) calls these latent reorganizations of these neuronal groups based on their branching arborizations *secondary repertoires*, as distinguished from their normal organization as *primary repertoires*.

At this point most of the elements for the probable neurobiological grounding of image schemata have been introduced. In the case of the owl we have examined how an experience-dependent, cross-modal map of space arises from the coordinated activity of primary visual and auditory maps. Because of the dual arborizations present in the cross-modal spatial map of the prism-reared owls, the prism-reared adult owl can switch between multiple degenerate neural arbors and learn a sensorimotor schema to hunt effectively with and without glasses.[11] The monkey evidence demonstrates how a more unimodal sensorimotoric schemata can be adaptively learned; in response to radical interventions the tactile and proprioceptive motor maps of the primary sensorimotor cortex reorganize. Once again this is accomplished by calling upon degenerate neural arbors to perform a new, slightly different mapping. Confronted with the new stimuli, the monkey cortex has reorganized to take advantage of latent secondary repertoires – but in this case, the interventions took place on adult monkeys and hence likely borrowed latent pre-extant, degenerate neural arborizations left over from unrelated developmental experiences. Unlike in the study of juvenile owls, the experimental interventions were not the precise cause of the degenerate and overlapping neural circuits which were then re-learned by the adult organism – the new learning required simply took advantage of latent organizational possibilities.

---

11. By contrast, the example of the frog in the previous footnote shows that in the absence of such dual arborizations, adaptive learning does not occur.

2.2.3. The neurobiological grounding of image schemata in humans

Though gathered using less invasive methodologies, similar findings hold for the human sensorimotor cortex. Analogous human studies show that similar cortical changes take place for the development of image schemata in the human sensorimotor cortices.

For example, the size and boundaries of neural maps can be changed from experience-dependent learning. Pascual-Leone and Torres (1993) studied differences in the hand somatosensory cortex of subjects who had learned to read Braille as adults. Using magnetoencephalography (MEG), they showed that compared to non-Braille reading adults the Braille-readers had a significantly larger scalp area over which potentials could be recorded for the right index finger. Further, the parts of the hand which were not used to read Braille were smaller in their somatosensory areas than in non-Braille readers. In another study, the somatosensory areas for the digits of the left hand of stringed-instrument players were larger than for their right hand or than for the left hand of control subjects who did not play a stringed instrument (Elbert et al. 1995). As in the case of the monkeys, the change in sensory experience causes a competitive reorganization of adjacent cortical areas so that the neural map of the fingers enlarges.

It is my contention that, similar to what was found for animals, the image schemata evidenced in human language and development are grounded in the sensorimotor cortices. While it is theoretically possible that every image schema is in fact simply physiologically encoded in an integrative secondary sensory cortical area (as in the owl's cross-modal map), I rather suspect this is not the case. Instead, suppose that image schemata rely on *functional* secondary repertoires which exist in the sensorimotor cortices, either in the primary sensorimotor cortex, in the more secondary "integrative" somatosensory cortex, the premotor cortex or in some combination of these.[12] In other words, when we grasp an object versus reading about grasping an object (or idea), we use a functioning secondary repertoire to mentally *simulate* – to imagine – performing the action using the same cortical area that we would use to perform the action. As the monkey mirror neurons have been divided into a number of subcategories, there is some support for this hypothesis in the mirror-neuron literature (Rizzolatti and Craighero 2004). Of the grasping neurons in area F5, approximately one third were classified as "strictly con-

---

12. It is possible that some particularly important image-schematic elements might have dedicated neural circuitry rather than a network of secondary repertoires.

gruent" neurons that code for precise hand shapes, while two thirds are "broadly congruent" mirror neurons that did not require observation of exactly the same action (Gallese et al. 1996). Some of these broadly congruent neurons appear to be responding to more abstractly general components of the hand shape or movement, such as being directed toward an end-goal. Thus one plausible proposal is that image schemata are the coordinated activation of secondary repertoires within the sensorimotor cortex consisting of some broadly congruent mirror neurons.

However, and whatever the exact neuronal mechanism might be, image-schema theory would predict that we understand language concerning the body and bodily actions by using the same cortical areas that map the sensorimotor activity for performing such actions. We would also expect that the activation course for language stimuli would be somewhat different – as understanding the sentence *I grabbed my knee* does not require my actually grabbing my knee, though pathological cases who do something similar have been reported (Schwoebel et al. 2002). Presumably, in the case of first-person action sentences, it is possible that there is either simultaneous inhibitory activation in the same cortical areas or, and more likely, an inhibitory firing in the spinal cord (as reported in Baldissera et al. 2001).

If this proposal for the neurobiological grounding of image schemata is correct, we should expect to see some areas within the primary sensorimotor, premotor and the more secondary integrative somatosensory cortices activated in fMRI studies by a range of linguistic tasks related to the body and bodily actions. Moreover, metaphoric versions of such language tasks ought to cause similar activation even when not literally describing bodily actions.

3. Metaphor in maps: convergent neuroimaging, electrophysiological and neurological studies of meaning

Recall first that the opening sentence of this chapter takes an abstract idea and gives it a concrete basis using the bodily metaphor of manipulating the idea-objects with the hands. As Lakoff and Johnson (1980) have shown, the conceptual metaphor IDEAS ARE OBJECTS is a commonplace way of speaking about intellectual matters. In English, there is a system of metaphoric expressions such as: *he handed me the project, the ideas slipped through my fingers, I found Lobachevskian geometry hard to grasp*, and so forth. Such expressions are instances of a related metaphor system, in which the image schemata of the source domain of object manipulation are systematically projected onto the target domain of mental activity. The inference patterns of the source can then be used to reason about the target. For example, if an idea slips through one's fingers, it means that we do not understand it; whereas, if we have a firm grasp on the idea, it means we do understand it. We understand what it means to grasp an idea much like we understand what it means to grasp an object.

In order to measure whether the same brain areas known to be involved in sensorimotor activity in monkeys and humans would also be activated by literal and metaphoric language about object manipulation, I compared the fMRI results from a hand stroking/grasping task to those from a semantic comprehension task involving literal and metaphoric hand sentences, as well as to a set of non-hand control sentences (Rohrer 2001b).[13] The sensorimotor areas active in the tactile task were congruent with previous studies of the somatotopy of the hand cortex (Moore et al. 2000), and were used to identify regions of interest for the two semantic conditions. As hypothesized, the results in the semantic conditions show that the participants exhibited several overlaps between the somatotopy found for a tactile hand stroking/grasping task and that found for both the literal hand sentence comprehension task and the metaphoric hand sentence comprehension task. These overlaps were concentrated particularly in the hand premotor cortex and in hand sensorimotor regions along both sides of the central sulcus, as well as in a small region of the superior parietal cortex (see figure 1). As expected, the overlaps were larger and more significant for literal than metaphoric sentences, though in most participants these same areas of overlap were observed. Furthermore, many of the cortical areas in which these overlaps were found are similar to those areas active in the hand/arm portion of the action-word experiments by Hauk et al. (2004). To provide a cross-methodological corroboration of these results, I also conducted related experiments with body-part word tasks in which I measured brain wave activity using event-related potential (ERP) methodologies (Rohrer 2001b). In short, I found that reading both metaphoric

---

13. Twelve right-hand dominant subjects participated in a block-design fMRI experiment on a 1.5T Siemens scanner at Thornton Hospital on the UCSD campus, using a small surface coil centered above the sensorimotor cortex with a TR of 4. Participants viewed eight alternating 32-second blocks of hand sentences and control sentences. Three such blocks were averaged together in each semantic comprehension condition. After the semantic data were obtained, one tactile right-hand stimulation block was performed. All data were analyzed using the FreeSurfer fMRI analysis package available from UCSD (Fischl et al. 1999).

and literal hand sentences activated many of the same sensorimotor areas as tactile stimulation of the hand did, as would be predicted by the image schemata hypothesis.

Of course, one standard objection to this interpretation of the fMRI evidence is that the neural activation might be merely an after-effect of "spreading activation" – that is, when we read the body-part term, we first understand it using some other region of the brain, and only after we understand it does the activation spread to the primary sensorimotor, premotor and secondary sensory cortices. Such an objection would thus suggest that the sensorimotor activation observed would not be functionally involved in semantic comprehension, but instead would be indicative of a preparatory response occurring after semantic comprehension has taken place elsewhere.

Fortunately much of the evidence already presented suggests that the after-effect proposal is likely not true. In the neurological literature, the dissociation of body-part knowledge observed in selective-deficit studies (Schwoebel and Coslett 2005; Suzuki et al. 1997; Shelton et al. 1998; Coslett et al. 2002) suggests that that the comprehension of body-part terms requires the undamaged and active participation of at least *some* of the somatotopic maps located in the sensorimotor cortices and the egocentric spatial neural maps located in the parietal cortices.[14] From experimental cognitive neuroscience, we know that the stimulation of the sensorimotor cortex (via TMS) can facilitate or inhibit the real-time comprehension of body-part action terms (Pulvermüller et al. 2002). Together with the other convergent psychological evidence for dynamic perceptual simulations also discussed in the introduction, these lines of evidence all suggest that these cortical areas are *functionally* involved in the semantic processing of body-part and bodily action terms and not a mere after-effect of it.

Finally, the spreading-activation objection to the fMRI overlap results is also explicitly addressed in my cross-methodological experiments using event-related potentials (ERPs). Using a single-word body-part task similar to that of Hauk et al. (2004), I examined the temporal dynamics and scalp distribution of the electrical signals from the sensorimotor cortices to measure first whether the ERPs are distributed across the sensorimotor cortices, and second whether the ERP response distributed across the sensorimotoric

---

14. Lesions can cause difficulties in tasks such as naming pictures of body parts, understanding body-part terms versus control terms, pointing to or naming contiguous sections of the body, naming the part of the body upon which a particular piece of clothing or jewellery is worn, etc.

cortex occurs concurrently with (or after) the ERP response to a list of control words (Rohrer 2001a). Thirteen right-handed participants read a list of single-word body-part terms such as *foot, ankle, calf, knee,* and so on. These language stimuli were grouped into four subcategories based on the somatotopic order as represented on the central sulcus and adjoining gyri: face, hand, torso, and legs/feet.[15] Each word was presented for 500 ms followed by a 500 ms blank interval. In the temporal window during which semantic comprehension most likely takes place (~400-600 ms after the presentation of the word), current source density (CSD) maps of the scalp distribution showed a only slightly lateralized bilateral distribution pattern ranging along the arc of the scalp above the central sulcus (see Figure 2a). This pattern was in direct contrast to a control condition of car-part terms (see Figure 2b), which showed the classic left-lateralized pattern of scalp distribution typically expected with single-word reading tasks. The response to body-part terms was closer to a second control condition in which participants were asked to imagine a movement in response to each body-part term read. Figure 2c shows a uniformly bilateral pattern in response to the movement visualization task.

Though the CSD maps in which all the body-part terms were averaged together may seem rather flat in amplitude compared to the control stimuli, this is an artifact of averaging the responses to all body-part terms. When the analysis of the ERPs to body-part terms is broken down into the four somatotopic subcategories (Figures 2d-2g), the resulting CSD maps show a sharply divergent pattern of somatotopic distribution measured across the electrode sites that cover the sensorimotor cortical areas; face at both edges near the temples, followed by hands, torso and feet as we move toward the midline.[16] Finally, note that the peak amplitudes to these four stimuli subgroups are concurrent with those of the control stimuli, suggesting that the sensorimotoric activation is not an after-effect of semantic comprehension

---

15. The genitals were omitted because reading genital terms can cause an emotional response (blinking) that would likely create oculomuscular artifacts in the ERPs. Each word was presented for 500 ms followed by a 500 ms blank interval.

16. Note that in comparing torso and foot scalp distribution maps (Figures 2f, 2g) there is also an inversion of polarity in the CSD map. This is likely a direct result of a sharp curvature in the primary sensorimotor cortex. As ERPs presumably record the summed firing of large pyramidal neurons lying perpendicular to the cortical surface, the polarity of the signal is likely to invert as the cortex curves where it descends along the medial wall of the brain.

but crucial to it. Together with the fMRI results, these CSD maps show not only where the response to body-part language occurs but also that it occurs during the appropriate time window for semantic comprehension. In short, the ERP evidence once again suggests that the activation in the sensorimotor cortices is functionally involved in the semantic comprehension of body-part terms.

4. Conclusion

Taken together, the converging results of these studies show that we now have an emerging body of compelling evidence which supports that the hypothesis that our semantic understanding takes place via *image schemata* located in the same cortical areas which are already known to map sensorimotor activity. The theory is robust enough to make a number of predictions about what we might expect to see in future studies.

Firstly, we can, with appropriately designed linguistic stimuli, expect to drive primary and secondary sensorimotor cortical maps. More specifically, we can predict that motion terms should activate motion maps, color terms should activate color map areas, object-centered versus egocentric sentences to activate the object-centered or ego-centered frame of reference maps in the parietal lobe, and so on. It is an open empirical question if such activation in relation to linguistic stimuli can be observed in other primary sensory cortices, or whether it will only be seen in more integrative secondary cortical areas (as might be expected in the visual modality).

Secondly, it remains to be seen whether one can ask similar questions about whether neural maps might also underlie a cognitive grammar. Langacker has argued that grammatical relations are derived from spatial relations (Langacker 1987); indeed he originally called his theory of cognitive grammar a "space grammar", and so we might design fMRI experiments to determine whether his proposals are reflected in the brain regions known to be involved in the neural mapping of spatial movement. For example, one could examine tense and aspect by examining the response in motion map areas to many paired constructions such as *Harry is walking to the store.* versus *Harry walked to the store.* Similarly, it may be possible that many of the current fMRI studies of syntax designed from outside cognitive linguistics may eventually be reinterpreted in terms of the embodied functions (mostly object recognition and manipulation) that the brain regions supposedly responsible for syntax primarily perform. Rizzolatti and colleagues (Rizzolatti and Buccino 2005; Rizzolatti and Craighero 2004), for instance, have recently suggested that the evidence for hand and mouth mirror neurons in and near Broca's area (inferior frontal gyrus) suggests that the disruption in the syntax of Broca's aphasiacs may result from the disruption of the ability to imitate actions and gestures.

Although it remains an open question how many of these related hypotheses will bear out, the converging evidence thus far for the participation of the sensorimotor cortices in language processing is undeniable. The ideas presented in this chapter may at first have seemed hard to handle, but my hope is that you no longer find my opening claim preposterous, though I will accept that it is bold. The most recent neurocognitive evidence shows that whenever you turn ideas over in your head, you are performing image-schematic simulations that take place in the hand sensorimotor cortices. Furthermore, converging research shows that semantic meaning is embodied and widely distributed throughout the brain, not localized to the classic "language areas."

Still, we are just at the beginning of explaining how semantic comprehension works, and our hypotheses are overly simplistic and gross in their scope. Future hypotheses in this field will undoubtedly become more abstract and refined as neuroimaging technology improves to the point where we can describe just the beginning of an action and measure its consequents – such abstractions, however, will not lead us away from the role of perception in language and cognition, but to it. Our theories of language and cognition will become more refined because our senses – and the image schemata which emerge from them – are even more refined than we yet know.

References

Allard, Terry, Sally A. Clark, William M. Jenkins and Michael M. Merzenich
    1991   Reorganization of somatosensory area 3b representations in adult owl monkeys after digital syndactyly. *Journal of Neurophysiology* 66: 1048-1058.
Arterberry, Martha E. and Marc H. Bornstein
    2001   Three-month-old infants' categorization of animals and vehicles based on static and dynamic attributes. *Journal of Experimental Child Psychology* 80: 333-346.
Baldiserra, Fausto, Paolo Cavallari, Laila Craighero and Luciano Fadiga
    2001   Modulation of spinal excitability during observation of hand actions in humans. *European Journal of Neuroscience* 13: 190-194.

Boroditsky, Lera and Michael Ramscar
    2002   The roles of body and mind in abstract thought. *Psychological Science* 13: 185-188.

Buccino, Giovanni, Ferdinand Binkofski, Gereon R. Fink, Luciano Fadiga, Leonardo Fogassi, Vittorio Gallese, Rüdiger J. Seitz, Karl Zilles, Giacomo Rizzolatti and Hans-Joachim Freund
    2001   Action observation activates premotor and parietal areas in a somatotopic manner: An fMRI study. *European Journal of Neuroscience* 13: 400-404.

Buonomano, Dean V. and Michael M. Merzenich
    1998   Cortical plasticity: From synapses to maps. *Annual Review of Neuroscience* 21: 149-186.

Brugman, Claudia
    1983   The use of body-part terms as locatives in Chalcatongo Mixtec. *Report 4 of the Survey of California and Other Indian Languages*, University of California: 235-90

Coslett, H. Branch
    1998   Evidence for a disturbance of the body schema in neglect. *Brain and Cognition* 37: 529-544.

Coslett H. Branch, Eleanor M. Saffran and John Schwoebel
    2002   Knowledge of the human body: A distinct semantic domain. *Neurology* 59: 357-363.

DeBello, William M., Daniel E. Feldman and Eric I. Knudsen
    2001   Adaptive axonal remodeling in the midbrain auditory space map. *Journal of Neuroscience* 21: 3161-3174.

DeCasper, Anthony J., Jean-Pierre LeCanuet, Marie-Claire Busnel, Caroyln Granierv-Deferre and Roselyn Maugeais
    1994   Fetal reactions to recurrent maternal speech. *Infant Behavior and Development* 17: 159-164.

Edelman, Gerald M.
    1987   *Neural Darwinism*. New York: Basic Books.

Elbert, Thomas, Christo Pantev, Christian Wienbruch, Brigitte Rockstroh and Edward Taub
    1995   Increased cortical representation of the fingers of the left hand in string players. *Science* 270: 305-307.

Ferrari, Pier Francisco, Vittorio Gallese, Giacomo Rizzolatti and Leonardo Fogassi
    2003   Mirror neurons responding to the observation of ingestive and communicative mouth actions in the monkey ventral premotor cortex. *European Journal of Neuroscience* 17: 1703-1714.

Fischl, Bruce, Martin I. Sereno, Roger B.H. Tootell and Anders M. Dale
    1999   High-resolution inter-subject averaging and a coordinate system for the cortical surface. *Human Brain Mapping* 8: 272-284

Fogassi, Leonardo, Vittorio Gallese, Giorgio Buccino, Laila Craighero, Luciano Fadiga and Giacomo Rizzolatti
    2001   Cortical mechanism for the visual guidance of hand grasping movements in the monkey: A reversible inactivation study. *Brain* 124: 571-586.

Gallese, Vittorio, Luciano Fadiga, Leonardo Fogassi and Giacomo Rizzolatti
    1996   Action recognition in the premotor cortex. *Brain* 119: 593-609.

Gibbs, Raymond W.
    1994   *The Poetics of Mind: Figurative Thought, Language and Understanding.* New York: Cambridge University Press.

Glenberg, Arthur M. and Michael P. Kaschak
    2002   Grounding language in action. *Psychonomic Bulletin and Review* 9: 558-565.

Guo, Yujin and Susan B. Udin
    2000   The development of abnormal axon trajectories after rotation of one eye in Xenopus. *Journal of Neuroscience* 20: 4189-4197.

Hauk, Olaf, Ingrid Johnsrude and Friedemann Pulvermüller
    2004   Somatotopic representation of action words in human motor and premotor cortex. *Neuron* 41: 301-307.

Jenkins, William M., Michael M. Merzenich, Marlene T. Ochs, Terry Allard and Eliana Guíc-Robles
    1990   Functional reorganization of primary somatosensory cortex in adult owl monkeys after behaviorally controlled tactile stimulation. *Journal of Neurophysiology* 63: 82-104.

Johnson, Mark
    1987   *The Body in the Mind: The Bodily Basis of Meaning, Imagination and Reason.* Chicago: University of Chicago Press.

Johnson, Mark and Tim Rohrer
    In press   We are live creatures: Embodiment, American pragmatism, and the cognitive organism. In *Body, Language, and Mind*, vol. 1, Jordan Zlatev, Tom Ziemke, Roz Frank, René Dirven (eds.). Berlin: Mouton de Gruyter.

Knudsen, Eric I.
    1998   Capacity for plasticity in the adult owl auditory system expanded by juvenile experience. *Science* 279: 1531-1533.
    2002   Instructed learning in the auditory localization pathway of the barn owl. *Nature* 417: 322-328.

Knudsen, Eric I. and Michael S. Brainard
  1991   Visual instruction of the neural map of auditory space in the developing optic tectum. *Science* 253: 85-87.
Knudsen, Eric I. and Masakazu Konishi
  1978   A neural map of auditory space in the owl. *Science* 200: 795-797.
Kohler, Evelyne, Christian Keysers, M. Alessandra Umiltá, Leonardo Fogassi, Vittorio Gallese and Giacomo Rizzolatti
  2002   Hearing sounds, understanding actions: Action representation in mirror neurons. *Science* 297: 846-848.
Lakoff, George
  1987   *Women, Fire and Dangerous Things.* Chicago: University of Chicago Press.
Lakoff, George and Mark Johnson
  1980   *Metaphors We Live By.* Chicago: University of Chicago Press.
  1999   *Philosophy in the Flesh: The Embodied Mind and Its Challenge to Western Thought.* New York: Basic Books.
Langacker, Ronald
  1987   *Foundations of Cognitive Grammar.* Stanford: Stanford University Press.
Lewkowicz, David J. and Gerald Turkewitz
  1981   Intersensory interaction in newborns: Modification of visual preferences following exposure to sound. *Child Development* 52: 827-832.
Matlock, Teenie, Michael Ramscar and Lera Boroditsky
  In press   The experiential link between spatial and temporal language. *Cognitive Science.*
Maurer, Daphne, Christine L. Stager and Catherine J. Mondloch
  1999   Cross-modal transfer of shape is difficult to demonstrate in one-month-olds. *Child Development* 70: 1047-1057.
Meltzoff, Andrew N.
  1993   Molyneux's babies: Cross-modal perception, imitation and the mind of the preverbal infant. In *Spatial Representation: Problems in Philosophy and Psychology,* Naomi Eilan, Rosaleen McCarthy and Bill Brewer (eds.), 219-235. Cambridge, Mass.: Blackwell.
Meltzoff, Andrew N. and Richard W. Borton
  1979   Intermodal matching by human neonates. *Nature* 282: 403-4.
Meltzoff, Andrew N. and Melanie K. Moore
  1977   Imitation of facial and manual gestures by human neonates. *Science* 198: 74-78.
Merzenich, Michael M., Randall J. Nelson, Michael P. Stryker, Max S. Cynader, A. Schoppmann and John. M. Zook
  1984   Somatosensory cortical map changes following digit amputation in adult monkeys. *Journal of Comparative Neurology* 224:591-605.

Merzenich, Michael M., Randall J. Nelson, Jon H. Kaas, Michael P. Stryker, Max S. Cynader, A. Schoppmann and John M. Zook
1987   Variability in hand surface representations in areas 3b and 1 in adult owl and squirrel monkeys. *Journal of Comparative Neurology* 258: 281-296.
Moore, Christopher I., Chantal E. Stern, Suzanne Corkin, Bruce Fischl, Annette C. Gray, Bruce R. Rosen and Anders M. Dale
2000   Segregation of somatosensory activation in the human rolandic cortex using fMRI. *Journal of Neurophysiology* 84: 558-569.
Pascual-Leone, Alvaro and F. Torres
1993   Plasticity of the sensorimotor cortex representation of the reading finger in Braille readers. *Brain* 116: 39-52.
Penfield, Wilder G., and Theodore B. Rasmussen
1950   *The Cerebral Cortex of Man*. New York: Macmillan.
Pulvermüller, Friedemann, Olaf Hauk, Vadim Nikulin and Risto J. Ilmoniemi
2002   Functional interaction of language and action processing: A TMS study. *MirrorBot: Biometric Multimodal Learning in a Mirror Neuron-based Robot*, Report #8.
Rizzolatti, Giacomo and Giorgio Buccino
2005   The mirror-neuron system and its role in imitation and language. In *From Monkey Brain to Human Brain*. Stanislas Dehaene, Jean-Réne Duhamel, Marc D. Hauser, and Giacomo Rizzolatti (eds.), 213-234. Cambridge, Mass.: MIT Press.
Rizzolatti, Giacomo and Laila Craighero
2004   The mirror neuron system. *Annual Review of Neuroscience* 27: 169-192.
Rizzolatti, Giacomo, Luciano Fogassi and Vittorio Gallese
2001   Neurophysiological mechanisms underlying the understanding and imitation of action. *Nature Review Neuroscience* 2: 661-670.
2002   Motor and cognitive functions of the ventral premotor cortex. *Current Opinion Neurobiology* 12: 149-54.
Rohrer, Tim
2001a   Pragmatism, ideology and embodiment: William James and the philosophical foundations of cognitive linguistics. In *Language and Ideology: Cognitive Theoretic Approaches*, Volume 1, René Dirven, Bruce Hawkins, and Esra Sandikcioglu (eds.), 49-81. Amsterdam: John Benjamins.
2001b   Understanding through the body: fMRI and of ERP studies of metaphoric and literal language. Paper presented at the *7th International Cognitive Linguistics Association* Conference, July 2001.
In press   The body in space: Embodiment, experientialism and linguistic Conceptualization. In *Body, Language, and Mind*, Vol. 2, Jordan

Zlatev, Tom Ziemke, Roz Frank, René Dirven, (eds.). Berlin: Mouton de Gruyter.

In press   Embodiment and Experientialism. In *The Handbook of Cognitive Linguistics*. Dirk Geeraerts, and Hubert Cuyckens (eds.). New York: Oxford University Press.

Rose, Susan A. and Holly A. Ruff
1987   Cross-modal abilities in human infants. In *Handbook of Infant Development*, Joy D. Osofsky (ed.), 318–362. New York: Wiley.

Rose, Susan A., M. S. Blank, and W. H. Bridger
1972   Intermodal and Intramodal retention of visual and tactual information in young children. *Developmental Psychology* 6: 482-486.

Schwoebel, John and H. Branch Coslett
2005   Evidence for multiple, distinct representations of the human body. *Journal of Cognitive Neuroscience* 4: 543-553

Schwoebel, John, Consuelo B. Boronat, and H. Branch Coslett
2002   The man who executed 'imagined' movements: Evidence for dissociable components of the body schema. *Brain and Cognition* 50: 1-16.

Shelton, Jennifer R., Erin Fouch, and Alfonso Caramazza
1998   The selective sparing of body part knowledge. A case study. *Neurocase* 4: 339-351.

Stern, Daniel
1985   *The Interpersonal World of the Infant.* New York: Basic Books.

Suzuki, K., A. Yamadori and T. Fujii
1997   Category specific comprehension deficit restricted to body parts. *Neurocase* 3: 193-200.

Talmy, Leonard
1985   Force dynamics in thought and language. *Chicago Linguistics Society* 21(2: *Possession in Causatives and Agentivity*): 293-337.
2000   *Toward a Cognitive Semantics*. Vol. 1. Cambridge, Mass.: MIT Press.

Umiltá, M. Alessandra, Evelyne Kohler, Vittorio Gallese, Leonardo Fogassi, Luciano Fadiga, Christian Keysers, and Giacomo Rizzolatti
2001   I know what you are doing. A neurophysiological study. *Neuron* 31: 155-165.

Wall, John T., Jon H. Kaas, Mriganka Sur, Randall J. Nelson, Daniel J. Felleman, and Michael M. Merzenich
1986   Functional reorganization in somatosensory cortical areas 3b and 1 of adult monkeys after median nerve repair: Possible relationships to sensory recovery in humans. *Journal of Neuroscience* 6: 218-233.

Warrington, Elizabeth K., and Tim Shallice
1984   Category specific semantic impairments. *Brain* 107: 859-854.

Woodward, Amanda L.
   1998   Infants selectively encode the goal object of an actor's reach. *Cognition* 69: 1-34.
   1999   Infants' ability to distinguish between purposeful and non-purposeful behaviors. *Infant Behavior and Development* 22: 145-160.
Woodward, Amanda L., and Jose J. Guajardo
   2002   Infants' understanding of the point gesture as an object-directed action. *Cognitive Development* 83: 1-24.
Zwaan, Rolf A., Carol J. Madden, Richard H. Yaxley, and Mark E. Aveyard
   2004   Moving words: Dynamic representations in language comprehension. *Cognitive Science* 28: 611-619.

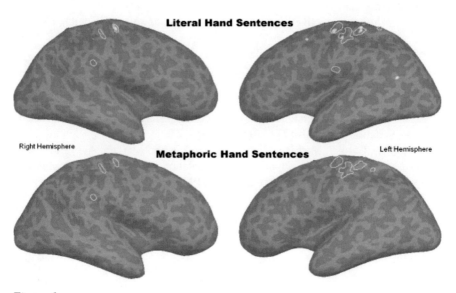

Figure 1.
Overlap of fMRI activation in the primary and secondary sensorimotor cortices between a sensorimotor task and two linguistic hand sentence tasks (literal and metaphoric). Areas active in the sensorimotor task are delimited by the white line. Only those areas which overlapped between the sensorimotor and particular language condition were traced (literal on top, metaphoric below). These are lateral views with the right hemisphere presented on the left side of the figure and the right hemisphere on the left side of the figure. The cortical surface has been inflated so that no data will be hidden in the cortical folds. Sulci are represented in the darker areas, while gyri are represented by the lighter areas. This figure represents individual data from one of the 12 subjects in the experiment. All data were analyzed using the FreeSurfer fMRI brain analysis package available from UCSD (Fischl, Sereno et al. 1999).

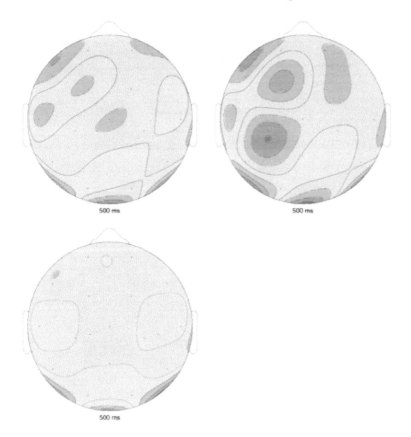

Figures 2a-c.
Current source density (CSD) maps of the scalp electrophysiological response to single word body-part and control (car-part) stimuli. The top left figure shows the response to all body-part terms averaged together, the top right figure shows the response to a list of car-part terms and the bottom figure shows the response of participants as they imagined moving the body part as they read each body-part term in sequence. The top right figure shows a classic left-hemisphere lateralized response to language stimuli, while the bottom figure shows a decentralized pattern of response which stretches across the sensorimotor cortices (an arc extending from each temple through a point roughly halfway between the nose and the top of the head). The response to a passive reading of a body-part word (top left figure) shows a distribution along this arc, as well as some left hemispheric bias. All figures are from an average of 13 participants, depict the averaged activity 500 ms after the onset of each stimulus and were collected using a 26-channel scalp electrode cap.

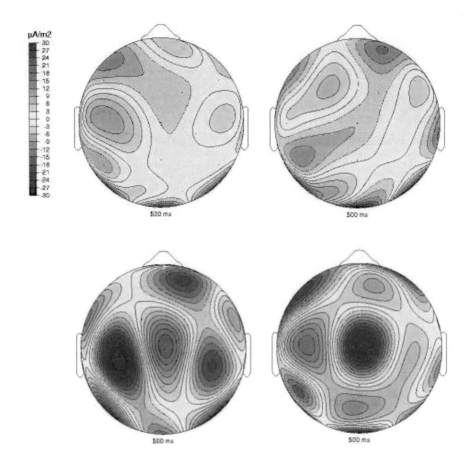

Figures 2d-g.
Current source density (CSD) maps of the scalp electrophysiological response to single word body-part stimuli divided into four subgroups. The upper leftmost figure shows the response to face body-part terms, the upper right figure shows the response to hand body-part terms, while the lower left figure shows the response to torso body-part terms and the lower right to foot body-part terms. These figures exhibit the distribution of the body image along the sensorimotor cortices with the face toward the temples, the hands slightly above them, the torso located near the midline with the legs and feet plunging down along the medial walls. The reversal of polarity between the torso and the feet is likely caused by this curvature of the cortex as it descends along the medial walls.

Part 3: Image schemas in spatial cognition and language

The fundamental system
of spatial schemas in language

Leonard Talmy

Abstract

Linguistic Research to date has determined many of the factors that govern the structure of the spatial schemas found across spoken languages. We can now integrate these factors and propose the comprehensive system they comprise for spatial structuring in language.This system is characterized by several features. At a componential level, it has a relatively closed universally available inventory of fundamental spatial elements. These elements group into a relatively closed set of spatial categories. And each category includes only a relatively closed small number of particular elements:the spatial distinctions that each category can ever mark. At a composite level, elements of the inventory combine in particular arrangements to form whole spatial schemas.Each language has a relatively closed set of "pre-packaged" schemas of this sort. Finally, the system includes a set of properties that can generalize and processes that can extend or deform pre-packaged schemas and thus enable a language's particular set of schemas to be applied to a wider range of spatial structures.

Keywords: spatial schema, spatial structure, spatial primitives

1. Introduction

1.1. Overview of the system of spatial schemas

Linguistic research to date has determined many of the principles that govern the structure of the spatial schemas represented by closed-class forms across the world's languages. Contributing to this cumulative understanding have, for example, been Gruber (1965), Fillmore (1968), Leech (1969), Clark (1973), Bennett (1975), Herskovits (1982), Jackendoff (1983), Zubin and Svorou (1984), as well as myself (Talmy 1983, 2000a, 2000b). It is now feasible to integrate these principles and to determine the comprehensive system they belong to for spatial structuring in spoken language.[1] The finding here is that this system has three main parts: the *componential*, the *compositional*, and the *augmentive*.

In the componential part of the system, there is a relatively closed inventory of fundamental spatial elements that in combination form whole schemas. Further, these elements fall into a relatively closed set of categories. Accordingly, there is a relatively closed number of particular elements in each category – hence, of spatial distinctions that each category can ever mark – and this number is generally small. The inventory is universally available. That is, any language can draw on the elements and categories of the inventory for its spatial schemas.

In the compositional part of the system, selected elements of the inventory are combined in specific arrangements to make up the whole schemas represented by individual closed-class spatial forms. Each such whole schema that a closed class form represents is thus a "pre-packaged" bundling together of certain elements in a particular arrangement. Each language has in its lexicon a relatively closed set of such pre-packaged schemas (larger than that of spatial closed-class forms, due to polysemy) that a speaker must select among in depicting a spatial scene.

Finally, the augmentive part of the overall system pertains to single whole schemas. Such already-formed individual schemas can exhibit various forms of generalization. Thus, a schema can either include a property that lets it cover a full family of schemas, or it can undergo a process that extends or deforms its basic form to yield certain non-basic forms. Such generalizations of schemas are a necessary part of the overall system so that the relatively closed set of spatial schemas in any given language can represent a greater range of spatial situations.

1.2. The target of analysis

The analysis to be undertaken here rests on a universal linguistic property. All languages exhibit two different subsystems of meaning-bearing forms. One is the "open-class" or "lexical" subsystem that, in any given language, comprises all of its open classes. An open class has relatively many forms

---

1. This paper is an expanded and more detailed version of the relevant section on spoken language in Talmy (2003).

that are readily augmented – for example, commonly, the roots of nouns, verbs, or adjectives. The other is the "closed-class" or "grammatical" sub-system. A closed class has relatively few forms that are difficult to augment – for example, bound forms like the case inflections on a noun, or free forms like conjunctions or prepositions. As argued in Talmy (2000a: 21-96), these subsystems basically perform two different functions: open-class forms largely contribute conceptual content, while closed class forms determine conceptual structure. Since our concern is with systematic spatial structuring in language, our examination focuses on the spatial schemas represented by closed-class forms. Thus, we do not examine the spatial configurations represented by open-class forms like the English noun *spiral*, the adjective *square*, or the verb *(to) zigzag*, which can be idiosyncratic without conforming to some organized framework. We instead examine only the spatial schemas represented by closed-class forms, as described next.

The spatial schemas represented by closed-class forms fall into two main groups.[2] The schemas of one group pertain to paths or sites. The closed-class forms for this group are of different types, as shown in (1).

(1)   a.   forms in construction with a nominal, e.g.:
        i.   prepositions like English across (as in across the field)
        ii.   noun affixes like the Finnish illative suffix -:n ('into')
        iii.   prepositional complexes like English in front of
        iv.   constructions with a "locative noun" like Japanese ue 'top sur-face' (as in teeburu no ue ni 'table gen top at' = 'on the table')
    b.   forms in construction with a verb, e.g.:
        i.   free verb satellites like English *out, back, apart* (as in *They ran out/ back/apart.*)
        ii.   bound verb satellites like Atsugewi *–ic't* ('into liquid')
    c.   deictic determiners and adverbs like English *this* and *here*
    d.   indefinites, interrogatives, relatives, etc., like English *everywhere/ whither/wherever*
    e.   qualifiers like English *way* and *right* (as in *It's way/right up there*)
    f.   adverbials like English *home* (as in *She isn't home*).

The schemas of the second group pertain to the shape or disposition of objects. Closed-class forms for this group include types like those in (2).

(2)   a.   markers for plexity or state of boundedness, like English -s for multi-plexing (as in *birds*) or -ery for debounding (as in *shrubbery*)

---

2. Closed-class forms can of course represent other conceptual domains than space, e.g., tense, aspect, gender, and causation.

b.   numeral classifiers like Korean *chang* ('planar object')
c.   forms in construction with the verb like some Atsugewi cause prefixes, e.g., *cu-* ('as the result of a linear object moving axially into the
Figure')

2.   The basic spatial elements and their categories

2.1. Methodology for determining the elements and categories

A particular methodology is here used to determine fundamental spatial elements in language. We start with any closed-class spatial morpheme in any
language, considering the full schema that it expresses and a spatial scene
that it can apply to. We then determine any factor that can be changed in the
scene so that the morpheme no longer applies to it. Each such factor must
accordingly correspond to an essential element in the morpheme's schema.

To illustrate, consider the English preposition *across* and the scene it refers to in *The board lay across the road* (ex 3). Let us here grant the first
two elements in the *across* schema (demonstrated Talmy 2000a: 184-254).
The first element, shown in (3a), is that a Figure object (here, *the board*) is
spatially related to a Ground object (here, *the road*). The second element,
shown in (3b), is that the Ground is ribbonal – that is, a plane with two
roughly parallel line edges that are as long as or longer than the distance
between them.[3] The remaining elements can then be readily demonstrated by
the methodology. Thus, a third element is that the Figure is linear, generally
bounded at both ends. If the board were instead replaced by a planar object,
say, some wall siding, one could no longer use the original *across* preposition, but would have to switch to the schematic domain of another preposition, that of *over*, as in (3c). A fourth element is that the axes of the Figure
and of the Ground are roughly perpendicular. If the board were instead
aligned with the road, one could no longer use the original *across* preposition
but would again have to switch to another preposition, *along*, as in (3d).
Additionally, a fifth element of the *across* schema is that the Figure is parallel to the plane of the Ground. In the referent scene, if the board were tilted
away from parallel, one would have to switch to some other locution such as
those in (3e). A sixth element is that the Figure is adjacent to the plane of the
Ground. If the board were lowered or raised away from adjacency, even

---

3. In Herskovits (1982) this is termed a "strip".

while retaining the remaining spatial relations, one would need to switch to locutions like those in (3f). A seventh element is that the Figure's length is at least as great as the Ground's width. If the board were replaced by something shorter, for example, a baguette, while leaving the remaining spatial relations intact, one would have to switch from *across* to *on*, as in (3g). An eighth element is that the Figure touches both edges of the Ground. If the board in the example retained all its preceding spatial properties but were shifted axially, one would have to switch to some locution like that in (3h). Finally, a ninth element is that the axis of the Figure is horizontal (the plane of the Ground is typically, but not necessarily, horizontal). Thus, if one changes the original scene to that of a spear hanging on a wall, one can use *across* if the spear is horizontal, but not if it is vertical, as in (3i).

(3)   target sentence: *The board lay across the road.* (F = Figure; G = Ground)
    a.   F is spatially related to G.
    b.   G is ribbonal.
    c.   F is linear (and generally bounded at both ends) – vs. *The wall siding lay over the road.*
    d.   The axes of F and G are roughly perpendicular – vs. *The board lay along the road.*
    e.   F is parallel to the plane of G – vs. The board is sticking out of/into the road.
    f.   F is adjacent to the plane of G – vs. The board lay (buried) in the road./The board was suspended above the road.
    g.   F's length is at least as great as G's width – vs. *The baguette lay on the road.*
    h.   F touches both of G's edges – vs. *The board lay over one edge of the road.*
    i.   The axis of F is horizontal (the plane of G is typically, but not necessarily, horizontal) *The spear hung across the wall.* – vs. *The spear hung up and down on the wall.*

Thus, from this single example, the methodology shows that at least the following elements figure in closed-class spatial schemas: a Figure and a Ground, a point, a line, a plane, a boundary (a point as boundary to a line, a line as boundary to a plane), parallelness, perpendicularity, horizontality, adjacency (contact), and relative magnitude.

In the procedure of systematically testing candidate factors for their relevance, the elements just listed have proved to be essential to the selected schema and hence, to be in the inventory of fundamental spatial elements. But it is equally necessary to note candidates that do not prove out, so as to know which potential spatial elements do not serve a structuring function in language. In the case of *across*, for example, one can probe whether the Figure, like the board in the referent scene, must itself be planar – rather than simply linear – and coplanar with the plane of the Ground. It can be seen, though, that this is not an essential element to the *across* schema, since this factor can be altered in the scene by standing the board on edge without any need to alter the preposition, as in (4).

(4)   The board lay flat/stood on edge across the road.

Thus, co-planarity is not shown by *across* to be a fundamental spatial element. However, it does prove to be so in other schemas, and so in the end must be included in the inventory. This is seen, for example, for one of the schemas represented by English *over*, as in (5a). Here, both the Figure and Ground must be planes and coplanar with each other. If the tapestry here were changed to something linear, say, a string of beads, it is no longer appropriate to use *over* but only something like *against*, as in (5b).

(5)   a.   The tapestry hung over the wall.
      b.   The string of beads hung *over/against the wall.

Now, another candidate element – that the Figure must be rigid, like the board in the scene – can be tested and again found to be inessential to the *across* schema, since a flexible linear object can be substituted for the board without any need to change the preposition, as seen in (6).

(6)   The board/cable lay across the road.

Here, however, checking this candidate factor across numerous spatial schemas in many languages might well never yield a case in which it does figure as an essential element and so would be kept off the inventory.

This methodology affords a kind of existence proof: it can demonstrate that some element does occur in the universally available inventory of structural spatial elements since it can be seen to occur in at least one closed-class spatial schema in at least one language. The procedure is repeated numerous times across many languages to build up a sizable inventory of elements essential to spatial schemas.

The next step is to discern whether the uncovered elements comprise particular structural categories and, if so, to determine what these categories are. It can be observed that for certain sets of elements, the elements in a set are mutually incompatible – only one of them can apply at a time at some point in a schema. Such sets are here taken to be basic spatial categories. Along with their members, such categories are also part of language's fundamental conceptual structuring system for space. A representative sample of these categories is presented in the next section.

It will be seen that these categories generally have a relatively small membership. This finding rests in part on the following methodological principles. An element proposed for the inventory should be as coarse-grained as possible – that is, no more specific than is warranted by cross-schema analysis. Correlatively, in establishing a category, care must be taken that it includes only the most generic elements that have actually been determined – that is, that its membership have no finer granularity than is warranted by the element-abstraction procedure.

To illustrate, the principle of mutual incompatibility yields a spatial category of "relative orientation" between two lines or planes, a category with perhaps only two member elements (both already seen in the *across* schema): approximately parallel and approximately perpendicular. Some evidence additionally suggests an intermediary "oblique" element as a third member of the category. Thus, some English speakers may distinguish a more perpendicular sense from a more oblique sense, respectively, for the two verb satellites *out* and *off*, as in (7). In any case, though, the category would have no more than these two or three members. Although finer degrees of relative orientation can be distinguished by other cognitive systems, say, in visual perception and in motor control, the conceptual structuring subsystem of language does not include anything finer than the two- or three-way distinction. The procedures of schema analysis and cross-schema comparison, together with the methodological principles of maximum granularity for elements and for category membership, can thus lead to a determination of the number of structurally distinguished elements ever used in language for a spatial category.

(7)   A secondary pipe branches out/off from the main sewer line.

2.2. Sample categories and their member elements

The fundamental categories of spatial structure in the closed-class subsystem of language fall into three classes according to the aspect of a spatial scene they pertain to: the segmentation of the scene into individual components, the properties of an individual component, and the relations of one such component to another. In a fourth class are categories of non-geometric elements frequently found in association with spatial schemas. A sampling of categories and their member elements from each of these four classes is presented next. The examples provided here are primarily drawn from English but can be readily multiplied across a diverse range of languages (cf. Talmy 2000a: 177-254).

2.2.1. Categories pertaining to scene segmentation

The class designated as scene segmentation may include only one category, that of "major components of a scene", and this category may contain only three member elements: the Figure, the Ground, and a Secondary Reference Object. Figure and Ground were already seen for the *across* schema. But schema comparison shows the need to recognize a third scene component, the Secondary Reference Object – in fact, two forms of it: one that is encompassive of the Figure and Ground and one that is external to them. The English preposition *near*, as in (8a), specifies the location of the Figure (*the lamp*) only with respect to the Ground (*the TV*) – it could be anywhere roughly within a sphere centered on the TV provided the distance between them is relatively small. But localizing the Figure with the preposition *above*, as in (8b), requires knowledge not only of where the Ground object is, but also of the encompassive earth-based spatial grid, in particular, of its vertical orientation. Thus, above requires recognizing three components within a spatial scene, a Figure, a Ground, and a Secondary Reference Object of the encompassive type.

(8)   a.   The lamp is near the TV.
       b.   The lamp is above the TV.

Comparably, the schema of *past*, as in (9a), only relates *John* as Figure to *the border* as Ground. An observer could felicitously say this sentence on viewing the event through binoculars from either side of the border. But (9b) with the preposition *beyond* could be said only by an observer on the initial side of the border, the side now opposite John. Hence, the *beyond* schema establishes a perspective point at that location as a Secondary Reference Object – in this case, one of the external type – in addition to its specifications for Figure and Ground.

(9)   a.   John is past the border.
       b.   John is beyond the border.

Closed-class schemas do not seem to require any further major scene components beyond the three just cited – Figure, Ground, and Secondary Reference Object – for example, something like a Tertiary Reference Object.

However, several scene components that are minor, or specialized, or derivatively dependent on the presence of certain other spatial phenomena, do occur in schemas. Examples of these – all illustrated below – are the path line formed by a moving-point Figure, the spin axis defined by a rotating object, and a "meta-Figure" such as an object that rotates or exhibits expansion or contraction. The main reason for recognizing such cases as kinds of scene components in their own right is that many of the same categories of basic spatial properties that belong to the remaining two classes, treated in the following sections, and that can apply to the three major scene components described above, can also apply to these newly proposed scene components. It is not clear how to treat such further scene components within our proposed framework. On the one hand, they could be added to the present category, which would then drop the term "major" from its label, or they could be placed in a new category, "minor components of a scene". Alternatively, the processes at work in the compositional part of the schema system in language – the ones that select and arrange the basic elements in the componential part of the system – can be considered capable of operating at least in part sequentially. Then one of the so-called minor scene components, such as the path of a moving Figure, can first be formed through the assembling of one set of basic components and then, as a new higher-level entity, be amenable to the addition of a further set of basic components.

2.2.2. Categories pertaining to an individual scene component

The second class of spatial categories comprises a number of categories that pertain to the characteristics of an individual spatial scene component. As just discussed, such a scene component can either be one of the three within the "major components of a scene" category, or one of the minor scene components, however these are assumed to arise. Several categories in this class are presented next. In addition to this sampling, some ten or so further categories pertaining to properties of an individual scene component, each category with a small number of fixed contrasts, can be readily identified.

One category in this class is that of "dimension". It has four member elements: zero dimensions for a point, one for a line, two for a plane, and three for a volume. Some English prepositions require a Ground object schematizable for only one of the four dimensional possibilities. Thus, the schema of the preposition *near* as in *near the dot* requires only that the Ground object be schematizable as a point. The preposition *along*, as in *along the trail*, requires that the Ground object be linear. *Over* as in *a tapestry over a wall* requires a planar Ground. And *throughout*, as in *cherries throughout the jello*, requires a volumetric Ground. It might at first be thought unfair to use this category as evidence of constrained membership since, after all, there are only four dimensions that could be members. But the noteworthy observation does emerge that each of these four dimensions can singly play a role in a spatial schema, so that all four – not some lesser number – must be included in the inventory. In any case, all the remaining spatial categories will have selective memberships.

A second category is that of "number". It seems to have only the following four members: one, two, several, and many. Some English prepositions require a Ground comprising objects in one or another of these numbers. Thus, *near* requires a Ground consisting of just one object, *between* of two objects, *among* of several objects, and *amidst* of numerous objects, as in (10). The category of number appears to lack any further members – that is, closed-class spatial schemas in languages around the world seem never to incorporate any other number specifications – such as 'three' or 'even-numbered' or 'too many'.

(10)   The basketball lay near the boulder/between the boulders/among the boulders/amidst the cornstalks.

A third category is that of "motive state". It has only two members: motion and stationariness. Several English prepositions mark this distinction for the Figure. Thus, in one of its senses, *at* requires a stationary Figure, as in (11a). But *into* requires a moving Figure, as in (11b).

(11)   a.   I stayed/*went at the library.
       b.   I went/*stayed into the library.

Other prepositions mark this same distinction, but for the Ground object (in conjunction with a Figure that is moving). Thus, *up to* requires a stationary Ground (here, *the deer*), as in (12a). But *after* requires a moving Ground, as in (12b). The issue of whether a Ground is stationary or moving itself can be understood in either of two ways. One way is to regard the terrain around the Ground as a Secondary Reference Object with respect to which the Ground is either fixed or moving. The other is to explain the moving Ground notion in terms of a nesting of one Figure-Ground situation within another – the solution adopted in Talmy (2000a: 311-344). By this interpretation, for example, in the sentence *The lion caught up with the deer*, *the lion* as Figure reaches *the deer* as Ground, at the same time that both lion and deer together as a distinct composite type of Figure move relative to the terrain as a distinct Ground. This nested arrangement holds as well for (12b) except that in the first Figure-Ground relationship, *the lion* as Figure remains fixed relative to *the deer* as Ground, since they retain the same distance from each other as they both run along.

(12) a.   The lion ran up to the deer.
      b.   The lion ran after the deer.

The motive state category seems to be limited to the two cited members, stationariness and motion. Apparently no spatial schemas mark such additional distinctions as motion at a fast vs. slow rate, or being located at rest vs. remaining located fixedly.

A fourth category is that of "state of boundedness". It too has only two members: bounded and unbounded. The English preposition *along* requires that the path of a moving Figure be unbounded, as shown by its compatibility with a temporal phrase with *for* but not *in*, as in (13a). But the spatial locution *the length of* requires a bounded path, as shown by its reverse compatibility with the two temporal constructions, as seen in (13b).

(13) a.   I walked along the pier for 10 minutes/*in 20 minutes.
      b.   I walked the length of the pier in 20 Minutes/*for 10 minutes.

As it happens, most motion prepositions in English have a polysemous range that covers both the unbounded and the bounded sense. Thus, *through* as in (14a) refers to traversing an unbounded portion of the tunnel's length. But in (14b), it refers to traversing the entire bounded length.

(14) a.   I walked through the tunnel for 10 minutes.
      b.   I walked through the tunnel in 10 minutes.

While some spatial schemas have the bounded element at one end of a line and the unbounded element at the other end, apparently no spatial schema marks any distinctions other than the two cited states of boundedness. For example, there is no cline of gradually increasing boundedness, nor a gradient transition. This is the case even though just such a "clinal boundary" appears elsewhere in our cognition, as in geographic perception or conception, e.g., in the gradient demarcation between full forest and full meadowland (Mark and Smith 2004).

Continuing the sampling of this class, a fifth category is "type of geometry" with two members: rectilinear and radial. The radial member itself is of two main kinds, motion or location either along a radius or about a center. The category as a whole can apply to a range of different scene components. For example, it can apply to an encompassive Secondary Reference Object to yield reference frames of the two geometric types. Thus, in a subtle effect, the English verb satellite *away*, as in (15a), tends to suggest a rectilinear reference frame in which one might picture the boat moving rightward along a corridor or sea lane with the island on the left (as if along the x-axis of a Cartesian grid). But *out*, as in (15b), tends to suggest a radial reference frame in which the boat is conceptualized as moving from a center point along a radius through a continuum of concentric circles.

(15)   a.   The boat drifted further and further away from the island.
        b.   The boat drifted further and further out from the island.

In addition to motion/location along a radius – the type just illustrated – radial geometry can as noted also apply to motion/location about a center. This circumcentric type in turn has three different geometric applications. First, it can apply to a "periphery", itself curved with respect to a center point. As seen in (16a), the preposition around can represent the spatial pattern of a moving Figure that describes a line roughly aligned with such a periphery as Ground. For comparison, the formulation in (16b) with *along(side)* can represent the same spatial event as conceptualized within the rectilinear type of geometry.

(16)   a.   I kept walking around the castle wall.
        b.   I kept walking along(side) the castle wall.

A second circumcentric application is to a moving Figure that, without hugging a preexisting curved periphery, describes a line that by itself is curved with respect to a center point. An example is in (17a), again with the preposition *around*. It is here set beside an attempt at a rectilinear example in (17b) to suggest a contrast.

(17)   a.   I walked around the maypole.
        b.   I walked past the maypole on one side and walked back past it on the other side.

A third circumcentric application is to the rotation of an object about a point within itself, prototypically its center, as in (18), here illustrated alone since there is no obvious rectilinear counterpart. In the analysis of rotation of this sort in Talmy (2000a: 311-344), what is truly figural in the situation is a set of multiple Figures: the points or parts of the rotating object. Each of these executes a circular path around the center, as treated in the preceding example. The object as a whole, then, is not a Figure, but what I term a "meta-Figure". This can in turn serve as a further type of scene component to which spatial categories and their member concepts might apply. Here, the relevant senses of the satellite *around* and the preposition *about* pertain to this meta-Figure.

(18)   The top spun around./The top spun about its central axis.

A sixth category is that of "state of consolidation" with apparently two members: compact and diffuse. This category applies to one-, two-, or three-dimensional regions of space. The compact member concept indicates that such a region is of relatively smaller ambit, and is typically associated with the further concepts that the region is bounded and that the speaker's measurement of it is relatively precisional. The diffuse member concept indicates that a region is of relatively larger ambit, and is typically associated with the further concepts that the region is unbounded and that the measurement of it is approximative. If an object is located in such a region, the two member concepts often have the further associations that the object's specific location within the region is relatively certain or uncertain, respectively.

To illustrate, the English preposition *at*, as in (19a), suggests a relatively compact 2-dimensional region surrounding a Ground object (*the landmark*) in which a Figure object (*the hiker*) is located and hence can be found with some certainty. By contrast, the preposition *around* in (19b) indicates that the region is relatively diffuse and hence that the Figure's specific location within it is relatively uncertain. Consistent with this distinction, the word somewhere can be readily added before the preposition in (19b) but not before the preposition in (19a).

(19)   a.   The other hiker will be waiting for you at the landmark.
        b.   The other hiker will be waiting for you around the landmark.

While the anaphoric locative pronoun *there* as in (20a) might be best considered neutral to the distinctions of the present category, its counterpart *thereabouts* as in (20b) surely includes the diffuse concept in its schema.

(20)   a.   Go to the market; you'll find her there.
        b.   Go to the market; you'll find her thereabouts.

For an example outside English, the distinctions of the present category can be seen marked in Malagasy (Imai 2003), by two demonstrative locative adverbs. They are distance-neutral, but to gloss them for proximal usage, *eto* means 'here within this bounded region', typically indicated with a pointing finger, while *ety* means 'here spread over this unbounded region', typically indicated with a sweep of the hand.

A final category in this sampled series is "phase of matter", which mainly pertains to a volume of space. It has three main members: vacancy (empty space/air), solid, and liquid, and perhaps a fourth member, fire. By another interpretation, this category could instead be placed in the class of non-geometric categories discussed in section 2.2.4. I place it here in a geometric class, though, on the grounds that the main distinction among the category members is between whether a volume of space is filled or not – a geometric property – and that, in the filled case, the category members differ on the basis of how the filling moves internally: largely immobile, readily movable, or actively moving – properties that are at least akin to those of the state of motion category.

This category can be readily illustrated in Atsugewi (Talmy 2000b: 21-146).The directional verb suffixes of Atsugewi, each of which represents a specific path followed with respect to a certain kind of Ground object, include a number of forms that are specific to a particular phase of matter. For example, among those that subdivide the English 'into' path concept, the suffix *-ipsnu* specifies motion into the empty space of a volumetric enclosure. The suffix *–ik's* specifies motion horizontally into solid matter (as in *chopping an ax into a tree trunk*). The suffix *-ic't* specifies motion into liquid. And *-caw* specifies motion into a fire.

The phase of matter category figures even in English in some of its prepositions, albeit covertly. Thus, *in* can apply to a Ground object of any phase of matter, whereas *inside* can apply only to one with empty space as in (21a), but not to one of any other phase of matter, as seen in (21b).

(21)   a.   The rock is in/inside the box.
       b.   i.   The rock is in/*inside the ground.
            ii.   The rock is in/*inside the puddle of water.
            iii. The rock is in/*inside the fire.

Other than the ones listed above, the present category apparently need not include as members any further phases or consistencies of matter, such as powder or viscous material or ooze (like mud).

2.2.3. Categories pertaining to one scene component's relation to another

A third class of categories pertains to the relations that one scene component can bear to another. In addition to the five categories presented below, some further ten categories of the same class can be readily identified, each with a relatively small number of members.

One such category was described earlier, that of "relative orientation", that is, the angle between two lines, two planes, or a line and a plane. This category appears to have two or three members: (roughly) parallel, (roughly) perpendicular, and perhaps oblique. For example, the linear path of the Figure (the caterpillar) in (22a) is represented as parallel to the linear Ground (the crack) by *along*, and as perpendicular to it by *across*. And, repeating an earlier example, the *out* of (22b) seems to contrast with the *off* in depicting a more perpendicular as against a more oblique angle, respectively.

(22)   a.   The caterpillar crawled along/across the crack in the sidewalk.
       b.   A secondary pipe branches out/off from the main sewer line.

Further evidence of a need to include a perpendicular/oblique distinction in the present category comes from the contrast between two cause prefixes in Atsugewi (see Talmy 2000b: 147-212). Both refer to a linear object impinging axially on a Figure in a way that causes it to move or remain located. But *cu-* refers to the linear instrument impinging on the Figure perpendicularly, as in such causal actions as 'by poking' or 'by prodding'. On the other hand, *ra-* refers to such an instrument impinging obliquely on the Figure, as in such actions as 'by poling a canoe', 'by piercing a needle through cloth as in sewing', or 'by propping something up with a stick leaned against it'.

The earth-based spatial grid incorporates a member of the present category in that its vertical axis is perpendicular to its horizontal plane. Further, spatial schemas often represent an element as being parallel to one or the other of these two earth-grid components. Thus, with the earth-grid functioning as the Ground, the satellites or adverbs in (23a) indicate that the path of the moving Figure (*the balloon*) is parallel to the earth's vertical axis. And with the earth-grid functioning as the Secondary Reference Object, the satellites in (23b) represent the path of the Figure (*the bat*) as parallel to the earth's vertical axis, while that in (23c) represents the path as parallel to the earth's horizontal plane. Finally, to reprise an earlier locative example, the preposition in (23d) indicates that the line connecting the Figure and the Ground (*the lamp* and *the TV*, respectively) is parallel to the earth's vertical axis.

(23)   a.   The balloon floated up(wards)/down(wards).
       b.   The bat flew up to the ceiling of the cavern/down to the floor of the cavern.
       c.   The bat flew over to a ledge in the cavern.
       d.   The lamp is above the TV.

A further application of orientation relative to the earth grid is seen for schemas involving the rotation of an object about its center, discussed above under the "type of geometry" category. Such rotation defines a "spin axis".

Specifically, the rotating object is a meta-Figure, as defined above; points in this object move in concentric circles that lie on a plane (or on a set of parallel planes); and the spin axis is a line through the center of those circles perpendicular to the plane(s). Now, the present category of relative orientation can be considered to include a subcategory, that of "orientation of spin-axis", which then has two members, vertical and horizontal. That is, the spin-axis is either parallel to the earth grid's vertical axis or to its horizontal plane. And English has two verb satellites that distinguish rotation about such differently oriented axes. These are *around* and *over*, respectively, as seen in (24). Thus, *the pail* in (24a) is understood to rotate about a vertical axis when *around* is used, but about a horizontal axis in (24b) when *over* is used.

(24) a.   I turned the pail around.
      b.   I turned the pail over.

A second category in the present class is that of "degree of remove" that one scene component has relative to another. This category appears to have four or five members, two with contact between the components – coincidence and adjacency – and two or three without contact – proximal, perhaps medial, and distal remove. Some pairwise contrasts in English reveal one or another of these member elements for a Figure relating to a Ground. Thus, the locution *in the front of*, as in (25a), expresses coincidence, since the carousel as Figure is represented as being located in a part of the fairground as Ground. But *in front of* (without a the) as in (25b) indicates proximality, since the carousel is now located outside the fairground and near it but not touching it.

(25) a.   The carousel is in the front of the fairground.
      b.   The carousel is in front of the fairground.

The distinction between proximal and distal can in turn be teased out by noting that *in front of* can only represent a proximal but not a distal degree of remove, as seen in the fact that one can say (26a) but not (26b). On the other hand, *above* allows both proximal and distal degrees of remove, as seen in (26c), and so does not serve to show the need for the distinction.

(26) a.   The carousel is twenty feet in front of the fairground.
      b.   *The carousel is twenty miles in front of the fairground.
      c.   The hawk is one foot/one mile above the table.

The distinction between adjacency and proximality is shown by the sense distinction between the prepositions *on* and *over*. Thus, the *on* in (27a) requires that the Figure be in adjacent contact with the Ground, whereas the *over* in (27b) requires that the Figure in fact not be in contact with the Ground but proximal to it.

(27)   a.   The fly is on the table.
       b.   The fly is over the table.

A need to include a fifth category member of medial degree of remove – midway between the proximal and distal degrees of remove – might come from languages with a 'here'/'there'/'yonder' kind of distinction in their deictic adverbs or demonstratives. English might covertly retain something of this three-way distinction in that the locative adverbial *away*, as used in an expression like that in (28) seems to indicate a distance greater than any proximal or medial distance that an adverbial or demonstrative uttered at that same location might ordinarily represent.

(28)   Mary is away. <said to someone asking for her at the door of her home>

A third category in this series is that of "degree of dispersion" with two members: sparse and dense. To begin with, English can represent a set of multiple Figures as being located adjacent to or coincident with a Ground object in a way that is neutral to the presence or absence of dispersion. This is seen, for example, in the sentences in (29) showing a set of 0-dimensional peas in relation to a 1-dimensional knife, a 2-dimensional tabletop, and a 3-dimensional portion of aspic.

(29)   There are peas on the knife/on the table/in the aspic.

But in representing dispersion as present, English can (or must) also indicate its degree. Thus, a sparse degree of dispersion is indicated by the addition of the locution *here and there*, optionally together with certain preposition shifts, as seen in (30).

(30)   a.   There are peas here and there on/along the knife.
       b.   There are peas here and there on/over the table.
       c.   There are peas here and there in the aspic.

To indicate a dense degree of dispersion, English has the three specialized forms *all along*, *all over* and *throughout*, as seen in (31).

(31)   There are peas all along the knife/all over the table/throughout the aspic.

Note that such representation of dense dispersion – despite the occurrence of the word *all* in some of the English forms – does not require an exhaustive covering or filling of the Ground object, but rather only a certain representative distribution relative to the Ground's total spatial extent. It appears that no closed-class forms across languages distinguish between such exhaustively dense distribution and merely representatively dense distribution, nor between any further distinctions of dispersion beyond the two cited concepts of sparse and dense.

The fourth category to be presented here rests on a prior category, "state of directedness" that has two members: non-directed and directed. This prior category could have been included under the preceding class of categories pertaining to an individual scene component, except that possibly no closed-class forms directly mark its two-way distinction, and it may come into play only for the present category. The prior "state of directedness" category is here considered only for a scene component with spatial extent, that is, with dimension above zero (though certain schemas might in fact involve a point). When an extended entity moves along its axis, plane, or radii, the property of directedness simply reduces to the direction of motion. But a stationary entity can also be conceptualized as having an intrinsic directedness or orientation throughout its extent. Returning to the present category, it can apply where a schema already includes an extended entity that is directed. The present category, then, is here termed "relation to directedness" and has two main members, co-directional and anti-directional, corresponding to whether the path of a moving object, or the locations of successive stationary objects, are in the same direction as the directed entity or in the reverse direction.

To illustrate a stationary directed entity first, such an entity can, as in (32), function as the Ground (*the chemical gradient*). Then the preposition *along* can indicate that the path of a moving Figure (*the axon*) is co-directional with the directedness of the Ground, while *against* indicates that it is anti-directional.

(32)   The axon grew along/against the chemical gradient.

A stationary directed entity can also function as a Secondary Reference Object, in particular, one of the encompassive type. In (33), this is the line (*queue*) which here inherits its directedness from the direction in which the people making it up are largely facing and intend to move. Here, *Mary* is the Figure while *John* is the Ground. The prepositional complex *ahead of* indicates Mary's location as being co-directionally further than John's location relative to the line's directedness. In its use here, this prepositional complex requires a directed Secondary Reference Object, and can occur in this sentence only because one is present. If both Mary and John retained their relative positions but were standing alone in a field, one could not say that Mary was *ahead of* John but only that she was *in front of* him. And this latter form can be used only in the case where he in fact faces toward her – a condition that *ahead of* did not require.

(33)   Mary is ahead of John in line.

The vertical axis of the earth grid is the most prominent case of a stationary directed extended entity. It is not clear whether the basic direction of the vertical axis should be the direction away from the earth or the one toward it – and metaphoric motivation could be argued either way. Nor is it clear whether a directed line must in fact have one direction as its basic direction, as long as a schema somehow establishes how, say, the motion of an external object relates to that directed line. For convenience here, though, it will be said that the direction away from the earth is the basic one. This directed vertical axis, then, can function either as a Ground or as a Secondary Reference Object. When it is the Ground, the English satellite *up* indicates that the path of a moving Figure is (prototypically parallel to and) co-directional with the vertical axis, while *down* indicates that it is anti-directional, as illustrated in (34a). When it is a Secondary Reference Object, among other prepositional options, English *above* indicates that a stationary Figure is at a location co-directionally greater than that of the Ground, while *below* indicates that it is anti-directionally greater, as illustrated in (34b).

(34)   a.   The eagle swooped up/down.
         b.   The lamp is above the TV./The TV is below the lamp.

The sentence in (35) illustrates the case where the directionality of an entity is determined by the direction of its motion. Here, the entity (*the current*), which functions as the Ground, is of linear extent and moves along its axis. The preposition *with* indicates that the path of the moving Figure (*the bear*) is co-directional with the moving Ground's directedness, while *against* indicates that it is antidirectional.

(35)   The bear swam with/against the current.

It is possible to maintain that the present category, "relation to directedness", has a third member, cross-directional, given that there do exist closed-class forms – like the English preposition *across*, as in (36a,b) – that can be used to indicate a path transverse to a linearly directed entity. The conclusion here, though, is that such a transverse path does not hinge on the linear entity's being directed, but only on the fact that the path is perpendicular to the linear entity's orientation, whether directed or not, and this is a relationship already covered under the category of "relative orientation".

(36)   a.   The axon grew across the chemical gradient.
       b.   The bear swam across the current.

A fifth category is that of "contour", which most prominently applies to the path of a moving object, but can apply as well to a static line or plane. It is treated here in the class of categories for one scene element relating to another because, at least in the case of a moving entity, its path is generally cognized in terms of its relation to other objects external to it. A schema that includes a path or static element can be neutral to its contour, as the schema for *through* is in sentences like *I made a bee-line/zig-zagged/circled through the woods*. But if the schema is contour-specific, there may be only four member concepts, that is, four available contour types for it to draw on: straight, arced, circular, and meandering. To illustrate, some English prepositions require one or another of these contour types for the path of a Figure moving relative to a Ground. Thus, *across* requires that the Figure's path be a straight line relative to the vertical axis (and, for that matter, the stationary Ground object must itself be a flat plane, that is, have a straight contour), as seen in (37a). By contrast, *over* – in its usage referring to a single path line – requires a contour arced relative to the vertical axis (and the stationary Ground must be comparably arced), as in (37b). In one of its senses, *around* indicates a roughly circular path, as seen in (37c). And about indicates a meandering contour in sentences like (37d).

(37)   a.   I drove across the plateau/*hill.
       b.   I drove over the hill/*plateau.
       c.   I walked around the maypole.
       d.   I walked about the town.

2.2.4. Non-geometric categories

All the preceding categories and their member elements have broadly involved geometric characteristics of spatial scenes or of the objects within them – that is, they have been genuinely spatial. But a certain number of non-geometric categories and elements are recurrently found in association with otherwise geometric schemas. Although definitionally outside the scope of a spatial analysis, their frequency of association calls for a treatment of them, and several of the most recurrent are described next. It remains to examine what it is about our cognitive structure that regularly associates such non-geometric concepts with the geometric ones.

One category of such elements is that of "force dynamics" (see Talmy 2000a: 410-470) with two members: present and absent. Thus, geometrically, the English prepositions *on* and *against* both represent a Figure in adjacent contact with a Ground. But in addition, on indicates that the Figure is supported against the pull of gravity through that contact, as is the case in (38a), while against indicates that it is not so supported, as in (38b).

(38) a.   The poster is on/*against the wall.
      b.   The floating helium balloon is against/*on the wall.

As in the preceding example, the two Dutch prepositions *op* and *aan* both indicate spatial contact between a Figure and a Ground, and both involve force dynamics in distinct ways (Melissa Bowerman, *p.c.*). But this distinction between them cuts force dynamics in a slightly different place. The form *op* indicates a Figure supported comfortably in what is conceptualized as a natural rest state through its contact with a Ground, whereas *aan* indicates that the Figure is being actively maintained against gravity through its contact with the Ground. Accordingly, flesh is said to be *op* the bones of a live person but *aan* the bones of a dead person.

A second non-geometric category that can occur in association with a geometric schema is that of "cognitive/affective state". Its extent of membership is not clear. But one recurrent member is the attitude toward a schematic feature that it is unknown, mysterious, or risky. This category member is associated with the English preposition *beyond*, perhaps in combination with the further concepts of inaccessibility or nonvisibility – themselves seeming to have part geometric and part non-geometric aspects. More specifically, these cognitive/affective concepts occur in association with the distal region of space specified by the *beyond* schema and with the locatedness of the Figure in that region, as seen in (39a). However, these concepts are absent from the otherwise parallel spatial locution *on the other side of*, as in (39b).

(39) a.   John is beyond the border.
      b.   John is on the other side of the border.

Thus, a speaker using *beyond* as in (39a) – in addition to specifying roughly the same spatial schema as that of *on the other side of* – also indicates that she in some way regards that region of space as being unfamiliar and the Figure located within it as accordingly being in potential jeopardy.[4]

---

4. Earlier, the schema for *beyond* was contrasted with that of *past* as including an external Secondary Reference Object, namely, an observer's point of view

A third nongeometric category – in the class that relates one scene component to another – is that of "relative priority". It has two members: coequal and main/ancillary. To illustrate, the English verb satellites *together* and *along* can both indicate joint participation and, when applied to motion through space, can both indicate that a moving Figure's path is executed coextensively with and parallel to a moving Ground's path. But *together*, as in (40a), indicates in addition to this spatial relation that the Figure and the Ground are coequal participants in the activity. On the other hand, *along*, as in (40b), indicates that the Figure entity is ancillary to the Ground entity, while the Ground entity is the main or determinative entity, one who would be assumed to engage in the activity even if alone (see Talmy 2000b: 213-288).

(40)   a.   I jog together with him.
       b.   I jog along with him.

2.3. Properties of the inventory

By the methodology adopted here, the universally available inventory of structural spatial elements includes all elements that appear in at least one closed-class spatial schema in at least one language. All such elements may indeed be equivalent in their sheer availability for use in schemas. Nevertheless, they appear to differ in their frequency of occurrence across schemas and languages, ranging from very common to very rare. Accordingly, the inventory of elements – and perhaps also that of categories – may have the property of being hierarchical, with entries running from the most to the least frequent.

Given such a hierarchy, the question arises whether the elements in the inventory, the categories in the inventory, and the elements in each category form fully closed memberships. That is, does the hierarchy end at a sharp lower boundary or does it trail off indefinitely? With many schemas and languages already examined, our sampling method may have yielded all the commoner elements and categories. But as the process slows down in the discovery of the rarer forms, will it asymptotically approach some limit of

---

on the side opposite that of the Figure. Here, the schema for the locution *on the other side of* shares the same viewpoint requirement with the *beyond* schema, but now these two schemas contrast with respect to the additional cognitive/affective state.

distinctions and maximum of constituents in the inventory? Or will it be able to go on uncovering sporadic novel forms?

The latter alternative seems likelier. Exotic elements with perhaps unique occurrence in just one schema in one language – or minimal occurrence in just a few such – can be expected. In fact, at least one such case can be observed in as close a language as English. Thus, both the prepositions *in* and *on* can refer to a Figure's location at the interior of a wholly or mostly enclosed vehicle. But, by one analysis, these two prepositions distinguish whether the vehicle respectively lacks or possesses a walkway. Thus, one is *in* a car but *on* a bus, *in* a helicopter but *on* a plane, *in* a grain car but *on* a train, and *in* a rowboat but *on* a ship. Further, Fillmore (1986) has observed that this *on* also requires that the vehicle be currently in use for transport. Accordingly, *in* becomes the preferred preposition for use with a nonfunctional bus, as in *The children were playing in/*on the abandoned bus in the junkyard*. Thus, schema analysis in English reveals the element '(mostly) enclosed vehicle with a walkway currently in use for transport'. This is surely one of the rarer elements in schemas around the world. But its existence, along with that of various others that can be found, suggests that indefinitely many more of them can sporadically arise. The theory that accounts for this arrangement cannot be of a type that requires a domain with well-defined boundaries and uniformly applicable principles, but rather of a type that can include gradients and fuzzy boundaries.

In addition to being only relatively closed at its hierarchically lower end, the inventory may include some categories whose membership seems not to settle down to a small fixed set. One such category may be that of "intrinsic parts", which could have been included under section 2.2.2 as another case of a category pertaining to an individual scene component, but which has been relocated here to help make the present point. Frequently encountered in this category are the five member elements: front, side, back, top, and bottom, as found in the English prepositions in (41).

(41)   The cat lay before/beside/behind/atop/beneath the TV.

But Mixtec, for one language, seems to distinguish a rather different set of intrinsic parts in their spatial schemas, ones dependent on the overall geometric shape of an object, e.g., one that might be glossed as 'at a main vertex of' (Brugman and Macaulay 1986). And Makah distinguishes many more and finer parts than the five cited above for English, such as with its verb suffixes for 'at the ankle of' and 'at the groin of' (Matthew Davidson, p.c.).

Apart from any such fuzzy lower boundary or noncoalescing categories, though, there does appear to exist a graduated inventory of basic spatial elements and categories that is universally available and that is relatively closed. This notion, however, has been challenged, with the main challenge raised by Bowerman (e.g., 1989). She notes, for example, that at the same time that children acquiring English learn its *in/on* distinction, children acquiring Korean learn its distinction between *kkita* 'put [Figure] in a snug fit with [Ground]' and *nehta* 'put [Figure] in a loose fit with [Ground]'. She argues that since the elements 'snug fit' and 'loose fit' are presumably rare among spatial schemas across languages, they do not come from any preset inventory, one that might plausibly be innate, but rather are learned from the open-ended semantics of the adult language. My reply is that the spatial schemas of genuinely closed-class forms in Korean may well still be built from the inventory elements I propose, and that the forms she cites are actually open-class verbs. Open-class semantics – whether for space or other domains – seems to involve a different linguistic subsystem, one that draws from finer cognitive discriminations within our overall processes of perception and conception. The Korean verbs are perhaps learned at the same age as English space-related open-class verbs like *hug* or *squeeze*. Thus, English-acquiring children probably understand that squeeze involves centripetal pressure from encircling or bi-/multi-laterally placed Antagonists, typically the arm(s) or hand(s), against an Agonist that resists the pressure but yields down to some smaller compass where it blocks further pressure, and hence that one can squeeze a teddy bear, a tube of toothpaste, or a rubber ball, but not a piece of string or sheet of paper, juice or sugar or the air, a tabletop or the corner of a building. Thus, Bowerman's challenge may be directed at the wrong target, leaving intact the proposal for a roughly preset inventory of basic spatial building blocks.

3.   Basic elements assembled into whole schemas

The last section was devoted to mapping out the componential part of the overall system of spatial schemas in language. The procedure was analytic, starting with the whole spatial schemas expressed by closed-class forms and abstracting from them an inventory of fundamental spatial elements. We turn now to the compositional part of the overall schema system. The procedure will now be one of synthesis, and will examine the ways in which individual spatial elements are assembled to constitute whole schemas.

The schemas represented by closed-class forms can range in complexity from the rather simple to the truly elaborate. Perhaps some few schemas consist of a single basic spatial element by itself. A possible candidate for this status is the schema of the English form *way* as in *The eagle flew way up*. This schema might consist solely of the (presumably) basic element 'of relatively great magnitude' – though an additional complexity might already be introduced if this schema is constrained to apply only to a linear extent. But most closed-class schemas are more complex than this – even ones that at first seem simple in form and usage. Thus, the schema of the seemingly simple *up* in the example sentence just cited was seen above under the "relation to directedness" category to consist of a fair-sized and fairly intricate assembly of elementary components. Moreover, the upper end of the schema complexity scale is quite well populated. Again, even common and seemingly innocuous forms can represent schemas of great complexity. This was already seen in the initial *across* example. We now go through another such example, but this time with specific focus on the assembly and arrangement of the schema components, while using only the categories and components already treated.

Consider the schema represented by the English preposition *past* in (42). Loosely characterized, this schema represents the ball as moving horizontally through a point near the side of my head. But its precise characterization is quite elaborate, and involves all the elements cited in (42) arranged with respect to each other exactly as indicated. Still, every one of the elements and of the relations among the elements that is presented in (42) is a member of one of the categories treated above – and here named within brackets. Thus, even though it is still rather partial, the inventory of basic spatial elements and categories proposed so far can already serve as an exhaustive source for some spatial schemas.

(42)   The ball sailed past my head at exactly 3 p.m.

    a.   There are a Figure object and a Ground object (here, *the ball* and *my head*, respectively) [members of the "major scene components" category].

    b.   The Figure is schematizable as a 0-dimensional point [a member of the "dimension" category].

    c.   This Figure point is moving [a member of the "motive state" category].

    d.   Hence it forms a one-dimensional line, its path [a member of the "dimension" category].

    e.   The Ground is also schematizable as a 0-dimensional point [a member of the "dimension" category].

f.   There is a certain point P at a proximal remove [a member of the "degree of remove" category] from the Ground point.

g.   Point P forms a 1-dimensional line [a member of the "dimension" category] with the Ground point.

h.   This line is parallel [a member of the "relative orientation" category] to the horizontal plane.

i.   In turn, the horizontal plane is a part [a member of the "intrinsic parts" category] of the earth-based grid.

j.   And the earth-based grid is a Secondary Reference Object [a member of the "major scene components" category].

k.   The Figure's path is perpendicular [a member of the "relative orientation" category] to the line between point P and the Ground.

l.   The Figure's path is also parallel to the horizontal plane of the earth-based grid [same as h/i/j above].

m.   If the Ground object has a front, side, and back [members of the "intrinsic parts" category], then it is the side part to which point P is proximal.

n.   There is a certain point Q of the Figure's path that is not one of its boundary points [a member of the "state of boundedness" category].

o.   Point Q becomes coincident [a member of the "degree of remove" category] with point P at a certain point of time.

The reasons for some of the inclusions in the *past* schema above can be made clearer. Thus, the Figure's path is specified as passing through a point P proximal to the Ground (42f, 42o) because if it instead headed directly toward the Ground, one would not say *The ball sailed past my head*, but rather *The ball sailed into my head*. And if the point through which the Figure passed were distal, one might instead say something like *The ball sailed along some distance away from my head*. The point P is further specified as being on a horizontal level with the Ground in (42g, 42h) because if it were instead, say, above the Ground, one would now have to say something like *The ball sailed right over my head*. And point P is specified as located at the side of the Ground in (42m) because if it were instead, say, at the front of the Ground, one would switch to saying something like *The ball sailed (by) in front of my head*. Finally, the Figure's path is specified as horizontal in (42l) because if it instead were vertical, one might rather say something like *The ball sailed down beside my head*.

The least understood aspect of the present investigation is what well-formedness conditions, if any, may govern the legality of the selection and arrangement of basic elements into whole schemas like the one just analyzed. As yet, no obvious principles based, say, on geometric simplicity, symmetry, consistency, or the like are seen to constrain the patterns of assembly. On the one hand, some seemingly byzantine combinations – like the schemas seen above for *across* and *past* – occur with some regularity across languages. On the other hand, much simpler combinations seem never to occur as closed-class schemas. For example, one could imagine assembling elements into the following schema: 'down into a surround that is radially proximal to a center point'. One could even invent a preposition *apit* to represent this schema. This could then be used, say, in a sentence like (43) to refer to my pouring water down into a nearby hole dug in the field around my house. But schemas like this one are not found.

(43)   *I poured water apit my house.

Similarly, a number of additional schematic distinctions in, for example, the domain of rotation are regularly marked by signed languages, as discussed in Talmy (2003), and could readily be represented with the inventory elements available to spoken languages, yet they largely do not occur. It could be argued that the spoken language schemas are simply the spatial structures most often encountered in everyday activity. But that would not explain why the additional sign-language schemas – presumably also reflective of everyday experience – do not show up in spoken languages. Besides, the different sets of spatial schemas found in different individual spoken languages are diverse enough from each other that arguing on the basis of the determinative force of everyday experience is problematic. Something else is at work, but it is not yet clear what that is.

4.   Properties and processes applying to whole spatial schemas

Dealing with the second *compositional* part of the overall system of spatial schemas in language, we just saw that selected elements of the universally available inventory are combined in specific arrangements to make up the whole schemas represented by individual closed-class spatial forms. Each such whole schema is thus a "pre-packaged" bundling together of certain elements in a particular arrangement. Each particular language has in its lexicon a relatively closed set of such pre-packaged schemas. This set is larger than that of its phonologically distinct spatial closed-class forms, because such forms are largely polysemous. A speaker of the language must in general select among this set of schemas in depicting a spatial scene.

Turning now to the third *augmentive* part of the overall system of spatial schemas in language, we can observe that such schemas, though composite, have a certain unitary status in their own right, and that certain quite general properties and processes can apply to them. In particular, certain properties and processes allow a schema represented by a closed-class form to generalize to a whole family of schemas. The terms "property" and "process" are here distinguished according to the way they perform this generalization. In the case of a generalizing property, all the schemas of a family are of equal priority. On the other hand, a generalizing process acts on a schema that is somehow basic, and either extends or deforms it to yield nonbasic schemas (see Talmy 2000a: 21-96, 177-254 and 2000b: 323-336). Such properties and processes are perhaps part of the overall language system so that any given language's relatively closed set of spatial closed-class forms and the schemas that they basically represent can be used to match more spatial configurations in a wider range of scenes.

4.1. Generalizing properties of spatial schemas

Looking first at generalizing properties of spatial schemas, under several such properties a schema exhibits a topological or topology-like neutrality to certain features of Euclidean geometry. Accordingly, a family of different schemas that range over all the variations of the feature that the basic schema is neutral to are equally represented by the same closed-class form. Three properties of this sort are described next.

For a first topological property, schemas are generally *magnitude neutral*. This property can be seen, for example, in the fact that the across schema can apply to a spatial situation of any size, as in (44a). Comparably, the two demonstratives *this* and *that* can contrast the different distances of two distinct objects from a speaker, but these distances can vary indefinitely in length, as seen in (44b).

(44)   a.   The ant crawled across my palm./The bus drove across the country.
       b.   This speck is smaller than that speck./This planet is smaller than that planet.

It was seen under the "contour" category in section 2.2.3 that a schema can require a particular contour at a certain locus and with respect to a specific orientation (e.g., an arced contour in the vertical plane).

Outside of such constraints, though, schemas largely exhibit a second topological property of being "shape-neutral". Thus, to reprise an earlier example, the *through* schema requires that the Figure form a path with linear extent, but it lets that line take any contour, as seen in (45).

(45)   I made a bee-line/zig-zagged/circled through the woods.

A third topology-like property of spatial schemas is that they are largely "bulk-neutral". This property is seen, for example, in the fact that the *past* schema requires a Figure and a Ground idealizable as points, regardless of the degree of spherical radial extension outward from those ideal points (provided only that the Ground does not then block the Figure), as seen in (46a). Comparably, the *along* schema requires that the Ground be idealizable as a linear extent, regardless of the radial extension outward from that ideal line, as in (46b).

(46)   a.   The ball sailed past my head./The asteroid sailed past the planet.
       b.   The caterpillar crawled up along the filament/tree trunk.

Thus, while holding to their specific constraints, schemas can vary freely in other respects and so cover a range of spatial configurations.

4.2.   Generalizing processes that extend spatial schemas

We turn now to generalizing processes, ones of the type that extend a basic form of a schema to nonbasic forms of it. Three such processes are described next.

One process of this kind is "extendability in ungoverned dimensions". By this process, a scene component of dimensionality N in the basic form of a schema can generally be raised in dimensionality to form a line, plane, or volume that is oriented and contoured in a way not conflicting with the schema's other requirements. To illustrate, it was seen earlier under the "type of geometry" category that, in the spatial schema of the English verb satellite *out* (in its radial sense), a Figure point is conceptualized as moving along a radius away from a central Ground point through a continuum of concentric circles, as in (47a). This schema with the Figure idealizable as a point is the basic form. But the same satellite can be used when this Figure point is extended to form a 1-dimensional line along a radius, as in (47b). And the *out* can again be used if the Figure point were instead extended as a 1-dimensional line forming a concentric circle, as in (47c). In turn, such a concentric circle could be extended to fill in the interior plane, as in (47d). Alternatively, the concentric circle could have been extended in the vertical dimension to form a cylinder, as in (47e). Or again, the circle could have been extended to form a spherical shell, as in (47f). And such a shell can be extended to fill in the interior volume, as in (47g). Thus, the same form *out* serves for this series of geometric extensions without any need to switch to some different form.

(47) a. The boat sailed further and further out from the island.
     b. The caravan of boats sailed further and further out from the island.
     c. A circular ripple spread out from where the pebble fell into the water.
     d. The oil spread out over the water from where it spilled.
     e. A ring of fire spread out as an advancing wall of flames.
     f. The balloon I blew into slowly puffed out.
     g. The leavened dough slowly puffed out.

A second schema-extending process is "extendability across motive states". A schema that is basic for one motive state and Figure geometry can in general be systematically extended to another motive state and Figure geometry. For example, a closed-class form whose most basic schema pertains to a point Figure moving to form a path can generally serve as well to represent a related schema with a stationary linear Figure in the same location as the path. Thus, probably the most basic *across* schema is actually for a point Figure moving along a path, as in (48a). By the present process, this schema can extend to the static linear Figure schema exemplified initially with the sentence in (48b). All the spatial properties earlier uncovered for that static schema hold as well for the present basic dynamic schema, which in fact is the schema in which these properties originally arise.

(48) a. The gopher ran across the road.
     b. The board lay across the road.

A possible third extensional process, "extendability from the prototype", actually covers no new cases, but is proposed here only as an alternative interpretation for some cases of neutrality, already treated above under generalizing properties. Thus, the *through* schema illustrated above in (45) was there treated as exhibiting shape neutrality. But this schema could alternatively be conceived as prototypically involving a strait path line for the Figure, one that can then be bent to any contour. Comparably, the schemas for *past* and *along* shown above in (46) to illustrate bulk neutrality could alternatively be thought to have as their prototypes a zero-dimensional point and a one-dimensional line, respectively, that can then be radially inflated.

4.3. Generalizing processes that deform spatial schemas

Continuing with generalizing processes, we turn now to ones of the type that derive nonbasic forms of a schema from the basic form not by extending it but by "deforming" it. That is, such processes alter the basic schema so that the result somehow deviates from its original basic character. Two such processes are described next.

One schema-deforming process is that of "stretching". This process allows a modest relaxation of one of the normal constraints otherwise present in a schema. Thus, in the *across* schema, where the Ground plane is either a ribbon with a long and short axis or a square with equal axes, a static linear Figure or the path of a moving point Figure normally must be parallel to the short axis or to one of the equal axes. But it cannot be parallel to the long axis of a ribbonal Ground. Accordingly, *across* can be used for a Figure's path along the short axis of a ribbonal Ground, as in (49a), or along one of the equal axes of a square, as in (49b), but it cannot be used for a path along the long axis of a ribbonal Ground, as in (49c). However, in this last case, the long axis is of much greater magnitude than the short axis. Consider now instead a Ground that is only slightly oblong in shape, where the Figure's path goes from one of its narrower sides to the other, as in (49d). Perhaps the longer axis here can be conceptualized as having been stretched from an equal-axis square shape. If so, the *across* schema can generally continue to apply to the longer axis if the stretch remains moderate, and becomes progressively less applicable as the stretch increases. But the fact that the schema can be used at all for such a stretched shape, rather than abruptly becoming inapplicable, is evidence for the existence of a cognitive process of schema deformation.

(49) a.   I swam across the canal. <from one side of the canal to the other>
      b.   I swam across the pool. <from one side of a square pool to its opposite>
      c.   *I swam across the canal. <from one end of the canal to the other>
      d.   ?I swam across the pool. <from one narrower side of a moderately oblong pool to the other>

Another schema deforming process is that of "feature cancellation", in which a particular element or complex of elements in the basic schema is omitted. To illustrate, the basic schema for the dynamic sense of *across* includes as features the fact that the path of a moving Figure point begins at one side of a Ground ribbon and terminates on the other side.[5] But the preposition *across* can still be used in a sentence like (50) even though, in the spatial scene represented by this sentence, the path of the moving Figure (*the shopping cart*) does not extend all the way to the distal side of the Ground ribbon (*the boulevard*). That is, one of the cited features of the schema – the Figure's path terminating on the distal side of the Ground ribbon – has been canceled or is left unrealized. Instead of needing to switch to some new preposition or paraphrase, the language here allows an extant preposition to have its schema altered and thus fit the novel spatial configuration.

(50)   The shopping cart rolled across the boulevard and was hit by an oncoming car.

The schema of this same preposition is seen to undergo an even more extreme case of feature cancellation in (51). Here, the two cited features – the Figure's path beginning on one edge of a bounded Ground and terminating on the opposite edge – are both canceled, leaving *across* to refer only to the Figure's path continuing along in coincidence with the plane of the Ground.

(51)   The tumbleweed rolled across the prairie for an hour.

5.   Relating the system of spatial schemas to other language systems

Closed-class forms that represent spatial structure are a subset of all closed-class forms representing conceptual structure generally. As such, they can be expected to exhibit the same properties possessed by the superset, as these were set forth in Talmy (2000a: 21-146). This in fact they do. For example, the superset has bequeathed to them its properties of having a componential part consisting of basic conceptual elements that fall into basic conceptual categories, which together constitute a relatively closed universally available inventory that individual languages draw from; a compositional part in which certain basic concepts are selected and set in particular relationships within conceptual complexes for representation by individual closed-class forms; and an augmentive part in which such conceptual complexes can be extended or deformed. Nevertheless, the spatial forms distinguish themselves

---

5. These features are in addition to the path's continuing in coincidence with the plane of the Ground ribbon, as well as to all the other features listed early on in (3).

as a subset by exhibiting certain greater constraints as well as certain greater elaborations in comparison with the rest of the superset.

The case of greater constraints can be seen in the componential part of the spatial schema system. In that part, certain conceptual categories are present that correspond to or are identical with conceptual categories in the componential part of the larger closed-class system – except that they are more constrained in their membership. One prominent example is the category of "number". In the spatial closed-class system, as discussed above, this category is apparently limited to just four member concepts: one, two, several, and many. But in the overall closed-class system, the number category includes additional concepts, including those expressed by such English closed-class determiners as *no, few, more, most, all* as well as such further concepts as 'three' in the trial inflections of some languages.

The case of greater elaboration can be seen in the compositional part of the spatial schema system. As just noted, the combining of basic conceptual elements into complexes for representation by single closed-class forms occurs not only in the compositional part of the spatial schema system, but also in the corresponding part of the general closed-class system. We saw earlier that what closed-class spatial schemas consist of can range from perhaps a single basic element, through an arrangement of moderate complexity, to a pattern of extreme intricacy. But while the referents of nonspatial closed-class forms can range over the first two degrees of this scale, they seem not to come up to the elaboration that spatial schemas are capable of.

To illustrate the nonspatial closed-class system first at the low end, consider the conceptual category of "gender" – say, in a language with just the two member concepts 'male' and 'female'. If we can abstract away from the application of this category to entities without natural gender and from various complications in its application even to entities with natural gender, perhaps we could conclude that the closed-class forms for masculine and feminine largely represent the single basic 'male' or 'female' concept alone.

More commonly, a nonspatial closed-class form represents a combination of several basic concepts in a particular relationship. Thus, still at the simpler end, the English plural suffix -*s*, as in *cats*, represents a shift within the conceptual category of "plexity" from one member concept 'uniplex' to another member concept 'multiplex'. But at the same time, it places the new multiplex referent within the sphere of relevance of another conceptual category, that of "state of boundedness", and in particular marks the new referent as unbounded. Thus, adding -*s* to *cat* changes its uniplex referent into an unbounded multiplexity.

For a more elaborate case, the English closed-class form *the*, as in *the cat*, represents a conceptual complex something like 'the speaker infers that the addressee can readily identify the referent of the adjoined noun.' This conceptual complex draws on the category of "speech participants" for the member concepts of 'speaker' and 'hearer', on a proposed category of "cognitive process" for the member concepts 'inferring' and 'identifying', and on the category of "force dynamics" for the member concept 'against little opposition' (for the 'readily' notion).

The conceptual complexes just seen represented by nominal -*s* and *the* exhibited integral patterns of basic concepts set into specific relationships with each other. In addition, though, some closed-class forms can represent what seem to be simple aggregations of basic concepts. An example is the English verb suffix -*s*, as in *Sue eats no meat*. This form represents together the concept 'one'(singular) from the "number" category, the concept 'third person' from the "person" category, the concept 'present' from the "tense" category, the concept 'factual' (indicative) from the "mood" category, and the concept 'habitual' from the "aspect" category. That is, this closed-class form appears to represent a selection of basic concepts that are juxtaposed as a simple set but that are not set into a particular arrangement with respect to each other.

But while nonspatial closed-class forms readily represent some four or five basic concepts combined in a complex – whether simply as an aggregate or in a structured relationship – they seem not to reach the extremities of elaboration and organization that occur with some frequency in the schemas represented by spatial closed-class forms.

So far in this section, the closed-class spatial schema subsystem has been compared with the closed-class subsystem for nonspatial conceptual structure. But this same closed-class spatial schema subsystem, as it has been analyzed in this chapter, has been looked at solely as it exists in spoken language. However, signed language has a particular subsystem – often termed the "classifier" subsystem – that is specifically dedicated to representing the motion or location of objects relative to each other in space. This is a subsystem within a different language modality that in turn invites comparison. It turns out that the properties we have found in the spatial schema subsystem of spoken language mostly do not hold for the classifier subsystem of signed language. The arguments and details are presented in Talmy (2003), but some highlights can be sketched here.

In its counterpart to the componential inventory of the closed-class spatial schema system of spoken language, the classifier subsystem of *signed language* generally has more basic spatial elements and more cate-

language generally has more basic spatial elements and more categories that they fall into. Further, though, these elements are often not the discrete concepts of the spoken system, but rather points along a gradient continuum. With regard to composition, where spoken languages have whole prepackaged schemas constituting specific selections and arrangements of basic elements, signed language largely lacks such preset schemas. Instead, each classifier expression can concurrently represent its own selection from some thirty distinct spatial parameters, and it can independently vary the values of these parameters, so that the whole complex accords in an individually tailored way with the current spatial structure needing representation. Finally, where the spoken language system has augmentive mechanisms that can extend and deform the preset schemas to adapt them to a wider range of spatial structures, the classifier subsystem largely lacks such mechanisms since they are generally not necessary: what would be extensions and distortions for a spoken language representation are simply represented directly in signed language. The cognitive and neural implications of these spoken-signed differences in spatial representation are examined in Talmy (2003), while their implications for the evolution of language are explored in Talmy (2004).

References

Bennett, David C.
  1975   *Spatial and Temporal Uses of English Prepositions: An Essay in Stratificational Semantics*. London: Longman.
Bowerman, Melissa
  1989   Learning a semantic system: What role do cognitive predispositions play? In *The teachability of language*, Mabel L. Rice, and Richard L. Schiefelbusch (eds.), 133-169. Baltimore: P.H. Brookes.
Brugman, Claudia, and Monica Macaulay
  1986   Interacting semantic systems: Mixtec expressions of location. *Berkeley Linguistics Society* 13: 315-328.
Clark, Herb
  1973   Space, time, semantics, and the child. In *Cognitive Development and the Acquisition of Language*, Timothy E. Moore (ed.), 27-63. New York: Academic Press.
Fillmore, Charles
  1968   The case for case. In *Universals in Linguistic Theory*, Emmon Bach, and Robert T. Harms (eds.), 1-88. New York: Holt, Rinehart and Winston.

Gruber, Jeffrey S.
   1965   Studies in lexical relations. Ph.D. Dissertation, MIT. [Reprinted as
            part of *Lexical structures in syntax and semantics*. Amsterdam:
            North-Holland, 1976.]
Herskovits, Annette
   1982   Space and the prepositions in English: Regularities and irregulari-
            ties in a complex domain. Ph.D. Dissertation, Stanford University.
Imai, Shingo
   2003   Spatial deixis: How demonstratives divide space. Ph. D. diss., Uni-
            versity at Buffalo, State University of New York.
Jackendoff, Ray
   1983   *Semantics and Cognition*. Cambridge, Mass.: MIT Press.
Leech, Geoffrey
   1969   *Towards a Semantic Description of English*. New York: Longman.
Mark, David M., and Barry Smith
   2004   A science of topography: From qualitative ontology to digital repre-
            sentations. In: *Geographical Information Science and Mountain
            Geomorphology*, Michael P. Bishop, and John F. Shroder (eds.),
            75-100. Berlin: Springer.
Talmy, Leonard
   1983   How language structures space. In *Spatial orientation: Theory,
            research, and application*, Herbert L. Pick, Jr., and Linda P.
            Acredolo (eds.), 225-282. New York: Plenum Press.
   2000a   *Toward a Cognitive Semantics*. Vol. 1. *Concept Structuring Sys-
            tems*. Cambridge, Mass.: MIT Press.
   2000b   *Toward a Cognitive Semantics*. Vol. 2. *Typology and Process in
            Concept Structuring*. Cambridge, Mass.: MIT Press.
   2003   The representation of spatial structure in spoken and signed lan-
            guage. In *Perspectives on Classifier Constructions in Sign Lan-
            guage*, Karen Emmorey (ed.), 169-195. Mahwah, NJ: Lawrence
            Erlbaum.
   2004   Recombinance in the evolution of language. In *Proceedings of the
            39th Annual Meeting of the Chicago Linguistic Society: The Panels*,
            Jonathon E. Cihlar, David Kaiser, Irene Kimbara, and Amy Frank-
            lin (eds.). Chicago: Chicago Linguistic Society.
Zubin, David A. and Svorou Soteria
   1984   Orientation and gestalt: Conceptual organizing principles in the
            lexicalization of space. In *Proceedings of the 20th Meeting of the
            Chicago Linguistics Society, Parasession on Lexical Semantics*,
            Veena Mishra Testen and Joseph Drogo (eds.), 333-345. Chi-
            cago: Chicago Linguistic Society.

Multimodal spatial representation:
On the semantic unity of *over*

Paul D. Deane

Abstract

The English preposition *over* appears to exemplify family resemblance networks (Brugman [1981] 1988; Lakoff 1987). The word combines semantic continuity with lack of a central definition and lexical idiosyncrasy – properties which, on standard views, ought not to cooccur. This paper presents a reanalysis, arguing that the word's meanings are more closely related than the Brugman-Lakoff account would suggest. To be precise, its polysemy derives from a central prototype via application of preference rules. But this unification depends critically on an image-based view of meaning in which apparent polysemy reflects concept-internal structure.

Keywords: polysemy, vagueness, image schema, prototype, lexical network

1. Introduction: The challenge of *over*

The analysis of Brugman (1988), inspired in part by the "space grammar" framework (Lindner [1981] 1983, 1982; Langacker 1987) has been described as an "outstanding contribution" to "the demonstration that prepositional usage is highly structured", as "one of the major achievements of the cognitive paradigm" (Taylor 1989: 110). It forms the basis for what is now termed *lexical network theory* (Norvig and Lakoff 1987; Brugman and Lakoff 1988; Hawkins [1984] 1985, 1988; Janda 1988; Taylor 1988; Geeraerts 1990, 1992; Cuyckens 1991; Schulze 1991). Lexical network theory claims: (i) that meaning is analogically represented by images and image schemas; (ii) that lexical meaning need not be centrally defined but subsists in a loose network of family resemblances, and rejects what Lakoff (1987: 157) terms *objectivist* views of meaning committed to necessary and sufficient conditions.

Brugman's analysis develops three key claims of lexical network theory: (i) chained sets of images make it possible to unite disparate meanings, even though (ii) such chains cannot be united under a single definition – contra the received view (Zwicky and Sadock 1974), according to which semantic contiguity entails vagueness and hence lexical identity, whereas lack of a unifying meaning entails lexical ambiguity. And (iii), the individual uses are primary, allowing for and predicting the existence of many fine-grained idiosyncrasies of distribution. The strength of Brugman's argument depends on the extent to which the uses of *over* appear to display these properties, thus challenging received views of lexical meaning.

However, certain aspects of the Brugman analysis, and lexical network theory in general, have been criticized extensively in the literature. Among the main issues that have been raised are (a) the unconstrained nature of lexical networks, most particularly the need for a methodology to delimit when one sense ends and another beings, and (b) the need to consider schematic rather than fully-specified senses, and take into account the possibility that sense variation can occur as a result of conceptual combination and inference (Kreitzer 1997; Sandra 1998; Sandra and Rice 1995; Rice et al. 1999; Tyler and Evans 2001, 2003.)

This study reflects a similar perspective: the analysis to be presented derives most of the semantic variability of *over* from a process of conceptual interpretation in which particular fully-specified interpretations are constructed in context from a lexical prototype, and thus will contend that the apparent lexical network structure found with prepositions like *over* reflects an underlying semantic unity. However, the analysis will argue that a full understanding of this process requires an image-based theory of spatial representation whose properties are compatible with – and often inspired by – what is known about the neuropsychology of spatial thought. The theory will be used to analyze – and predict – patterns of polysemy (or more accurately, perhaps, at least flexibility of conceptual interpretations) displayed by *over* and other prepositions, including *on, across,* and *above.*

1.1. The Brugman-Lakoff analysis of *over*

Over covers an extraordinarily wide semantic range. It can be paraphrased variously as 'above', 'across', 'above and across', or 'on', to name only the most frequent paraphrases. Various themes recur, including:

I.   *Verticality*: The lamp hangs over the table; the plane flew over the city; He jumped over the wall; he walked over the hill.

II.   *Boundary-Traversal*: The plane flew over the city; he walked over the hill; he walked over the street; he got over the border; the spark jumped over the gap.

III. *Surmounting*: He jumped over the wall; he fell over the lamp; he pushed her over the balcony; the water flowed over the rim of the bathtub.

IV.   *Covering*: He put his hands over his face; he laid the tablecloth over the table; the child threw his toys (all) over the floor; he walked all over the city.

V.   *Potential interaction*: Pull the lamp over the table; the bomber is over the city; he stood over the prisoner; we will discuss it over lunch.

VI.   *Contact (or its absence)*: Some uses saliently imply that the TR is separated from the LM by a gap; others, that they are in contact or indeed coincide (Examples may readily be observed above).

As Brugman (1988) observes: (i) none of these characteristics is semantically necessary; (ii) no one use seems to combine all of them; in fact some features, such as covering and boundary-traversal, seem not to cooccur. Lakoff (1987) restates Brugman's analysis as a lexical network of schemas:

Schema 1. The plane flew over.
   Schema 1.X.NC. The plane flew over the yard.
   Schema 1.VX. NC. The plane flew over the hill.
   Schema 1.V.NC. The bird flew over the wall.
   Schema 1.X.C. Sam drove over the bridge.
   Schema 1.VX.C. Sam walked over the hill.
   Schema 1.V.C. Sam climbed over the wall.
   Schema 1.VX.C.E. Sam lives over the hill.
   Schema 1.X.C.E. Sausalito is over the bridge.
Schema 2. Hang the painting over the fireplace.
   Schema 2.1DTR. The power line stretches over the yard.
Schema 3. The board is over the hole.
   Schema 3.P.E. The city clouded over.
   Schema 3.MX. The guards were posted all over the hill.
   Schema 3.MX.P. I walked all over the hill.
   Schema 3.RO. There was a veil over her face.
   Schema 3.P.E.RO. Ice spread all over the windshield.
   Schema 3.MX.RO. There were flies all over the ceiling.
   Schema 3.MX.P.RO. The spider had crawled all over the ceiling.
Schema 4. Roll the log over.
   Schema 4.RFP. The fence fell over.
Schema 5. The bathtub overflowed.
Schema 6. Do it over.

Each schema is labeled for its salient properties. The label begins with a numeral: 1 for 'above and across', 2 for pure 'above', 3 for 'covering', 4 for 'curved trajectory', 5 for 'excess', and 6 for 'repetition'. Additional specifications vary along several dimensions: the *landmark* (LM, or reference object), may be horizontally (X) or vertically (V) extended. It may also be one dimensional (1DTR) or not. There may be contact (C) or noncontact (NC) between the landmark and the *trajector* (TR, or located object). The trajector may be multiplex (multiple entities or locations) or mass (a continuous medium). Various remaining distinctions are indicated: P indicates a connecting path, E indicates location at the end of a trajectory (*end-point focus*), and RO indicates a relation rotated from its normal orientation.

As with Brugman's original account, Lakoff's analysis claims that *over* occupies a semantically continuous range but possesses no centrally defining properties In addition, Lakoff (1987) and Brugman and Lakoff (1988) are careful to note idiosyncrasies in the data:

> One might suggest that instead of rotation from the vertical, there is simply a lack of specification of orientation. If there were, we would expect that the contact restrictions would be the same in all orientations. However, they are not. The rotated versions of the MX schemas – 3.MX and 3.MX.P – require contact, while the unrotated versions do not. Here are some typical examples that illustrate the distinction:
> *Superman flew all over downtown Metropolis.* (TR above LM, noncontact)
> **Superman flew all over the canyon walls.* (TR not above LM, noncontact)
> *Harry climbed all over the canyon walls.* (TR not above LM, contact)

Another idiosyncrasy appears with the 'endpoint focus' schemas 1.X.C.E and 1.VX.C.E. Lakoff (1987: 424) states:

> In these cases, *over* has the sense 'on the other side of' as a result of endpoint focus. However, *over* does not in general mean 'on the other side of'. For example, sentences like *Sam lives over the wall* and *Sam is standing over the door*, if they occur at all, cannot mean that he lives, or is sitting on the other side of the door and the wall. And a sentence like *Sam is sitting over the spot*, can only mean that he is sitting on it, not that he is sitting on the other side of it.

1.2. Criticisms of the Brugman-Lakoff analysis

The Brugman-Lakoff analysis is open to a variety of objections. Several points are critical:

(i) An imagistic semantic theory presupposes a rigorous theory of images; lacking such, semantic description becomes an informal exercise lacking in predictive power. This objection is particularly important since Brugman and Lakoff's discussion refers only generally to results from the relevant disciplines (e.g., psychology and neuropsychology).

(ii) Lexical network theory uses context-bound interpretations as the basic unit of analysis. This creates clear risks of misanalysis. For example, the sentence *John jumped over the wall* implies a curved trajectory. On what grounds is this fact attributed to the meaning of *over* rather than to common knowledge about walls or jumping? As Tyler and Evans (2003) argue, one must actually demonstrate the point, just as Kreitzer (1997) argues that one must demonstrate whether contact is lexically associated with the preposition or with general world knowledge as applied to particular scenes.

(iii) Family resemblance networks are extremely powerful descriptive devices: one simply notes the observed uses of the words and arranges them in an intuitively natural way. The skeptic might very well wonder how the Brugman-Lakoff analysis represents an advance over purely descriptive catalogues of semantic variation, such as Lindkvist's (1972) description of the semantics of *over*, *above* and *across*. This objection is particularly relevant since lexical network theory does not place clear constraints on the overall shape of a network; relations are locally defined over pairs of adjacent images.

Informed by such criticism of polysemy networks, Choi and Bowerman (1991) observe that some uses of the same path particles are probably unrelated and other uses only loosely related. If all that binds the various meanings together is loose similarity or weak overlap, it is by no means clear, what is actually to be gained by saying that they form a single category. Rosch (1978: 28-29) postulates that categories obey what she terms the *Principle of Economy*, according to which

> ... what one wishes to gain from one's categories is a great deal of information about the environment while conserving finite resources as much as possible.

It is far from obvious how it is informative to include such concepts as 'above and across' and 'covering' within a single category. This point has been developed further in the subsequent literature (cf. Sandra and Rice 1995), where the difficulty of delimiting fine-grained senses from one another raises issues concerning which of many possible network analyses is cognitively realistic.

It has been suggested that lexical networks can be modeled as connection-ist networks (Harris 1989; cf. Munro et al. 1991), but this is not necessarily a recommendation, since unrestricted neural networks can model virtually any phenomenon, whether or not the results provide a realistic model. For instance, in a study which employed connectionist models to simulate control of eye movements, Arnold and Robinson (1990: 825) concluded:

> ... in so many neural-network models the units in one, two, or all the lay-ers bear no resemblance to real neurons in the central nervous system. In many applications this is irrelevant; in others, there exists no data base of what real neurons do for comparison. In the vestibulo-ocular reflex, we have a relatively large data base. We know quite well what the input and output neurons do, and we know enough about the interneurons to know what they do not do. Thus, we are in the relatively unique position of, in-stead of admiring the incredible agility of such networks, rejecting them because they are too fanciful. These networks are amazingly imaginative and will find ingenious ways to get around one's constraints and discover unrealistic solutions.

This is not to disparage the value of connectionist simulation; there are very interesting connectionist studies of prepositional semantics, such as Regier (1992). Regier's study has shown that a properly constrained neural network can provide interesting accounts of key facts, such as the fact that preposi-tions frequently conflate location with goal but seldom conflate location with source. A critical property of Regier's study, however, is that his network incorporates known facts about the neural organization of spatial vision. The point, rather, is that unconstrained neural networks do not provide cognitive grounding.

And yet as Brugman and Lakoff take pains to point out, there may not be obvious places to draw the line between senses. If the [+vertical, -contact] uses form a lexical item, there would have to be a great divide between (1) (which is [-contact]) and (2) (which is +contact]). Similarly, iIf all the [+vertical] uses form a single lexical entry, there would have to be a funda-mental distinction between (3) (which is [+vertical]) and (4) (which is [-vertical]:

(1)   Mary jumped over the fence.
(2)   Mary climbed over the fence.
(3)   John wandered over the field.
(4)   The dot wandered over the screen.

The problem is that the uses of *over* vary continuously (if somewhat irregularly).

2.   Attempts to handle the challenge of *over*

This is the challenge of *over*: to develop a model which can account for the way in which *over* combines extreme polysemy with semantic continuity. We will consider the following analyses in detail: (i) the analysis of Jackendoff (1991: 72-74, 292-293), which illustrates the difficulties intendant upon a schematic analysis; and (ii) the analysis of Tyler and Evans (2001, 2003). These illustrate two poles: a relatively traditional formal analysis, and an alternative cognitive analysis. The issues which confront these analyses carry *over* through the intervening literature, including Cuyckens (1988), Vandeloise (1990), Sandra and Rice (1995), Kreitzer (1997) and Rice et al. (1998).

2.1. Jackendoff's analysis of *over*.

Jackendoff's (1991) analysis takes for granted the static, locative sense in (5):

(5)   The plane is now over the city.

In a footnote he suggests that *over* is unspecified with respect to contact. It thus appears that Jackendoff analyzes core *over* as the lexical conceptual structure (6), with OVER standing for the feature [+vertical]. Jackendoff accounts for other meanings of *over* by optionally embedding core *over* within various locative functions. These include (7), where OVER specifies goal rather than location. It also includes (8), where OVER specifies route rather than goal. And it includes so-called "end-point focus", i.e., location at the end of a route (cf. 9):

(6) $[_{place}$ OVER $[_{thing}]_j]$

(7) $[_{path}$ TO $[_{place}$ OVER $[_{thing}]_j]]$

(8) $[_{path}$ VIA $[_{place}$ OVER $[_{thing}]_j]]$

(9) $[_{place}$ AT-END-OF $([_{path}$ VIA $([_{place}$ OVER $([_{thing}]_j)])])$

Jackendoff abbreviates these into a single lexical entry using independently motivated conventions. Certain additional meanings fall out automatically. For instance, schema 3.MX.RO involves "distributive location", cf. Jackendoff (1991: 101-106).

Jackendoff's account entails that certain meanings are lexically distinct whereas others merely reflect pragmatic inferences. These consequences create serious difficulties. First, such an account is committed to the claim that (10) contains at least two lexically distinct senses of *over*. It must postulate a similar lexical distinction in (11). But where does one draw the line?

(10)   a.   Jane climbed over the fence.
       b.   Jane walked over the hill.
       c.   Jane walked over the field.
       d.   Jane glided over the field.
       e.   A shadow glided over the field.
       f.   A shadow glided over the screen.
       g.   A shape glided over the screen.

(11)   a.   Hold the tablecloth over the table.
       b.   Place the tablecloth over the table.
       c.   Drape the tablecloth over the table.
       d.   Drape the tablecloth over the chair.
       e.   Drape the tablecloth over the wall.

There is a second problem. Features like boundary traversal or surmounting are occasionally criterial. Consider (12):

(12)   a.   The truck is over the bridge. (AT-END-OF PATH VIA OVER)
       b.   The plane is over the house. (*AT-END-OF PATH VIA OVER)

As Brugman and Lakoff (1988) observe for examples like (12), end-point focus is only possible in (12a), where the landmark is construed as spatially extended. This restriction is entirely unexplained within Jackendoff's account. Thus the problem Jackendoff's account has greatest difficulty with is the general continuity among uses, a continuity which makes it difficult to draw the line between where one sense ends and the next begins.

2.2. The Tyler-Evans analysis of *over*

The Tyler-Evans (2001, 2003) analysis follows the most recent literature in rejecting the very high number of context-bound sentences of classical lexical network theory, assuming a limited number of lexical senses, and arguing that most of the variations in meaning modeled by lexical network theory are in fact not senses of the word at all, but context-specific interpretations derived by a combination of schema-filling and pragmatic inference.[1]

Thus, in particular, Tyler and Evans argue that the 'above and across' sense found in sentences like *The rabbit jumped over the wall* is entirely derived by inference from knowledge of the real world and the meanings of the other words in the sentence. Similarly, they argue that the contact/no-contact distinction drawn by Brugman and Lakoff is a matter not of the meaning of *over* but reflect differences in the construed scenes. In short, for Tyler and Evans a large portion of the Brugman-Lakoff network are subsumed under a single prototypical scene involving the idea that the trajectory is (a) higher than and (b) within the sphere of influence of the landmark. The picture they draw is one in which the core prototype covers almost the entire range of spatial uses, with distinct senses being separated out only where they cannot be handled by filling in details not specified by the central schema. Thus they distinguish the covering senses as a distinct sense (since the covering uses do not require that the trajectory be higher than the landmark), and they separate out the endpoint-focus and related traversal senses.

In other words, the basic unit of representation is a schema, filled in by contextual inference. Polysemy is a relationship between two independent schemas, related by inference and reanalysis. The core sense of *over* is one schema; its frequent cooccurrence with certain other schemas, such as movement along a path, or covering, is then adduced as motivation for the development of additional schemas. Because the schemas are cognitive schemas, and have image-schematic properties such as respecting topological and/or functional rather than metric similarity, this mode of analysis

---

1. Some historical historical connections are worth noting. An early version of the analysis presented here was pre-printed by the L.A.U.D. in 1992 but remained otherwise unpublished, as I left university shortly after to work in industry for several years. This early analysis of *over* (including he broader issues surrounding it) was presented around the same time at a seminar on cognitive semantics at the University of Florida, in which A. Tyler participated. However, A. Tyler's conclusions – particularly about the relationship between fully specified senses and the core lexical prototype – differ significantly from mine (see above) in that I (still) view most of the variations in interpretation to which the purely spatial uses of *over* are subject as consequences of the internal conceptual structure of the image schemas which define the prototypical scene.

buys quite a lot of flexibility. However, it has one property which is worth considering.

On this account, the connection between senses appears to be incidental, contingent upon inferential processes that remain relatively open and unspecified. For instance, the development of trajectory senses is contingent upon the fact that the preposition *over* is often used with verbs that specify a trajectory. The trajectory information is not part of the prototypical scene at all, yet because of its frequency with a subset of the word's uses, it motivates the development of a series of trajectory schemas (on-the-other-side-of, above-and-beyond, completion, transfer, temporal). Similarly, the development of covering senses is viewed as contingent upon the fact that covering often cooccurs with instances of *over*, particularly when the appearance of three-dimensional scenes from multiple viewpoints is taken into account.

It is certainly true that semantic change can operate in this fashion, but the implication is that the covering schema and the transfer schema are not connected to the core *over* schema in any intrinsic way. The relationship is exactly the reverse of classic prototype accounts: in a prototype account, the extensions keep parts, but not all, of the features associated with the prototype. In this account, the extensions share nothing with the prototype, and the connections are essentially historically driven by usage. It may be that this is the correct view, but I shall argue below that a more dynamic view is possible, a view which derives most of the range of interpretations possible for a preposition like *over* from its prototype.

In its basic spirit, in fact, Tyler and Evan's view of prepositional polysemy is not at all that different from the more formal schematic analysis proposed in Jackendoff (1991), and, like that analysis, it is vulnerable where the issue of sense continuity comes into play. For instance, there are uses which straddle the boundary between pure trajectory senses and the above-and-across sense, which Tyler and Evans argue is entirely derived by inference:

(13)   a.   The cat jumped over the hole.
        b.   The spark jumped over the gap.

It is hard to see how a schema which accounted for the meaning *over* has in (13b), where the core sense cannot apply, would fail to account for the meaning it has in (13a), where the core sense would apply. And if we postulate the presence of a trajectory in the latter case, why should it not be part of the conceptual representation for the former case? Similarly, compare (14a) and (14b):

(14)   a.   The wig is over his head.
       b.   The wig is over his face.

It is hard to see how the 'covering' schema which motivates (14b) would not also apply to (14a), to which the core schema clearly applies. Now, if the core sense of *over* and the covering schema are distinct word meanings, (14a) should be ambiguous; but the whole point of Tyler and Evan's account is that it is not, that the covering relationship derives from normal conceptual interpretation of the context. To keep the essence of Tyler and Evan's account in place, we have to posit multiple schemata which are simultaneously active without ambiguity. Once we allow this, though, the logic of the analysis appears to lead inexorably back toward something like the Brugman/Lakoff lexical network analysis, where the points in the network are locations within a lattice of overlapping schemas.

3.   Reformulating the problem

The semantic analysis of *over* must confront two distinct issues. (i) *Over* is prototypically spatial; its analysis thus presupposes a theory of spatial concepts. (ii) *Over* is highly polysemous; its analysis thus presupposes a theory of polysemy. These issues are linked, since meanings that seem similar in one representation may seem unrelated in another. In other words, the apparent polysemy of *over* and other spatial prepositions may reflect inadequate assumptions about the representation of spatial meaning.

Examination of the literature reveals the pervasive assumption that prepositions evoke a common-sense geometry: one less explicit than Euclidean geometry, but sharing many of its basic properties. The Brugman-Lakoff analysis, for example, postulates geometrically defined images. Jackendoff (1991) defines prepositions by geometric functions. Herskovits (1986) assumes idealized geometric meanings underlying actual use. Such authors as Bennett (1975), Leech (1974), and Wege (1991) define prepositions as bundles of geometric features. While ordinary geometric descriptions are intuitively natural and culturally salient, there are other ways to define spatial structure, such as the principle on which draftsman's sketches are based. A draftsman's sketch displays how a building will appear at standard angles of view. The resulting portfolio of sketches appears two-dimensional yet indicates three-dimensional structure precisely. Spatial position can also be indicated in terms of action potential. For example, an object touched without walking or turning must be close and to the front.

The literature also suggests that prepositions resist purely geometric analysis. Vandeloise (1991) claims that prepositions can be described in terms of: (i) localization; (ii) concepts of naive physics; (iii) potential encounter; (iv) general and lateral orientation. For the most part, these are functional not geometric concepts. For example, Vandeloise observes that there is a significant contrast between (15a) and (15b). (15a) displays the same geometric relation as (15b): what differs is the functional relation, the presence or absence of forceful containment.

(15)   a.   The thread is in the pliers.
       b.   *The thread is in the clothes-peg.

Similar points apply to Herskovits (1986). Although Herskovits postulates ideal geometric meanings, she is forced to ascribe a dominant role to extrageometrical factors, such as function, perspective, and topological structure. Such factors force Herskovits to postulate multiple "use types" for each geometric ideal.

Common-sense geometry is easily accessible to introspection, but this fact entails that it is a high-level construct, the product of complex preconscious computations. Moreover, spatial position is inferred from a variety of cues – visual, vestibular, auditory, and somesthetic; the process by which such inferences are computed is extraordinarily complex. We find neuropsychologists positing multiple spatial representations which vary in part with the modality and in part with the task; we find that information from the same sensory channel is divided among different parts of the brain; it appears, in short, that the apparent simplicity of common-sense geometry dissolves on closer inspection into internal complexity and multiplicity. If the meaning of prepositions depends in any way upon preconscious spatial thought, we would expect to find exactly the same paradox: apparent simplicity dissolving into extraordinary complexity on closer examination.

3.1. Spatial vs. visual imagery

One complexity arises from the role of sensory modality. The term *image* automatically suggests visual imagery, although auditory, olfactory, or kinesthetic images are also possible. But there are also *supramodal* images which define spatial relations without depending solely on visual perception. The distinction between visual and spatial images is well-supported (Farah et al. 1988); this conclusion is reinforced by the competence of blind individuals on spatial tasks (Landau and Gleitman 1985). Spatial imagery is obviously relevant even in the absence of visual information, since it is a prerequisite to formulating and carrying out motor plans. An immediate consequence is that the same spatial relation may receive distinct representations in multiple representational modalities.

3.2. Egocentric vs. allocentric representation of space

Another complexity lies in the brain's ability to localize objects either by reference to the external world (i.e., in *allocentric* terms), or egocentrically, in terms of their relation to the body. Different parts of the brain seem to be implicated in this difference. On the one hand, Stein (1991) argues that the posterior parietal cortex is the substrate for egocentric representation of space; on the other, the hippocampus is critical for one type of allocentric representation – *cognitive maps*, long-term memory for places and scenes and for their spatial arrangement across the landscape (cf. O'Keefe 1991; Thinus-Blanc et al. 1991). The distinction between egocentric and allocentric representation is a broad one, and authors posit a variety of more specific representations of spatial relations. For example, the brain apparently distinguishes between at least three types of egocentric space: *personal space*, the space occupied by the body; *peripersonal space*, that which is accessible to direct manipulation by the body; and *extrapersonal space*, more distant regions accessible by sight or hearing but not touch (cf. Stein 1991: 211; Duhamel, Colby and Goldberg 1991; Regan, Beverly and Cynader 1979).

3.3. Multiple reference frames.

While some languages encode spatial position in terms of absolute, or allocentric reference systems, it is clear that English prepositions are part of an egocentric system centered on the body. Both linguistic (e.g., Vandeloise 1991) and psychological studies (e.g., Bisiach et al. 1985) conclude that the primary reference frames for humans are tied (i) to the line of sight, (ii) to frontal vs. lateral orientation of the torso, as well as to the direction of (potential) movement or bodily interaction, and (iii) to true vertical as defined by gravity. It is thus important to allow for multiple reference frames. Such frames may reflect multiple modes of spatial thought, as suggested in Paillard (1991b: 472).

3.4. What vs. where systems

Another complexity is that the brain separates information about object identity from information about object position. Visual information for instance flows along two very different channels (Livingstone and Hubel 1988). One channel originates in the so-called *magnocellular* layers of the lateral geniculate body, an early visual center; the other channel, in the *parvocellular* layers. The parvocellular layers are very sensitive to color, position, and brightness and receive most of their input from the fovea, the eye's center of focus. They feed higher-level structures which classify shapes and identify objects, culminating in the cerebral cortex at the inferior temporal lobe. The magnocellular layers, by contrast, are much less sensitive to static features but are very sensitive to rapid visual changes at the edge as well as at the center of vision. They feed higher-level structures which detect movement and position in space, culminating in the cerebral cortex at the inferior parietal lobe – i.e., the lower part of the posterior parietal cortex. Ungerleider and Mishkin (1982) term these two channels the *what* and *where* systems. Jackendoff and Landau (1991) argue that the processing of prepositions is mediated by the inferior parietal cortex, the highest level of the *where* system. However, it should be noted that the two systems are not entirely separated; each does receive some inputs from the other.

3.5. Sensory vs. motor coding of spatial coordinates

Another complexity lies in the fact that the brain apparently uses a variety of coordinate systems. Only the vestibular system of the middle ear correlates directly with the vertical axis defined by gravity (Berthoz 1991). Otherwise, the brain primarily employs egocentric *sensory* and *motor* coordinates (Gilhodes et al. 1991; Paillard 1987, 1991a). One type of sensory coordinate involves a *retinotopic* system, such as the 2-1/2 D representation of Marr (1982) in which spatial location is defined by retinal position and depth information. Visual motor coordinates also exist; these are oculomotor coordinate systems based on movement of the eye muscles (cf. Goldberg et al. 1990). In such a system the motor commands for fixation of gaze are equivalent to a system of angular coordinates. There are a variety of motor coordinate systems, each of which defines an implicit egocentric space: a *haptic* space for hand movements, a *reach* space for arm movements, etc.

Motor spaces can be defined either by the actions needed to reach a location or by the actions possible there (Arbib 1991).

There is little evidence that the brain constructs a single abstract representation of three-dimensional space (Arbib 1991: 379; Stein 1991: 186-187). Instead, sensory and motor coordinates seem to be transformated into one another in ways which simulate higher-order representations. In particular, there is evidence that certain regions of the brain encode *sensory* information in *motor* coordinates (or *motor* information in *sensory* coordinates). Such hybrid representations stabilize perceived location by taking movement into account – or, conversely, they guide movement by taking sensory information into account. For example, parts of the inferior parietal lobe encode location of visual percepts by the *saccade*, or shift in eye position, necessary to place that item in focus (Anderson 1989). As the eye moves, saccade coordinates shift to take the altered perspective into account. The effect is a shift from *retinotopic* representation (which will shift every time the eye moves) to a more truly spatial representation – in this case, to a coordinate system defined in terms of the line of sight.

3.6. Spatial frequency; lateralization

Another complication is that specific brain regions are differentially sensitive to *spatial frequency* (Robertson and Lamb 1991: 307-310). As the spatial frequency of an image increases, its *resolution*, or capacity to distinguish similar images, increases. It appears that the brain tends to channel information at low spatial frequencies to the right hemisphere, reserving higher spatial frequencies for analysis by the left hemisphere of the brain. The brain appears, in other words, to "split" its representation of space into images that differ in resolution.

3.7. Multiple representations; converging cues

The literature on the neurology of vision (e.g., Livingstone and Hubel 1988; Zeki and Shipp 1988; Zeki 1992) emphasizes: (i) separation of different kinds of visual information into distinct representations; (ii) the idea that the brain employs multiple cues to identify spatial configurations. Usually the cues converge; but each can be interpreted singly. For example, there are multiple representations of shape: one representation depicts static form; the other depicts dynamic form, shape as reconstructed from patterns of movement (Zeki 1992). The resulting system is what Jackendoff (1983) terms a *preference rule system* – a prototype defined by the convergence of multiple cues. Even within a single representational modality, similar considerations arise. For example, Ullman (1990) proposes a model of object recognition employing collections of images representing the same object from different viewing angles.

3.8. Implications for the semantics of prepositions

Since most prepositions encode spatial relations (even if they also possess various metaphorical interpretations), we may reasonably assume that their meanings will be organized along lines compatible with the neuropsychological representation of space. Several consequences follow:

(i) The multiple images postulated in lexical network theory might represent not distinct lexical senses but different aspects of the same complex concept.

(ii) The semantic variability of prepositions might directly reflect the brain's redundant use of multiple cues.

(iii) The interleaving of visual and functional information discussed by Herskovits (1986) and Vandeloise (1991) might reflect the neurological interleaving of sensory and motor coordinates.

These considerations suggest a strategy: to define prepositions as clusters of sensorimotor representations. It is not appropriate to import a specific neuropsychological model, since the study of spatial cognition is still in its early stages, and the available models are quite primitive. However, the constraints imposed by neuropsychology provide a useful guide to develop more highly articulated and more readily testable theories of prepositional semantics.

The present article will pursue these goals, subject to various constraints. One constraint is that we shall be concerned primarily with the *motivation* and *derivation* of potential interpretations, as opposed to the problem of disambiguation among senses.2 Another constraint is that the analysis will

---

2. The analysis to be presented below implicitly supports a view of word sense disambiguation in which relevant aspects of word meaning are activated, and irrelevant ones are suppressed, through interaction and integration of lexical concepts with the surrounding context (cf. Hirst 1988 for a similar approach).

focus primarily on the preposition *over* and a selection of other English prepositions. Two considerations motivate this choice: (i) the exceptionally detailed information available with respect to the semantics of English prepositions generally and with respect to *over* in particular; (ii) the need to explore a limited test case in detail. A third constraint is that analysis will be limited to the spatial domain. While prepositions play an important role in spatial metaphor (Heine 1989; Heine, Claudi and Hünnemeyer 1991: 113-118, 123-147; Rubba 1992; Svorou 1986), extensive consideration of metaphoric senses would carry the discussion too far afield. A final constraint, primarily a consequence of space considerations, is that attention will be focused on the use of *over* as a preposition, and not on its uses as a particle or a prefix. An extensive discussion does not appear to be warranted, since except for a few outlying cases, the particle or prefix *over* and the preposition *over* display a similar range of meanings.

4.   Visual space: Spatial relations as image-complexes

4.1.   Indirect definition of spatial relationships.

Consider sentence (16). In geometric terms, (i) the balloon is higher than the table; (ii) the balloon is placed on a vertical line extending upwards from the table. But the same information can be captured by a set of image-schemas, which we can express as in (17):

(16)   The balloon is over the table.

(17)   a.   From the side: the trajector is separated from the landmark by a
                vertical gap.
         b.   From above: the trajector occludes the landmark.

By itself, (17) is compatible with a variety of three-dimensional relationships. But (17a) and (17b) combined specifies precisely the three-dimensional relationship in which the preposition *over* is appropriate. Note that while (17a) and (17b) could be characterized as features rather than images, they carry specifically visual information, making use of concepts like occlusion and visual separation; and their relation to one another requires use of the concept of visual point-of-view. Such images are essentially 2 1/2 D representations in the sense of Marr (1982), involving what Livingstone and Hubel (1988: 746) label *depth cues* and attribute to the *where*, or magnocellular system.

Much of the literature on mental images is precisely on this kind of image (cf. Block 1981; Gibson 1979; Kosslyn 1980; Talmy 1983; Osherson, Kosslyn and Hollerbach 1990). Drawing on this literature, we may note that spatial images implicitly include a distinction between *figures* (elements which must be located) and a background *field* (the space in which elements are located). To define an image, we must specify (i) what properties the figure(s) possess; (ii) what properties the field possesses; (iii) how the figure(s) relate to the field; (iv) how figures in the field relate to one another; (v) image transformations, that is, what relations may hold among different images which describe the same scene. In the case of 2 1/2 D images, the follwing operating assumptions seem reasonable:

(18)   (a)   The coordinate system is *gaze-based*: up and down, left and right are relative to the line of gaze, as is apparent depth.

(b)   Images differ by *resolution* – how fine-grained they are, rather than by some absolute notion of perspective or distance from the object of gaze.

(c)   Important features of images include *occlusion* – whether or not one entity blocks the visibility of another.

(d)   Object-centered information is represented by multiple images which indicate how the object appears from different *viewpoints*, such as from above or from the side.

Certain aspects of this merit discussion. First, there is every reason to believe in the accuracy of the coordinate system used. Experimental research on the neurology of human and primate visual perception (e.g., Anderson 1989; Anderson and Mountcastle 1982; Anderson et al. 1985; O'Reilly et al. 1990; Zipser and Anderson 1988) has shown that visual neurons are responsive to line of gaze, perceived depth, and viewpoint orientation as far up as the posterior parietal cortex, where they function to compensate for shifts in eye and head position. There is a basic difference between the gaze coordinates (which strictly speaking specify stimulus position on the retina) and the depth and viewpoint orientation coordinates (which provide egocentric coordinates in 3D space). One of the functions of 2 1/2 D images is precisely to coordinate the two kinds of information.

Second, according to Livingstone and Hubel (1988), the *where* system is insensitive to details of form; this concurs with Jackendoff and Landau's (1991) observations concerning the minimal shape specifications of prepositions. (18) builds these limitations into its definition of images. In addition, relations among figures are limited to relative orientation and the visual relations of overlap, contact, and separation.

Third, many of the most important cues for depth perception are dependent upon a comparison of distinct images of the same object, such as *disparity* and *optical flow*. Other cues, such as perspective, can be recovered from a single image but require detailed information about apparent shape – information which we have assumed, on the basis of neurological evidence, not to be available to the system of images under consideration. A clear implication emerges: to the extent that depth perception depends upon disparity and optical flow, it has to operate on pairs or larger collections of images which represent different views of the same object. Such images would require an object-centered field; thus we will assume that object-centered fields contain at least two images.

The key to the system, then, is that it allows images to be bound together as alternative representations of the same three-dimensional scene. Relations among images are based on image transformations which shift either the angle of view or the resolution. Here, as with the use of gaze coordinates and viewpoint orientation, the system is functionally motivated: the brain must automatically compensate for predictable changes in order to stabilize an image and achieve true 3D representation of space. It is important, for example, to recognize that a scene viewed from above is identical to the same scene viewed from the side, or to recognize a blurred image as representing the same scene previously viewed in close detail. In other words, the mind must form spatial categories transcending angle of gaze and point of view; according to the present proposal, it does so by directly storing key images and their transformational relationships.

Finally, note that the current system is adequate only for describing static spatial relations. It is thus but one of several representational modes, a fragment of a complete description, whose strength lies in its representation of depth information.

4.2. An application: *on, over, above.*

With these provisos, let us apply the framework to *over* and the two closely contrasting prepositions *above* and *on*. The static interpretation of *over* minimally presupposes the pair of image-scehmas, (17a) and (17b), which together constrain *over* to be used in situations where the trajector is directly above the landmark. By contrast, we can define *above* in its prototypical geometric sense as involving only the vertical separation image, (17a). That is, the obvious difference between static *over* and prototypical *above* is the horizontal position of the trajector. (19) illustrates this contrast:

(19)   a.   The balloon is over the table.
      b.   The balloon is above the table.

(19a) will be true only if the balloon is placed on a vertical line which intersects the table – a fact captured in the present framework by the fact that the trajector occludes the landmark in the second, vertically oriented image. By contrast, (19b) will be true as long as the balloon is higher than and separated from the table.

However, according to one of the operating assumptions set forth above, there are no isolated images in an object-centered field, since two images are necessary to indicate stereoscopic depth. The most likely source of a second image would be a shift in resolution, since the *above* relation always involves vertical separation. We thus define *above* in terms of the following pair of image-schemas:

(20)   a.   From the side at high resolution: the trajector is separated from
          the landmark by a vertical gap.
      b.   From the side at low resolution: the trajector is separated from the
          landmark by a vertical gap.

That is, the gap between trajector and landmark remains visible at low resolution. Notice the effect of adding the second image: we have a representation which carries information about perceived distance. What (20) represents as the meaning of *above* is a physical situation in which the trajector and landmark are separated by a large enough visual angle that the gap is still visible at a distance.

It should be noted at this point that the "vertical" position of the trajector in (20) is an egocentric vertical defined by the observer's body. It is therefore relative, not absolute, susceptible to shifts in viewpoint. Thus, the headboard of a bed may correctly be described as being *above* its occupant's head. Of course in the absence of specific contextual cues to the contrary there is a strong presumption that the observer's body is in its normal vertical stance.

Consider next the English preposition *on*. *On* would be represented (at least in part) by the image-complex (21):

(21)   a.   From the side: the trajector is not separated from the landmark by
          any gap.
      b.   From the top: the trajector partially occludes the landmark.

In other words, if we represent prototypical *on* and static *over* using visual images, the two words differ only in one particular: the presence of contact rather than separation on a horizontal view. Matters are not quite so simple, however. The difference between contact and separation depends critically on resolution. Suppose, for example, that a balloon is placed a few inches over a table. If the scene is viewed up close, the separation will be clear. On the other hand, if we view the same scene from a distance, the balloon will seem to be in contact with the table. That is, to be accurate, we should represent high- and low-resolution versions of both views, and the difference between the prototypical uses of *over* and *on* is that there is a gap at high resolution (but not at a lower resolution consistent with viewing the scene at a distance.) Thus the image complex for *over* would be (22):

(22)   a.   From the side at high resolution: the trajector is separated from the landmark by a vertical gap.
       b.   From the side at low resolution: the trajector is not separated from the landmark by a gap.
       c.   From the top: the trajector partially occludes the landmark.

(22) has advantages we have not yet discussed. In many of its uses, *over* carries the implication that trajector and landmark are relatively close. (22) guarantees this result, for if the trajector is too high above the landmark, the gap will remain visible even at low resolution. This fact accounts for the significant contrast between *over* and *above* in (23):

(23)   a.   The helicopter is over the city.
       b.   The helicopter is above the city.

(23a) and (23b) imply that the city and the helicopter are separated, respectively, by a small or a large visual angle. This contrast is directly explained by the contrast between (20) and (22): a large separation will still be visible at low resolution; a small one will not.

We should also consider what happens when resolution changes for the vertically oriented image. Decreased resolution is equivalent to loss of focus, which entails fuzziness and a loss of depth perception. Thus the occlusion boundary – the line at which the trajector interrupts perception of the landmark – should be hard to localize precisely. If the resolution is less than the distance between the occlusion boundary and the landmark boundary, the two will be assigned the same coordinates. The second consequence is that the depth contrast between trajector and landmark will be reduced, perhaps even to zero. Thus, the net effect of a loss of resolution is an image in which the trajector appears to cover the landmark. This is a striking result, since 'covering' is a meaning whose motivation has thus far been unclear.

The image-complex (24) results. (24) is a category specified by its perceptual correlates. It describes a scene in which the trajector is comparable in size to the landmark and is just above it. Thus, if (24) is taken as a set of necessary-and-sufficient features, it is too restrictive, though it exactly specifies the prototypical visual scene for *over*.

(24)   a.   From the side at high resolution: the trajector is separated from the landmark by a vertical gap.
       b.   From the side at low resolution: the trajector is not separated from the landmark by a gap.
       c.   From the top at high resolution: the trajector partially occludes the landmark.
       d.   From the top at low resolution: the trajector occludes the landmark entirely.

However, as discussed in section 2, the brain employs multiple cues, or a preference rule system, to infer higher-level representations. Let us therefore make the following assumptions:

(i)   *Preference rule principle.* A variant construal may be formed by combining a subset of images from the prototype.
(ii)   *Stereoscopic Principle.* Representations employing object-centered fields are stereoscopic images, and must therefore consist of at least two images which represent the same scene but differ in the coordinates or resolution from which they view the scene.
(ii)   *Distinctiveness Principle.* If an image or an image-complex is part of the prototype for a preposition, it cannot be used as a semantic variant of another preposition.

The first constraint is simply the definition of a preference rule system; the second, a modality-specific representational constraint; the third instantiates the principle of paradigmatic opposition. These principles predict a range of uses (technically, instances, not linguistically distinct senses) for static *over*.

There are four combinations employing three of the four images in the prototype. The first is (25):

(25)   a.   From the side: the trajector is not separated from the landmark by a gap.
       c.   From the top at high resolution: the trajector partially occludes the landmark.

    d.   From the top at low resolution: the trajector occludes the landmark entirely.

(25) differs from the prototype by the elimination of the image that *over* shares with *above*. Loss of this image eliminates the contrast between separation at high resolution and apparent contact at low resolution, yielding an interpretation very close in meaning to *on*. However, the remaining images specify that the trajector must virtually cover the landmark. This meaning could be instantiated either by placing one object on top of a slightly larger object, or by spreading a collection of objects across the upper surface of the landmark. In either case, shifting to low resolution will create the appearance of covering:

(26)   a.   Put the little block over that big block.
           b.   There are crumbs scattered over the table.

In (26)a, low resolution blurs the region between the edges of trajector and landmark. In (26b), low resolution blurs the boundaries among the multiple elements of the trajector, thus also motivating instances like (27). Another possible variant is (28):

(27)   a.   There is a funny pattern that goes over most of the rug.
           b.   As I looked down, I saw enemy squadrons scattered over the city.

(28)   a.   From the side at high resolution: the trajector is separated from the landmark by a vertical gap.
           b.   From the side at low resolution: the trajector is not separated from the landmark by a gap.
           d.   From the top: the trajector occludes the landmark entirely.

(28) reduces the top-view to an image of covering. The result is that (28) licenses any use of *over* in which there is covering plus a vertical gap, motivating uses like (29), or else (30):

(29)   a.   The roof is over my head.
           b.   There is an awning over the sidewalk.

(30)   a.   From the side: the trajector is separated from the landmark by a vertical gap.
           c.   From the top at high resolution: the trajector partially occludes the landmark.
           d.   From the top at low resolution: the trajector occludes the landmark entirely.

(30) eliminates the requirement that the trajector be relatively close to the landmark; it maintains, however, the requirement that the trajector occlude and virtually cover the landmark when viewed from above. (30) thus allows uses like (31):

(31)   a.   There were clouds over the desert.
        b.   There is a satellite over London now.

The last possibility which maintains three of the four images is (32):

(32)   a.   From the side at high resolution: the trajector is separated from the landmark by a vertical gap.
        b.   From the side at low resolution: the trajector is not separated from the landmark by a gap.
        c.   From the top at high resolution: the trajector partially occludes the landmark.

(32) abandons virtual covering as a requirement; it thus allows for major size discrepancies while still requiring closeness of trajector and landmark. It thus motivates uses like (33):

(33)   a.   The lamp is hanging over the table.
        b.   The fly is hovering over the floor.

In principle, variants employing fewer images would expand the word's range considerably. However, the Distinctiveness Principle eliminates some possibilities. Recall that (21) was the representation for *on*. It is thus not a possible variant of *over*.

However, other pairings are possible, including (34), which requires that the trajector appear to touch – and cover– the landmark at all resolutions, entailing actual contact and actual covering, as in (35).

(34)   b.   From the side: the trajector is not separated from the landmark by a gap.
        d.   From the top: the trajector occludes the landmark entirely.

(35)   a.   He had a cloak over his shoulders.
        b.   There is a tablecloth over the table.

Another possibility is (36):

(36)   a.   At high resolution: the trajector is separated from the landmark by a vertical gap.
        b.   At low resolution: the trajector is not separated from the landmark by a gap.

(36) retains the requirements of superiority and relative closeness, but drops the requirement that the trajector be directly above the landmark. (36) thus motivates uses like (37); particularly interesting is (37c), where the massiveness of the mountains entails that one is very close to them on the visual scale that they imply:

(37) a. She sat for a long time over the breakfast table.
      b. He stood over the prisoner.
      c. The mountains loomed over us.

The last two-image possibility is (38):

(38) a. From the side: the trajector is separated from the landmark by a vertical gap.
      b. From the top: the trajector partially occludes the landmark.

This set of images simply extends the interpretation in which *over* means 'directly above' indefinitely upward vertically, allowing cases like (39):

(39)   There was a bird hovering half a mile over his head.

At this point we have accounted for the static, locational uses of the preposition *over*. In terms of the Brugman-Lakoff analysis, we have accounted for schema 2 (the 'above' interpretation of *over*) and the static nonrotated versions of schema 3 (the 'covering' interpretations 3 and 3.MX). The analysis also appears to yield appropriate results for *above* and *on*. Within the visual image system *on* and *above* are minimal categories defined by a pair of images. The analysis therefore predicts that their polysemy derives from other components of their meaning. This is a reasonable prediction; it directly reflects the clear intuition speakers of English seem to have that *over* is semantically more complex than *on* and *above*. The remaining meanings of *above*, *on* and *over* involve dynamic elements: movement along a path, location of a path, position at the end of a path, rotation of the coordinate system. To deal with these concepts, we must shift our attention from visual images to images which represent orientation and movement.

5. The representation of action and force dynamics: Kinetic space

What I will describe below as kinetic space is inspired in part by Talmy's (1985) theory of *force dynamics* and in part by the concepts of dynamically defined spaces and vector fields discussed in Arbib (1991). The focus is on movements, paths, and forces interacting in space. Kinetic space may be defined as follows:

(40) (a)   Coordinates are defined with respect to a reference entity *ego* in three-dimensional space where 'up'/'down' is defined by gravity and 'forward'/'back' and 'left'/'right' by the orientation of *ego*.

    (b)   Ego is located on the *locomotor surface* of the *base*, e.g., the surface of the earth, though other objects can be substituted if the usual physical circumstances do not apply.

    (c)   Objects, including ego, have an *impetus*, a potential direction of motion, with a resultant *path* of motion. The potential interactions of an object with other objects are defined in terms of combinations of impetus, resisting forces, and resultant paths.

By moving from a visual representation of three-dimensional space to a kinetic one, we perforce move to a completely different way of representing three-dimensional relationships: one in which the relevant images reflect paths of motion or force and their resultant states. In the case of the three-dimensional prototype for *over*, three image-sequences or potential force-dynamic interactions are critical:

(41) *First Kinetic Image Sequence*:

    (a)   The landmark forms part of the base, where it functions as a boundary on the locomotor surface. The trajector is in open space, has force-dynamic impetus parallel to the base, and is on one side of the landmark relative to the locomotor surface.

    (b)   Resultant state: the trajector is on the far side of the landmark from its initial position.

(42) *Second Kinetic Image Sequence*:

    (a)   The landmark forms part of the base, where it functions as a barrier for movement over the locomotor surface. The trajector is in locomotor space and has force-dynamic impetus which carries it to a location higher than the landmark.

    (b)   Resultant state: the trajector is higher than the landmark.

(43) *Third Kinetic Image Sequence*:

    (a)   The trajector has force-dynamic impetus downward toward the landmark.

    (b)   Resultant state: the trajector exerts force upon the landmark.

Note that if we assume prototypical alignment between images, such that visual vertical aligns with the gravitational vertical, visual occlusion and vertical separation entail the same three dimensional relationship as (41) through (43), which naturally apply to the prototypical three-dimensional scene in which a trajector must first get over the landmark, then pass over it (or else fall and strike against it.)

(41) provides a direct account for cases with boundary-traversal or end-point focus, as in Brugman (1988):

(44) a. *Schema 1.X.C.* Sam drove over the bridge.
      b. *Schema 1.VX.C.* Sam walked over the hill.
      c. *Schema 1.V.C.* Sam climbed over the wall.
      d. *Schema 1.VX.C.E.* Sam lives over the hill.
      e. *Schema 1.X.C.E.* Sausalito is over the bridge.

What is critical to note is that the constraints on this set of uses follow directly from their being defined in kinetic space rather than visual space and thus making use of concepts like the base, the locomotor surface, and force-dynamic interaction. That is, most of the gaps in usage for these can be explained by the requirement that the landmark (a) be part of the base, and (b) be construed as a boundary or barrier for force-dynamic interaction. That is, while *over* is generally licensed for abstract nouns like *border* and *boundary*, cf. (45)-(46) and (47b), it is less applicable to concrete nouns, cf. the absence of endpoint focus in (48)-(49).

(45) a. We drove over the border.
      b. We walked over the boundary.

(46) a. They live over the border in Georgia.
      b. Sausalito is (just) over the boundary.

(47) a. Flight 101 has just passed over the Korean border.
      b. You can't shoot at those jets – they're already over the border.

(48)   Tibet is to be found over the Himalayas.

(49) a. *Sam lives over the wall.
      b. *Sam is hovering over the rock.
      c. *John is over the chess board

Note further that nouns like *threshold* and *cliff* denote boundaries. We thus predict endpoint focus interpretations:

(50) a. Sam stepped over the threshold.
      b. Sam is standing just over the threshold.

(51) a. The train hurtled over the (edge of the) cliff.
      b. The train is over the (edge of the) cliff, about a hundred feet down.

On the other hand, nouns like *turnstile* or *gate* do not denote part of the base and so do not readily obtain endpoint focus interpretations:

(52)   a.   Sam stepped over the turnstile.
       b.   *Sam is standing just over the turnstile.

(53)   a.   Sam stepped over the gate.
       b.   *Sam is standing just over the gate.

Brugman and Lakoff (1988) argue that sentences such as (54) lack an endpoint focus construal. It is true that they are incompatible with purely subjective motion. But note (55):

(54)   a.   Sam climbed over the wall.
       b.   *Sam lives over the wall.

(55)   They're over the wall!

(55) has all the earmarks of an endpoint focus use: it describes position at the end of a path and it is related to another interpretation which describes motion along the same path. But the implied status and orientation of the landmark are different. Sentences like (55) are appropriate when the landmark is construed as a barrier; the trajector proceeds up the barrier and ultimately surpasses it. That is, a different kinetic-space image is required, that of (42), where the landmark is viewed as a barrier and the trajector's motion is viewed as taking it higher than the landmark rather than across it. For instance, (55) would be entirely appropriate to describe balloonists whose balloons have finally cleared the top of a wall; likewise (56):

(56)   a.   The river is over its banks.
       b.   In a final growth spurt, he shot up over all his classmates.

Finally, note examples like (57) which instantiate a locus-of-impact construction:

(57)   They hit me over the head.

(58)   a.   They kissed each other on the cheek.
       b.   I grabbed the bike by the handlebars.
       c.   They hit me on the head.

Certain metaphorical senses of *over* also exploit the idea of potential impact from above, as in the phrase *their power over me*.

   An important point to note is that these kinetic-space interpretations of *over* potentially combine all three kinetic images: there is nothing to prevent all three force-dynamic interactions from happening in a single event of passing over an object.

(59)   The elephant climbed over the wall, knocking it down, and continued on its way.

We end up with a kinetic-space representation which, while motivated by polysemy, is an accurate force-dynamic description of prototypical *over*. Horizontal movement proceeds over the base and hence over the boundary defined by a landmark on the base. If the landmark is a barrier, one must raise oneself at least as high as the object's upper surface to get over it. And if one is over an object, downward movement leads to impact upon it.

6. Representing space in motor coordinates: Maneuver space

Neuropsychological theories of motor control postulate multiple systems of motor coordinates. For example, a distinction is made (cf. Arbib 1991: 383-386; Jeannerod 1991) between *haptic space* (the space of hand movements) and *reach space* (the space of arm movements.) Grasping and reaching involve very different coordinate systems. Grasp space is an allocentric system: it coordinates delicate wrist, palm and finger movements whose configurations must match the shape of the object to be grasped. Reach space, by contrast, is egocentric: it defines an object's position by the arm movements necessary to bring the hand within grasping distance. This distinction between reach space and haptic space is far more specific than will actually be required to analyze the semantics of prepositions, but it illustrates two very different ways in which motor information defines spatial relationships. The kinds of force-dynamic interactions described in the previous section form one such system of representation, an egocentric one. In the section which follows additional uses of *over* will be accounted for by postulating *maneuver space*: an allocentric system used for close-range coordination of spatial position and orientation.

Maneuver space is defined by the fact that every object places limits on the movement of nearby objects, limits defined by its size and shape. In other words, every object functions as the reference element, or *ground*, for a maneuver space, which we may think of as that object's field of influence. The chief concerns in maneuver space are distance, relative orientation, and the consequences of manipulation. The basic concern for this type of manipulation-based image system is whether there is *clearance*, the open space from a point within the edge of a figure to the nearest point on the ground. An object's position may therefore be defined by systematically mapping its clearance under different manipulations, such as rotation, motion toward the ground, or motion parallel to the ground.

Consider for the moment the rotated covering uses of the word *over*:

(60)   a.   I put my hand over my face.
       b.   I hung drapes over the walls.
       c.   There is a screen over the window.

These uses of *over* can be motivated from the visual representation, by assuming a point of view in which visual vertical is not aligned with the vertical of gravity. Yet such an account does not fully explain the properties of these uses. Why, in particular, is the covering meaning *necessary when* we abandon a normal spatial vertical? In (60a), for example, the hand must be aligned parallel to the face, maximizing occlusion, and must be quite close to the face, consistent with a covering interpretation; none of the other combinations of visual image schemas work. Moreover, there is no obvious reason – in purely visual terms – why we should assume a visual vertical perpendicular to the surface of the face.

On the other hand, if we think in terms of maneuver-space images, an object-centered, or allocentric, coordinate system falls out automatically. Near the surface of an object, we can define a local vertical perpendicular to that surface, and calculate another object's clearance and orientation relative to that surface. The association between *over* and covering turns out to be natural in such a coordinate system. *Over* and *above* thus contrast in a context with a rotated vertical, such as (61):

(61)   a.   I held my hand above the dot on the wall.
       b.   I held my hand over the dot on the wall.

The difference between *over* and *above* is parallel to the difference in other contexts – *over* implies a closer relationship than *above* – but in maneuver-space terms, the difference is that in (61b), the trajector has to be close enough to the landmark that there isn't any clearance to spare; any rotation of the trajector, or movement of the trajector towards the landmark, will reduce clearance to zero. Similarly with the contrast between *over* and *on*:

(62)   a.   My hand is on the dot on the wall.
       b.   My hand is over the dot on the wall.

In (62a), *on* requires actual contact – in maneuver-space terms, zero clearance, whereas (62b) implies clearance while allowing the possibility of contact. These contrasts suggest the following maneuver-space image complex for *over*:

(63) a. Initial position: there is clearance between the trajector and the landmark, with the trajector oriented parallel to the ground.
  b. Image after vertical displacement: zero clearance.
  c. Image after horizontal displacement: no change in clearance.
  d. Image after rotation: zero clearance.

Very different (and much simpler) image-complexes would be postulated for *on* and *above*. For *on* the maneuver-space image complex would be:

(64) a. Initial position: there is zero clearance between the trajector and the landmark, with the trajector oriented parallel to the ground.
  b. Image after rotation: zero clearance.

For *above* the maneuver-space image complex would be:

(65) a. Initial position: there is significant clearance between the trajector and the landmark, with the trajector oriented parallel to the ground.
  b. Image after rotation: there is still significant clearance.

That is, *on* requires contact in maneuver space, regardless of orientation, while *above* requires the lack of contact – clearance – regardless of orientation. *Over* contrasts with both, occupying an intermediate position where clearance may be present but is not guaranteed if the orientation or position of the trajector changes.

  This interpretation is reinforced if we consider differences in the compatibility of *above* and *over* with verbs of motion when a local object provides an object-centered frame of reference. First, consider *above*:

(66) a. His finger rose (high) above the dot on the wall.
  b. His finger drifted above the dot on the wall.
  c. #His finger dropped above the dot on the wall.

That is, *above* is not compatible with a loss of clearance, whereas *over* prefers it:

(67) a. #His finger rose (high) over the dot on the wall.
  b. His finger drifted over the dot on the wall.
  c. His finger dropped over the dot on the wall.

If we adopt the strategy we have before, of assuming a preference-rule system, with combinations of images forming possible interpretations, unless they intersect with the prototype for another word, we get interesting predictions. *Above* occupies the prototype where the trajector and landmark have significant clearance from the landmark; *on* occupies the prototype where the trajector and landmark are necessarily in contact. The range of interpretations possible for *over* is constrained by that fact. Let us quickly consider the possible interpretations. We cannot isolate (63a), (63b) or (63c) from the image-complex, because they are part of the prototypes for *above* and *on*. Similarly, (63c) is arguably part of the maneuver-space prototype for *across*. The combination of (63a) plus (63b) – movement toward contact – is arguably part of the prototype for *onto*. Other combinations which do not necessarily imply covering are possible, however. For instance, *over* can describe a scene in which (63a) and (63b) hold true without covering:

(68)   He waved the pencil over the dot on the wall.

Or we can isolate (63b), (63c) and (63d), which entail movement with contact, as in (69):

(69)   He slid the pencil over the wall.

Or we can isolate (63b), and (63c), allowing two-dimensional images like (70):

(70)   The dot moved over the wall from left to right.

In short, when we create a scene which requires a maneuver-space image, the image-complex (63) allows a range of meanings in which covering is prominent but not strictly necessary, but in which covering falls out naturally from the contrast between *over* and related prepositions.

6.1. Further complications: Landmark as ground versus contextual ground

One point we have not focused upon thus far is the relationship between the landmark (as required by the preposition) and the ground (which provides the frame of reference in maneuver space). In the simple cases they are one and the same thing:

(71)   a.   I held my hand over the wall (and felt the heat radiating from it.)
         b.   I waved my hand over the wall.

(72)   A tapestry is hanging over the wall.

But the interpretation of landmark as ground appears to be a matter of contextual interpretation, and not part of the image-complex which defines *over* in maneuver space. For example, we may say:

(73) a.   I put my hand over the pimple.
      b.   I hung a drape over the hole.
      c.   There is a screen over the decal.

The acceptability of (73) depends upon the presence of a contextually defined ground. I.e., pimples are oriented relative to the skin, holes are oriented relative to the surface they interrupt, and a decal, when attached (as 79c implies), is oriented to the ground it adjoins.

The landmark need not be part of the ground if it is otherwise oriented in maneuver space:

(74)   I held my hand over a penny.

While (74) would normally be oriented with respect to the Earth, other orientations are possible. Consider the following situation: There is a wall on the right. The speaker holds the penny a quarter inch to the left of the wall. At the same time, the speaker's other hand is held a quarter inch to the left of the penny. In this situation, one can truthfully assert (74), since the wall provides a suitable ground.

Close examination reveals that (74) is ambiguous between two maneuver space interpretations: one in which the penny is the ground, and another in which the ground is contextually supplied. Consider the following situation:

(75)   The penny is held in midair a quarter inch to the left of the hand. The palm of the hand is parallel to the surface of the penny.

In (75), the hand is over the penny. But a rotation of the penny changes the situation. In (76), the hand is not 'over' the penny:

(76)   The penny is held in midair a quarter inch to the left of the hand with its edge pointing toward the palm of the hand.

However, if hand and penny are next to a wall, the situation changes again. In (77), the hand clearly is over the penny.

(77)   The penny is held a quarter inch to the left of the hand, with its edge pointing toward the palm of the hand. The penny itself is a quarter inch to the right of a wall.

In (77), *over* is acceptable because the wall provides an alternate ground. Notice, however, that the wall and the penny behave differently with respect to contact. If the penny provides the ground, contact is impossible. Thus, *over* does not apply to (78):

(78)   The penny is held in midair parallel to the palm, which directly touches it.

When the ground is contextually supplied, contact is possible; thus, *over* applies to (79):

(79)   The penny is held with one edge touching the wall; the palm of the hand touches the other edge.

6.2. A note on combinations of images from different modalities

Nothing in the discussion precludes the possibility of having uses of the prepositions motivated by images from multiple modalities at the same time, and one in fact expects that they will normally cooccur. Note, however, that there is a principle of egocentric alignment involved: to use kinetic space images with visual images, for instance, one must align visual vertical with gravity vertical; to use the maneuver space images with kinetic images, the base in kinetic space must be equated with the ground in maneuver space, and so forth. These are the prototypical correspondences among modalities in any case. But it is worth noting cases in which the combinations of these images account for particular shades of meaning. For instance, (80) is the prototypical combination of kinetic space vertical (defined by gravity) with maneuver-space images, whereas (81) is a pure maneuver-space equivalent.

(80)   He found an an old rug lying over the bare concrete floor.
(81)   He found old drapes hanging over the bare cinder block walls.

If we keep the kinetic images entailing motion of the trajector, over describes directional covering of the entire ground (82). It too has a rotated variant (83):

(82)   The spilled milk spread over the rug.
(83)   The spilled milk spread over the wall.

Another variant describes static covering of an entity on the ground; (84a) is the version which is oriented in kinetic space; (84b) is the rotated, maneuver space version:

(84)   a.   I put my foot over the burn mark in the rug.
        b.   I put my hand over the telltale mark on the wall.

A final variant describes directional covering of an entity on the ground; like the preceding versions, it can be oriented either in visual space or in maneuver space:

(85) a. I passed my foot over the burn mark in the carpet.
      b. I passed my hand over the telltale mark on the wall.

This kind of pattern – where similar spatial relationships can be normally oriented, or oriented in one of the specific modalities – accounts for a large range of the possible variations in usage. Interactions among the modalities accounts for other peculiarities in usage. In particular, note the contrast between (86) and (87):

(86) a. There are flies all over the ceiling.
      b. Superman crawled all over the walls of the canyon.

(87) a. *There are flies hovering all over the ceiling.
      b. *Superman flew all over the walls of the canyon.

Brugman and Lakoff use a gap like this to motivate a network account in which individual uses have to be represented as distinct (but connected) nodes. Another explanation is possible given our analysis in terms of images in multiple modalities. The multiplex-to-mass transformation requires us to represent *over* in (86) as involving occlusion at high resolution (because the gaps among the multiple trajectors are visible) but as involving covering at low resolution (because the multiple trajectors have blurred into a single mass). The fact that (86) and (87) evoke rotated 'covering' interpretations means that they involve maneuver space representations where the trajector is represented as being parallel to the landmark and close enough to it that vertical displacement or rotation are likely to yield contact.

Up to this point, everything has worked out normally. (86) and (87) are special, however, because they make use of a visual image-transformation, namely, the ability to view a collection of distinct entities or positions at low resolution and thus to blur them into a single, indistinct mass. This transformation allows the situations described in (86) and (87) to be perceived as involving covering – but only in visual space. In maneuver space, the multiplex-to-mass transformation is not obviously well-defined; it is an essentially visual relationship. Thus, if (86) and (87) are to work, the maneuver-space images must apply correctly to each individual element in the group trajector.

The relevant images are those which require that the trajector be positioned where it will (a) touch the ground after a minimal vertical displacement and (b) touch the ground after rotation. If each individual trajector touches the landmark, these conditions are met automatically. By contrast, these conditions are pragmatically very difficult to meet in sentences like (87). In (87a), the difference between contact and potential contact after rotation is a matter of millimeters; each fly must therefore be hovering millimeters from the ceiling without ever flying further away. Similarly, in (87b), Superman must be close enough to the canyon wall that any rotation of his body would cause him to touch it: a matter of inches. And this position must be maintained throughout his path if *over* is to apply to the entire trajectory (which it must for the multiplex-to-mass tranformation to apply). But the verb *flying* does not suggest that kind of motion; flying is movement through three dimensional space not movement with continuous near-contact.

These considerations suggest that sentences like (87) are unacceptable only for pragmatic reasons. This analysis is confirmed when we consider sentences like (88):

(88) a. There are balloons drifting about all over the ceiling.
      b. Superman skimmed about over the walls of the canyon, looking for veins of kryptonite.

A similar sort of point can be made about one interesting peculiarity of over: its interaction with verbs of upward and downward movement. As we noted briefly earlier, the 'directly above' interpretations of *over*, by contrast, are distinctly incompatible with verbs of upward movement, but combine readily with verbs of downward movement:

(89) a. *John rose over the hand grenade.
      b. John fell over the hand grenade.

Such sentences display an instructive peculiarity: they describe movement toward covering:

(90) a. I dropped the handkerchief over the hot dog.
      b. The net descended over me.

In fact, if the sentence cannot describe covering, the results are distinctly unacceptable, as in (91), which would only be acceptable uttered by an entity far smaller than a speck of dust:

(91) *The dust speck dropped over me.

The cooccurrence of downward orientation and covering can be explained very easily within the present theory: they are a consequence of the maneuver-space image-cluster associated with covering. That is, the primary images within the prototype which describe motion toward the landmark or ground are the maneuver space images which specify the lack of clearance after rotation or vertical displacement, and these directly imply a covering relationship. Either the trajector is vertically displaced toward the ground, resulting in covering, or it is rotated toward the ground, as in (92):

(92)   a.   Jane tripped over a step.
       b.   John fell over the threshold.

Note, however, that the association with covering is not absolute, since there is one image which allows downward movement without covering: the kinetic image-schema (43) for downward force. This motivates such uses as (93) where covering is not necessary:

(93)   The plane dropped a bomb over its target.

Thus the general pattern we see is very much in the spirit of the preference-rule system we have postulated: a wide range of interpretations are possible as long as they are compatible with a distinctive set of images associated with the prototype.

7. Conclusion

7.1. Polysemy theory

This study proposes a predictive model of polysemy in a limited but fundamental domain. It provides a method for specifying prototypical meanings for prepositions (and, presumably other spatial predicates.) It then provides an account of the mechanisms which relate a word's polysemy to its prototype (e.g., the preference rule system, correspondence rules, and the Distinctiveness Principle.) The effect is to enforce a close relationship between a word's conceptual representation and its potential for polysemy.

Comparison with other theories demonstrates the importance of this result. Despite significant progress in the last decade, polysemy is still (as it has traditionally been) the problem child of lexical semantics. While it is always easy to provide a *post hoc* explanation for any particular pattern of polysemy, it is difficult to demonstrate that such explanations are any more reliable than folk etymologies. Within structural theories of language, this problem surfaces as the difficulty of making a principled distinction between polysemy and homonymy, or (using a slightly different terminology) between ambiguity and vagueness (cf. Binnick 1970; Gragg 1978; Lakoff 1970; Lehrer 1974; Nunberg 1980; Zwicky and Sadock 1974). The result is that structural theories of meaning typically force the analyst to make a Hobson's choice. If a wide range of polysemous senses are lumped together, there may be no satisfactory definition which covers the entire range of meanings. If polysemous senses are kept apart, i.e., treated as distinct lexical items, individual senses are easier to define but their coherence as senses of the same word will be obscured. Section 1 showed that this issue remains problematic for structural theories of meaning, even in relatively sophisticated versions like Jackendoff's Conceptual Semantics. Lexical network theory sidesteps the issue of ambiguity vs. vagueness by eliminating the distinction altogether, but it is still open to the charge that it draws essentially *post hoc* connections among the word senses. In fact, major proponents of usage-based models, e.g., Lakoff (1987: 460) and Langacker (1991: 56) explicitly claim that polysemy is motivated but not so regular that it can be predicted by rule.

Willingness to postulate polysemy ranges to extremes, from the extreme polysemy of lexical network theory to the relentless monosemy championed by Ruhl (1989). This study should not be interpreted as advocating either extreme. There is ample evidence (Deane 1984, 1987, 1988; Geeraerts 1993; Langacker 1991: 268-271; Persson 1988; Tuggy 1981) that polysemy is not a homogeneous phenomenon. Following the arguments of Deane (1988) we may distinguish at least three types of "polysemy": *allosemy*, *regular polysemy*, and *lexical polysemy*. Allosemy (such as the relation between *arm* 'normal biological arm' and *arm* 'prosthetic') occurs when a coherent meaning is modulated in context. Regular polysemy (such as the metonymy which justifies *sail* for 'ship') occurs when a word productively acquires a conceptually distinct sense. Lexical polysemy (such as the relation between *crown* 'royal headgear' and *crown* 'royal government') occurs when two distinct lexical items are closely related in meaning, so that each motivates – that is, functions as a weak mnemonic cue for – the other. Lexical polysemy would be unpredictable by definition; regular polysemy at least to some extent depending on the productivity of the relation involved.

This study argues that most of the observed spatial uses of the preposition *over* can be accounted for by the operation of preference rules upon structured sets of images to produce contextually induced semantic interpretations. It is important to note that this analysis does not cover all meanings of the word. For example, the use of *over* meaning 'again' is best viewed as lexically distinct, motivated more or less as Tyler and Evans (2003) postulate.

7.2. Language and spatial cognition

This study seeks to link spatial language and the neuropsychology of spatial cognition. While the proposed model is not a neuropsychological theory, its design features are compatible with what is known about visual and spatial image processing. It thus suggests lines of research that might be fruitfully exploited on an interdisciplinary basis. For example, we might find that disorders in spatial comprehension correlate in interesting ways with aberrant patterns of polysemy. As a purely hypothetical example, consider what would happen if an individual had brain damage which severely compromised maneuver space representations, but which left visual and kinetic space representations intact. Presumably, maneuver space representations are employed in fine motor tasks, such as hand-eye coordination. But a person with compromised maneuver space representations should also have difficulty with 'rotated' construals of spatial prepositions. If the semantics of prepositions is based upon the where system in the human brain, and is localized in the inferior parietal lobe, as Jackendoff and Landau (1991) suggest, such difficulties might be associated with inferior parietal lobe lesions. The theory thus opens up interesting prospects.

7.3. Image-based semantic representations

The framework presented in this study avoids many of the traditional arguments against image-based semantic theories. It is often argued, for example, that images are inappropriate for the description of abstract concepts because they must be specific enough to be visualized (cf. Aitchison 1987: 42-43; Palmer 1981: 25-26). It is impossible, for example, to imagine a piece of fruit without imagining some specific shape, color, and so forth. A second, related objection is that images do not intrinsically encode functional information. And yet the present theory has no difficulty describing abstract spatial relationships characterized by functional properties like 'covering' or 'support'. Such objections obtain their apparent force from the assumption (i) that there is a one-to-one relation between meanings and images; (ii) that images are simple perceptual experiences, without complex (and abstract) internal structure. This study thus reinforces arguments for the adequacy of image-based models of meaning (e.g., Langacker 1987, 1991), even if it argues against the application of lexical network models to fine-grained semantic variation.

References

Aitchison, Jean
    1987   *Words in the Mind: An Introduction to the Mental Lexicon.* Oxford/ New York: Basil Blackwell.
Anderson, Richard A.
    1989   Visual and eye-movement functions of the posterior parietal cortex. *Annual Review of Neuroscience* 12: 377-403.
Anderson, Richard A., and Vernon Mountcastle
    1982   The influence of the angle of gaze upon the excitability of the light-sensitive neurons of the posterior parietal cortex. *The Journal of Neuroscience* 3: 532-548.
Anderson, Richard A., Greg K. Essick, and Ralph M. Siegel
    1985   Encoding of spatial location by posterior parietal neurons. *Science* 230: 456-458.
Arbib, Michael A.
    1991.   Interactions of multiple representations of space in the brain. In *Brain and Space*, Jacques Paillard (ed.), 379-403. Oxford: Oxford University Press.
Arnold, D.B., and D.A. Robinson
    1990   Teaching neural networks to process temporal signals for oculomotor control. In *Cold Spring Harbor Symposia on Quantitative Biology.* Vol. 55. *The Brain*, 823-826. Plainview, N.Y.: Cold Spring Harbor Laboratory Press.
Bennett, David C.
    1975   *Spatial and Temporal Uses of English Prepositions: An Essay in Stratificational Semantics.* London: Longman.
Berthoz, A.
    1991   Reference frames for the perception and control of movement. In *Brain and Space*, Jacques Paillard (ed.), 81-111. Oxford: Oxford University Press.
Binnick, Robert I.
    1970   Ambiguity and vagueness. In *Papers from the Sixth Regional Meeting*, Mary Anne Campbell (ed.), 147-153. Chicago: Chicago Linguistic Society.

Bisiach, Edoardo, Erminio Capitani and Eduardo Porta
1985   Two basic properties of space representation: Evidence from unilateral neglect. *Journal of Neurology, Neurosurgery, and Psychiatry* 48: 141-144.
Block, Ned (ed.)
1981   *Imagery*. Cambridge, Mass.: MIT Press.
Brugman, Claudia
1988   *The Story of* Over: *Polysemy, Semantics, and the Structure of the Lexicon*. (Outstanding Dissertations in Linguistics.) New York/ London: Garland. [M.A. Thesis, University of California, Berkeley, 1981].
Brugman, Claudia, and George Lakoff
1988   Cognitive topology and lexical networks. In *Lexical Ambiguity Resolution: Perspectives from Psycholinguistics, Neuropsychology, and Artificial Intelligence*, Steven I. Small, Garrison W. Cottrell, and Michael K. Tanenhaus (eds.), 477-508. San Mateo, CA: Morgan Kaufmann Publishers, Inc.
Choi, Soonja, and Melissa Bowerman
1991   Learning to express motion events in English and Korean: The influence of language-specific lexicalization patterns. *Cognition* 41: 83-122.
Cuyckens, Hubert
1988   Spatial prepositions in cognitive semantics. In *Understanding the Lexicon: Meaning, Sense, and World Knowledge in Lexical Semantics*, Werner Hüllen and Rainer Schulze (eds.), 316-328. Tübingen: Max Niemeyer Verlag.
1991   The semantics of spatial prepositions in Dutch. Ph.D. diss., Universitaire Instelling Antwerpen.
Deane, Paul D.
1984   Three types of polysemy. In *Papers from the 18th Mid-America Linguistics Conference at Boulder,* David Rood (ed.), 136-143. Department of Linguistics, University of Colorado at Boulder, Colorado.
1987   Semantic theory and the problem of polysemy. Ph.D. diss., University of Chicago.
1988   Polysemy and cognition. *Lingua* 75: 325-361.
Duhamel, Jean-Rene, Carol L. Colby, and Michael E. Goldberg
1991   Congruent representations of visual and somatosensory space in single neurons of monkey ventral intra-parietal cortex (area VIP). In *Brain and Space*, Jacques Paillard (ed.), 223-236. Oxford: Oxford University Press.

276 *Paul D. Deane*

Farah, Martha J., Katherine M. Hammond, David N. Levine, and Ronald Calvanio
1988   Visual and spatial mental imagery: Dissociable systems of representation. *Cognitive Psychology* 20: 439-462.
Garrod, Simon C., and Anthony J. Sanford
1988   Discourse models as interfaces between language and the spatial world. *Journal of Semantics* 6: 147-160.
Geeraerts, Dirk
1990   The lexicographic treatment of prototypical polysemy. In *Meanings and Prototypes: Studies in Linguistic Categorization*, Savas L. Tsohatzidis (ed.), 195-210. London/New York: Routledge.
1992   The semantic structure of Dutch *over*. *Leuvense Bijdragen* 81: 205-230.
1993   Vagueness's puzzles, polysemy's vagaries. *Cognitive Linguistics* 4: 223-272.
Gibson, James J.
1979   *The Ecological Approach to Visual Perception*. Boston: Houghton Mifflin.
Gilhodes, Jean-Claude, Yves Coiton, and Jean-Luc Velay
1991   Sensorimotor space representation: a neuromimetic model. In *Brain and Space*, Jacques Paillard (ed.), 433-445. Oxford: Oxford University Press.
Goldberg, M.E., C.L. Colby, and J.-R. Duhamel
1990   Representation of visuomotor space in the parietal lobe of the monkey. In *Cold Spring Harbor Symposia on Quantitative Biology*. Vol. 55. *The Brain,* 729-740. Plainview, N.Y.: Cold Spring Harbor Laboratory Press.
Gragg, Gene B.
1978   Redundancy and polysemy: Reflections on a point of departure for lexicology. In *Papers from the Parasession on the Lexicon, Chicago Linguistic Society, Apr. 14-15 1978*, Donka Farkas, Wesley M. Jacobsen and Karol W. Todrys (eds.), 174-183. Chicago: Chicago Linguistic Society.
Harris, Catherine
1989   A connectionist approach to the story of *over*. *Berkeley Linguistics Society* 15: 126-138.
Hawkins, Bruce W.
1985   *The Semantics of English Spatial Prepositions*. Trier: L.A.U.T. [Ph.D. Dissertation, University of California, San Diego, 1984].
1988   The natural category MEDIUM: An alternative to selection restrictions and similar constructs. In *Topics in Cognitive Linguistics*, Brygida Rudzka-Ostyn (ed.), 231-270. Amsterdam: Benjamins.

Heine, Berndt
1989   Adposition in African languages. *Linguistique Africaine* 77-127.
Heine, Berndt, Ulrike Claudi, and Friederike Hünnemeyer
1991   *Grammaticalization: A conceptual framework*. Chicago: University of Chicago Press.
Herskovits, Annette
1986   *Language and Spatial Cognition: An Interdisciplinary Study of the Prepositions in English*. Cambridge: Cambridge University Press.
Hirst, Graeme
1988   Resolving lexical ambiguity computationally with spreading activation and polaroid words. In *Lexical Ambiguity Resolutions*, Steven Small, Garrison Cottrell, and Michael Tanenhaus (eds.), 73-107. Los Altos, CA: Morgan Kaufmann.
Jackendoff, Ray
1983   *Semantics and Cognition*. Cambridge, Mass.: MIT Press.
1991   *Semantic Structures*. Cambridge, Mass: MIT Press.
Jackendoff, Ray, and Barbara Landau
1991   Spatial language and spatial cognition. In *Bridges between Psychology and Linguistics: A Swarthmore Festschrift for Lila Gleitman*, Donna Jo Napoli, and Judy Anne Kegl (eds.), 145-170. Hillsdale, N.J.: Lawrence Erlbaum Associates.
Janda, Laura
1988   The mapping of elements of cognitive space onto grammatical relations: An example from Russian verbal prefixation. In *Topics in Cognitive Linguistics*, Brygida Rudzka-Ostyn (ed.), 327-344. Amsterdam: Benjamins.
Jeannerod, M.
1991   A neurophysiological model for the directional coding of reaching movements. In *Brain and Space*, Jacques Paillard (ed.), 49-69. Oxford: Oxford University Press.
Kosslyn, Stephen Michael
1980   *Image and Mind*. Cambridge, Mass.: Harvard University Press.
Kreitzer, Anatol
1997   Multiple Levels of Schematization: A study in the conceptualization of space. *Cognitive Linguistics* 8: 291-325.
Lakoff, George
1970   A note on ambiguity and vagueness. *Linguistic Inquiry* 1: 351-359.
1987   *Women, fire and dangerous things: What categories reveal about the mind*. Chicago: University of Chicago Press.
Landau, Barbara, and Lila R. Gleitman
1985   *Language and Experience: Evidence from the Blind Child*. Cambridge, Mass.: Harvard University Press.

Langacker, Ronald W.
  1987   *Foundations of Cognitive Grammar*. Vol. 1. *Theoretical Prerequi-sites*. Stanford: Stanford University Press.
  1991   *Concept, Image, and Symbol: The Cognitive Basis of Grammar*. Berlin/ New York: Mouton de Gruyter.
Leech, Geoffrey
  1974   *Semantics*. Harmondsworth, U.K.: Penguin Books.
Lehrer, Adrienne
  1974   Homonymy and polysemy: Measuring similarity of meaning. *Language Sciences* 32: 33-38.
  1990   Polysemy, conventionality and the structure of the lexicon. *Cognitive Linguistics* 1: 207-246
Lindner, Susan
  1983   *A Lexico-Semantic Analysis of Verb-Particle Constructions with* up *and* out. LAUT Series A: Paper 101. Trier: L.A.U.T. [Ph.D. Dissertation, The University of California, San Diego, 1981].
  1982   What goes up doesn't always come down: The ins and outs of opposites. *Chicago Linguistic Society* 18: 305-323.
Lindkvist, Karl-Gunnar
  1972   *The Local Sense of the Prepositions* Over, Above, *and* Across. Stockholm: Almqvist and Wiksell.
Livingstone, Margaret, and David Hubel
  1988   Segregation of form, color, movement, and depth: Anatomy, physiology, and perception. *Science* 240: 740-749.
Marr, David
  1982   *Vision: A computational investigation into the human representation and processing of visual information*. New York: W.H. Freeman and Company.
Marr, David, and H. Keith Nishihara
  1978   Visual information processing: Artificial intelligence and the sensorium of sight. *Technology Review* 81: 2-23.
Munro, Paul, Cynthia Cosic, and Mary Tabasko
  1991   A network for encoding, decoding, and translating locative prepositions. *Connection Science* 3: 225-240.
Nikanne, Urpo
  1990   *Zones and Tiers: A Study of Thematic Structure*. (Studia Fennica Linguistica 35.) Helsinki: Suomalaisen Kirjallisuuden Seura.
Norvig, Peter, and George Lakoff
  1987   Taking: A study in lexical network theory. In *Berkeley Linguistics Society* 13: 195-206.

Nunberg, Geoffrey D.
1980   The non-uniqueness of semantic solutions - polysemy. *Linguistics and Philosophy* 3: 143-184.
O'Keefe, John
1991   The hippocampal cognitive map and navigational strategies. In *Brain and Space*, Jacques Paillard (ed.), 273-295. Oxford: Oxford University Press.
O'Reilly, Randall C., Stephen M. Kosslyn, Chad J. Marsolek, and Christopher F. Chabris
1990   Receptive field characteristics that allow parietal lobe neurons to encode spatial properties of visual input: A computations analysis. *Journal of Cognitive Neuroscience* 2: 141-155.
Osherson, Daniel N., Stephen M. Kosslyn, and John M. Hollerbach (eds.)
1990   *An Invitation to Cognitive Science.* Vol. 2. *Visual Cognition and Action.* Cambridge, Mass.: MIT Press.
Paillard, Jacques
1987   Cognitive vs. sensorimotor coding of spatial information. In *Cognitive Process and Spatial Orientation in Animal and Man.* Vol 2. *Neurophysiology and Developmental Aspects*, P. Ellen, and C. Thinus-Blanc (eds.), 43-77. Dordrecht: Martinus Nijhof.
1991a   Motor and representational framing of space. In *Brain and Space*, Jacques Paillard (ed.), 163-182. Oxford: Oxford University Press.
1991b   Knowing where and knowing how to get there. In *Brain and Space*, Jacques Paillard (ed.), 461-481. Oxford: Oxford University Press.
Palmer, F. R.
1981   *Semantics.* Second Edition. Cambridge: Cambridge University Press.
Regan, David, Kenneth Beverley and Max Cynader
1979   The visual perception of motion in depth. *Scientific American* 241: 136-151.
Regier, Terrance P.
1992   The acquisition of lexical semantics for spatial terms: A connectionist model of perceptual categorization. Ph.D. Dissertation, University of California, Berkeley.
Rice, Sally, Dominiek Sandra, and Mia Vanrespaille
1999   Prepositional semantics and the fragile link between space and time. In *Cultural, Psychological and Typological Issues in Cognitive Linguistics: Selected Papers of the Bi-annual ICLA Meeting in Albuquerque, July 1995*, M. Hiraga, Chris Sinha, and Sherman Wilcox (eds.), 108-127. Philadelphia: John Benjamins.

Robertson, Lynn C., and Marvin R. Lamb
    1991   Neuropsychological contributions to theories of part/whole organi-
            zation. *Cognitive Psychology* 23: 299-330.
Rosch, Eleanor
    1978   Principles of Categorization. In *Cognition and Categorization*,
            Eleanor Rosch, and B. Lloyd (eds.), 27-48. Hillsdale, N.J.: Law-
            rence Erlbaum Associates.
Ruhl, Charles
    1989   *On Monosemy: A Study in Linguistic Semantics.* Albany: State
            University of New York Press.
Rubba, Jo
    1994   Grammaticization as semantic change: A case study of preposition
            development. In *Perspectives on Grammaticalization*, William
            Pagliuca (ed.), 81-101. Amsterdam/Philadelphia: Benjamins.
Sandra, Dominiek
    1998   What linguists can and can't tell us about the mind: A reply to
            Croft. *Cognitive Linguistics* 9: 361-378.
Sandra, Dominiek, and Sally Rice
    1995   Network analyses of prepositional meaning: Mirroring whose mind
            – the linguist or the language user's? *Cognitive Linguistics* 6: 89-
            130.
Schulze, Rainer
    1991   Getting round to *(a)round*: Towards the description and analysis of
            a 'spatial' predicate. In *Approaches to Prepositions*, Gisa Rauh
            (ed.), 253-274. Tübingen: Gunter Narr Verlag.
Stein, J.F.
    1991   Space and the parietal association areas. In *Brain and Space*,
            Jacques Paillard (ed.), 185-222. Oxford: Oxford University Press.
Svorou, Soteria
    1986   On the evolutionary paths of locative expressions. *Berkeley Linguis-
            tics Society* 12: 515-527.
Talmy, Leonard
    1983   How language structures space. In *Spatial Orientation: Theory,
            Research, and Practice*, Herbert L. Pick, Jr., and Linda P. Acredolo
            (eds.), 225-282. New York/ London: Plenum Press.
    1988   Force dynamics in language and thought. *Cognitive Science* 12: 49-
            100. [original publication 1985]
Taylor, John R.
    1988   Contrasting prepositional categories: English and Italian. In *Topics
            in Cognitive Linguistics*, Brygida Rudzka-Ostyn (ed.), 299-326.
            Amsterdam: Benjamins.

1989   *Linguistic Categorization: Prototypes in Linguistic Theory.* Oxford: Oxford University Press.

Thinus-Blanc, C., E. Save, M.-C. Buhot, and B. Poucet
1991   The hippocampus, exploratory activity, and spatial memory. In *Brain and Space*, Jacques Paillard (ed.), 334-352. Oxford: Oxford University Press.

Tuggy, David
1981   The Transitivity-related Morphology of Tetelcingo Nahatl: An Exploration in Space Grammar. Ph.D. Dissertation, The University of California, San Diego.

Tyler, Andrea, and Vyvyan Evans
2001   Reconsidering prepositional polysemy networks: the case of *over*. *Language* 77: 724-65.
2003   *The Semantics of English Prepositions: Spatial Scenes, Embodied Meaning, and Cognition.* Cambridge: Cambridge University Press.

Ullman, Shimon
1990   Three-dimensional object recognition. In *Cold Harbor Symposia on Quantitative Biology.* Vol. 55. *The Brain*, 889-898. Plainview, N.Y.: Cold Spring Harbor Laboratory Press.

Ungerleider, Leslie G., and Mortimer Mishkin
1982   Two cortical visual systems. In *Analysis of Visual Behavior*, David J. Ingle, Melvyn A. Goodale, and Richard J. W. Mansfield (eds.), 549-586. Cambridge, MA: MIT Press.

Vandeloise, Claude
1990   Representation, prototypes, and centrality. In *Meanings and Prototypes: Studies in Linguistic Categorization*, Savas L. Tsohatzidis (ed.), 403-437. London and New York: Routledge.
1991   *Spatial Prepositions: A Case Study from French* [Translated by Anna R.K. Bosch.] Chicago: University of Chicago Press.

Wege, Barbara
1991   On the lexical meaning of prepositions: A study of *above, below*, and *over*. In *Approaches to Prepositions*, Gisa Rauh (ed.), 275-296. Tübingen: Gunter Narr Verlag.

Zeki, Semir
1992   The visual image in mind and brain. *Scientific American* 267: 68-77.

Zeki, S., and S. Shipp
1988   The functional logic of cortical connections. *Nature* 335: 311-317.

Zipser, David, and Richard Anderson
1988   A back-propagation programmed network that simulates response properties of a subset of posterior parietal neurons. *Nature* 331: 679-684.

Zwicky, Arnold, and Jerrold Sadock
   1974   Ambiguity tests and how to fail them. *Working Papers in Linguistics* (Columbus) 16: 1-34.

Part 4: Image schemas and beyond:
Expanded and alternative notions

Culture regained:
Situated and compound image schemas

Michael Kimmel[*]

Abstract

The hallmark of a genuinely socio-cultural perspective on image schemas must be its ability to account for their variation both across cultures and in situated cognition. To counterbalance the prevalent research strategies which have highlighted highly generic cognitive resources that cross-cut a broad range of different contexts, I propose two complementary analytical strategies that make nuances in image schema usage more visible: The first lies in focusing more on how image schemas interact at the level of whole scenes, at which they form compound gestalts – a step allowing the analyst to get a handle on complex tropes. The second lies in evading the practice of endowing image schemas with a *maximally* decontextualized ontology – a step opening an avenue to augmented descriptions of image schemas and their context-bound usage. This analytical strategy produces "situated image schemas", descriptions capturing how "primitive" image schemas are actualized with regard to the kind of embodiment they involve, as well as their intentional, emotional and motivational nature within specific settings, or their embedding within wider action scenarios and even a cultural ethos.

Keywords: augmented image schemas, gestalts, image schema ontology, situated cognition, cultural variation

[*] For generous feedback to previous versions of this chapter I am indebted to the editor of this volume, two anonymous reviewers, Roslyn Frank, Kathryn Geurts, Veronika Koller, Zoltán Kövecses, Anja Minnich, Irene Mittelberg, Svetla Pacheva, and Naomi Quinn.

> The term imagery highlights the fact that concepts originate as representations of sensory experience, even though they may subsequently undergo complex processes of formation and re-combination.   (Palmer 1996: 46)

> ... if you attend only to structure ... [y]ou lose, or at least over-look, the very thing that gives image schemas their life, motivat-ing force, and relevance to human meaning, namely their em-beddedness within affect-laden experience.
>
> (Johnson, *this volume*)

1.   The socio-cultural situatedness of image schemas

In cognitive linguistics, the claims staked in understanding meaning are cur-rently widening. In a recent interview Johnson defined meaning as "located in the complex, dynamic arc of interactions that includes brains, bodies, environments, and cultural artifacts and institutions" (Pires and Bittencourt, to appear). A firm recognition of the cultural side of this arc will affect the way we use image schemas as descriptive devices in several important ways that have not be discussed comprehensively yet. This chapter elaborates what is cultural about image schemas or, more precisely, how the notion of image schema can be better adapted to an analysis that takes into account cultural context. When I speak of culture here I wish to highlight the inher-ent *situatedness* of cognitive forms in the shared interaction between hu-mans (cf. Gibbs 1999; Zlatev 1997); hence we will only become fully aware of the cultural nature of image schemas through a situated and context-sensitive analysis of their usage.

Given these brief preliminaries, this chapter will expound two major per-spectives that a cultural analysis of image schemas should bring into play. In order to move beyond the classical view sketched in Section 1, I will make a case for widening the ontology of image schemas and the methodology of their study (see 1.2). Section 2 contends that we need to direct more empiri-cal efforts to the study of "compound image schemas" and their cognitive effects, while Section 3 argues for developing more context-adaptive de-scriptors of "situated image schemas". The latter argument will draw on developmental and ethnographic studies indicating that image schema acqui-sition may be in interesting ways cultural, and that seemingly universal im-age schemas may become culturally augmented or nuanced through their usage context.

1.1. From the classical to a socio-cultural view on image schemas

Ever since Johnson's (1987) landmark publication, cognitive linguists have treated image schemas as simple topological structures of trans-modal imagery, which are acquired as the child negotiates the environment with her body. They (minimally) encompass the kinesthetic, the visual and auditory modalities. From a functional viewpoint image schemas support the topology of metaphorical mappings, categorization, and many aspects of grammar. The notion has also been used to explain how conceptual thought developmentally emerges from embodied (i.e., proprioceptive and kinesthetic) imagery, thus giving us an interface mechanism, holding one foot in either. The canonical understanding of image schemas strongly relies on a list of prototypical examples like CONTAINER, UP-DOWN, NEAR-FAR, or PATH, and two or three dozens other ones (Johnson 1987: 126; Cienki 1997: 3). All these are cognitive structures of a very basic and simple sort.

Image schemas, qua schemas, are acquired not through the specifics of individual episodes humans encounter, but through feature-overlaps between many experiential contexts. Hence, image schemas comprise primary building blocks of cognition, regardless of how these units combine in any given setting. There is also a certain concurrent tendency to focus on image schemas as structures of cognitive competence entrenched in long-term memory,[1] although Johnson also devoted some thought to their inherently intentional nature and thus demonstrated interest in how they are enacted in situ. Not surprisingly, although image schemas are recognized by Johnson as being "relatively malleable" with varying contexts (1987: 30), descriptive techniques for contextual adaptation are largely left unspecified.

All this points to the standard account's dominant interest in the situation-independent repertoire of imagery that members of a cultural group share or, beyond that, in cross-cultural universals. Thereby, the classical account has overlooked that image schemas are not *only* generalized mental entities, but also ones that are instantiated in socio-cultural contexts (cf. Gibbs 1999). Rather than rejecting what I see as the canonical view, I will furnish it with a dialectical partner here, a complementary, more context-sensitive vantage point to address matters. Thus, the socio-culturally situated perspective embraced in this chapter aims to return "qualitative flesh and

---

1. Cf. Johnson's (1987: 183-190) discussion of the Searlean notion of "background".

blood to our image-schematic skeletons", something that Johnson (*this volume*) recognizes as desirable, but remains skeptical about.

1.2. A cluster of biases

Self-imposed limitations hold sway over much of cognitive linguistics, which mar its potential as a full-fledged socio-cultural account of cognition, despite recent attempts to remedy this state of affairs (e.g., Jensen de López and Sinha 2000; Sinha 1999). These limitations have also left their imprint on the dominant notion of image schema. As I shall argue, the ontology and methodology of image schema research remains grounded in mutually strengthening biases which are not exactly congenial to a socio-cultural view.

– *The universalist acquisition bias*: Image schemas are, by virtue of universal pre-linguistic embodiment in infancy, developmental universals.
– *The feed-forward bias*: Embodiment is rooted in general kinesthetic experience in space, whereby the body shapes culture, but not vice versa.
– *The micro-unit bias*: The simple image-schematic building-blocks of cognition are ontologically or functionally prior to higher-level gestalts.
– *The maximal schematicity bias*: Image schemas are what settings share at the widest schematic level; their cognitive profile does not stem from being situated in narrower kinds of settings.
– *The de-contextualized methods bias*: Image schemas are supported by experimental and linguistic data centering on the word and phrase level, less so by discourse-analytic and ethnographic analyses of larger units of data with a sensitivity for pragmatic usage and contextuality.

After this short preview, I will now turn to some prerequisites for a socio-culturally situated analysis of image schemas and, in the course of the argument, discuss the biases further and suggest alternatives. The two decisive steps for a socio-culturally situated analysis I see are (a) widening the focus by studying *compound image schemas* and (b) developing a theory of *situated image schemas*.

2.   Compound image schemas

A culturalized view requires a closer look at the transformational and combinatory capacities image schemas exhibit in usage contexts of some complexity. This section attempts to discuss and sub-classify under the heading
of "compound" effects of complex image-schematic processes both in short
and in temporally more extended cognitive events.

Beginning with a general division, image-schematic gestalts may occur as
primitive (basal) units or as compounds: Image schemas like CONTAINER,
LINK, FORCE, CENTER-PERIPHERY, or BALANCE are primitive to the extent
that their topological structure cannot be meaningfully decomposed into yet
simpler gestalts.[2] Most image schemas discussed in the literature (cf. Oakley,
to appear) are primitive ones.

Compound image schemas, by contrast, emerge when several simpler
ones hook up in time or space to create more complex groupings that are
reducible into simpler gestalts. I follow Cienki's (1997: 9) view that "image
schemas ... usually do not occur in an isolated fashion in experience, but
rather are experienced grouped as gestalts or wholes", many of which prototypically occur together "in an experiential gestalt structure". For example,
CENTERY-PERIPHERY, NEAR-FAR, SCALE, and FORCE co-occur in the bodily
experience of being a center of force which decreases with distance in a scalar fashion, like when a hand is extended (Cienki 1997: 7-9). Other compounds, I would add, though less familiar from embodied experience, may be
created in the imagination.

I will subsume under "compound image schemas" those that add topological structures within a single static locus and those that dynamically
construe a mental scene as one image schema following upon another. Applying a photographic metaphor, the difference between these two kinds of
compound is much like that between a multiple-exposure of the same negative and a movie-clip of sequentially unfolding images.[3] The former type
involves static superimpositions of image schemas, while the latter, more
dynamic type relies on our ability to perform what Lakoff (1987: 440-444)
and Johnson (1987: 26) call image schema transformations, e.g., zooming in

---

2. Image-schematic primitives constitute "irreducible gestalts" (Johnson 1987:
    44, 62) whose integrity is destroyed by breaking down their internal structure.
3. As I define it here, the feature of compound-ness may also be distributed in
    time, even when each snapshot conforms to a primitive image schema.

and out between MULTIPLEX and MASS, or anticipating the trajectory of a moving object in a specific construal of the PATH schema.

We can often process a complex scene *either* as a static configuration in which all facets are conceived as coexistent and simultaneous *or* as a dynamic series of successively transforming states.[4] Thus, image schemas like BALANCE, MATCHING, MERGING, CONTACT, LINK, SPLITTING and others can be understood either as a process or, when receiving "end-point focus", as a state achieved (Cienki 1997: 7). This makes the static-dynamic distinction usage-dependent and a matter of degree.

2.1. Static compound schemas

One first type of compound image schema is (relatively) static. It results from stacking simpler image schemas on top of each other in a single imaginative locus through image-schematic superimposition. An example is superimposing a connective CONDUIT (i.e., a FORCE moving an ENTITY through a LINK) onto the space between two CONTAINERS to create the well-known folk-model of communication.

Compound image schemas are inherently present in any complex posture which activates primitive image schemas in various body parts simultaneously. For example, the spine can be STRAIGHT, the arms in BALANCE, the shoulders UP, the chest a rigid CONTAINER, etc., all at the same time and in the single integrative locus of one's body image. Arguably, such configurations are stored and recalled as a complex image-schematic gestalts. An analysis of body-related image schemas has been indirectly suggested by Gibbs (cf. 2003: 11) who had experimental subjects rate the various meanings of the expression *to stand* and found that the word combines the image-schematic profiles of BALANCE, VERTICALITY, CENTER-PERIPHERY, RESISTANCE, and LINKAGE (with varying situational emphases).

Furthermore, compound image schemas of the static usage type frequently appear in philosophical or cosmological models and metaphors (Kimmel 2002). Examples are image schemas of SYSTEMS (Kövecses 2002) characterized by LINK or BALANCE relations, or hierarchic action chains

---

4. This mirrors the difference between Langacker's (1987:144-146) construal types of "summary/sequential scanning".

from God via the church to the layman which involve a passing of FORCE through a CONDUIT-like chain from ABOVE.[5]

2.2. Dynamic compound schemas

A second type of compound image schema is more dynamic. It occurs when simple image schemas are lined up in a scenario-like sequence whose contour we imagine. This may be thought of as a multi-frame clip passing the mind's eye, in which sizes, relations or vantage points undergo change by virtue of image schema transformations.

The simplest dynamic compounds are probably elicited by words. The processing of such verbs like *narrow* or *approach* requires imagining various points in time over which a trajector and a landmark move closer to each other. Other relatively simple dynamic contours occur when we manipulate a real context so that it keeps its match with an imaginative standard. Gibbs and Colston (1995) mention the example of a shepherd maneuvering his herd to keep it close enough together not to fall apart but dispersed enough to keep them moving. The shepherd continually gauges the present state of affairs against a MULTIPLEX-MASS transformation in a certain BALANCE. In a slightly more complex situation, when the whole herd has to be driven so that one escapee can be caught, the multiplex is superimposed on an imaginary TRAJECTORY anticipating where the renegade can be picked up again.

In dynamic compounds, the modality or direction of movement may change. Thus, by adding CONTRACTION to EXPANSION, we get the more complex image-schematic gestalt of PULSATION. A very similar, though slightly different image-schematic scenario is well known from the study of anger metaphors (Lakoff and Kövecses 1987). Here, the metaphor scenario of a pressurized container can be imagined as a sequence of gradual WELLING UP, rapid EXPLOSION, and the resulting DEFLATION.[6] In this and similar ways, dynamic contours often underlie what D'Andrade calls "social scripts" (1995).

---

5. Langacker (1987: 304-306) posits the combination of imagistic and schematic units as basic functional principle of language processing. Grammatical structure mentally sets up an *elaboration-site*, i.e., an analog topology that begins weakly specified but is gradually enriched as new words are processed and leave an "imprint".

6. I introduce these new terms because they capture a specific modality of more general schemas like EXPANSION and CONTRACTION.

How we imagine emotions more generally also relates to dynamic compounds. Johnson (1999: 92) argues for the image-schematic nature of so-called "vitality affect contours" of various kinds. We experience bodily activation contours over time like "the felt quality of anger or fear – the 'rush' of fear, the 'crescendo' of anger that leads to an angry 'outburst', the 'fading away' of one's joyful exuberance".

Although all examples so far involve relatively short scenario-like contours, it has been hypothesized that extended events evoke imagistic clips with similar contours. This can mean enacting an entire dance choreography or ritual, perceiving a piece of music (Cook 1990), or imaging a story's plot (cf. Turner 1996) as an extended image-schematic contour. Taking narrative as a testbed, Kimmel (2005) develops a full cognitive model of how such macro-image schemas may be created.[7] Simple image schemas found in the text-base are compounded in the readers' mind. One cognitive purpose of the resulting image-schematic contour is to create an extended mnemonic of the plot dynamics.[8] Moreover, as with musical forms, esthetic meaning and emotionality may reside in this contour, e.g., through the imagistic build up of tension and its subsequent resolution. Finally, the model suggests that the build-up of image-schematic compounds serves inferential purposes, by enabling multiple readings as well as the recovery of implicit meaning. Thus compounds facilitate or constrain the creation of emergent cognitive structure.

2.3. Interacting image schemas: Irony frames and gestalt switches

Image-schematic thought allows for further complex effects, which nuance the compositionality of image schemas in interesting ways. Quite simply, it is not always the case that compounds create a perfect match between their constituents. Text cues may encourage us to integrate image-schematic elements not compatible in a straightforward way. I will exemplify two related such effects, irony frames and gestalt switches.

---

7. This case-study of the novel "Heart of Darkness" purports to illustrate how the joint work done by metaphors is largely based on the affinities and combinatory fit of the image schemas inherent in them.

8. Specifically, I argue for the possibility that spatial, temporal, intentional agent-related, and emotive/mood-related features may be integrated in a single compound structure.

Turner (1996: 64-67) suggests that the perception of irony may depend on holding two inverted image schemas in focus simultaneously. Analyzing a scene of Shakespeare's *King John* he speaks of an "ironic tension between the image schemas". The powerful king, who senses his impeding decline, commands the messenger foreboding ill news (who is probably kneeling before him) "pour down thy weather", thus ironically likening him, who is a mere subject, to powers beyond the king's own, those of nature and fate. According to Turner, the scene involves a juxtaposition of two inverse UP-DOWN predications. Werth (1999) discusses a similar juxtaposition of two conflicting metaphors of the type GOOD IS UP. In one text passage of Forster's *A Passage to India*, the topography of a city in India is predicated on power (CONTROL IS UP, POWERFUL IS UP), because the colonial English-men live on a hill rising above the rest of the city. This may be seen as an axiology in which one end of the scale is defined as positive, the other as negative (Krzeszowski 1993). Another axiology, antithetical to the first, presents a SCALE of vitality, ranging from the least animate Englishmen to the vegetation as most animate, with the natives situated in between. Both axiologies together create an ironical image of the powerful, but, as it were, lifeless English. This particular irony frame superimposes (or co-aligns) two axiological schemas, one of which is the inversion of the other, thus setting up a double-axiology.

Secondly, complex thought processes may also rely on "gestalt-switches" (cf. Wittgenstein 1953). Although previous uses of the notion choose other foci, I will define a gestalt-switch as the imaginary oscillation between two incompatible image-schematic configurations that are nonetheless under-stood as integral. The skill of performing gestalt-switches is notably involved in certain mental operations in philosophy, theology, and mathematics. An example discussed by Arnheim (1969: 287) and Blumenberg ([1979] 1996: 445) is Nicolas Cusanus' "Sprengmetapher" ('explosive metaphor') of God as a sphere with an infinite radius and its center everywhere. This idea makes the circumference converge with a perfect line, yet, so we are told, it belongs to a circle. As I interpret this, what our mind's eye is encouraged to do is to move away from this line to make the curvature become visible. Whenever we think that the curvature should be visible, we remember the paradoxical instruction that it cannot be so and correct our image by super-imposing a line to make it conform. Thus we try moving even further out-wards, ad infinitum. Of course our imaginative act will not continue end-lessly, but its effect will be to suggest infinite distance through the corrective gestalt switch from curve to line.

Olds (1991: 18) discusses a comparable example from the Chinese Buddhist philosopher Fa-Tsang (A.D. 643-712). For teaching the notion of infinite progression the sage used the image of the Golden Lion "each of whose hairs contains another golden lion, such that all lions and all the hairs together enter into each other in infinite progression". In addition, all the lions embraced by all the hairs simultaneously enter each single hair, filling it with an infinite numbers of lions. This complex image elicits what we may call a recurring NESTING relation within a multi-level PART-WHOLE image schema and *simultaneously* an IDENTITY image schema (as a shorthand for the involved structure matching). Simultaneously with nesting there is structural replication, a kind of micro-macro iconicity between PARTS and WHOLES. Fa-Tsang's goal is to intimate the idea of unending mutual inclusion and a radically non-hierarchic view of reality. We can start out on every conceivable level of reality and all other levels will always be contained within it. Fa-Tsang's ontological statement is, of course, paradoxical. According to our everyday knowledge, something can either include something else *or* be identical with it, never both. The paradox is realized through jumping between an image schema of PART-WHOLE/NESTING on the one hand and one of structural IDENTITY on the other, while understanding both as integral. This gestalt-switch occurs as soon as we direct our attention from the inclusion hierarchy to the isomorphism between the different levels. As an emergent effect, the nested levels appear interchangeable because they can be topologically matched.

In concluding this brief sampling of more complex effects of image-schematic compounding, we may compare irony frames and gestalt switches. The two are apparently sibling phenomena in that both match what appears incoherent, with irony frames representing more static images of tension, whereas gestalt switches tend towards the opposite pole of dynamically oscillating images. Studying these and similar cognitive effects is highly instructive: First, they point towards a usage-based analysis rooted in the insight that, rather than being topological givens with narrow combinatory constraints, image schemas are often used in fluid ways and undergo complex reshapings. Secondly, we can glean from the examples how image schema analysis might be applied at the higher level of dynamic thought models (cf. Kimmel 2002). While characterizing complex thought as mere collections of image schemas may often prove inadequate, the perspective remains eminently useful when it instead chooses as a descriptive topic the *interaction of several image schemas* and their effects.

2.4. Compounds and theory

After this typological survey we may return to the wider issue of how we define the ontology of image schemas. Without question, compound image schemas move back to center stage the notion of "gestalt," which has been somewhat neglected since Lakoff (1987) and Johnson (1987) introduced it to cognitive linguistics. It thus seems timely, even though prosaic, to remind readers of the fact that not only primitive configurations such as the CONTAINER schema have gestalt features like the in-out relation and a boundary. Many interesting gestalts in perception, thought, and action are higher-level gestalts like the ones just discussed.

I will examine further along how, by dint of cultural learning, complex image-schematic gestalts – though structurally more complex than highly intuitive pet examples like the CONTAINER – may gradually become "psychologically simple" – one of Lakoff's (1987: 489, 525) criteria for a successful image-schematic gestalt. While it may be an overgeneralization that image schemas need to be "cognitively simple, easy to learn", they will probably remain "easy to remember, and easy to use" once they are acquired (Lakoff 1987: 538). An alternative hypothesis would be that image schemas are encoded at multiple mental hierarchies, out of which combinatory high-level gestalts can be just as easily generated as simpler ones.

One research bias that seems to be characteristic of cognitive linguistics is that the canonically listed CONTAINER, CENTER-PERIPHERY, UP-DOWN, LINK, PATH, or BALANCE schemas remain the primary object of attention. A focus on these primitive schemas is a logical consequence of looking for situation-independent patterns in grammar or the non-situated meanings of words. While reducing the scope of an image-schema analysis that might be potentially interesting to the humanities and social sciences or, for that matter, to linguists concerned with larger chunks of discourse, the practice in itself is, of course, perfectly legitimate. However, behind this may stand an implicit ontological bias that is untenable. The sole focus on primary image-schematic building-blocks makes these primary image schemas seem either functionally or ontologically more basic than complex, culture-specific packages. Implicitly, an analytic ontology is preferred to a more holistic one. Overall, I can see no ontological grounds for excluding compound gestalts from the image schema notion. Their psychological reality in a given context, however, is an empirical issue.

3.   Situatedness and image schemas

Socio-cultural situatedness becomes manifest in studying the interdependence of individual cognitive dispositions and specific cultural contexts. Current cognitive-science approaches emphasize "structural coupling" of the cognitive system with the environment as a general property of cognition (cf. Gibbs 1999). As I see it, two avenues are open to scholars who accept the importance of a situated perspective on image schemas: We can leave image schemas narrowly defined by proposing other theoretical descriptors for capturing their dynamic interaction with situated themes in discourse (e.g., Quinn 1991). Alternatively, we can frame the image schema notion itself more widely by describing situation-adaptive subvariants of generic schemas. Taking this second route here, I will argue for fleshing image schemas out by specifying situated aspects of their acquisition and usage. In other words, I will discuss ways of descriptively specifying how image schemas structurally couple with cultural (or natural) environments and thus take on a situated ontology.

3.1.   Image schemas in memory and in on-line use

Situating image schemas requires looking at on-line cognition. In the past, there was a certain tendency to understand image schemas exclusively as permanent structures in long-term memory. While entrenched image-schematic dispositions are a valid hypothesis to consider (cf. Gibbs and Berg 2002), we may also stress the fluidity of image schemas or even argue against viewing them as stable representations and for seeing them as assembled "on the fly" in on-line use, as Gibbs (*this volume*) does. The least we can say is that to *exclusively* consider image schemas as transcontextual constructs which reflect general properties of the human cognitive inventory is reductionist. Applied ethnographic contexts like symbolic healing underscore this possible double perspective:

> ... [d]emonic possession ... begins with a inchoate (pre-objectified) feeling of loss of control over the body ... This is then objectified by a healer in terms of what Johnson calls the "container schema" and is diagnosed as an intrusion across a boundary, to be corrected by a suitable form of embodied action in response. What emerges, then, is *something quite particular and also something comparable to other contexts in which the container schema is similarly activated.* (Strathern 1996: 188-89 [emphasis added])

Thus, I would not yet go so far as to say that image schemas are *only* and *always* fluid structures without fixed memory traces of any sort. Instead, what we need to cultivate more is a stereoscopic view on context-bound and transcontextual functions that image schemas fulfill (Kimmel 2002: 165-68), a double ontology.

3.2. Situated image-schema acquisition

For fleshing out the context-adaptive aspects of the ontology of image sche-mas, it is useful to look first at the mechanisms whereby their acquisition reveals cultural and contextual facets.

The cognitive linguistic mainstream to date retains a relatively a-cultural take on how basic cognitive forms emerge from embodiment (Sinha 1999). What looms large are universal patterns of bodily experience that develop-mentally prefigure conceptual discourse. This is conceived either as ground-ing of simple images in transcontextual kinesthetic experiences like the FORCE schema (Johnson 1987) or as the grounding of metaphoric mappings in primary scenes – co-occurrences of source and target – like RELATION-SHIPS ARE ENCLOSURES, DIFFICULT IS HEAVY, PLEASING IS TASTY, or IM-PORTANT IS BIG (Grady 1997, *this volume*). Image schemas are thus thought of as acquired through kinesthetic, spatial, and sensory experiences of a general nature. A universalist acquisition bias inheres in this, assuming that image schemas are, by virtue of pre-linguistic embodied experience in in-fancy, developmental universals. Yet, image schemas are also acquired or refined in more specific interactions with other bodies, social space, social interaction or rituals, and culture-specific artifacts. Studies with a develop-mental or acquisition focus document at least four kinds of culture-specific concept formation that involve the body.

First, learning particular and complex image schemas is often *mediated by formative special practices or settings*. Shore (1991) describes ritualized postural techniques that are instrumental in acquiring the twin concepts *mana* ('generative potency', 'luck') and *tapu* ('sacred', 'bound', 'set-aside'). When *tapu* is imposed on people or objects "in the interest of rendering these people or objects intelligible and redirecting personal potency for general or cosmic ends" (Shore 1991: 17), body techniques are involved that can be connected with BINDING, CONTAINMENT, CENTEREDNESS, RIGIDITY and STASIS schemas, which must be co-activated in body awareness. Clearly, this is a compound or superimposition of several simpler image schemas, which is difficult to master and in which each aspect further nuances body aware-ness. Learning this contained body style begins in infancy with the encour-agement of stress impulse control and a technique of sitting in the *fata'i* position (legs crossed and arms resting on the thighs). The same embodied style later informs postural attributes of chiefs, dance, ritual and gender styles.[9] Elsewhere, Shore (1996: 207-261) discusses complex learning through specialized cultural practices in great detail. He argues that aborigi-nal novices, over several years, distill a complex "walkabout" schema (ar-guably to do with CYCLE, ITERATION and INSIDE-OUTSIDE) of geographical and epistemic relevance, from a multitude of overlapping episodic memories. In a parallel process, ritual experiences are gradually transformed into pro-cedural schemas, while mythological narratives are transformed into seman-tic schemas.

Second, image schema acquisition is *mediated through a mix of overt and covert body practices* that are ubiquitous in everyday life. Geurts (2003) studies the image schema of BALANCE across contexts in the Anlo-Ewe culture of Ghana (see below). Bourdieu's (1977: 90-92), ethnography of the Algerian Kabyles, while not introducing the notion of image schema itself yet, describes a complex system of gendered homologies in which pos-tures, practices, and social space together define OUTWARD and UP schemas as male and INWARD and DOWN schemas as female. Bourdieu's theory of embodied cultural knowledge – couched in terms of generative principles called "habitus" and concretely manifested in bodily "hexis", i.e., posture and movement patterns – sees ritual and everyday activities as continuous "structural exercises" for particular schemas.

Third, image schema acquisition is *mediated through the cultural envi-ronment of artifacts or spatial arraying* (cf. Toren 1993). According to Sinha and Jensen de López (2000: 31), children employ social knowledge of the canonical use of objects *in conjunction with* their innate capacity for schematizing spatial relations. The image-schematic nature of cultural ob-jects may be a prototypical ecological affordance that influences language (Sinha and Jensen de López 2000: 22). Thus, Zapotec children are not as quick as Danish or English children to notice linguistic differences between

---

9. Shore (1991: 17) calls this learning by "sensory metonymy". It is triggered, as with Grady's (1997) account of "primary scenes", by feature co-occurrence in a setting. But whereas Grady emphasizes co-occurring attributes in infancy in basic nurturing or kinesthetic experience, Shore's formative co-occurrences continue throughout adolescence and are culturally orchestrated.

senses of *under* and *in* because they are not encouraged to play with upright cups, and more generally because Zapotecs use a smaller variety of containers they tend to use more multi-functionally.

Finally, acquisition is *mediated through language itself* (Bowerman 1996; Zlatev 1997). For example, probably due to linguistic marking, Yucatec Maya pay more attention to what something is made of in categorizing, while English speakers pay attention to shape (Lucy 1996: 49-52).

All this suggests that image schema acquisition inherently involves a dialectical relationship between bodily and socio-cultural dispositions. For a balanced view, cognitive linguistics must overcome a tendency to unidirectionally theorize how image schemas shape discourse, while neglecting how discourse, ritual, and material culture shape image schemas. To remedy this "feed-forward bias" – perhaps deriving from the "universalist bias" previously discussed – we need to develop frameworks (cf. Kövecses 2000: 160-163) that capture how image-schematic metaphors, for example, are doubly constrained by embodied experiences *and* by cultural ideology. Finally, a strong connection between compoundness and situatedness suggests itself for further exploration: Compound image schemas may often be acquired though exposure to culture-specific scenes that create situation-bound knowledge packages, that is, quite specific experiential gestalts.

3.3. Image schemas with context-selective origin and context-adaptive use

For opening the notion of image schema to a socio-culturally situated ontology, we had best begin with a caveat: If we want to study recurrent and schematic aspects of cognition, we cannot throw out the baby with the bathwater and focus exclusively on the finest ethnographic details of how people act in a single context or say that this context is so unique it has nothing noteworthy in common with other contexts. However, the issue hinges on the question just how transcontextual the origin of an image has to be in order to make it an image *schema*. The simple image schemas usually enumerated only capture schematic commonalities across the *widest possible* scope of differing situations. Every CONTAINER schema is described quite like any other, even though a container like our body's trunk, a thermos flask, and the religious model of an all-encompassing entity have notable differences, and these perhaps even extend to the schematic level: one we can feel inside, the other touch with our hands and see, and the third only imagine with reference to a complex cosmological model. Still image schemas are usually discussed as schematically as our own abstractive imagination allows, without a trace of contextuality and without specifying situation-specific subvariants or the loci of the image schemas.

But do image schemas qua schemas need to be described as maximally schematic entities? Clearly, the notion of schema per se does not force a commitment to *maximal* schematicity. Schemas are spoken of at various levels of embeddedness. Hence, calling something an "image schema" may be perfectly legitimate, even if it captures commonalities *of a limited set of (typically culture-specific) experiential settings* like some kinds of healing, a class of religious rituals, or a type of body posture.

3.4. Cultural augmentations of "primitive" image schemas

How may we then capture in which way a relatively limited set of experiences produces a corresponding set-specific, and thus "situated" image schema? I propose that the descriptive adaptation of primitive image schemas to specific types of action should involve several aspects, notably their intentionality, motivation/emotion, and embodied quality.

3.4.1. *Fully intentional image schemas*

The ontological status of image schemas is, despite the possibility that they create transcontextually entrenched structures of cognition, inherently also that of contextual significance-bestowing devices. As Alverson's (1991: 117, 1994) cognitive-phenomenological work points out, image schemas are never actualized as pure idealizations or Euclidean abstractions. Rather than actualistic shapes they are intentional tools through which we *make* sense. Take the simple example of intending one's glass half FULL and intending it half EMPTY. Clearly, our viewpoint lends a different intentionality to the same scene. What I am getting at is that any simple image schema will appear in a more situated way once we specify the intentionally of its usage. Although an Euclidean bias may still prevail (due to the interest in situation-independent cognition), descriptions of image schemas should, for several reasons, not remain entirely devoid of the intentionality they are enacted with:

First of all, culture may determine fairly stable general modes of bestowing intentionality. Linguistic worldviews may produce a strong bias to construe a scene as moving, as Palmer (1996: 148) notes for the Yaqui speakers of northern Mexico and Arizona, whereas English speakers tend to construe the very same spatial scene as static. The same drawing is seen as representing a static or a moving person depending on culture. Similarly, Alverson (1994: 22-23) shows that Bantu-speaking cultures see anchor points based on object size 'into' the spatial line-up of three objects, while Europeans treat them 'on a par', independent of size. Furthermore, Bantu speakers may scan the scene beginning with the remotest object, Europeans must do so from ego's viewpoint.

Second, intentionality means that image schemas are always embedded in a concrete type of usage context. Recurrent context-types always add something to the decontextualized ontology of basic image schemas, as Gibbs (1999: 154) expresses it:

> … containment is not just a sensori-motor act, but an event full of anticipation, sometimes surprise, sometimes fear, sometimes joy, each of which is shaped by the presence of other objects and people that we interact with. Image schemas are therefore not simply given by the body, but constructed out of culturally governed interactions.

While Johnson (1987: 181-190), when he first developed the notion, was at pains to describe image schemas as inherently intentional, he may have understood intentionality in a more transcontextual sense than Gibbs or I would understand it. What Johnson seemed to be emphasizing then is the fact that we cannot conceive of a schema like CONTAINER devoid of a usage-context or aim of *some* sort. Through this valuable insight alone we do not yet achieve a particularly thick description of any actual intentionality, or one that is fully context-adaptive. By conceiving of intentionality as pertaining to the general class of events where a CONTAINER occurs, its description will include in-out and boundary dimensions, but nothing beyond. This still *relatively* unspecified intentionality remains open to further specification according to a particular usage-type.

Any image schema's intentionality depends on its locus with relation to the individual, i.e., on whether it is perceived/imagined in one's own body or perceived/imagined in the external world. Usually, our actions directed at the body-container feel noticeably different from such directed at a balloon, and definitely different from mental operations undertaken with a category-container.[10] Similarly, image schemas, though ensuring transmodal map-

---

10. There is perhaps some truth to the claim that, say, the imaginative and metaphorical FORCE of reason (e.g., acting on an idea-object) and an external

pings, may also differ slightly in each sensory modality that actualizes them in experience (cf. Grady, *this volume*).

Specificity also issues from the fact that intentionality may primarily be bound to holistic image-schematic scenes, in which other image schemas are co-present, not to an image-schematic primitive per se (cf. Alverson 1991: 112). A STRAIGHT FORCE feels intentionally different from a FORCE CYCLE. Whenever experiential co-occurrence results in an "integral relation" between image schemas, the intentionality should be tied up with the entire scene, like MASS, NEAR-FAR, and MERGING related in seeing something recede in the distance (Cienki 1997: 8). As Alverson's Bantu example showed, further specificity arises from different construals of such a complex spatial setting. In discourse, a quite different kind of holistic determination may obtain. Quinn (1991), in a study of marriage discourse, observed that distinct image-schematic metaphors may occur in a tightly packed fashion within a single passage. One interviewee, for example, smoothly switches between ontological construals of marital lastingness as *unbreakable bond* (LINK), *well-made product* (ENTITY), *permanent location* (CONTAINER), and *ongoing journey* (PATH). To capture how themes like marriage and sub-themes like lastingess are organized, Quinn posits higher-level "cultural models". If image-schema selection and grouping is indeed governed by these, then image schemas may inherit from them part of their complex intentionality. Finally, cultural styles of relating to an image schema, i.e., its embedding in a holistic ethos, may also shape its intentionally (see 3.4.4).

In sum, we should recognize that the generic fact of intentionality can be fleshed out through the situated intentionalities real people act on. This notwithstanding, we also need to retain Johnson's insight that something connects all ontological sub-variants of an image schema. Recognizing this more decontextualized level of ontology remains indispensable for explaining what provides the cognitive basis for transmodal mappings and the (re-) combination of gestalts.

FORCE acting on our physical body may be phenomenologically similar in that something belonging to us feels displaced in some way? Yet, we should not be too quick to equate them as intentionally identical.

3.4.2. *Fully emotional and motivational image schemas*

The affinity of image schemas to emotion and evaluation has been discussed by Krzeszowski (1993), Palmer (1996), and Johnson (1999). First of all, image schemas may be said to become imbued with emotion to the degree that they also constitute motivations (cf. D'Andrade and Strauss 1992). Palmer (1996: 107, 109) argues that "[all] concepts are imbued, to varying degrees, with emotional values that constitute part of their imagery" and that, conversely, "emotions are complex configurations of goal driven imagery that govern feeling states and scenarios, including discourse scenarios." This two-way connection sits well with Paul's (1990: 439) definition of drives as "cognitive mental images already endowed with an affective tone that renders them motivational." Hence, to become emotion-imbued, an image schema must be motivational and intentionally linked to a specific action-goal. While a decontextualized, stripped down image schema will hardly become emotion-imbued, putting it to a human task in some context can produce this surplus quality. Emotion and motivation thus tend to occur as emergent properties of image-schematic compounds, because these are typically the outcome when an emotion-triggering social setting is construed as a complex scene.

3.4.3. *Fully embodied image schemas*

Image schemas have always been claimed to be of an inherently embodied nature (for limitations, cf. Kimmel, to appear). Therefore, a final layer of endowing an image schema with situatedness relates to how we describe its embodied quality. In my view, richer phenomenological and qualitative descriptions of bodily experience can be part of understanding image schemas. This should involve looking at how an image schema is embedded into a particular way of the body's "engagement with the world". Here, we can look to Csordas' (1994) cultural phenomenology, a recent trend in the anthropology of the body that is intensely concerned with imagery in embodied experience. Csordas' strategic focus is the enactive"lived body" and notably involves the study of "somatic modes of attention". These are culture-specific modes of attending to one's own body, the others' bodies, and of reacting to the others' attention to ones own body.

The approach is context-adaptive in that it describes embodiment in a richer and more qualitative fashion than image schemas alone would allow.

However, it does so in a way that can accommodate these, as Csordas' ethnography of symbolic healing in a Pentecostal community illustrates: By way of causal-explanatory objectification, the expert-healer interprets the lay-client's diffuse state of embodied discomfort or guilt as "demon" (of masturbation, etc.). This means that an external AGENT who has taken possession of the body CONTAINER through PENETRATION is predicated onto the client's subjective feeling, thus enabling the expert to EXPEL it by applying spiritual FORCE. Apparently, important aspects of Csordas' account may be reframed as an image-schematic social script functioning as a medium of the symbolic act. More generally, infusing the analysis of image-schematic practices with phenomenological context sensitivity often requires a holistic analysis of embodied social scripts as well as a discussion of the styles of embodied awareness and beliefs surrounding them.[11]

3.4.4.   A case study of a situated image schema

Image schemas can become culturally situated, because the goals they are directed at are embedded in holistic cultural meanings. Their intentionality forms part of an ethos or worldview. Within the ethnographic literature on cultural sensoria, Geurts' (2003) study of the Anlo-Ewe of South Ghana breaks new ground by giving a careful culture-sensitive description of modes of embodied engagement. Combing ethnographic, linguistic and developmental aspects, her goal is to illustrate the role of kinesthetic and proprioceptive schemas related to the Anlo-Ewe theory of *seselelame* ('attending to feeling-within-the-body'). Within this general cultural mode of being, BALANCE is a powerful generative principle. Cultivating proper balance is ubiquitous in Anlo-Ewe life: To begin with, balance is quite simply required to carry heavy loads on the head, so as to be able to move freely and naturally. But achieving balance is not only a goal of explicit learning as a transportation technique; someone's posture and gait also index a person's moral fortitude and psychological disposition. Metaphors expressing this are linguistically more varied and performatively more elaborated than similar Euro-American

---

11. What kind of embodiment one may discover inherently depends on the situatedness of the analysis: Clues about "strong" embodiment (in the sense of a full "engagement with the world") emerge from looking at ongoing acts of experiencing *in toto*. Experiments on the co-activation of embodied imagery with words, however, generate a "weaker" sense of embodiment, at least as long as phenomenological specifications are not attempted.

counterparts such as "having backbone". Not surprisingly, the head-balancing of objects is also elaborated in ritual. Moreover, special social practices ensure that children develop a proper sense of BALANCE: Infants often get their joints flexed to develop an awareness of graceful movement; and toddlers are continually exhorted to balance.

The Anlo-Ewe also perceive balance as a diachronic relation and there-fore as something that can obtain between different events: Balance schemas inform a specific ritual dramaturgy where dancing alternates between a heated and a cool mode. Another schema encourages each Anlo-Ewe person to achieve balance between extra- and introverted modes of being across time. Finally, balance is not strictly intra-individual; it also refers to the necessary balance of the social and cosmic bodies (= systemic relations). Living in balance therefore requires a sensitivity to family relations and ex-tends, as it were, beyond the individual's skin.

Geurts' account underscores that Anlo-Ewe BALANCE is at all times situ-ated in contexts ranging from mundane ones such as the fetching of water to highly elaborate ones such as ritual. The view from a detailed ethnography ipso facto turns out to be different from the early Johnsonian image schema of BALANCE that children all over the world acquire in a roughly similar way. The balance ethos of the Anlo-Ewe brings to the fore how an image schema like BALANCE may be culturally refined. Especially because it par-takes of a cultural disposition for cultivating the proprioceptive sense, it is a perfect example for my proposed descriptive strategy of specifying how the intentionality of general image schemas is fine-tuned. Even though Anlo-Ewe BALANCE has in itself obvious image-schematic sub-variants (e.g., various loci), these different instantiations hang together via the cultural ethos that makes balance so salient and produces a strong resonance in body aware-ness.[12] Thus, the generic BALANCE schema is refined with regard to a cul-tural ethos, which constitutes a wider intentional field.

3.5. Situated image schemas and situated analysis

Image schemas, as I propose to understand them, are tools of situated cogni-tion and action (Zlatev 1997; Gibbs 1999). Together intentionality, emotion,

---

12. This partly mirrors Strauss and Quinn's (1997) theory of discursive metaphor use, which spells out how, against the backdrop of a shared cultural ethos, subvariants in conceptualization emerge.

motivation and full phenomenological embodiment define what I call situatedness in usage. From an acquisition perspective we may additionally direct our focus onto how specific image schemas are learned or refined in culturally recurrent settings.

For all practical purposes, speaking of *situated schemas* means striking a healthy balance between isolating unique cultural occurrences too rich for a schema and positing maximally schematic, general image schemas devoid of anything context-bound. To make this work, I propose to fine-grain the ontology of the more basic image schemas by moving center stage their situated *sub-variants* and their connection to particular context *types*. While neither subvariants nor context types need to be universal, they do form parts of the *recurrent experience* of a group of people. Thus, for a situated analysis, image schemas must be specified at least at the level of some scenario-type, i.e., a kind of recurrent action goal, with regard to some or all of the above criteria: their meshing with other image schemas, their sensory modality, their locus in the body, their intentional, motivational and emotional role. This specification may be put into practice either by sub-indexing familiar image schemas to create terms like FORCE-CYCLE, or by describing them in their qualitative context.

3.6. Situated methods

Finally, to understand *how people do things with image schemas* in contexts (like framing a discursive topic in a processual or, alternatively, in an entified ontology) we will have to open up to situated methods of data collection. Presently, linguistic and experimental methods which tend to generate rather de-contextualized data dominate. Much of the ontology of how linguists understand image schemas has emerged from looking at such data. This may have created a bias towards overemphasizing the situation-independent cognitive inventory or even cultural universals. The danger is that, without applying context-sensitive methods as a counadcheck against research artifacts, it remains difficult to gauge to what extent assumptions of universality are influenced by the scholar's own abstractions from situated data and how much subtle variation in image schema usage escapes the analysis. Here, the rise of ethnographic (Geurts 2003) and discourse-analytic approaches (Quinn 1991; Strauss and Quinn 1997; Liebert et al. 1997) points in the right direction.

4. Conclusion

Picking up the various loose ends, a larger picture of the perhaps dominant view of image schemas in Cognitive Linguistics emerges. The logic of the ontological biases enumerated above – universal acquisition, feed-forward, micro-unit, maximal schematicity – is mirrored in the methodological preference for situation-independent data. These biases hamper a socio-cultural view, probably because they tend to mutually support one another: First, studying micro-units like CONTAINER pure and simple, especially when conceived as maximally schematic, is congenial to the search for situation-independent cognitive structure precisely *because* primitives devoid of situated characteristics are what different contexts are likely to share. Second, experimental and linguistic methods which invite the elimination of situated nuances of intentionality mirror this predominant aim. Third, a rather universalist view of image schemas is itself partly due to this abstraction from cultural context. Fourth, screening out ethnographic methods for studying image schema acqusition and usage means neglecting how cultural environments and practices feed back into image schemas, a fact which further reinforces universalism.

All of the biases discussed are thus part of an academic gestalt in its own right, which cognitive linguistics seems to have lived by for some time. While this gestalt does not need to be replaced completely, it needs to be given a dialectical partner, perhaps through honing our own capacity for performing a gestalt-switch between seeing image schemas as situated *and* as maximally transcontextual entities.

References

Alverson, Hoyt
    1991   Metaphor and experience. Looking over the notion of Image Schema. In *Beyond Metaphor. The Theory of Tropes in Anthropology*, James Fernandez (ed.), 94-119. Stanford: Stanford University Press.
    1994   *Semantics and Experience. Universal Metaphors of Time in English, Mandarin, Hindi, and Sesotho.* Baltimore: Johns Hopkins University Press.
Arnheim, Rudolf
    1969   *Visual Thining.* London: Faber.

308   *Michael Kimmel*

Blumenberg, Hans
  1996   Reprint. Ausblick auf eine Theorie der Unbegrifflichkeit. In
          Theorie der Metapher, Anselm Haverkamp (ed.), 438-454.
          Darmstadt: Wissenschaftliche Buchgesellschaft [original 1979].
Bourdieu, Pierre
  1977   *Outline of a Theory of Practice*. Cambridge: Cambridge University
          Press.
Bowerman, Melissa
  1996   Cognitive versus linguistic determinants. In *Rethinking Linguistic
          Relativity*, John J. Gumperz, and Stephen Levinson (eds.), 145-176.
          Cambridge: Cambridge University Press.
Cienki, Alan
  1997   Some properties and groupings of image schemas. In *Lexical and
          Syntactical Constructions and the Construction of Meaning*, Mar-
          jolijn. Verspoor, Kee Dong Lee, and Eve Sweetser (eds.), 3-15.
          Amsterdam: John Benjamins.
Cook, Nicholas
  1990   *Music, Imagination and Culture*. Oxford: Oxford University Press.
Csordas, Thomas (ed.)
  1994   *Embodiment and Experience: The Existential Ground of Culture
          and Self*. Cambridge: Cambridge University Press.
D'Andrade, Roy G.
  1995   *The Development of Cognitive Anthropology*. Cambridge: Cam-
          bridge University Press.
D'Andrade, Roy G., and Claudia Strauss (eds.)
  1992   *Human Motives and Cultural Models*. Cambridge: Cambridge Uni-
          versity Press.
Geurts, Kathryn L.
  2003   *Culture and the Senses. Bodily Ways of Knowing in an African
          Community*. Berkeley: University of California Press.
Gibbs, Raymond W.
  1999   Taking metaphor out of our heads and putting it into the cultural
          world. In *Metaphor in Cognitive Linguistics*, Raymond Gibbs, and
          Gerard Steen (eds.), 145-166. Philadelphia/ Amsterdam: John Ben-
          jamins.
  2003   Embodied experience and linguistic meaning. *Brain and Language*
          84: 1-15.
Gibbs, Raymond W., and Eric Berg
  2002   Mental imagery and embodied activity. *Journal of Mental Imagery*
          26: 1-30.

Gibbs, Raymond W., and Herbert L. Colston
1995   The cognitive psychological reality of image schemas and their transformations. *Cognitive Linguistics* 6: 347-378.
Grady, Joseph E.
1997   Foundations of meaning: Primary metaphors and primary scenes. Ph.D. Dissertation at The University of California, Berkeley.
Jensen de López, Kristine, and Chris Sinha
2000   Culture and the embodiment of spatial cognition. *Cognitive Linguistics* 11: 17-41.
Johnson, Mark
1987   *The Body in the Mind: The Bodily Basis of Meaning, Imagination, and Reason.* Chicago: University of Chicago Press.
1999   Embodied Reason. In *Perspectives on Embodiment: The Intersections of Nature and Culture*, Gail Weiss and Honi Haber (eds.), 81-102. London: Routledge.
Kimmel, Michael
2002   Metaphor, imagery, and culture. Ph.D. Dissertation at the University of Vienna.
2005   From metaphor to the "mental sketchpad": Literary macrostructure and compound image schemas in 'Heart of Darkness'. *Metaphor and Symbol* 20: 199-238.
To appear   Properties of cultural embodiment: Lessons from the anthropology of the body. In *Body, Language and Mind*, Vol. 2, Roslyn Frank, René Dirven, Enrique Bernárdez, and Tom Ziemke (eds.). Berlin/New York: Mouton de Gruyter.
Kövecses, Zoltán
2000   *Metaphor and Emotion. Language, Culture, Body in Human Feeling.* Cambridge: Cambridge University Press.
2002   *Metaphor: A Practical Introduction.* Oxford: Oxford University Press.
Krzeszowski, Tomasz P.
1993   The axiological parameter in preconceptual image schemata. In *Conceptualizations and Mental Processing in Language*, Richard Geiger, and Brigyda Rudzka-Ostyn (eds.), 307-330. Berlin/New York: Mouton de Gruyter.
Lakoff, George
1987   *Women, Fire and Dangerous Things. What Categories Reveal About the Mind.* Chicago: Chicago University Press.
Lakoff, George, and Zoltán Kövecses
1987   The cognitive model of anger inherent in American English. In *Cultural Models in Language and Thought*, Dorothy Holland and

Naomi Quinn (eds.), 195-221. Cambridge: Cambridge University Press.

Langacker, Ronald
1987   *Foundations of Cognitive Grammar*. Vol. 1. Stanford: Stanford University Press.

Liebert, Wolf-Andreas, Gisela Redeker, and Linda Waugh (eds.)
1997   *Discourse and Perspective in Cognitive Linguistics*. Amsterdam/ Philadelphia: John Benjamins.

Lucy, John A.
1996   The scope of linguistic relativity: An analysis and review of empirical research. In *Rethinking Linguistic Relativity*, John J. Gumperz, and Stephen C. Levinson (eds.), 37-69. Cambridge: Cambridge University Press.

Oakley, Todd
To appear   Image schema. In *The Oxford Handbook of Cognitive Linguistics*, Dirk Geeraerts, and Hubert Cuyckens (eds.). New York: Oxford University Press.

Olds, Linda E.
1991   Chinese metaphors of interrelatedness: Re-imaging body, nature, and the feminine. *Contemporary Philosophy* 13: 16-22.

Palmer, Gary
1996   *Toward a Theory of Cultural Linguistics*. Austin: University of Texas Press.

Paul, Robert
1990   What does anybody want. Desire, purpose, and the acting subject in the study of culture. *Cultural Anthropology* 5: 431-451.

Pires de Oliveira, Roberta, and Robson de Souza Bittencourt
To appear   Embodiment: From neurons to sociocultural situatedness. In *Body, Language and Mind*, Vol. 2, Roslyn Frank, René Dirven, Enrique Bernárdez, and Tom Ziemke (eds.). Berlin/ New York: Mouton de Gruyter.

Quinn, Naomi
1991   The cultural basis of metaphor. In *Beyond Metaphor. The Theory of Tropes in Anthropology*, James Fernandez (ed.), 56-93. Stanford: Stanford University Press.

Shore, Bradd
1991   Twice born, once conceived: Meaning construction and cultural cognition. *American Anthropologist* 93: 9-27.
1996   *Culture in Mind.* Oxford: Oxford University Press.

Sinha, Chris
   1999   Grounding, mapping and acts of meaning. In *Cognitive Linguistics: Foundations, Scope and Methodology*, Theo Janssen, and Gisela Redeker (eds.), 223-255. Berlin: Mouton de Gruyter.
Strathern, Andrew
   1996   *Body Thoughts*. Ann Arbor: University of Michigan Press.
Strauss, Claudia, and Naomi Quinn
   1997   *A Cognitive Theory of Cultural Meaning*. Cambridge: Cambridge University Press.
Toren, Christina
   1993   Making history: The significance of childhood cognition for a comparative anthropology of mind. *Man* 28: 461-478.
Turner, Mark
   1996   *The Literary Mind*. Oxford/New York: Oxford University Press.
Werth, Paul
   1999   *Text Worlds: Representing Conceptual Space in Discourse*. Harlow: Longman.
Wittgenstein, Ludwig
   1953   *Philosophical Investigations*. New York: Macmillan.
Zlatev, Jordan
   1997   Situated Embodiment: Studies in the Emergence of Spatial Meaning. Stockholm: Gotab.

What's in a schema?
Bodily mimesis and the grounding of language

Jordan Zlatev[*]

> Mimetic skills or mimesis rests on the ability to produce conscious,
> self-initiated, representational acts that are intentional but not lin-
> guistic.   Merlin Donald, *Origins of the Modern Mind*

Abstract

The chapter defines *mimetic schemas* as dynamic, concrete and preverbal representations, involving the body image, which are accessible to consciousness, and
pre-reflectively shared in a community. Mimetic schemas derive from a uniquely
human capacity for *bodily mimesis* (Donald 1991; Zlatev, Persson and Gärdenfors
2005) and are argued to play a key role in language acquisition, language evolution and the linking of phenomenal experience and shared meaning. In this sense
they are suggested to provide a "grounding" of language which is more adequate
than that of image schemas. By comparing the two concepts along six different
dimensions: representation, accessibility to consciousness, level of abstractness,
dynamicity, sensory modality and (inter)subjectivity the term "image schema" is
shown to be highly polysemous, which is problematic for a concept that purports
to be foundational within Cognitive Linguistics.

Keywords: bodily mimesis, consciousness, "grounding", intersubjectivity, mimetic schemas, representation, language acquisition.

1. Introduction

The concept of image schema is central to Cognitive Linguistics, as demonstrated by the contributions to this volume. At the same time, there is little
agreement on the exact nature of the phenomenon that it should apply to.
While some define image schemas as representational structures (Lakoff
1987; Grady, *this volume*; Mandler 2004, *this volume*), others emphasize

---

[*] I am indebted to Beate Hampe, Esa Itkonen, Vyv Evans and two anonymous
     reviewers for helpful comments on an earlier version of this chapter.

their non-representational, "interactional" character (Zlatev 1997; Johnson and Rohrer, in press; Johnson, *this volume*; Gibbs, *this volume*). Some see them as part of the "Cognitive Unconscious" (Lakoff and Johnson 1999; Johnson, *this volume*), but others claim that image schemas possess phenomenal contours and hence cannot be completely unconscious (Gibbs, *this volume*). Most often image schemas are thought to be rather abstract structures such as PATH and VERTICALITY (Johnson 1987; Mandler 2004), or even more abstract ones such as CYCLE and PROCESS (Johnson 1987; see also the survey in Grady, *this volume*). On the other hand, "basic level" experiential structures such as PUSH and GRASP are sometimes given as illustrations of image-schematic structure (Gibbs, *this volume*). Finally, even their "embodied" nature, in the sense of being based on physical experience, has been questioned in some definitions (Clausner and Croft 1999), while Grady (*this volume*) argues for limiting the notion strictly to sensorimotor experience.

Clearly, image schemas cannot have all of these properties at the same time, and consequently we have not one but a number of different, more or less overlapping concepts: the term "image schema" is therefore highly polysemous. While polysemy may be a central characteristic of language, it is hardly a desirable property for a *scientific* concept, which furthermore is supposed to be foundational within Cognitive Linguistics. If there is one core feature that all the different "senses" of the term share, it is that image schemas should provide *a ground for linguistic meaning* – including, for some authors, even grammar (Lakoff 1987; Deane 1994). But of course, the manner in which image schemas are supposed to "ground" language depends on how the concept is defined in the first place.

Instead of adding one more sense to the term "image schema", I will employ a related, but distinct concept, namely that of *mimetic schema*. My goal in this chapter will be twofold: First, I will show how my concept compares to the different definitions of image schemas proposed in the literature along six different "parameters", two of which are also discussed by (Grady, *this volume*). Second, I will explicate and explore some of the evidence for the hypothesis that *linguistic meaning is grounded in mimetic schemas*. The realization of these two goals gives rise to the inference that mimetic schemas provide an alternative (and arguably better) account of what image schemas were designed to do: explain the possibility for linguistic meaning to arise. The presented analysis also has implications for the nature of image schemas of the more abstract type, e.g., CONTAINMENT, that are similar to those suggested by Dewell (*this volume*): Rather than being prior to and independent of language as claimed by, e.g., Dodge and Lakoff (*this volume*), they are largely constituted by language itself.

2. Bodily mimesis and mimetic schemas

Over the past three years, I have carried out research within an interdisciplinary group of linguists, semioticians, cognitive scientists and philosophers in which we have studied the interrelationship between language, gestures and pictures in a phylogenetic and ontogenetic perspective.[1] A key concept in our project has been that of *bodily mimesis*, particularly in the manner explicated by Donald (1991), presented summarily in the chapter motto. We have proceeded to elaborate the concept, and at the same time relate it to similar theoretical proposals such as Piaget's ([1945] 1962) concept of *symbol* and Tomasello's (1999) notion of *imitative learning*. While our research has been collaborative, I will in the following express my individual take on the story, so my colleagues should not be held responsible for my, possibly controversial, statements.

The key notion can be defined as follows: A particular bodily act of cognition or communication is an act of *bodily mimesis* if and only if:

(i)   it involves a cross-modal mapping between proprioception (kinaesthetic experience) and exteroception (normally dominated by vision), unless proprioception is compromised (*cross-modality*).
(ii)   it consists of a bodily motion that is, or can be, under conscious control (*volition*).
(iii)   the body (part) and its motion correspond – either iconically or indexically – to some action, object or event, but at the same time are differentiated from it by the subject (*representation*).
(iv)   the subject intends the act to stand for some action, object, or event for an addressee (*communicative sign function*).

But it is not an act of bodily mimesis if:

(v)   the act is fully conventional, i.e., a part of mutual knowledge, and breaks up (semi)compositionally into meaningful sub-acts that systematically relate to other similar acts (*symbolicity*).

---

1. For a description of our project (mostly in Swedish), see <www.arthist.lu.se/kultsem/pro/sgb.html>.

While this definition is formulated as a "classical" list of necessary and (jointly) sufficient conditions, it allows for a stage-like interpretation that can be seen in an evolutionary perspective that we call the *mimesis hierarchy*. Acts which only fulfill the first condition, but not the others can be defined as *proto-mimetic*. Neonatal face-mirroring and cross-modal matching (Meltzoff and Moore 1977, 1983, 1994) can be regarded as such, and these have been witnessed in newborn chimpanzees as well (Myowa-Yamakoshi et al. 2003). On the other hand, both *deferred imitation* and *mirror self-recognition* fulfill conditions (i)-(iii) and thus show a full form of bodily mimesis. However, if condition (iv) is not fulfilled, it is bodily mimesis only of a *dyadic* sort. Skills such as these presuppose that the subject can both differentiate between his own (felt) bodily representation, and the entity that this representation corresponds to, and to see the first as standing for the latter. This is what Piaget (1962) called "the symbolic function", appearing at the end of the sensorimotor period of the child's development. Sonesson (1989, in press) uses this as the crucial criterion to distinguish between true signs, which display it, and pre-sign meanings, which do not. A recent review of the non-human primate evidence (Zlatev, Persson and Gärdenfors 2005a) shows that contrary to previously held views (e.g., Tomasello 1999), apes are capable of dyadic mimesis in the domains of imitation (e.g., do-as-I-do), intersubjectivity (e.g., shared attention) and gesture (e.g., imperative pointing). Therefore it is most likely that the common ape-human ancestor was also capable of dyadic mimesis.[2]

The crucial step in human evolution appears to involve (iv), or *triadic mimesis*, such as that involved in *pantomime* or *declarative pointing*, which has not been clearly demonstrated in apes in natural environments or even zoos. However, "enculturated" or "cross-fostered" apes, including chimpanzees (Fouts 1973), gorillas (Patterson 1980), an orangutan (Miles 1990) and bonobos (Savage-Rumbough and Lewin 1994) have shown that when provided with a high degree of social interaction involving intentional communication, the communicative sign function is not completely beyond the grasp of our nearest relatives in the animal kingdom. These findings can be taken as supporting Donald's (1991) original proposal of an intermediary mimetic

---

2. Note that our distinction between dyadic and triadic mimesis is not identical with Tomasello's (1999) notions of dyadic/triadic engagements: we classify e.g. imperative pointing as dyadic mimesis since it does not involve communicative intentions, even though there are three entities in the scene. On the other hand, we treat e.g. pantomime as triadic mimesis, even if it only depicts the (desired) actions of mimer and interpreter, i.e., a "dyadic" engagement.

stage in hominid evolution, approximately coinciding with the high days of *Homo erectus/ergaster* between 2 million and 500,000 years ago (with one descendant, the recently discovered *Homo floresiensis*, possibly surviving until as late as 18,000 years ago).

Finally, condition (v) distinguishes between intentional gestural communication, and *signed language*, which also possesses the properties of conventionality and systematicity (Singleton, Goldwin-Meadow and McNeill 1995). Some have proposed that such a *post-mimetic* stage, utilizing the manual-brachial rather than the vocal modality, intervened in hominid evolution (Stokoe 2001; Corballis 2002). Their claim is, in other words, that our ancestors initially communicated in a (simple) signed language, prior to vocal language taking the upper hand in hearing populations. However, the evidence does not require such a strong view, and the findings that have been marshaled in its support, e.g., the ubiquity of co-speech gestures (McNeill 1992), or the homology between Broca's area and areas of the monkey's pre-motor cortex controlling motor skills, and even their recognition in conspecifics using "mirror neurons" (Rizzolatti and Arbib 1998; Arbib 2003), can also be explained assuming a stage of triadic bodily mimesis, lacking full conventionality and systematicity.

While bodily mimesis, both in its dyadic and even more so in its triadic forms, is an essentially interpersonal phenomenon, it can also be *internalized* and used for thought, as argued by Piaget (1962) making the concept rather "Vygotskyan", in the sense of the general principle of the *inter*personal preceding the *intra*personal (Vygotsky 1978). But internalized, or what we might call *covert* mimesis, corresponds to what has recently been discussed in terms of "mental simulation" (Barsalou 1999; Gallese 2003; Gibbs, *this volume*; Rohrer, *this volume*). The major difference is that simulation is most often described as an unconscious, "neural" process (Dodge and Lakoff, *this volume*; Gallese and Lakoff 2005), while in our account all but proto-mimesis is at least potentially conscious. Notice also that the concept of "representation" used in our account (cf. also Ikegami and Zlatev, in press) presupposes a differentiation between expression and content, or mental image and (perceptual) reality *from the standpoint of the subject* (Piaget 1962), implying conscious awareness of the representation as such.

Given this characterization of bodily mimesis, mimetic schemas can be defined as *categories of acts of overt or covert bodily mimesis*. Examples of mimetic schemas are so-called action concepts, such as EAT, SIT, KISS, HIT, PUT IN, TAKE OUT, RUN, CRAWL, FLY, FALL, etc., which represent everyday actions and events. Let us summarize their properties.

(i) Mimetic schemas are *bodily* – in the very literal sense of the word, (usually) involving proprioception even if the action is "simulated" rather than actually re-enacted.

(ii) Mimetic schemas are *representational* – "running" the schema (either in reality or in imagination) is differentiated from the object, action or event to which is corresponds, "from the standpoint of the subject".

(iii) Mimetic schemas are *dynamic* – again in the literal sense of involving motion in both expression and content.

(iv) Mimetic schemas are *accessible to consciousness* – even though it need not be a matter of focal consciousness, which in the case of signs is directed at the represented rather than at the representation itself (Sonesson in press). Even so, mimetic schemas would qualify as structures of marginal consciousness (Gurwitsch 1964) rather than the "Cognitive Unconscious" (Lakoff and Johnson 1999).

(v) Mimetic schemas are *specific* – each one is a generalization of a particular bodily *act*, even if this act is carried out in the imagination rather than actually performed.

(vi) Mimetic schemas are, or at least can be, *pre-reflectively shared* – since they derive from imitating culturally salient actions and objects, both their representational and experiential content can be "shared" by the members of the community.

As we will see in the next section, most of these properties have been adopted within at least *some* account of image schemas. No account has, to my knowledge, included all of these properties, making the notion of mimetic schema a novel concept.

3.   Mimetic schemas vs. image schemas

It is not my goal here to argue against image schemas and in their place try to sell my concept of mimetic schema. Rather, my concern is with explicating the essential features of mimetic schemas. In the process of doing so, I will show that these features contrast with some characterizations of image schemas, but not with others. Thus, these properties and their contrasts can be seen as values along parameters along which different accounts of (image) schemas vary. While I will urge for a particular set of values along these parameters, I do not mean to exclude other possible sets: These other kinds of (image) schemas may have theoretical value in cognitive science and Cognitive Linguistics, but (a) they are not mimetic schemas, and (b) their role is less directly related to providing a ground for language. I will not argue for this second statement explicitly, but will try to show that mimetic schemas are more consistent with both empirical evidence and conceptual considerations concerning the nature of language. At the same time, if the reader would agree with my attribution of values along the following six dimensions, but insist on the term "image schema", then I would reply: "What's in a name?"

3.1. Representation

While the notion of *mental representation* was the most fundamental concept of "classical" cognitive science (e.g., Fodor 1981), "second generation" cognitive science of the 1990s (e.g., Varela, Thompson and Rosch 1991) witnessed a justified reaction against the overuse of the term, relying on such notions as *embodiment* (cf. Ziemke, Zlatev and Frank, in press) and *interaction*. Some image schema theorists adopt such an anti-representationalist stance explicitly:

> As we said in *Philosophy in the Flesh*, the only workable theory of representations is one in which a representation is a flexible pattern of organism-environment interactions, and not some inner mental entity that somehow gets hooked up with parts of the external world by a strange relation called 'reference'. (Johnson and Lakoff 2002: 249-250)

But redefining "representation" as "interaction" is a bit too strong. Admittedly, much of animal and (even) human cognition is non-representational, in the sense of "representation" used by Piaget ([1945] 1962) and adopted in the definition of mimetic schemas in Section 2. But is (drawing) a picture of an apple an "interaction" with it of the same kind as eating it? Furthermore, if we adopt a characterization of image schemas as non-representational structures, as stated explicitly by Johnson and Rohrer (in press), image schemas become structures of general animal sensorimotor cognition, and are in no way specific to human beings:

> Image schemas are thus part of our non-representational coupling with our world, just as barn owls and squirrel monkeys have image schemas that define their types of sensorimotor experience.

Johnson (*this volume*) similarly defines image schemas as "structures of sensory-motor experience" and Gibbs' (*this volume*) characterization as "attractors within human self-organizing systems" appears to be similar, at least in this respect.[3] In previous work (Zlatev 1997), I also urged for an interpretation of image schemas as *sensorimotor schemas* in the sense of Piaget (1952): goal-directed structures of practical activity, emerging from the child's physical interaction with the environment.

However, there is a serious problem for these accounts to the extent that they purport to provide an explanation of (the rise of) language. Sensorimotor schemas are non-representational, while language *is* representational in two different, though related, respects: it has expression-content structure and statements are *about* states of affairs, they have what Searle (1999) refers to as a "mind-to-world direction of fit" (cf. Zlatev, in press).

Piaget was very much aware of this problem, and while he argued that sensorimotor structures play an important part in the "construction of reality for the child", he also claimed that they have inherent limitations:

> … sensorimotor activity involves accommodation only to present data, and assimilation only in the unconscious practical form of application of earlier schemas to present data. (Piaget 1962: 278)

Therefore Piaget distinguished between sensorimotor schemas and what he referred to as *symbols*. The latter emerge at the end of the sensorimotor period and serve as a prerequisite to the learning of linguistic *signs*. However, Piaget's term "symbol" is confusing (to the modern reader) since what it refers to is neither *conventional*, nor interconnected in a *system*.[4] In fact, Piaget's account of "symbol" is very close, if not identical to that of mimetic schema: both emerge through imitation, but can be internalized as a form of mental simulation. Several accounts of image schemas presented in this volume, most notably that of Gibbs (*this volume*), likewise regard these as simulations: "simulators of action that are based on real-life actions and potential actions that a person may engage in". But the notion of simulation begs the question: simulation of *what*?

Other accounts of image schemas (Grady, *this volume*; Mandler 2004, *this volume*) are more explicitly representational:

---

3. Notice, however, that Gibbs (*this volume*) inserts the adjective "human" and later on urges that image schemas "should not be reduced to sensorimotor activity", which is also true of mimetic schemas. He also refers to image schemas as "simulators" and "simulations", which would appear to make his notion of image schemas representational anyway.

4. These influential characterizations of symbols, which I have argued should be combined (Zlatev 2003b), were made by Peirce (1931-1935) and Deacon (1997), respectively.

Image-schemas, such as SELF-MOTION, form the earliest meanings that the mind represents. ... This representational system creates a conceptual system that is potentially accessible; that is, it contains the information that is used to form images, to recall, and eventually to plan. (Mandler 2004: 91).

Mimetic schemas are thus in accordance with accounts of image schemas which treat the latter as representational structures, but not with those which treat them as (merely) sensorimotor, "interactional" structures, and even less so with those which treat them as neural structures (Rohrer, *this volume*; Dodge and Lakoff, *this volume*), since in themselves neurons, or even "neural circuits" do not stand for anything.[5]

3.2. Consciousness

Mimetic schemas are recurrent acts of bodily mimesis, and since mimesis rests on consciousness (Donald 1991), mimetic schemas are structures of consciousness. The notion of "consciousness" is of course vexed with riddles, but since consciousness became again a (scientifically) respectable topic over the last 20 years,[6] considerable advances have been made in both philosophical discussions, e.g., of the "hard problem" of the irreducibility of qualitative experience (Chalmers 1996), in distinguishing between different kind of consciousness, e.g., *affective* from *reflective* consciousness, as well as in understanding the neural underpinnings of this often mysterious phenomenon (e.g., Edelman 1992; Damasio 2001). In this respect, Cognitive Linguistics, with some notable recent exceptions (e.g., Talmy 2000; Evans 2003), is lagging behind, and (usually) shying away from referring to consciousness as an *explanans* for linguistic meaning and structure. Instead, the bedrocks of language, including image schemas, are sought in problematic

---

5. Dodge and Lakoff (*this volume*) appeal to the work of Regier (1996) in seeking a neural basis for image schemas, but I would argue that this is misguided. Regier does not interpret his model as an implementation of image schemas and repeatedly points out that it is only inspired by some properties of nervous systems, as well as by "high level" structures such as Source, Path and Goal, deriving from linguistic analysis. For a very different interpretation and a minor modification of Regier's model, see Zlatev (1997, 2003a).
6. As testified by a number of journals including *Journal of Consciousness Studies*, *Consciousness and Cognition*, and PSYCHE: *An Interdisciplinary Journal of Research on Consciousness*, as well as annual conferences such as "Towards a Science of Consciousness" (TSC).

notions (cf. Zlatev, in press) such as the "Cognitive Unconscious", characterized as "completely and irrevocably inaccessible to direct conscious introspection" (Johnson and Lakoff 1999: 103).

Johnson (*this volume*), however, is considerably more careful in pointing
out that structures such as image schemas "*typically* operate beneath the
level of our conscious awareness" [my emphasis], which does not imply that
they are inaccessible. In an even stronger departure from earlier formulations, he admits that, by regarding image schemas as (unconscious) structures,

> ... you lose, or at least overlook, the very thing that gives image schemas
> their life, motivating force, and relevance to human meaning, namely, their
> embeddedness within affect-laden and value-laden experience.

But this is nothing else but an aspect of affective consciousness, and thus of
"phenomenological embodiment" (Lakoff and Johnson 1999), rather than the
Cognitive Unconscious. Gibbs' (*this volume*) remark that an image schema
is a "simulator [that] provides something close to what it actually feels like
in a full-bodied manner" similarly includes a reference to phenomenology.
Lakoff, on the other hand, seems to be moving in the opposite direction and
seeking not just neural substrates, which is a justified scientific enterprise,
but actually "viewing image schemas as neural circuits" (Dodge and Lakoff,
this volume). This is another matter, both philosophically and empirically, as
it is not my hippocampus that sees or feels an object moving along a path to
a landmark, I do. The argument that "linguistic structure is below the level
of consciousness because the brain structures that compute them are unconscious" (Dodge and Lakoff, *this volume*) is, metaphorically speaking, a
(conceptual) *short*-circuit.

Whereas Johnson (*this volume*) worries that "there may be no way
around this problem", i.e., of how to include (affective) consciousness into
image-schematic structure, I would venture to claim that the problem does
not even appear with respect to mimetic schemas. This is so, firstly, because
mimetic schemas exist at the level of specific real or imagined bodily actions. Since they are by their nature *experiential* structures, each mimetic
schema has a different emotional-proprioceptive "feel", or affective tone
(Thompson 2001) to it. Consider, for example, the affective contrast between the mimetic schemas X-KICK-Y and X-KISS-Y. In this way they capture
what Johnson (*this volume*) refers to as "the flesh and blood of meaning".

Secondly, since mimetic schemas can be decoupled from perception and
actual action, they can be used in imagination, and thus become an aspect of
reflective consciousness. This makes them "accessible" in Mandler's terms

(2004, *this volume*), which is a property that she considers definitional of *concepts*. On the other hand, Mandler (*this volume*) also points out that image schemas "are not themselves accessible", i.e., conscious, but that is because she considers image schemas a representational "format" that gives rise to specific content, the latter being consciously accessible. It appears that she envisages image schemas to be part of an innate mechanism called "perceptual meaning analysis", which "extracts the spatial and movement structure of events in image-schematic form to represent them". Thus, there seems to be another parameter along which image schema accounts differ: bottom-up, "empiricist" accounts starting with actual full-blooded experience such as those of Johnson and Gibbs (in affinity with mimetic schemas) and top-down, "rationalist" accounts such as Mandler's and Lakoff's. This is, however, closely related to the next dimension, so I will not discuss it separately.

3.3. Level of abstractness

In the Cognitive Linguistics literature there has been some considerable debate concerning the level of abstractness of image schemas. In his contribution to this volume, Grady makes a set of valuable distinctions: there are at least three different levels of abstractness involved: (i) concrete schemas such as UP (HEIGHT), for which Grady reserves the designation "image schema", (ii) more abstract schemas such as MORE (QUANTITY), which Grady calls "response schemas" since he regards them as being the outcome of *primary metaphors* (Grady 1997), mappings from concrete domains due to correlations in experience in early childhood, and (iii) "superschemas" such as SCALAR PROPERTY, which capture the shared structure between (i) and (ii), guaranteeing a degree of isomorphism or "invariance" (Lakoff 1990). This hierarchy is very useful, but Grady fails to specify the nature and origin of such superschemas serving as constraints on metaphorical mappings. In a complementary contribution, Dewell (*this volume*) argues that schemas such as CONTAINMENT, and I would add UP, are not "purely preverbal" but rather shaped by language itself due to:

> ... the influence of language generally toward maximally precise and differentiated linear shapes that can be explicitly profiled and publicly accessed from a flexible perspective.

I am in general agreement with both of these accounts, and furthermore believe that the approach endorsed in the present chapter can help provide a synthesis. Mimetic schemas such as CLIMB and JUMP are (at least) one level below Grady's image schemas (of the HEIGHT and PROXIMITY type). Similar to Johnson (1987, *this volume*), I consider the latter to be formed in part *inductively*, i.e., by extracting generalizations over shared features of particular mimetic schemas, e.g. both CLIMB and JUMP involve motion along a VERTICAL dimension. But such generalizations are hardly formed purely "pre-verbally". First there is the famous "problem of induction" (Hume [1739] 2000). Concerning the present example: why generalize on the basis of verticality rather than some other "dimension", e.g., using both hands/feet? If, on the other hand, the child is simultaneously exposed to the morpheme *up* or *down* in conjunction with actions involving motions in the corresponding direction, then this generalization would be facilitated. This is exactly what Regier's (1996) connectionist model requires in order to converge on the corresponding "image schema" (see note 2 above, concerning the contrary interpretations of Regier's model). On the other hand, if the child is exposed to the verbs *kkita* and *nehta*, then (s)he will learn to discriminate TIGHT FIT from LOOSE FIT, as is the case in Korean (Choi and Bowerman 1991; Bowerman 1996), and it has been shown that Korean adults do, but adult English speakers do not make conceptual distinctions on the basis of the dimension 'tightness-of-fit' (Mandler 2004, *this volume*). This implies that, contrary to the most common view, "image schemas" of the kind most often discussed in the literature do *not* "exist independently of the linguistic forms used to express them" (Dodge and Lakoff, *this volume*). In the terms introduced in Section 2, such schemas are symbolic, i.e., conventional and systematic, and thus post-mimetic.

Further evidence for this possibly controversial analysis comes from studies of the spontaneous emergence of Nicaraguan Sign Language (NSL) during the past 25 years. Senghas, Kita, and Özyürek (2004) compared the co-speech gestures of Nicaraguan speakers of Spanish, with the signing of three "cohorts", or generations, of learners of NSL and documented the emergence of the differentiation between MANNER and PATH along with the emergence of the language: the more fluent the signers were in NSL, the more likely they were to express these as separate units in communication. Since this concerns "schemas" that are very dear to cognitive linguists, and whose apparently universal expression in separate units of language (Talmy 2000, Vol I: 21-146) is often given as evidence of their "preverbal" and in some cases even "neural" nature, I quote the analysis of Senghas, Kita, and Özyürek (2004: 1781) at length:

The movements of the hands and body in the sign language are clearly derived from a gestural source. Nonetheless, the analyses reveal a qualitative difference between gesturing and signing. In gesture, manner and path were integrated by expressing them simultaneously and holistically, the way they occur in the motion [event] itself. Despite this analogue, holistic nature of the gesturing that surrounded them, the first cohort of children, who started building NSL in the late 1970s, evidently introduced the possibility of dissecting out manner and path and assembling them into a sequence of elemental units. As second and third cohorts learned the language in the mid 1980s and 1990s, they rapidly made this segmented, sequenced construction the preferred means of expressing motion events. NSL thus quickly acquired the discrete, combinatorial nature that is the hallmark of language.

This passage illustrates very clearly the transition from iconic gestures, which can be regarded as fairly transparent externalizations of mimetic schemas, to "discrete, combinatorial" cognition, which has its origin in language (e.g., Tomasello 1999). Thus, image schemas even of the most concrete type in Grady's hierarchy cannot provide a ground for language, since they are themselves constituted by it. Mimetic schemas, on the other hand, can, since they correspond to much more concrete actions and events. This conclusion is bound to be resisted since it goes against a prevalent assumption within Cognitive Linguistics concerning the "non-verbal" nature of foundational concepts like image schemas and conceptual metaphor. But as Dewell's contribution to this volume testifies, the belief in this assumption seems to be wearing off.

Why it is that language brings about the qualitative difference is itself a matter of heated controversy. Nativists of the generative tradition such as Siegal (2004: 9) have seen the NSL phenomenon as evidence for "the fundamental innateness of grammar", but Senghas, Kita and Özyürek (2004: 1782) prefer a scenario in which the first languages and children's learning abilities have co-evolved. It is also possible to seek more functional explanations, such as the "pressures to insure successful communication" (Dewell, *this volume*).

To return to Grady's (*this volume*) hierarchy: if even the most concrete image schemas that he presents are language-based at least to some degree, there is even more reason to believe that this is also the case with the more abstract ones. "Superschemas", such as ONTOLOGICAL CATEGORY (EVENT, PROCESS, THING), SCALARITY/DIMENSIONALITY, ASPECT, BOUNDEDNESS, etc., are all reflected in the grammatical systems of the worlds' languages. Do we need to explain their universality on the basis of "preverbal" structures and processes as is customary in Cognitive Linguistics? I would argue not. As claimed by Heine and Kuteva (2002) grammaticalization processes can lead not only to language change, but to an increase in language complexity through the *evolution* of grammatical (and hence semantic) categories, though this itself challenges the dogma of language "uniformitarianism" (cf. Newmeyer 2003). If this is furthermore coupled with a co-evolutionary scenario in which children's learning abilities have themselves been changed/shaped over the millennia since the dawn of (proto)language, as suggested by Senghas, Kita, and Özyürek (2004), it would explain why Nicaraguan children constructed the representational categories (schemas) MANNER and PATH so easily when they created NSL.

As for the metaphorical "mapping" between image schemas and "response schemas", that can be naturally explained as deriving from (conscious) processes of *analogy* (Itkonen 2005), performed by speakers (and signers) under the constraints of the shared structure (the "superschemas") in the source and target domains. As suggested above, it is likely that this structure is induced in part by language itself.

In sum, mimetic schemas are relatively concrete, "analogue" and "holistic" representations. As such, they qualify for the adjective "pre-verbal", and are therefore a possible ground for language. The kind of structures that cognitive linguists have termed "image schemas" come in different levels of specificity, but to the extent that they constitute semantic primitives such as CONTAINMENT, PATH and MANNER, they are not a ground, but rather a product of language – in probably both phylogenetic and ontogenetic terms.

3.4. Dynamicity

At first glance, this parameter of variance is easier to deal with than the preceding three, since nearly all image schema theoreticians ascribe some form of "dynamicity" to the concept. One possible exception is Mandler (2004, *this volume*), who – when describing image schemas as a "format" for concepts – suggests some sort of "mold" in which experience is poured, and molds are static things. But that may be a (metaphorical) misinterpretation, since what leads to (consciously accessible) concepts for her is "perceptual meaning analysis", which is nothing but a process (see also Section 3.2). Still, Mandler (*this volume*) notes that "image-schemas are not iconic... An image-schema of PATH does not contain information about speed or direction." This would imply that Mandler's concept of PATH (and other schemas) is a rather abstract structure which, contrary to her analysis, may be based on language rather than serving as a basis for it, as suggested above.

However, the issue of dynamicity is not so simple, as shown by Dewell (*this volume*), who argues that truly dynamic image schemas, in both "structure" and "content" have been rather "underappreciated" in the cognitive linguistic literature in the quest for semantic primitives such as CONTAINER. Dewell provides an analysis in which even such apparently static structures (usually given as meanings to prepositions such as *in*) are ontogenetically preceded by dynamic schemas such as ENTRY:

> It is much more likely that the earliest image schemas will involve activities and paths, with little clear differentiation between trajectors (TRs), landmarks (LMs) and relations, between paths and resulting states, or between space and time.

Mimetic schemas are likewise "dynamic in structure and content", but are in comparison still more undifferentiated, e.g., there is not yet any differentiation between "activity" and "path", as shown in iconic gestures. In contrast to Mandler's notion, mimetic schemas are highly *iconic* (or *indexical*) structures,[7] resembling the represented activity in not only speed and direction, but in the features GAIT, BODY PART and EFFORT, discussed by Dodge and Lakoff (*this volume*).

At the same time, since mimetic schemas are defined as "*categories of acts* of bodily mimesis", they are (expected to be) relatively stable and well-defined. This has two implications: (i) there is likely to be a relatively limited set of mimetic schemas within a cultural community – which is relevant for their capacity to be shared (see 3.6 below), and (ii) while they are not identical with verb meanings, mimetic schemas can serve as a likely candidate to ground the latter in ontogeny.

In an analysis of the "first verbs" of a child acquiring English, Tomasello (1992) classifies the motion predicates acquired by the child during the period from 16 to 24 months, i.e., the period of the "vocabulary explosion", as shown in Table 1. During her first 8 months of (productive) language acquisition the child learned a total of 84 verbs denoting activities involving different forms of bodily motion (see the first two rows of Table 1). *Each one of these can be taken to correspond to a mimetic schema.* Contrasting with

---

7. The various forms of pointing found in different cultures, e.g. with the index finger, the whole hand, with the mouth, may be regarded as realizing *indexical* mimetic schemas.

these are 17 other "verbs" expressing more schematic relations, of the type that would presumably involve image schemas such as UP and CONTAIN-MENT.[8] While some of the latter were also acquired very early, one can notice that all of them form contrastive pairs: *move/stay (stuck), go/come, put/get-out, bring/take, up/down, on/off, in/out, over/under, here/there.* This is further evidence for the hypothesis that language itself played a crucial role for their differentiation, as opposed to assuming that the expressions are just "labels" being mapped to "pre-existing schemas".[9] No such contrasts are discernable in the activity verbs.

Table 1. Classification of the first motion predicates of a child during the period 16 to 24 months, based on data provided by Tomasello (1992: 187-221)

Category	Examples	Total No.
Activities with objects	sweep, cut, hammer, drive, kick…	48
Activities without objects	cry, pee-pee, jump, swim…	36
Change-of-state, focus on motion	move, stay, stuck, go, come, put, get-out, bring, take	9
Change-of-state, focus on goal	up, down, on, off, in, out, over, under, here, there	8

The conclusion, again, is that mimetic schemas, which are dynamic representations of everyday actions and events, are ontogenetically more basic than image schemas, even when the latter are taken as inherently dynamic structures.

3.5. Sensory modality

Image schemas are nearly always characterized as "bodily", but it is less often explained what this actually means, since "embodiment" is a highly

---

8. The items in the fourth row were classified as verbs because the context of use showed that they involved motion, even though they are not verbs but prepositions/adverbial particles and deictic adverbs.
9. In Regier's (1996) model, such contrastive pairs or sets needed to be given to the model simultaneously so that the model could converge on its representations. Otherwise, it did not – unless presented with explicit "negative evidence" of the kind that children do not in general receive (e.g., Braine 1971).

ambiguous concept (cf. Ziemke, Zlatev and Frank, in press). If it only means that they are based on neural structures and functioning, a matter of "neural embodiment" (Lakoff and Johnson 1999; Dodge and Lakoff, *this volume*; Rohrer, *this volume*), then their bodily status becomes rather trivial, since all mental functioning has the brain as a *sine qua non*. The alternative (or complementary) and more fruitful approach has been to regard the "embodiment" of image schemas as constituted by sensorimotor activity and experience (Johnson 1987, *this volume*). In previous work (Zlatev 1997) I argued that this makes them identical to Piaget's (1952) *sensorimotor schemata* – except that they are defined at a higher level of abstraction. Piaget's formulation in the preface to the second edition of *The Origins of Intelligence in Children* could well be taken from a publication by Mark Johnson, but surprisingly, Piaget is seldom given credit within Cognitive Linguistics:

> It is primarily preverbal sensorymotor activity that is responsible for the construction of a series of perceptual schemata, the importance of which in the subsequent structuring of thought cannot, without oversimplification, be denied. (Piaget 1952: 10)

Thus understood, image schemas are *cross-modal* (as apposed to amodal) structures, involving sensorimotor coordination. However, we need to probe deeper and ask: which modalities are *essential* for their formation. The first candidate is *vision*, which is plausible, given the relatively dominant role played by vision in the primate, and even more so human, brain (Watt 1991). Mandler (2004, *this volume*) argues that perceptual meaning analysis of visual data "provides the main route of our concept of physical force" and similarly for other image schemas. But if vision is so crucial, then blindness from birth should invariably lead to serious mental disfunctioning and this is not the case. In their detailed study of a blind child, Landau and Gleitman (1985) report only slight delays in cognitive development and language onset, but otherwise a completely normal developmental pattern in language acquisition. The child learned the meanings of words such as *see* and *look*, though she applied them differently for herself, referring to haptic exploration, and for her seeing parents, with apparently the same meanings as in English. So while vision is undoubtedly a very important source of experience for normal children, it cannot be a *necessary* ground for language. A key to the puzzle could be the fact that the child received extraordinary amounts of haptic and verbal interaction from her caregivers, which appeared to compensate the lack of vision.

Similarly, certain handicaps show that actual sensorimotor *activity* itself is not necessary for the development of intelligence, which presents problems for Piaget's, as well as Mark Johnson's, emphasis on sensorimotor (image) schemas. Consider the episode recounted by Jordan (1972: 379-380):

> ... while visiting an institution for the aged and incurable, I was attracted by a patient there: Her head was that of a normal adult – in the early 40s – but her body was that of a neonate – albeit about two to three times the size of a month old infant. Her arms and hands were 'absolutely' infantile. They stuck out from her body exactly as an infant's do, moving occasionally but showing no purpose whatsoever. ... I asked about the patient and was told that she was one of the most popular and intelligent of the patients, serving as a regular discussion reader, and being of great help to both the other patients and the staff in filling out income tax returns.

Jordan concludes that this case poses a challenge to Piaget's theory:

> Given the fact that the patient never used her body since birth and interpreting sensory-motor activity as action in and upon the environment, it follows that the patient never did engage in sensory-motor activity. Yet, the patient did exhibit a normal adult functioning intelligence. (Jordan 1972: 380)

Orthodox piagetians usually dismiss such objections by pointing out that even paralyzed patients can at least move their eyes, and that *sensorimotor activity* should be taken more generally, but this seems to water down the whole notion, distancing it from the "the flesh and blood of meaning". Some recent research (Riviére and Lècuyer 2002) conducted on children with spinal muscular atrophy (SMA), who are severely motorically impaired, shows that they do not differ in their performance on tasks involving spatial cognition compared to healthy controls.[10] Furthermore, such children display a normal IQ and language skills. Therefore if (a) image schemas, or for that part mimetic schemas, need to be acquired through *actual* physical experience, and (b) they are a necessary prerequisite for the development of (spatial) cognition and language, then patients with SMA would be expected to be at least linguistically retarded, if not impaired. Since this is not the case, logic tells us that either (a) or (b) must be retracted. Mandler's (largely)

---

10. In a follow-up study Riviére and Lècuyer (2003) even report significantly higher performance on a 3-location search task for SMA children compared to healthy controls, and interpret this in terms of better developed inhibitory mechanisms in the SMA children, allowing for a "more reflective approach to the problem" (Riviére and Lècuyer 2003: 290).

vision-based account would seem compatible with this perspective, but then it is problematic due to the results from blindness. I believe there is a way out by modifying, rather than abandoning statement (a), in a way showing that Jordan is wrong in claiming that the patient "never used her body since birth" in the final quotation.

Mimetic schemas in normal cases have their *origin* in a cross-modal mapping between exteroception (dominated by vision, unless there is blindness) and proprioception. However, in contrast to the way Gibbs (*this volume*) defines image schemas, mimetic schemas are not *exhausted* by proprioception, and if the latter would be compromised, then only proto-mimesis would be impossible, but not mimesis itself. Gallagher (2005: 37-38) argues that proprioception serves as the basis for the *body schema*: "a system of sensory-motor processes that constantly regulate posture and movement – processes that function without reflective awareness or the necessity of perceptual monitoring". Gallagher describes a patient who has lost tactile and proprioceptive input from the neck down, but can consciously control his movements, especially by visual guidance. In Gallagher's (2005: 37-38) analysis the patient performs this through the *body image*, which is "a (sometimes conscious) system of perceptions, attitudes, beliefs and dispositions pertaining to one's own body." The two systems normally interact, but can be doubly disassociated. From these definitions, it becomes clear that bodily mimesis, and thus mimetic schemas as *conscious, dynamic representations*, should be expected to utilize the body *image,* serving as a kind of *virtual* body rather than the pre-conscious body schema.

Returning to the patient described by Jordan (1972), it is fair to conclude that due to her handicap, she must have had a dysfunctional body schema. Nothing is, however, said about her body image, which also appears to correspond to the "mimetic controller" hypothesized by Donald (1991). Thus, she would still have been able to form mimetic schemas, albeit of the *covert* type. In other words, she would have been able to perform mental "simulations" of actions and events, matching these to the bodily motions of others, possibly through the often mentioned, but (still) not completely well understood "mirror neuron system" (e.g. Gallese, Keysers and Rizzolatti 2004). Observing the actions of others, she would have been able to "imitate" them in a covert way, making her mimetic schemas intersubjective in a way to be explicated below.

I am aware that this reply to the challenge to claims of necessity for any kind of body-based schemas (be they image, sensorimotor or mimetic schemas) provided by the mentioned clinical evidence is tentative. Nevertheless, since mimetic schemas are not sensorimotor structures but bodily concepts, it seems that they offer a promising way to reconcile the various sorts of evidence. The meta-conclusion is that clinical evidence should be taken more seriously prior to postulating particular sensory modalities as necessary grounds for cognitive and linguistic development.

3.6. Intersubjective vs. private

The final dimension is one that unfortunately has received very little atten-tion in the Cognitive Linguistics literature. Image schemas, as all forms of mental structures, are usually conceived as private, individual phenomena, irrespective of how they are treated otherwise. But this poses a problem if they are to serve as a ground for, or even constitute, linguistic meanings, since the latter are public, *conventional* entities (Clark 1996; Tomasello 1999; Itkonen 2003; Zlatev, in press). As clearly stated by Tomasello (1992: 215): "Linguistic symbols are social conventions that package cognition in a way that human beings have found useful for communication". The problem is both conceptual and empirical: Since 18-month-old children lack the meta-linguistic capacity for establishing full-fledged conventions, which are struc-tures of common knowledge (Lewis 1969), it remains a mystery how chil-dren move from the (private) sensorimotor to the symbolic (i.e., conventional and systematic) level to learn a language as a "socially shared symbolic system" (Nelson and Shaw 2002).

Mimetic schemas can help resolve this puzzle since they possess the property that Arbib (2003) calls "parity": they are, or at least can be, shared among the members of a community who engage in face-to-face (or rather body-to-body) interaction. In his theory of "the emergence of symbols", Pia-get proposed that the latter crucially involve *imitation*. Piaget distinguished between three types of imitation, which form an epigenetic progression (i.e., a developmental sequence, where later forms necessarily build on earlier forms): (a) *sensorimotor imitation* – in which the model's action is imitated directly; (b) *deferred imitation* – in which the imitated action – either of another, or of oneself – is displaced in time; and (c) *representative imitation* – in which:

> ... the interior image precedes the exterior gesture, which is thus a copy of an "internal model" that guarantees the connection between the real, but absent model, and the imitative reproduction of it. ... Imitation, with the

help of images, provides the essential system of "signifiers" for the purpose of individual or egocentric representation (Piaget 1962: 279-280).

As pointed out earlier, Piaget's "symbols" and "images" are practically identical with my concept of mimetic schemas. Piaget's characterization of such representations as "individual and egocentric" should not be taken to mean that they are *private*, since Piaget defines "egocentrism" as "failure to differentiate between the ego and the group, or confusion of the individual view-point and that of others" (Piaget 1962: 290). In other words, it is more correct to say that mimetic schemas are *pre-reflectively shared* or perhaps *proto-conventional*. Since the child's mimetic schemas derive from imitating salient actions and events in the community, both their representational and experiential content will be "shared" with those of his caregivers and peers. In this way, they can serve as a bridge to developing true symbols, which are not just shared but known to be shared, i.e., post-mimetic.

This, however, could be taken to imply that children who cannot engage in imitation due to various sorts of motoric handicaps, such as the cases discussed in Section 3.5, will fail to develop mimetic schemas. Piaget's account of the origin of representations through imitation therefore needs to be modified. The *overt* sequence of sensorimotor-deferred-representative imitation cannot be a necessary epigenetic progression. What I earlier called *covert* imitation would be a way to resolve this impasse. The mirror neuron system of the child would presumably allow for this even in the absence of body movements, undergoing a developmental sequence similar to that proposed for the *evolution* of the mirror system by Rizzollati and Arbib (1998): from action recognition to (covert) imitation to representation, by decoupling the image and its content. Whether the *experiential* content of the mimetic schemas of motorically impaired children would differ from those of the rest of us is an interesting philosophical and empirical question to which I do not think there is any answer at present.

Finally, this account would correctly predict that children with autism, who in general do not imitate in an adequate manner despite full motoric proficiency will (whatever the underlying reason) fail to develop intersubjective mimetic schemas, and consequently will have various degrees of language impairment. This account is similar to that of Tomasello et al. (2005) who propose that children with autism, as well as non-human primates, fail to develop "dialogic cognitive representations". Zlatev, Persson and Gärdenfors (2005a,b) point out this similarity, and suggest that bodily mimesis and mimetic schemas can explain the nature of human cognitive specificity, being what allows (non-autistic) children to co-construct a world of meaning that is shared with their elders and peers.

4.   Summary and conclusions

In this chapter I have presented the notion of mimetic schemas, and compared it to different formulations of what appears to be the most fundamental notion in Cognitive Linguistics, image schemas. The comparison was done on six different dimensions: *representation, consciousness, level of abstractness, dynamicity, sensory modality and (inter)subjectivity*, showing that accounts of "what's in a schema" differ along each one of these. I have argued, mostly rather briefly due to limitations of space, for a particular set of values along the dimensions, and thereby explicated mimetic schemas as *dynamic, concrete and preverbal representations, involving the body image, which are accessible to consciousness, and pre-reflectively shared in a community*. In conclusion, I wish to summarize their value as an explanatory concept for Cognitive Linguistics and cognitive science.

First and foremost, they can help explain the "grounding of language". This metaphorical expression which figures in the title of the chapter is often used but seldom defined, and it is high time for me to do so. Mimetic schemas constitute a *ground* for language in the sense that they constitute preverbal mental representations which make language acquisition possible by (a) constituting the first "accessible" concepts (similar to the role that image schemas play in Mandler's model), (b) allowing the insight that others have similar mental representations, which is a prerequisite for having communicative intentions and (c) bootstrapping the acquisition of the meaning of verbs, which is essential for the acquisition of grammar, as pointed out by Tomasello:

> ... the acquisition of verbs as single-word lexical items during the 2nd year of life is the major turning point in children's transition to adultlike competence. The grammatical valencies contained in children's first verbs simply "beg" to be completed into sentences. (Tomasello 1992: 7)

At the same time, mimetic schemas do not *constitute* linguistic meanings (see also Dewell, *this volume*), as the latter are not only pre-reflectively shared, but conventional and systematic in a way that mimetic schemas are not. Thus, the transition from mimetic schemas to image schemas – as defined by, e.g., Grady (*this volume*) – is the transition from pre-verbal to verbal, and from mimetic to post-mimetic.

Second, mimetic schemas can help explain the source of human cognitive uniqueness, providing a "ground" for the evolution of language. In line with Donald's (1991) original proposal, the notion of bodily mimesis can help explain why language is so difficult for our animal relatives, including even "enculturated" apes. In contrast, if image schemas are defined as structures of general *animal* sensorimotor cognition (Johnson and Rohrer *in press*; Dodge and Lakoff, *this volume*) which "map" onto linguistic meanings, it becomes a mystery why animals are not language users...

Third, if mimetic schemas continue to operate even after language acquisition (as assumed within the present model), rather than only play the role of Wittgenstein's famous ladder that is "kicked away" after climbing it, that could explain the ubiquity of co-speech gesture (McNeill 1992). My hypothesis is that mimetic schemas underlie both speech and gesture, thereby accounting for the close synchronization of the two modes of expression. However, while speech is conventionalized and (semi-) compositional, gesture is largely analogue and "holistic", since it is more closely based on the structure of mimetic schemas. At the same time, co-speech gestures are at least partly *post*-mimetic, since due to their synchronization with speech they gain some language-specific characteristics (Kita and Özyürek 2003).

Fourth, mimetic schemas are consistent with evidence concerning cognitive development and language acquisition in impaired populations. They predict that deaf children should not be affected, and would create a language even if lacking "linguistic input", and that blind children given bodily and verbal interaction will not be cognitively and linguistically retarded. Since they are not sensorimotor structures but conscious "simulations", even children with severe motor impairments would be relatively unaffected. Conversely, image schemas – either in Mandler's largely vision-based model, or in the Piaget/Johnson sensorimotor activity-based model – are relatively more problematic to reconcile with the clinical evidence. On the other hand, the problems of children suffering from *autism*, with difficulties in socialization, communication and imagination could possibly be explained as the result of impairment in bodily mimesis, which should be crucially implicated in these three cognitive domains.

Fifth, if language is based on (without being reduced to) mimetic schemas, one would expect exactly the kind of evidence that has been accumulating from research in experimental psychology and neuroscience lately, showing that language use engages "motor representations", as well as the corresponding brain regions (Barsalou 1999; Rohrer, *this volume*). At the same time, this evidence does not imply that all symbolic and inferential processing is carried out by sensorimotor categories and brain regions, as claimed by, e.g., Lakoff and Johnson (1999), or Johnson and Rohrer (in press), since that would make it impossible to explain the qualitative difference between animal and human cognition.

Sixth and finally, mimetic schemas as a ground for public, conventional symbols can help explain how both "cognitive" (representational) and "affective" (experiential) meaning can be communicated through language, since both aspects can be – to various degrees – shared by communicators with similar bodily experiences, giving rise to the "the flesh and blood of meaning" (Johnson, *this volume*). At the same time, since mimetic schemas involve the body image and not (only) the body schema, they could explain the (unfortunate) possibility of a disassociation between denotation and connotation, which both clinical and everyday experience bears witness to.

Finally, it is possible that I am aiming too high and that by proposing a concept, and the outline of a theory, that is meant to explain so much, I have failed to acknowledge many problematic issues in each one of the fields involved in the discussion. But this is something that only further research can show. All that I claim to have offered is a *promising* concept, and in particular one that does not suffer from some of the problems of the various accounts of image schemas that exist in the Cognitive Linguistics literature, most of which have been gathered in the present volume.

References

Arbib, Michael
　　2003　　The evolving mirror system: A neural basis for language readiness. In *Language Evolution*, Morten Christiansen, and Simon Kirby (eds.), 182-200. Oxford: Oxford University Press.
Barsalou, Lawrence W.
　　1999　　Perceptual symbol systems. *Behavioral and Brain Sciences* 22: 577-660.
Bowerman, Melissa
　　1996　　Learning how to structure space for language – A cross-linguistic perspective. In *Language and Space*, Paul Bloom, Mary A. Peterson, Lynn Nadel, and Merrill Garret (eds.), 385-436. Cambridge, Mass.: MIT Press.
Chalmers, David
　　1996　　*The Conscious Mind.* Oxford: Oxford University Press.

Clark, Herbert
1996   *Using Language.* Cambridge: Cambridge University Press.
Clausner, Timothy, and William Croft
1999   Domains and image schemas. *Cognitive Linguistics* 10: 1-32.
Corballis, Michael C.
2002   *From Hand to Mouth: The Origins of Language.* Princeton: Princeton University Press.
Choi, Sonya, and Melissa Bowerman
1991   Learning to express notion events in English and Korean: The influence of language-specific lexicalization patterns. *Cognition* 41: 83-121.
Damasio, Antonio
2001   *The Feeling of What Happens. Body, Emotion and the Making of Consciousness.* London: Vintage.
Deacon, Terry
1997   *The Symbolic Species: The Co-Evolution of Language and the Brain.* New York: Norton.
Deane, Paul
1994   *Grammar in Mind and Brain. Explorations in Cognitive Syntax.* Berlin: Mouton de Gruyter.
Donald, Merlin
1991   *Origins of the Modern Mind. Three Stages in the Evolution of Culture and Cognition.* Cambridge, Mass.: Harvard University Press.
Edelman, Gerald
1992   *Bright Air, Brilliant Fire: On the Matter of the Mind.* London: Basic Books.
Evans, Vyv
2003   *The Structure of Time. Language, Meaning and Temporal Cognition.* Amsterdam: Benjamins.
Fodor, Jerry A.
1981   *Representations.* Cambridge, Mass.: MIT Press.
Fouts, Roger
1973   Acquisition and testing of gestural signs in four young chimpanzees. *Science* 180: 978-980.
Gallese, Vittorio
2003   A neuro-scientific grasp of concepts. From control to representation. *Philosophical Transactions of the Royal Society of London, B, 358*: 1231-1240.
Gallese, Vittorio and George Lakoff
2005   The brain's concepts: The role of the sensory-motor system in conceptual knowledge. *Cognitive Neuropsychology* 22: 455-479.

Gallese, Vittorio, Christian Keyners, and Giacomo Rizzolatti
2004   A unifying view of the basis of social cognition. *Trends in Cognitive Sciences* 8: 396-403.
Gallagher, Shaun
2005   *How the Body Shapes the Mind.* Oxford: Oxford University Press.
Gurwitsch, Aron
1964   *The Field of Consciousness.* Pittsburgh: Duquesne University Press.
Grady, Joseph E.
1997   Foundations of meaning: Primary metaphors and primary scenes. Ph.D. dissertation at the University of California, Berkeley.
Heine, Bernard, and Tanya Kuteva
2002   On the evolution of grammatical forms. In *The Transition to Language*, Alison Wray (ed.), 376-397. Oxford: Oxford University Press.
Hume, David
2000   Reprint. *A Treatise of Human Nature.* David Norton, and Mary Norton (eds.). Oxford: Oxford University Press. Original edition, 1739.
Itkonen, Esa
2003   *What is Language? An Essay in the Philosophy of Linguistics.* Turku: University of Turku Press.
2005   *Analogy.* Amsterdam: Benjamins.
Johnson, Mark
1987   *The Body in the Mind.* Chicago: University of Chicago Press.
Johnson, Mark, and George Lakoff
2002   Why cognitive linguistics requires embodied realism. *Cognitive Linguistics* 13: 245-263.
Johnson, Mark, and Tim Rohrer
in press   We are live creatures: Embodiment, American pragmatism, and the cognitive organism. In *Body, Language and Mind.* Vol 1. *Embodiment*, Tom Ziemke, Jordan Zlatev, and Roslyn Frank (eds.). Berlin: Mouton de Gruyter.
Jordan, N.
1972   Is there an Achilles heel in Piaget's theorizing? *Human Development* 15: 379-382.
Kita, Sotaro, and Asli Özyürek
2003   What does cross-linguistic variation in semantic coordination of speech and gesture reveal? Evidence for an interface representation of spatial thinking and speaking. *Journal of Memory and Language* 48: 16-32.

Lakoff, George
1987   *Women, Fire and Dangerous Things: What Categories Reveal About the Mind.* Chicago: University of Chicago Press.
1990   The Invariance Hypothesis: Is abstract reason based on image-schemas? *Cognitive Linguistics* 1: 39-74.
Lakoff, George, and Mark Johnson
1999   *Philosophy in the Flesh: The Embodied Mind and Its Challenge to Western Thought.* New York: Basic Books.
Landau, Barbara, and Lila Gleitman
1985   *Language and Experience. Evidence from the Blind Child.* Cambridge, Mass.: Harvard University Press.
Lewis, David K.
1969   *Convention: A Philosophical Study.* Cambridge Mass.: Harvard University Press.
Mandler, Jean
2004   *The Foundations of Mind: Origins of Conceptual Thought.* Oxford: Oxford University Press.
McNeill, David
1992   *Hand and Mind: What Gestures Reveal about Thought.* Chicago: University of Chicago Press.
Meltzoff, Andrew, and M. K. Moore
1977   Imitation of facial and manual gestures by human neonates. *Science* 198: 75-78.
1983   Newborn infants imitate adult facial gestures. *Child Development* 54: 702-709.
1994   Imitation, memory, and the representation of persons. *Infant Behavior and Development* 17: 83-99.
Miles, H. Lynn
1990   The cognitive foundations for reference in a signing orangutang. In *"Language" and Intelligence in Monkeys and Apes*, Sue T. Parker, and Kathleen R. Gibson (eds.), 511-539. Cambridge: Cambridge University Press.
Myowa-Yamakoshi, Masako, Masaki Tomonaga, Masayuki Tanaka, and Tetsuro Matsuzawa
2004   Imitation in neonatal chimpanzees (Pan troglodytes). *Developmental Science* 7: 437-442.
Nelson, Katherine, and Lea Kessler Shaw
2002   Developing a socially shared symbolic system. In *Language, Literacy and Cognitive Development*, James Byrnes, and Eric Amseli (eds.), 27-57. Mahwah, NJ: Lawrence Erlbaum.

Newmeyer, Frederick
  2003   What can the field of linguistics tell us about the origin of lan-
          guage? In *Language Evolution*, Morten Christiansen, and Simon
          Kirby (eds.), 58-76. Oxford: Oxford University Press.
Patterson, Francis
  1980   Innovative use of language in a gorilla: A case study. In *Children's
          Language*, Volume 2, Katherine Nelson (ed.), 497-561. New York:
          Gardner Press.
Piaget, Jean
  1962   *Play, Dreams, and Imitation in Childhood*. English translation of
          La formation du symbole chez l'enfant by G. Gattegno and F. M.
          Hodgson. New York: Norton [French original 1945].
  1952   *The Origin of Intelligence in the Child*. New York: Basic Books.
Peirce, Charles S.
  1931-35 *The Collected Papers of Charles Sanders Peirce*. Volumes 1-4.
          Cambridge, Mass.: Harvard University Press.
Regier, Terry
  1996   *The Human Semantic Potential: Spatial Language and Constrained
          Connectionism*. Cambridge, Mass.: MIT Press.
Riviére, James, and Roger Lècuyer
  2002   Spatial cognition in young children with spinal muscular atro-
          phy. *Developmental Neuropsychology* 13: 165-184.
  2003   The C-not-B error: A comparative study. *Cognitive Development*
          18: 285-297.
Rizzolatti, Giacomo, and Michael Arbib
  1998   Language within our grasp. *Trends in Neurosciences* 21: 188-194.
Savage-Rumbough, Sue, and Roger Lewin
  1994   *Kanzi: The Ape at the Brink of the Human Mind*. New York: John
          Wiley.
Searle, John
  1999   *Mind, Language and Society. Philosophy in the Real World*. Lon-
          don: Weidenfeld and Nicolson.
Senghas, Ann, Sotaro Kita, and Asli Özyürek
  2004   Children creating core properties of language: Evidence from an
          emerging sign language in Nicaragua. *Science* 305: 1779-1782.
Siegal, Michael
  2004   Signposts to the essence of language. *Science* 305: 1720-1721.
Singleton, Jenny, Susan Goldin-Meadow, and David McNeill
  1995   The cataclysmic break between gesticulation and sign: Evidence
          against a unified continuum of gestural communication. In *Lan-
          guage, Gesture and Space*, Karen Emmorey, and Judy Reilly (eds.),
          287-332. Hillsdale: Laurence Erlbaum.

Sonesson, Göran
 1989 *Pictorial Concepts.* Lund: Lund University Press.
 in press From the meaning of embodiment to the embodiment of meaning:
  A study in phenomenological semiotics. In *Body, Language and
  Mind.* Volume 1. *Embodiment,* Tom Ziemke, Jordan Zlatev, and
  Roslyn Frank (eds.). Berlin: Mouton de Gruyter.
Stokoe, William C.
 2001 *Language in Hand. Why Sign Came Before Speech.* Washington,
  D.C.: Gallaudet University Press.
Talmy, Leonard
 2000 *Toward a Cognitive Semantics.* Volumes 1-2. Cambridge, Mass.:
  MIT Press.
Thompson, Evan
 2001 Empathy and consciousness. *Journal of Consciousness Studies* 8: 1-
  32.
Tomasello, Michael
 1992 *First Verbs: A Case Study of Early Grammatical Development.*
  Cambridge: Cambridge University Press.
 1999 *The Cultural Origins of Human Cognition.* Cambridge, Mass.:
  Harvard University Press.
Tomasello, Michael, Malinda Carpenter, Josep Call, Tanya Behne, and Henrike
  Moll
 2005 Understanding and sharing intentions: The origins of cultural
  cognition. *Behavioral and Brain Sciences* 28: 675-735.
Varela, Francisco, Evan Thompson, and Eleonor Rosch
 1991 *The Embodied Mind. Cognitive Science and Human Experience.*
  Cambridge, Mass.: MIT Press.
Vygotsky, Lev S.
 1978 *Mind in Society. The Development of Higher Psychological Processes.* Cambridge, Mass.: Harvard University Press.
Watt, Roger
 1991 *Understanding Vision.* New York: Academic Press.
Ziemke, Tom, Jordan Zlatev, and Roslyn Frank (eds.)
 in press *Body, Language and Mind.* Volume 1: *Embodiment.* Berlin: Mouton.
Zlatev, Jordan
 1997 *Situated Embodiment. Studies in the Emergence of Spatial Meaning.* Stockholm: Gotab Press.
 2003a Polysemy or generality? Mu. In *Cognitive Approaches to Lexical
  Semantics,* Hubert Cuyckens, René Dirven, and John Taylor (eds.),
  447-494. Berlin: Mouton de Gruyter.

2003b   Meaning = Life (+ Culture). An outline of a unified biocultural theory of meaning. *Evolution of Communication* 4: 253-296.

in press   Embodiment, language and mimesis. In *Body, Language and Mind.* Volume 1. *Embodiment,* Tom Ziemke, Jordan Zlatev, and Roslyn Frank (eds.). Berlin: Mouton de Gruyter.

Zlatev, Jordan, Tomas Persson, and Peter Gärdenfors

2005a   *Bodily Mimesis as "the Missing Link" in Human Cognitive Evolution.* LUCS 121. Lund: Lund University Cognitive Studies.

2005b   Triadic bodily mimesis is the difference. Commentary to Tomasello et al. *Behavioral and Brain Sciences* 28: 720-721.

Image schemas vs. "Complex Primitives" in cross-cultural spatial cognition

Margarita Correa-Beningfield,* Gitte Kristiansen, Ignasi Navarro-Ferrando and Claude Vandeloise

Abstract

This paper constitutes an attempt to evaluate the relative adequacy of the notion of *image schema* (Lakoff 1987; Johnson 1987; Mandler 1992) in the cross-cultural analysis of spatial cognition and language. The paper contrasts this notion with that of *Complex Primitive* (Vandeloise 1994, 2003) and argues that the latter notion is better equipped to deal with socially, functionally and physically motivated configurations than the former, and more suitable to describe spatial conceptualizations and their linguistic reflections in different languages. Two of its advantages are presented by its increased analytical precision on the one hand, and the reduction of excessive polysemy on the other.

Keywords: image schemas, complex primitives, cross-cultural spatial cognition, language acquisition, experiential semantics.

1. On the relative (in)adequacy of the notion of image schema

Work by Leonard Talmy (1983), Johnson (1987) and Lakoff (1987) established the notion of "image schema" as one of the most basic concepts in cognitive semantics. Image schema theory maintains that image schemas are the most basic units upon which more elaborate concepts can be built. As

*   The order of authors is alphabetical, please send correspondences to the first author. The project on which part of this paper draws (BFF 2002-01056) was funded by the Spanish Ministry of Culture and Technology. We would like to thank the editor and Robert Dewell, as well as two anonymous reviewers for their helpful comments. The positions advocated in this paper engage only their authors.

gestalts,[1] they are not atomistic structures. They can be "analyzed", since they have parts and dimensions, but as Johnson (1987: 62) observes:

> ... any such attempted reduction will destroy the unity (i.e., meaningful organization) that made the structure significant in the first place.

Image schemas are claimed to be deeply grounded in general human bodily *and* social experience, but the claim that they should grow out of successful *bodily* experience has undoubtedly received far more attention than that which involves *social* experience.

1.1. Image schemas as universals

It was Leonard Talmy (1983) who first made the observation that in spite of the fact that spatial relations terms have different meanings in the languages of the world, those meanings can be decomposed into primitive "images" which recur across languages. Talmy surmised that this set of primitives was universal (cf. also Lakoff 1987; Talmy, *this volume*; Dodge and Lakoff, *this volume*). Typical examples from early image schema theory include CONTAINMENT, SOURCE-PATH-GOAL, CONTACT, ENCIRCLEMENT, etc.

In line with this thought, image schemas are generally thought to be acquired by human beings because we are *physiologically, neurally and experientially predisposed* towards the acquisition of such basic configurations. Physiologically, because humans perceive the world from a vertical perspective, possess a variety of specific senses, and have symmetrical bodies. Experientially, the physical and emotional world we encounter as infants is characterized by gradable dimensions: cold-heat, light-dark, softness-roughness. Scalarity thus really exists and is detectable by humans. We also have very early experience with 'up-down', 'front-back' orientations, and crucially with functional dimensions such as 'constraint', 'containment' or 'support'.

There is nothing wrong with such a search for uniting factors, for what characterizes the human species as such, and the findings need not be at odds with issues concerning cultural and linguistic relativity – at least as long as we (a) engage in large-scale comparisons of as many languages as possible, (b) take no specific language – English included – as the model

---

1. Cf. Shepard and Metzler's (1971) work on mental rotation, according to which mental images preserve their basic topology in spite of being rotated. Cf. also Lakoff (1987), Johnson (1987).

against which the other languages are to be compared, and (c) bear in mind that the social world of different cultures places severe constraints on just what is successful for the individual within a given social group (cf. Lucy 1992; Levinson and Gumperz 1996).

In this respect let us recall the cross-linguistic and cross-cultural study between Danish and Zapotec by Sinha and Jensen de López (2000). The authors examined the use of the body-part term *láani* (i.e., English *stomach*) in San Marco Tlapazola Zapotec to lexicalize both the schematic spatial relation of English *in* and *under*. While in English the spatial relation of canonical containment (enclosure within a canonically oriented container such as a cup, e.g. *in*) is differentiated lexically from the spatial relation of enclosure within the bounded space of an inverted container (e.g. *under*), in Zapotec no such lexical distinction is made. The authors (Sinha and Jensen de López 2000: 34-35) hypothesize that the Danish and English prepositions *i* and *in* are both organized around a core or "impetus" meaning (Vandeloise 1991) equivalent to canonical containment, while the Zapotec term is organized around a core meaning that equals full enclosure without profiling the orientation of the container. A plausible explanation would take account of socio-cultural differences regarding artifact use in the two societies: the Zapotec culture makes use of a limited number of artifacts (such as baskets) and employs them flexibly and multi-functionally, often in inverted orientation. Providing that the core CONTAINMENT schema of Zapotec involves *constraint* of the location of the trajector by the landmark, the schema would as readily be associated with an orientation of the container with its cavity upwards as with its cavity downwards. In conclusion, the CONTAINER/CONTENT schema is undoubtedly operative in many languages, English included, but it is not universal. In other cultures the corresponding spatial conceptualization is encoded at the more general level of a 'controller/controlled' relationship, subsuming the senses of English *in* and *under*, as in the case of Zapotec, or of English *in* and *on*, as in the case of Spanish (see below).

Spatial schemas and the linguistic representations associated with them are thus culturally situated, and cultural situatedness also constitutes a kind of embodiment.[2] At the same time, viewing spatial cognition as embodied and situated (cf. Ziemke 2002, 2003; Kristiansen 2003, in prep.) – rather

---

2. Cf. Frank, Bernárdez, Dirven and Ziemke (in prep.) and Ziemke, Zlatev and Frank (in prep.) for an overview of different approaches to cultural situatedness and embodiment.

346   *Margarita Correa-Beningfield et al.*

than as a series of out-of-context, universal processes – necessarily brings cultural and group-related factors into the picture: real people interacting with other people at a specific historical moment and in a specific physical environment, with a series of real resources at their disposal. Another pertinent group-related factor is normativity. Not only social practices, but also linguistic practices and conventions have a bearing on the acquisition of spatial prepositions (cf. Rice 2003, as quoted in Section 4 below).

1.2. Image schemas as schemas

The prelinguistic basis necessary for the linguistic description of space consists of schemas, which are abstracted by perceptual analysis or by "perceptual meaning analysis", as Mandler puts it more explicitly in this volume. These schemas are "dynamic analogue representations of spatial relations and movements in space" (Mandler 1992: 591).[3] Even though image schemas have been abundantly used in Cognitive Linguistics, their definition in the spatial domain has never been very carefully spelled out. Despite Mandler's (1992) efforts to make the definition of Lakoff's (1987) image schemas more explicit, there remains space for further specifications. True, they are schematic, but schematicity is not their exclusive privilege, and it does certainly not constitute a sufficient condition.

Because Mandler's definition of image schema is so sketchy, one might try to figure it out by looking for commonalities between her examples. A first group of schemas in the infant's conceptualization of space is kinetic, that is related to movement. They include ANIMATE MOTION, INANIMATE MOTION, SELF-MOTION and CAUSED MOTION. These concepts are, in keeping with Mandler's way of characterizing image schemas, highly schematic and, admittedly, analogue. A second group of prelinguistic concepts like 'containment' and 'support', however, seems different. Following Lakoff (1987), Mandler characterizes CONTAINMENT by three structural elements:

---

3. Notice that by "dynamic", Mandler refers to movements and not to forces. This is in contrast with the terminology of Vandeloise (2005), in which movements are "kinetic" relations and "dynamic" refers to forceful relations. There, a spot of light moving on a wall is a kinetic but not a dynamic event.

interior, boundary, and exterior.[4] SUPPORT, on the other hand, according to Mandler, requires only a representation of contact between two objects in the vertical domain. As we will see in Section 2, 'containment' and 'support' as we understand them are very different.

The common point between such prelinguistic concepts as 'self-motion', 'animate motion', or 'self-moving-animate' on the one hand and 'containment' and 'support' on the other hand is not so much their schematic structure as their utmost importance in the interaction of the child with her environment. The interest of new-borns in self-moving objects may be directly related to their survival. 'Containment' and 'support' are equally pervasive in young children's behavior. These concepts are determined by their high degree of basic utility and need not be simple abstract schemas. As far as schematicity is concerned, prelinguistic concepts in the first group, like 'self-motion' and 'animate motion', may to some extent meet Mandler's description of image schemas. We do not believe, however, that the schematic representations of CONTAINMENT and SUPPORT proposed by Lakoff (1987) and Mandler (1992) capture the *complexity* of these concepts. As we will see in Section 2, 'containment' – or the relationship *C(ontainer)/ c(ontent)*, as it is called in this paper – belongs to "Complex Primitives" (CP), a different type of prelinguistic concept.

1.3. Image schemas as images

The fact that image schemas were coined the way they were constitutes a problem to more than one scholar. It was George Lakoff (1987), who in *Women, Fire, and Dangerous Things* subsumed Talmy's original topological, orientational and force-dynamic "primitives" under one general heading, or cover term, namely that of "image schema". As Mandler (1998: 263) rightly emphasizes, image-schemas are not images. Their name, then, is confusing and not very well chosen. In order to clarify the description, "imagistic" is sometimes used instead of "image" but, as long as "imagistic" is not defined, the shift does not help much.

---

4. As image schemas are gestalts, there is no reason to believe that 'interior' or 'exterior' are more primitive concepts than 'containment'. For a study of the concept 'interior', see Vandeloise (1999).

Figure 1 shows schemas illustrating CAUSED MOTION, SUPPORT, and CONTAINMENT (cf. Mandler 1992) as well as an adaptation of the last schema by Bowerman (1996b: 420):

Figure 1. CAUSED MOTION, SUPPORT, CONTAINMENT (M/B)

The problems posed by diagrams have been recognized by Johnson (1987: 23) who finds it "extremely important to recognize the way in which all diagrams are misleading". Also Lakoff (1987: 453) points out that "the drawings we gave are not the schemas themselves". In this way, he establishes a distinction between the meta-language about image schemas and image schemas themselves.

We would like to reply that a difference between chairs and talk about chairs is relatively easy to establish, because chairs are objects that can be seen and manipulated. We can also make a difference between talk about language (i.e., meta-language) and language itself because, even though language is not an object, we are aware of its reality. But it is more difficult to make a difference between the meta-language about unicorns and unicorns as objects because all we know about unicorns is their representation: if we change the meta-language about unicorns, we change unicorns. And we believe that we are in the same situation with image schemas. All we know about a speaker's mental representation is a graphic representation (or perhaps a propositional description) as offered by its proponent – be it a linguist or a psychologist. Unless we can meet image schemas otherwise, image schemas *are* what their representation tells us about them.

An obvious difficulty for pictorial representations is that they are doomed to represent properties which are irrelevant for the relationship.[5] For example, CONTAINMENT is indifferent to CONTACT between the container and the content but a graphic representation must commit itself either to contact or to separation. Mandler's schema chooses the latter solution. Pictorial representations also impose a choice between open containers (as in Mandler's

---

5. For further shortcomings of pictorial representations, see criticism of Lakoff's analysis of the preposition *over* in Vandeloise (1990) and in Dewell (1994).

schema) or closed containers (as in Bowerman's adaptation of Mandler's schema). The drawings proposed by Mandler to represent SUPPORT and CONTAINMENT also hide the functional complexity of these concepts; a fact which is difficult to reconcile with the high degree of abstraction she attributes to image schemas. This remains the case even when she makes it clear that image schemas are "primitive" not in the sense of being unitary and indivisible symbols, but in the sense of being "foundational" (Mandler 1992: 591), i.e., the most basic meanings on which language is grounded.

Though surely very "basic" indeed, image schemas cannot be elements of "basic-level" categorization, for two reasons: (i) they do not operate at the conceptual level (as they are "pre-"conceptual); (ii) if they were basic-level categories, then what would appear at the superordinate level? We maintain that it is only at the level of spatial prepositions – i.e., language- and culture-specific spatial encodings – that we have concepts that we can depict or describe in more precise ways by means of a propositional definition. In this respect, the alternative description of 'containment' proposed in Section 2 is an attempt to go beyond the characterization proposed in the pictorial representations for the image schemas of CONTAINMENT.

Not all of the image schemas represented by Mandler in Figure 1 do require the same type of information. First, her schemas of SUPPORT and CONTAINMENT are static, whereas the schema of CAUSED MOVEMENT is kinetic. As long as they apply to static shapes, the pictures representing image schemas may be considered iconic or analogue, but when they represent kinetic schemas, this is no longer so. Only a camera could represent movement and speed in an analogous way. We may be as familiar with the representation of movement by an arrow as we are familiar with writing – but the former representation is as conventional as the second. Therefore, the analogue virtue of many diagrams is delusive. Once they introduce conventional symbols like arrows to represent movement or dashed lines to represent virtual closures, pictures create a meta-language as conventional as language itself. Schemas are abundantly used by, for instance, Ronald Langacker in his Cognitive Grammar, as well as in Gilles Fauconnier's representations of mental spaces. Both are fully explicit, however, in emphasizing that their meta-language is partly conventional and would not consider their drawings as analogous representations.

Pictures may represent static relations like ABOVE or BELOW in an analogous way. As we saw above, this is more difficult for kinetic relations. While image schemas for static and kinetic relations may be built upon perceptual information only, this is not true for SUPPORT and CONTAINMENT because, as we will see in Section 2, FORCES and CONTROL have an essential role in the understanding of these concepts, which require the handling of objects in order to be completely assimilated. Even though Mandler (2000, *this volume*) suggests that, because of the limitations on infants' manual abilities, early analyses are more spatial than force-related, force unavoidably plays a role in the acquisition of CONTAINMENT. This becomes clear in the analysis of CONTAINMENT proposed by Dewell (*this volume*). Compared to the static image schemas proposed for 'containment' so far (Mandler 1992; Lakoff 1987), Dewell's attempt at introducing the dynamic dimension is certainly to be applauded. However, the representation of CONTAINMENT as "entry-enclosing", forces Dewell (*this volume*: Figure 3) to introduce new conventional devices in his representation: curved dashed arrows representing forces and straight dashed arrows representing virtual movement. While Dewell's pictures represent a step forward in the sense of more precision as far as pictorial representations are concerned, the propositional representations we will propose for the representation of CPs in the next section represent a step forward in the non-pictorial descriptive direction. As a matter of fact, the frequent use of pictures in the representation of image schemas, and the difficulty of representing force and function graphically may partly account for the neglect of these two important factors in the literature on image schemas – and so may the relative lack of cross-cultural studies: what the pictorial representations in question aim at reflecting are the specific conceptual encodings of no more than a few languages.

2. Complex Primitives as family resemblances vs. image schemas

"Complex Primitives" (CPs) (Vandeloise 1987, 1990, 1991, 1994, 2003), like 'containment' and 'support', are called "primitives" because they are prelinguistic. In this respect they are to be understood globally (or holistically) in terms of the general needs, i.e., the well-being and even survival, of the child. They are called "complex" because the fulfillment of these needs usually presupposes the presence of several conditions, involving perception, kinetics and interaction[6]. An ideal container, for example, is concave, solid, partially hides its content, etc. These properties are described by a set of propositions that represent the CP.

---

6. The primitives proposed by Wierzbicka (1972), in contrast, are atomistic.

While investigating independently the distribution of spatial expressions like *dans* or *sur* (as in a *est dans/sur* b) in French, Vandeloise (1986) realized that all these propositions were instrumental in validating their use. In this way, CPs provide a basis for the development of prepositional polysemy, with different languages allowing different combinations of propositions to extend the use of the word corresponding to the (originally holistic) CP.

The sets of propositions representing CPs are organized as the traits of a family resemblance. Situations characterized by all the traits of the family constitute prototypical examples of the Complex Primitive. Marginal examples of the CP are characterized by a few propositions only. In this sense, the traits representing the CP acquire for the linguist the status of theoretical axioms or basic hypotheses.[7] Vandeloise (1991), for instance, analyses the concepts of 'containment' and 'support' as expressed by prepositions (*in* and *on*, respectively) in terms of the Complex Primitives *C/c* (*container/content*) and *B/b* (*bearer/burden*). In this way, the conditions under which the expression *a is in b* is used are presented (Vandeloise 2005: 224), with 'a' and 'b' representing the entities designated by *a* and *b*:

(a)　The position of *a* relative to *b* does not change when *b* is moving.

(a')　The container *b* prevents the content *a* from transgressing its limits in more than one direction[8]

(b)　If there is movement, *a* moves toward *b* rather than the reverse

(c)　*b* surrounds *a*

(d)　*b* protects *a*

(e)　[...]

Condition (c) is an attempt to describe the prototypical shape of containers. In Vandeloise (1991: 225), this property was presented as follows: "*a* is included, at least partially, in the convex closure of the containing part of *b*."

---

7. As such, empirical testing is undoubtedly called for, but the advantages are already numerous: (a) being more specific than the pictures representing image schemas in figure 1, CPs can be falsified in a Popperian sense, (b) they are specifically geared towards a deeper understanding of cross-linguistic and cross-cultural differences, (c) they take social and functional factors governing spatial configurations into account, and (d) they reduce polysemy to manageable proportions (cf. Sandra and Rice 1995).

8. The conditions (a) and (a') are a development of proposition (a) proposed in Vandeloise (2003: 398): "*b* controls the position of *a* in more than one direction."

The presence of "containing" in the proposition, however, shows that topological inclusion cannot satisfactorily describe this property of containment independently of containment itself. Finally, the unspecified proposition (e) in the list shows that the list is open. None of these properties is understood as a necessary or sufficient condition. For example, condition (c) is only partially met by sentence (1), and condition (b) is not met by sentence (2):

(1)   The bulb is in the socket.
(2)   The soup is in the ladle.

These properties, then, are not necessary. Neither are they sufficient. For example, condition (a) is not sufficient, since a soccer player controls the football, but the football is obviously not *in* the soccer player. However, according to Vandeloise (2003), each situation in which *in* is used shares at least one property with the other situations allowing for the use of this preposition. The properties describing the use of the preposition *in*, then, are structured like traits in a family resemblance set.

The spatial configurations in the categories *C/c* and *B/b* (Vandeloise 1994: 6) play an important role in our survival and our well-being. From a functional perspective, the need to control the objects which surround us operates as a driving unifying factor for the meaning of *in* and *on,* and shapes, motions and forces constitute the different ways in which the functions of containment and support realize themselves, as means towards a purpose. As we will see in Section 4, Vandeloise (2003: 411) furthermore suggests that 'containment' and 'support' are functional elaborations of 'control'. Whereas CPs globally conceived may be universal because of their vital importance for our survival, the family resemblance representing their function and the choice of combinations sanctioning the use of the corresponding word are largely language-dependent.

If we now compare the notion of CP with that of image schema, it is easy to observe that they obviously have things in common. They are both prelinguistic and both serve as a foundation to which basic words are anchored. 'Containment', for example, is certainly the same concept whether it is viewed as image schema (Lakoff 1987; Mandler 1991; Dewell, *this volume*) or CP (Vandeloise 1991). The difference is that the analogue representation of image schemas is rather unspecific, whereas the representations of CPs are more falsifiable since their linguistic description is propositional in nature. A proposition like (b) in the family resemblance *C/c* might as well be represented in an analogue way, in keeping with Mandler's image schema of

CAUSED MOVEMENT. As we noticed above, the analogue representation of force and function is more difficult.

These affirmations provided, we will take a special interest in the Spanish spatial-relations term *en* (see Section 4), which triggers the spatial concepts of both 'containment' (English *in*, French *dans*) and 'support' (English *on*, French *sur*).

3. A three-dimensional approach to the family resemblances representing CPs

CPs are *global functional concepts* represented by family resemblances at the analytical level. Focusing on the preposition *in*, which conveys the CP of 'containment' represented by the family resemblance *C/c*, we will try to understand the nature of the traits in the family resemblance better, and to sort them out in three dimensions. People perceive and are aware of the topology of objects given the human perceptual apparatus. But people are also aware of the movement of entities and of the patterns of interaction that allow for object recognition, use and categorization. The latter are not intrinsic to the situation but "observer-relative", and include "social facts" (Searle 1995). Thus, the spatial relationships expressed linguistically do not represent situational or real-world relations, but rather aspects of the "projected world" (Jackendoff 1983), which are relevant for the observers' (/speech community's) aims, goals or interests in a particular environment. Clark (1973), Deane (1993), and Talmy (1983) constitute early views of spatial semantics that point in the direction of explaining and accounting for "projected" and "social" aspects of spatial meanings of linguistic expressions.

According to Clark (1973), human beings perceive space following several parameters in order to construe perceptual space (P-space). Accordingly, (i) *physical space* implies the perception of three dimensions defined by three axes (length, height and width); (ii) *geological space* emerges from the perception of gravity and the ground level as constant features of our experience; (iii) *biological space* is defined in relation to the human body, with a head on the top, symmetrical organs for perception (eyes, ears, hands, etc.), motion forwards, and standing position, which constitutes the human canonical position; and finally, (iv) *social space* is determined by the way human beings interact with each other, i.e. face-to-face, performing what Clark calls the "canonical encounter". In addition, there is *linguistic space* (L-space). L-space is the semantics that each language uses to reflect and conceptualize P-space. It is assumed that there must be a direct correlation between P-space and L-space. Linguistic meanings cannot contradict the organization of human perception, a principle expressed in Clark's correlation hypothesis: "the structure of P-space will be preserved in L-space" (Clark 1973: 28). Therefore, L-space shows the conceptualization of points, lines, and planes of reference, the ground level with positive and negative poles, up-down, right-left, and front-back distinctions, and finally, canonical position, as well as canonical encounter (reflected in egocentric meanings and deixis). The universality of perceptual principles, however, does not imply that L-space should have the same form and structure for all languages.

Deane (1993: 115, *this volume*) proposes a multimodal conception of meaning for prepositions that could be viewed as a new version of Clark's P-space. In Deane's terms, human beings perceive and conceptualize three aspects of space: *Visual space images*, which correspond to Clark's physical space. They represent spatial relationships in terms of separation, contiguity, angle of vision, and any aspect related to the position of entities in relation to each other, i.e. their topological relationship. *Manoeuver space images*, which roughly correspond to social and biological spaces. This kind of perception processes information relative to motor control and the capacity to interact with other people and manipulate objects, as well as the body itself. *Kinetic space images*, which encode the information necessary to calculate dynamic interaction, in terms of paths, directions, axes, gravity, relative orientation of the participants, etc. According to Deane, these modes of perception occur together in human experience. They are prelinguistic in character, and form part of the human bodily experience that prompts the emergence of new concepts in the child's mind.

Talmy (1983, *this volume*) suggests a series of different aspects of meaning expressed by spatial terms that go beyond the mere physical location of objects, and introduces biosocial aspects such as trajector orientation, intentionality, the conceptualizer's perspective and point of view, site, path, the scope and reference frame of the scene, and force-dynamic patterns of interaction between the participants, as well as many of Clark's distinctions. A conception of spatial meaning that goes beyond the description of mere location (topology) or mere movement (kinetics) is all the more convincing if we take into account that language acquisition and cognitive development are processes in which perception, action, and interaction play a crucial role. Piaget and Inhelder (1969) already viewed such processes as individual construction of reality and language through mechanisms of accomodation and assimilation. Beyond that, Vygotsky's (1986 [1934]) conception of dialogical development claimed that primary pseudo-conceptual thinking aims at interaction with other people, so that the child's earliest speech is already social. Thus, perceiving the world equals (inter)acting in it, a conception which converges with Merleau Ponty's (1943) phenomenology of perception, where perception, self-motion and interaction co-occur as a single phenomenon.

Recent research in language acquisition (Bowerman 1996b) gives support to both the Vygotskyan and the Piagetian approach. Bowerman shows that children's initially vague spatial concepts become more subtle with progressive language usage. Despite the absence of empirical data, the temporal priority of certain non-linguistic experiential knowledge patterns (whatever name we want to give them, "image schemas" or (holistic) "Complex Primitives") over language-specific spatial knowledge is an overall accepted hypothesis in Cognitive Linguistics. Mandler's (1992) distinction between perceptual categories and conceptual categories points in the same direction. Mandler sees infants as young as 3 months as having schematic concepts, and claims that development goes from the abstract to the concrete in concept formation rather than from the concrete to the abstract.

We also conceive of the development of CPs in the child's mind as a process from globally conceived CPs to conscious family resemblance discrimination in later stages. CPs are viewed here as a functionally inspired improvement of the notion of image schemas as highly schematic, prelinguistic patterns. The traits of family resemblance sets representing spatial CPs can be viewed along three experiential dimensions contributing to conceptual development: perception (*sensory*), action (*motor*) and interaction (*purposive*). Though the purposive dimension is the most relevant to human beings, it is the most neglected one in image schema theory.

Concerning the acquisition of these three-dimensional CPs, Vandeloise (2003: 412-420) suggests that, in *stage 1*, they are first understood globally by infants, and that their prototypical manifestations are later, in *stage 2*, associated to a word of the acquired language. In *stage 3*, the word begins to be used for marginal situations that imply only part of the family resemblance set. However, at this stage, CPs are still understood globally, as long as children rely on their memory to recognize the marginal situations for which they use the word. It is only at *stage 4* that children finally begin to analyze the complexity of the CP in a "conscious" way. Then, children are able to use each single feature in the family resemblance that models the CP, so that they apply it to marginal situations they meet for the first time. Such a use of the associated words makes meaning extension possible.

Whether the analysis of the global CP in the mind of the child is analogue or propositional is a question that goes beyond the linguist's possibilities. We would like to stress, however, that even mental representations that *are* analogical cannot be fully modeled by means of (static) pictures/diagrams. From the point of view of linguists, as well as lexicologists trying to represent words, however, we believe that propositions provide the most explicit and falsifiable alternative for an account of (prelinguistic) meaning.

Thus, while image schemas – or CPs at the global level – are generally accepted as prelinguistic universal constructs, the representation of CPs by linguists may be viewed as a set of traits, from which different meaning extensions can occur in different languages. Therefore, for linguistic analysis, we suggest that the family resemblance features representing the CPs should be considered and used for the purpose of describing and explaining further semantic extensions. The global CP of a given preposition would appear as a "proto-concept".

The sets of traits describing CPs may be divided according to the three experiential factors suggested above in accordance with the proposals made by Clark, Deane and Talmy:

Perception: The *perception* of *topological* arrangements, determined by human perceptual capacities, which in the case of spatial semantics are mainly visual capacities.[9]

Kinetics: *Sensory-motor experience* about the *kinetic* action of objects determined by human motor capacities.

Interaction: *Assimilation of the environment*, as well as *accommodation of the body*, in order to facilitate survival, determined by human interaction, including social interaction.

We assume that every trait within a family resemblance will correlate with one of these three experiential dimensions. In the case of the relationship *C/c* (see Section 2), the five traits would be distributed in the following way:

Perception: (c) b (partially) surrounds a.

---

9. Since we are dealing with spatial meanings (*in*, *on*, *at*, etc.), the perceptual dimension has to do with the perception of topology by means of the human visual apparatus. By "visual" we do not refer to the notion of mental images (Lakoff 1987: 444-445).

Kinetics:	(b) If there is movement, a moves toward (the interior zone of) b rather than the reverse.
Interaction:	(a') The position of *a* relative to *b* does not change when *b* is moving.
	(a") The container (b) prevents the content *a* from transgressing its limits in more than one direction.
	(d) b protects a.

For each usage of the preposition, at least one of the traits appears, or is more prominent. In sentence (3), trait (a) is the most prominent, in sentence 4 trait (b) is the most prominent, and in sentence (5), trait (c) is the most prominent. Notice that the traits of the family resemblance are expressed propositionally as *a/b* relationships.

(3)   The fish is in the hand
(4)   Hit him in the stomach
(5)   I am singing in the rain

Let us consider the case of the English preposition *at*, as it is analyzed by Navarro-Ferrando (2002). The author suggests that the family resemblance that represents its CP should consist of at least three features that would correlate with a perceptive relation, a kinetic relation, and an interactional relation between trajector and landmark, and possibly of more than one feature for each type of experiential dimension. The *Container/content* CP can be understood as a functional elaboration of Mandler's CONTAINER image schema and the *Bearer/burden* CP is conceived as a functional elaboration of Mandler's SUPPORT image schema. The functional elaboration implies the incorporation of traits that refer not only to mere topological or kinetic arrangements, but also interactional configurations in terms of accommodation and assimilation. Image schemas are usually explained in terms of entities and movement, but other kinds of relations between the elements have not been described, for example the asymmetrical relation of intentionality. In a similar way, the *Operator/artifact* CP for the preposition *at* can be viewed as a linguistic instantiation of *encounter* (a prospective CP) which defines, more than a physical pattern, a multidimensional and dynamic pattern involving aspects such as agentivity, intentionality, asymmetry and functional orientation (cf. Talmy 1983, *this volume*).

As a tentative proposal, we will draw our family resemblance traits from Navarro-Ferrando's (2002) description of *at* so as to elaborate the idea of an *Operator/artifact* CP. Thus, the senses of the preposition *at* could be derived from a family resemblance expressed propositionally in terms of *a/b* relationships, which in turn derive from sensory-motor and social experience (visual, kinetic or interactional). Let us consider sentence 6:

(6)   The engineers gathered at the computer

Here "the engineers" is identified as element *a* and "the computer" is identified as element *b*. The *Operator/artifact* CP could then be defined as:

(a)   a is contiguous to b (a feature of visual perception)
(b)   a is oriented towards b (a feature of perceived intentionality (interaction)
(c)   If there is movement a moves towards b and not the reverse (a feature of perceived kinetics)
(d)   a uses b in a conventional or canonical way (a feature of interaction)

Example (6) can be considered a prototypical example of the preposition *at*, attending to the proposed family resemblance – attributes a) to d) above. In other cases, as in (7) to (10), only one or more traits might be more prominent than the rest. The three dimensions of experience thus provide a frame for family resemblances as candidates to be accepted as prepositional CPs.

(7)   The point is at the centre of the circle (trait a)
(8)   The students kept looking at the blackboard (trait b)
(9)   The soldiers ran at the enemy (trait c is the most prominent, though trait a also contributes to the choice of *at*, instead of *towards*)
(10)   John was at church (trait d is the most prominent)

In this section we have tried to ground the notion of CP as an experientially-based principle. CPs anchor language to prototypical situations at stage 1 and allow extensions to marginal situations at stage 4. We have argued that the same kind of grounding is plausible not only for previously proposed CPs, such as *Container/content* or *Bearer/burden*, but also for new ones such as *Operator/artifact*.

4.   Cross-cultural cognition: Spanish *en* and English *in* and *on*

Whereas all languages have an element corresponding to English *on* to describe spatial relations involving a horizontal surface, some languages, like Japanese and Korean, do not use the same element in those relations involving a vertical surface. This extended use, the use of *on* or its equivalent in other languages in relation to a vertical surface, is characteristic of languages like Chinese, English and Spanish. Spanish is especially interesting in this regard, because not only does it have a single word *en* for expressions that imply contact with a horizontal surface and for expressions that imply contact with a vertical surface, both corresponding to English *on*, but it also has the same word *en* for expressions that imply position in a container and in an enclosure, corresponding here to the English preposition *in*.

Spanish *en*	
English *in*	English *on*
There is a ball in the box.. *Hay una pelota en la caja.*	*The pencil is on the floor.* *El lápiz está en el suelo.*
María lives in Spain. *María vive en España.*	*That picture goes on that wall.* *Ese cuadro va en esa pared.*

Figure 2. Spanish *en* vs. English *in/on*

Besides the discrepancies between *en* (Spanish) and *in* and *on* (English), Choi and Bowerman (1991) and Bowerman (1996) also point out that words like *op* and *aan* (Dutch), and *kkita* (Korean) may convey some kind of support and/or containment but that their distributions are very different, with *aan* expressing attachment and *kkita* conveying tight fit. Vandeloise (2003: 402-404) claims that these discrepancies can be motivated by hierarchical connections between the concept of 'control' and the concepts of 'containment', 'support', 'tight fit' and 'attachment'.

The hierarchical connections between 'containment' and 'support' are reflected by the Spanish preposition *en*, which covers the domains of the prepositions *in* and *on* in English. This preposition *en* suggests the existence of a concept of 'control', which captures what is shared by 'containment' and 'support'. Indeed, whereas *in* and 'containment' involve control in more than one direction (cf. trait (a) in family resemblance C/c), *on* and support involve control along one axis only, usually the vertical axis corresponding to gravity (Vandeloise 1991). The common denominator between these two traits determining the distribution of *on* and *in* is the more abstract concept of 'control'. 'Tight fit' and 'attachment', on the other hand, may be considered as elaborations of 'containment' and 'support' respectively. The hierarchical connections between these concepts are illustrated in Figure 3.

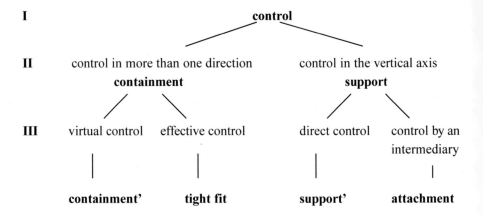

Figure 3. A hierarchy of concepts involving 'control'

At the highest level of generality, *b* controls *a* if *b* prevents *a* from moving in at least one direction. At the second level of elaboration, 'containment' and 'support' can be defined as "control in more than one direction" and "control in the vertical axis", respectively. Finally, at the third level of elaboration, we find 'tight fit' and 'attachment', as well as 'containment' and 'support'. Both 'Tight fit' and 'containment' are elaborations of 'containment', while 'attachment' and 'support'' are elaborations of 'support'. For 'containment', control may be either actual (if there is contact between the content and the container) or potential as in the case of a bee *in* the middle of a cup or a prisoner *in* the middle of his cell. Even though there is no contact between the container and the content (the bee and the prisoner are free to move inside the limits of the cup or the cell), their moves are limited by the container. 'Tight fit', in contrast, implies contact *and* direct control. Similarly, for 'support', control may be direct or through an intermediary. As such, 'attachment' may be roughly defined as "support with an intermediary between a non-horizontal bearer and the burden".

Children learning the words conveying support in English, Dutch, and Spanish are confronted with different linguistic clues coming from adults speaking their language. In English, the child learning *on* will be confronted with situations in which this word is associated with attachment. Such will not be the case for a child learning *op* in Dutch or *auf* in German since for attachment, adults use the prepositions *aan* or *an* respectively. In this way, different languages confront their learners with different repertories of uses susceptible to modify the concepts children have initially attached to a word. Languages with general meanings, like Spanish, may lead to concept extension whereas languages with more specific meanings are more likely to lead to concept restriction. At this point, these assessments are speculative and call for empirical confirmation. As Rice (2003: 248) states:

> It is incumbent upon cognitive linguistics to lead the way in asking psychologically testable questions of its theory and identifying relevant experimental stimuli.

In addition to variation across languages in children's acquisition of spatial terms, the data proposed by Rice show that children speaking the same language may not necessarily follow the same path of acquisition either. Indeed, the level at which a child connects spatial words with prelinguistic concepts may account for individual variation in one language. By way of example, imagine a Spanish child learning the preposition *en*. She might first associate the preposition with the concept of 'control' or, at a different level of granularity, with 'containment' or 'support'. There are good reasons for each of these two concepts to emerge first. Indeed, 'containment' has the advantage of control in several directions, while 'support' puts the vertical axis to the fore, a direction to which three-month-old infants already pay special attention. Suppose this Spanish child chooses 'support' first. Then, she might be expected to underextend the preposition *en* to the circumstances in which an English child would use the preposition *on*. For that child, all the circumstances for which *en* is used to describe 'containment' will sound as marginal usages for which she has to make adjustments. The reverse would be true for a Spanish child that first associates *en* to 'containment', in that the Spanish child will underextend *en* to circumstances in which the English child uses *in*. This situation of English children acquiring *in* compared to Spanish children acquiring *en* is similar to English children learning the preposition *on* compared to Dutch children learning the preposition *op*. Indeed, Dutch children will never get linguistic clues tempting them to associate *op* to 'attachment' since this does not occur in their language. The situation is different however because, in contrast to 'containment' and 'support', which are functionally equally important, the function of 'attachment' may be less pervasive.

Which is the relationship between concepts like 'control' (highest degree of abstraction), 'support' (intermediary level) and 'attachment' (most specific level)? If they are all complex primitives, the concepts at the most specific level are obviously more complex than those at the most abstract level. 'Attachment' is certainly a spatial relation which is rarer and more complex than 'support'. The case of 'tight fit', corresponding to Korean *kkita*, is more puzzling. Indeed, even though 'tight fit' is more complex than 'containment', it might also be considered as a prototypical case of 'containment' since control is more efficient when there is contact and exchange of energy than in the case of loose containment, where control is virtual. Language acquisition research might help to clarify the connections between these concepts (cf. Choi et al. 1999).

5. Conclusions

Complex Primitives and image schemas are notions which undoubtedly have things in common. 'Containment' may be viewed in terms of an image schema (Lakoff 1987) or of a CP (Vandeloise 1991). The difference is that image schemas as theoretical constructs constitute rather unspecific, imagistic representations, while CPs are functional concepts represented by a set of propositions (family resemblances).

Both notions are supposedly "embodied", but not in the same way. While image schemas are grounded in successful bodily (and social) experience, CPs take cultural situatedness seriously and aim at a deeper understanding of language-specific spatial encodings. Moreover, while a radial network analysis based on image schema transformations results in an overwhelming number of slightly different senses, CPs on the contrary reduce polysemy and thus possess a unifying power. In this respect, determining CPs for several prepositions in English and Spanish will allow us, at the analytical level, to test the relative importance of single sense features in both languages, to compare them, and to test the degrees of sense feature transfer in learners of a foreign language.

In addition, we suggest that functional and dynamic relationships are more primary than topological ones in the process of language acquisition (see also Dewell, *this volume*). Therefore, our standpoint considers functional meaning as primordial. In adult usage the three dimensions related to *topology, kinetics,* and *purposive interaction* are active to varying degrees and contribute in different measure to the meanings of diverse prepositions, as has been suggested by experimental evidence.[10] Furthermore, we suggest

---

10. Navarro-Ferrando and Tricker (2001) show that, in adult usage, uses conveying intentional interaction predominate for *at* and *on*, whereas topological perception is much more prominent for *in*.

that the three of them develop simultaneously in children's language acquisition, while being intimately linked to each other in human experience, resulting in language-specific analyzed CPs.

The incorporation of the functional element to semantic description and explanation can contribute to get beyond sensorimotor/perceptual processes into processes involved in complex communication and social interaction. On the other hand, CPs as family resemblances expressed in propositional form allow for a more accurate analysis of linguistic polysemy than image schemas (taken as a representational device), since the former make possible an analysis of concept formation and extension, from the prelinguistic stage to conscious sense discrimination. Furthermore, CPs could facilitate cross-linguistic concept comparison, as well as the analysis of gradual concept learning in foreign language learning processes.

References

Bowerman, Melissa
    1996a   The origins of children's spatial semantic categories: cognitive versus linguistic determinants. In *Rethinking Linguistic Relativity*, John J. Gumperz and Stephen C. Levinson (eds.), 145-176. Cambridge: Cambridge University Press.
    1996b   Learning how to structure space for language: A crosslinguistic perspective. In *Language and Space*, Paul Bloom, Mary A. Peterson, Lynn Nadel and Merrill F. Garrett (eds.), 385-436. Cambridge, MA: MIT Press.
Choi, Soonja, and Melissa Bowerman
    1991   Learning to express motion events in English and Korean: The influence of language specific lexicalization patterns. In *Lexical and Conceptual Semantics,* Beth Levin and Steve Pinker (eds.), 83-121. Oxford: Basic Blackwell.
Choi, Soonja, Laraine McDonough, Melissa Bowerman and Jean M. Mandler
    1999   Early sensibility to language specific categories in English and Korean. *Cognitive Development* 14: 241-268.
Correa-Beningfield, Margarita
    1985   *Prototype and Language Transfer: The Acquisition by Native Speakers of Spanish of Four English Prepositions of Location.* Ann Arbor, MI: University Microfilms International.
Deane, Paul
    1993   *At, by, to,* and *past*: An essay in multimodal image theory. *Berkeley Linguistics Society* 19: 112-124.

Dewell, Robert B.
    1994   'Over' again: On the role of image-schemas in semantic analy-
           sis. *Cognitive Linguistics* 5: 351-380.

Frank, Roslyn M., Enrique Bernárdez, René Dirven and Tom Ziemke (eds.)
    in prep. *Body, Language, and Mind.* Vol. 2: *Cultural Situatedness.* Ber-
           lin/New York: Mouton de Gruyter.

Geeraerts, Dirk
    1997   *Diachronic Prototype Semantics. A Contribution to Historical Lexi-
           cology.* Oxford: Clarendon Press.

Gumperz, John, and Stephen Levinson (eds.)
    1996   *Rethinking Linguistic Relativity.* Cambridge: Cambridge University
           Press.

Jackendoff, Ray
    1983   *Semantics and Cognition.* Cambridge, MA: MIT Press.

Johnson, Mark
    1987   *The Body in the Mind: The Bodily Basis of Meaning, Imagination
           and Reason.* Chicago/London: The University of Chicago Press.

Kristiansen, Gitte
    2003   How to do things with allophones: Linguistic stereotypes as cogni-
           tive reference points in social cognition. In *Cognitive Models in
           Language and Thought: Ideologies, Metaphors and Meanings*,
           Dirven, René, Roslyn M. Frank and Martin Pütz (eds.), 69-120.
           Berlin/New York: Mouton de Gruyter.
    in prep. Idealized cultural models: The group as a variable in the develop-
           ment of cognitive schemata. In *Body, Language, and Mind.* Vol. 2:
           Cultural Situatedness, Frank, Roslyn M., Enrique Bernárdez, René
           Dirven and Tom Ziemke (eds.), Berlin/New York: Mouton de
           Gruyter.

Lakoff, George
    1987   *Women, Fire, and Dangerous Things: What Categories Reveal
           about the Mind.* Chicago/London: The University of Chicago Press.

Lucy, John R.
    1992   *Grammatical Categories and Cognition: A Case Study of the Lin-
           guistic Relativity Hypothesis.* Cambridge: Cambridge University
           Press.

Mandler, Jean M.
    1992   How to build a baby: II. Conceptual primitives. *Psychological Re-
           view* 99: 587-604.
    1994   Precursors of linguistic knowledge. *Philosophical Transactions of
           the Royal Society of London* 346: 63-69.
    2000   Perceptual and conceptual processes in infancy. *Journal of Cogni-
           tion and Development* 1: 3-36.

Merleau-Ponty, Maurice
1945   *Phénoménologie de la Perception*. Paris: Gallimard.
Navarro-Ferrando, Ignasi
2001   Is function part of the literal meaning of English prepositions? In *On Prepositions*, Ljiljana Saric and Donald F. Reindl (eds.), 39-62. University of Oldenburg: BIS.
2002   Towards a Description of the meaning of *at*. In *Perspectives on Prepositions*, Hubert Cuyckens and Günter Radden (eds.), 211-230. Tübingen: Max Niemeyer Verlag.
Navarro-Ferrando, Ignasi and Deborah Tricker
2001   A comparison of the use of *at*, *in* and *on* by EFL students and native speakers, *Revista Española de Lingüística Aplicada* 14: 295-324.
Olson, David R., and Ellen Bialystok
1983   *Spatial cognition: The structure and development of the mental representation of spatial relations*. Hillsdale, NJ: Lawrence Erlbaum.
Piaget, Jean, and Bärbel Inhelder
1969   *The Psychology of the Child*. New York: Basic Books.
Rice, Sally
2003   Growth of a lexical network: Nine English prepositions in acquisition. In *Cognitive Approaches to Lexical Semantics*, Cuyckens, Hubert, René Dirven and John Taylor (eds.), 243-260. Berlin/New York: Mouton de Gruyter.
Rosch, Eleanor, and Carolyn B. Mervis
1975   Family Resemblances: Studies in the Internal Structure of Categories. *Cognitive Psychology* 7: 573-605.
Sandra, Dominiek, and Sally Rice
1995   Network analyses of prepositional meaning: Mirroring whose mind – the linguist's or the language user's? *Cognitive Linguistics* 6: 89-130.
Searle, John. R.
1995   *The Construction of Social Reality*. New York: Free Press.
Shepard, Roger N., and Jacqueline Metzler
1971   Mental rotation of three dimensional objects. *Science* 171: 701-704.
Sinha, Chris, and Kristine Jensen de López
2000   Language, culture and the embodiment of spatial cognition. *Cognitive Linguistics* 11: 17-41.
Talmy, Leonard
1983   How language structures space. In *Spatial Orientation: Theory, Research and Application,* Herbert L. Pick, Jr., and Linda P. Acredolo (eds.), 225-281. New York: Plenum Press.

Vandeloise, Claude
   1987   CP in language acquisition. *Belgian Journal of Linguistics* 2: 11-36.
   1990   Representation, prototypes and centrality. In *Meanings and Proto-types: Studies in Linguistic Categorization,* Savas L. Tsohatzidis (ed.), 403-437. London/New York: Routledge.
   1991   *Spatial Prepositions: A Case Study from French.* Chicago: The University of Chicago Press.
   1992   Structure of lexical categories and family resemblances. Duisburg: LAUD (Series A, Paper No 325).
   1994   Methodology and analyses of the preposition *in. Cognitive Linguistics* 5: 157-184.
   1995   Cognitive linguistics and prototypes. In *Advances in Visual Semiotics: The Semiotic Web 1992-1993*, Thomas A. Sebeok and Jean Umiker-Sebeok (eds.), 423-442. Berlin/New York: Mouton de Gruyter.
   2003   Containment, support and linguistic relativity. In *Cognitive Approaches to Lexical Semantics*, Hubert Cuyckens, René Dirven and John R. Taylor (eds.), 393-426. Berlin/New York: Mouton de Gruyter.
   2005   Force and Function in the Acquisition of the preposition *in.* In *Functional Features in Language and Space*, Laura Carson and Emile van der Zee (eds.), 219-231. Oxford: Oxford University Press.
Wierzbicka, Anna
   1972   *Semantic Primitives.* Frankfurt: Athenäum.
Wittgenstein, Ludwig
   1953   *Philosophical Investigations.* New York: Macmillan.
Vygotsky, Lev S.
   1986   Reprint. *Thought and Language.* Cambridge, MA: MIT Press [original publication 1934].
Ziemke, Tom
   2002   Situated and embodied cognition. *Cognitive Systems Research* 3: 271-554.
   2003   What's that thing called embodiment? In *Proceedings of the 25th Annual Meeting of the Cognitive Science Society,* Richard Alterman and David Kirsh (eds.), 1305-1310. Mahwah, N.J.: Lawrence Erlbaum.
Ziemke, Tom, Jordan Zlatev and Roslyn M. Frank (eds.)
   in prep.   *Body, Language, and Mind.* Vol. 1: *Embodiment.* Berlin/New York: Mouton de Gruyter.

Part 5: New case studies on image schemas

Dynamic patterns of CONTAINMENT

Robert B. Dewell[*]

Abstract

This chapter advocates a return to Johnson's (1987) original notion that image schemas are "dynamic patterns". Using CONTAINMENT as an example, it makes the case that even static locational relations are structured as dynamic processes that incorporate image-schema transformations and scanning processes by a ceaselessly active conceptualizer.

CONTAINMENT is analyzed as a merger of two basic experiential patterns, ENTRY and ENCLOSURE, and both patterns are grounded originally in the construal of motion events. The construal processes that originally accompany objective motion acquire schematic status of their own and come to characterize even timeless locational relations. Unlike proposals in which image schemas have a static structure, the analysis accounts for the basic relational nature of CONTAINMENT and provides a plausible account of its many important functional and force-dynamic implications.

Positing a fundamentally dynamic structure for image schemas has significant theoretical implications. It implies that language plays a much greater role in the development of image schemas than is often assumed, contributing not only to cross-linguistic variation but also to some universal similarities in the structure of image schemas. It also calls into question some of the most basic assumptions of the "standard view of cognition".

Keywords: containment, image-schema transformations, *in*, cross-linguistic variation

[*] I would like to thank the editor of this volume and two anonymous reviewers for their helpful comments on an earlier version of this chapter.

Though it is customary – and I think innocuous – to use nominal expressions to designate mental phenomena (e.g. mind, thought, concept, perception, etc.), such terms must always be understood as convenient reifications. Mind is the same as mental processing; what I call thought is the occurrence of a complex neurological, ultimately electrochemical event; and to say that I have formed a concept is merely to note that a particular pattern of neurological activity has become established, so that functionally equivalent events can be evoked and repeated with relative ease. ... Mental experience is thus a flow of events: it is what the brain does.   (Langacker 1987: 100)

1.   Image schemas as dynamic patterns

From the beginning, Johnson (1987: 29) stressed that image schemas are "dynamic patterns rather than fixed and static images". Image schemas are "structures *of an activity* by which we organize our experience in ways that we can comprehend", and they are "flexible in that they can take on any number of specific instantiations in varying contexts" (Johnson 1987: 29-30). I believe that this fundamentally dynamic nature of image schemas has been underappreciated in the literature since Johnson (1987). For a variety of reasons having to do with the particular overriding concerns of the leading researchers and with some generally unchallenged basic assumptions, image schemas have been analyzed largely as static structures. They have come to be considered dynamic only in the sense that they can and typically do "represent continuous change in location, such as an object moving along a path" (Mandler 1992: 591). In other words, image schemas are taken to represent dynamic *content*, but that content is considered separate from their *structure*.

This chapter will advocate a return to Johnson's core notion that image schemas are intrinsically dynamic patterns. As an example of what such a dynamic structure might be like, I will speculate in some detail about the nature and development of CONTAINMENT, which is one of the most commonly cited image schemas in the literature. Employing an "informal phenomenological analysis" (cf. Johnson, *this volume*) of basic recurring experiences related to containment, I will argue that CONTAINMENT cannot be a static structure like the ones typically proposed. Even when they represent static locational relations, image schemas are themselves active scanning processes, cognitive pathways that are grounded in the perception of motion.

The key to thinking of image-schematic structure dynamically is to recognize a much more essential role for construal processes such as image-schema transformations. Rather than thinking of these processes as relatively independent operations *on* image schemas, we need to think of them as integral or extended parts *of* image-schematic structure itself. Most fundamentally of all, we need to acknowledge the crucially important role of a ceaselessly active conceptualizer in any dynamic construal. That means not only that a conceptual viewpoint is "part of the structural relations" of any image schema (Johnson 1987: 36); it also means that the conceptualizer is not a static observer that stands passively apart from the image. As we will see below, image schemas consist fundamentally of conceptual scanning processes like those described by Langacker (1987: 166-177).

After illustrating the role of these processes in CONTAINMENT, I will turn to some theoretical implications of having a truly dynamic conception of image-schematic structure. To begin with, a dynamic pattern is not an explicitly encoded mental object (compare also Gibbs' contribution to *this volume*). That means that an image schema cannot simply be "mapped" onto a language construction; the relation between image schemas and language is more complex than that. In fact, language turns out to play a surprisingly active role in the development and organization of image schemas, contributing not only to cross-linguistic variation but also to some universal similarities among image-schematic concepts. Finally, all of these considerations will call into question some of the most basic assumptions of what Jones and Smith (1993: 129) have called the "standard view of cognition".

2. Containment

2.1. Background

CONTAINMENT has been a parade example in the image-schema literature for several reasons. It seems to characterize a universally important semantic concept that is remarkably similar across languages and develops very early across languages. It is fundamentally important in metaphorical structuring and in inferential reasoning. It is also grounded in a wide range of common basic experiences.

Take for example a child in a red dress who watches her mother put cookies into a jar. The child then takes the lid off of the jar and looks inside to search for the cookies. She reaches into the jar, reaches down into the cookies to find a particular cookie near the bottom, grasps the cookie (so that the cookie is now in her hand), and takes it out. She wraps the cookie in a napkin. She walks with the cookie through a door into another room, where she is picked up in her mother's arms and put into a high chair. She watches the mother pour milk into a glass. She then dunks her cookie into the milk (which is itself contained in the glass), and puts the cookie into her mouth.

According to Johnson (1987: 21-22), such experiences share a common structure that involves "spatial boundedness" and is especially related to "being limited or held within some three-dimensional enclosure, such as a womb, a crib, or a room". Lakoff (1987: 271) developed that notion into a CONTAINER schema that consists of "a *boundary* distinguishing an *interior* from an *exterior*" and "defines the most basic distinction between IN and OUT". He thus abstracts away from the functional aspects – such as restriction and limitation – that are usually connected with the notion of "containment", distilling it essentially to what Vandeloise (1991) calls topological INCLUSION/EXCLUSION.

Given the developmental focus of her research, Mandler (1992: 597-598) is naturally more concerned to link containment realistically and in detail to the experiences of preverbal infants. She posits "a cluster of related image-schemas", one of which "expresses the meaning of CONTAINMENT itself" – i.e. the Lakoffian CONTAINER schema (which she represents as a horseshoe-shaped landmark) with a trajector inside. She also tends to emphasize the role of functional notions such as SUPPORT, and of motion events such as GOING IN or GOING OUT and OPENING or CLOSING.

Like Lakoff and Johnson, Mandler notes a child's subjectively embodied experiences with things going into and out of containers, e.g. eating, drinking, spitting, being clothed and unclothed, being taken in and out of rooms, etc. Unlike Johnson and Lakoff, she also stresses the importance of observing one object containing another even when the child is not subjectively involved in the relation. She notes (Mandler 1992: 597, see also *this volume*) that "it is not obvious that bodily experience per se is required for perceptual analysis to take place" and adds: "Indeed, I would expect it to be easier to analyze the sight of milk going into and out of a cup than milk going into and out of one's mouth."

2.2. Earliest schemas as paths

In adult semantic systems, pure static locations are generally considered to be simpler and more basic than motion events. Paths are taken to consist of complex sequences of locations structured in terms of starting locations, medial locations and ending locations as reflected in the common SOURCE-PATH-GOAL analysis. For example, CONTAINMENT defines a location, and paths can then be structured to go *into, out of* or *through* that basic location.

While this organization makes good sense in an adult semantic system, it is not likely to reflect the developmental sequence by which a young child originally arrives at the most basic image schemas grounded directly in experience. As Mandler (*this volume*) reports, infants appear to have a dynamic conception of containment that emphasizes the motion of going in and going out. What is most salient to a child will presumably involve visually observed motion, the sensorimotor routines of self-motion, and the sensations of being touched or moved by external forces.

Children's attentive bias toward motion is reflected in a range of reported observations. The earliest uses of locational expressions such as English *in* are primarily or exclusively for motion (Choi and Bowerman 1991: 96). Tomasello (1987: 83) comments that children's typical uses of words like *in* are more like verb-particles than like adult locative prepositions. Thiel (1985) maintains that 18-month-olds do not distinguish objects from the activities they associate with them, and even older children learn to differentiate them only gradually. When asked to identify what an object is, the young children Thiel studied would say things like *in(to)* (German *rein*) if it was a typical container or *on(to)* (*rauf*) if it had a salient surface to put things on. They would also use object terms such as *table* or *chair* to characterize activities. Thiel further observed that children would consistently carry out an associated act – at least by simulating with an empty hand gesture – when asked the name of an object. All in all, Thiel argues convincingly that young children exhibit a lack of cognitive differentiation between object and activity. It is unlikely then that their earliest image schemas would be static locations (or containers) with no path involved.

Returning specifically to CONTAINMENT, we might also observe that many actual containers do not really define a location in space the way that jars and cribs and rooms do. In our cookie example, hands, napkins and red dresses are clearly not experienced simply as bounded regions in space.

If we take a realistic developmental perspective then, it seems unlikely that a child's earliest image schemas related to CONTAINMENT will be pure static relations in timeless space, i.e., a notion like Lakoff's CONTAINER that is bounded and separates an interior region from an outside. Such notions may become primitives in a sophisticated and linguistically influenced adult system, but they are not developmental primitives. It is much more likely that the earliest image schemas will involve activities and paths, with little clear differentiation between trajectors (TRs), landmarks (LMs) and relations, between paths and resulting states, or between space and time.

2.2.1. Entry

The most obvious path type related to containment can be called "entry". Children repeatedly observe other people inserting something into an open container such as a jar or a drinking glass, or reaching into such a container to retrieve something; they learn to execute such actions themselves; they experience being inserted into (or removed from) open containers such as cribs; they observe people walking into and out of houses and rooms; and they eventually learn to do so themselves. The pattern that develops might look something like Figure 1, which is similar to Mandler's "CONTAINMENT itself" except that a path is part of the image and there is not yet a clearly differentiated TR.[1]

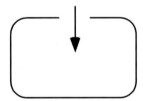

Figure 1. ENTRY.

The pictorial representation in Figure 1 is misleading in several ways though, making the image appear less schematic and less dynamic than it actually is. In particular, the image presumes a whole range of image-schema transformations that have to be considered a part of the structure of the image schema. To begin with, the LM in the child's actual experience would obviously be three-dimensional rather than the two-dimensional image used here for diagrammatic convenience. Moreover, the image is schematic

---

1. Cf. also the initial concept of containment posited by Hespos and Baillargeon (2001) for infants as young as 2.5 months.

with respect to the angle of inward approach. Although many common early experiences involve downward motion through an open top, the image in Figure 1 can be freely rotated so that the entry could be through any side (such as the door to a room).[2]

Another transformation allows the opening in the LM's surface to vary in size so that it might take up a whole side. Again, it is easy to imagine the development of a separate schema for large and small openings, particularly since the relative sizes of the TR and the opening are important for the motor routines for insertion being learned by small children. Similarly, the schema can be extended to include penetrating paths that have to create their own openings in the LM surface. Many other general transformations are of course involved in the pattern, such as those that result in a more precise shape and extent for a particular path and a particular LM. The image could also be linked with associated schemas to form more complex routines such as first creating the opening (e.g. by removing the jar lid).[3]

Further development of the image schema will eventually involve differentiation into a distinct TR, LM, and path – each of which can be profiled separately. The TR is left maximally schematic here, although we can easily imagine languages that come to differentiate TRs according to how they need to be shaped and aligned for insertion. There will also be a salient resulting state corresponding to the final stage of the path, and this state can be profiled with endpoint focus (Lakoff 1987) as in Figure 1.1, which is understood to profile the TR in its final location more prominently than in its prior locations represented by the arrow.

---

2. While the English word *in* allows this transformation to operate freely, we can easily imagine a language that constrains its operation and differentiates downward insertion from lateral insertion. Interestingly though, I am not aware of any languages other than sign languages that do make such a distinction.
3. An image based primarily on the subjective experience of reaching into a container would of course look somewhat different from the purely visual image of observing someone else do so. The schematic image in Figure 1 could still apply though, augmented by image-schema transformations that allow the conceptualizer to adopt various vantages that include identification with an implicit agent or with the TR or with the LM. See the discussion below on the general influence of language.

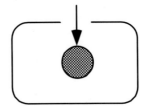

Figure 1.1. TR location resulting from ENTRY.

2.2.2. Stative inclusion based on entry

The path arrow in Figure 1 actually depicts a *summary scan* of a path (Langacker 1987: 144-146), i.e. it is a cumulative scan of a dynamic temporal sequence of locations that begins somewhere outside the LM and ends inside it. The shaped single image of a path pattern corresponds to a memory trace of past locations – Talmy's (2000: 149) "sensing" of "path structure".[4] An often neglected but absolutely crucial aspect of such a construal is that the path of the moving object is accompanied by a corresponding *conceptual movement*. In experiential terms, a person who watches an object move into a container will track the course of the object through space and time by moving the head and eyes, so that the person's gaze takes a course that corresponds to that of the objective path. In other words, the arrow in Figure 1 also depicts a purely conceptual tracking path that accompanies the objective motion. We already know from discussions of fictive motion (Langacker 1987; Talmy 2000) that purely conceptual scanning processes have the potential to become independent of the objective physical motion that they originally accompany. I will now claim that these purely conceptual scanning paths are an essential element not only for path schemas such as ENTRY and for fictive motion, but for purely stative relations as well. In fact, nearly all image-schematic structure is characterized most fundamentally by recurring patterns in the ceaseless flow of conceptual motion.

To see why such an approach is necessary, consider the most obvious alternative account of how a stative CONTAINMENT image might result from ENTRY experiences. After an image such as that in Figure 1.1 has become established as a salient resulting state, the child can form a purely stationary locational image that becomes distinct from whatever path preceded it. At

---

4. See also Cienki's (1997) discussion of stative path traces.

that point we might imagine that the child has developed an image like that of Figure 1.2, which would result from removing the path arrow from the image in Figure 1.1. This is of course the pure static inclusion schema as it is usually portrayed ("CONTAINMENT itself").

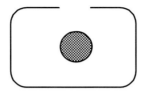

Figure 1.2. Pure inclusion?

The problem with this account is that it does not specify what makes the configuration "containment" – or inclusion or any other locational relation. We accept Figure 1.2 as a representation of containment because *we supply* that relation by a dynamic pattern of scanning. We construe the configuration *as* containment not simply because the configuration exists objectively, but because we process it in a particular way. And it is precisely that defining *dynamic process* which is missing in the misleadingly static image of Figure 1.2. As such, Figure 1.2 can only represent a meaningless configuration of unrelated entities.

If we begin instead with an event schema like that in Figure 1.1, which combines objective motion with an accompanying conceptual scanning pattern, we can trace a process of abstracting from spatiotemporal paths to stative locational relations that differentiates the scanning pattern from the objective motion and thus allows it to apply to stative configurations. As a first step from Figure 1.1, the child might imagine a purely hypothetical entry path, or a hypothetical act of reaching into the LM to search for an object and retrieve it. More abstractly still, the child might imagine a purely visual search path that corresponds to the schematic entry path, as if following the gaze of someone who is looking into the LM.[5] The most abstract way of all to construe a stative relation based on an entry path would be to divorce the image even from a real person's directed gaze and imagine a purely conceptual search path that begins outside the LM and moves inward

---

5. According to Johnston (1985: 970) children "can conceptualize the path of sight and decide what someone else is looking at by age three", and children think in terms of goal-directed paths by the second half of the first year (Mandler, *this volume*).

until the TR has been located. This kind of subjective gaze-based construal is in effect the same pattern of conceptual motion that accompanies normal entry paths (Figure 1) – but now completely differentiated from any objective motion (and from conceived time).[6]

We could draw the resulting relation as in Figure 1.3, which is the same as 1.1 except that the dashed arrow is meant to represent pure conceptual motion with no necessary corresponding motion by the TR (or by any other entity actually participating in the scene). Figure 1.3 represents a locational relation between the TR and its setting. We could think of it as an instruction to find the TR by searching from a random point outside of the LM, moving past the opening in the LM surface and continuing on inward toward the center.[7] (Recall that the schema in Figure 1 allows entry from any angle.)

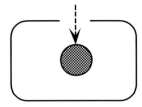

Figure 1.3. Stative inclusion based on ENTRY.

Thus we can arrive at a basic schema for stative inclusion that is thoroughly grounded in the experience of realistic containment events, and which is also fundamentally a dynamic pattern with an active role for the conceptualizer. Before we turn to the theoretical implications of this kind of dynamic image

6. As an indication of the course of development from physical paths to stative locational search paths, consider this incident reported by Thiel (1985: 202). He describes a child who put two model chairs next to a model bathtub and then said *raus* ('out'). I take this as an indication that the projective prepositions begin in effect as hypothetical paths that move 'out of' the LM and thus have the effect of locating where the TR is now. The 'out' path will later become more refined by distinguishing *neben* 'next to' from *über* 'above', *vor* 'in front of' and so on – all of which describe scanning paths beginning at the LM and moving in a specified pattern.

7. The role of a scanning path grounded in ENTRY even for stative relations is reflected in the special status of TRs that extend in the direction of entry, such as flowers in a vase or a man standing in shallow water. The partially included TRs are not considered contained when the scanning of their extent does not coincide with an entry path. A man sitting on the edge of a pool may have his feet in the water, but we would not say that *he* is "in" the water.

schema though, we need to add another important image to the cluster of patterns that make up CONTAINMENT.

2.2.3. Enclosing

The basic experiences reflected in our cookie example are actually more diverse than most discussions imply, and many of them cannot be adequately accounted for in terms of topological inclusion or the simple entry of a mobile figure into a stationary container. That is especially true of containers that actively enclose an object by grasping (a cookie in the hand, a child in its mother's arms) or wrapping (a cookie in a napkin, a child in a red dress). There is in effect a continuum of experiential patterns that are commonly classed together as CONTAINMENT, with the primary variable being how active the container and the contained are relative to each other. At one pole are jars and cribs and houses that are for the most part stationary receptacles with stable shapes – fixed regions of the setting where things can be located. At the other pole are hands and napkins, which are not intrinsic containers at all in their canonical states. Containing is something that these things actively do on a particular occasion by bending and closing in on the contained object. Between the two poles are many other containers – such as socks, canvas bags and container substances – that involve both entry by the contained object and active enveloping by the container.

We might represent the active enclosing pattern of a grasping hand or a wrapping napkin crudely as in Figure 2. The image suggests an originally open configuration that allows the container to begin to surround the contained object as it moves toward it. From there the container curves in on itself so that it tends eventually to enclose the object completely. An enclosing container thus engages in two types of inward motion simultaneously. It closes in on the object it contains, and it also closes in on itself. The righthand image particularly profiles the concluding phase in which the container is completing its own closure.

Figure 2. Active ENCLOSING.

If interpreted sufficiently abstractly with primary focus on the concluding phase, this image actually applies to most typical containers. Its relevance to flexible containers such as socks, canvas bags and liquids is apparent. Even relatively stationary containers with relatively inflexible sides are usually associated with some kind of closing event before containment in them is complete.[8] For example, putting something *in* a suitcase normally implies that the suitcase will eventually be closed (even if that closure is temporally remote). Similar comments apply to jars (putting the lid back on), houses and rooms (closing the door), desk drawers (pushing them back into the desk), and many other common containers.

A stative resulting image can develop for enclosing just as it did for entry. The arrows in Figure 2 can become memory traces of the scan that accompanied actual motion by the container, or they can correspond to hypothetical or potential closing motion (e.g. of suitcases or of jars that regain their lids), or they can correspond to the purely imaginary closure of a container's open side.

2.3. Combining ENTRY and ENCLOSING

Most instances of containment seem to involve elements of both ENTRY by the TR (resulting in a pure locational relation with functional implications associated with insertion or removal) and active ENCLOSING by the LM (re-

---

8. Figure 2 is meant to be neutral as to whether enclosing results in contact between the LM and the TR. That will depend on the flexibility of the entities involved. Grasping hands and wrapping napkins and immersing substances will continue moving inward until contact is established from all relevant directions; relatively rigidly shaped LMs will not normally reach contact except to the extent that the TR itself initiates it, e.g. by resting on the bottom of the container or by spreading (milk in a glass).

sulting in functional and force-dynamic implications such as restricted motion). Apparently, people are inclined to combine the two images into a single coherent image schema for CONTAINMENT.

The most obvious problem with combining ENTRY and ENCLOSING is that they have opposing figure-ground relations. In ENCLOSING the container is the moving figure, while ENTRY requires the contained object to be the relatively mobile entity. Reaching to grasp a cookie would more naturally be described with the container as TR and a verb such as English *grab*, *grasp*, *catch*, *enclose*, or *surround* (resulting in having the hand *around* the cookie). Only when the cookie is in the enclosed state does it become more natural to say that it is *in* someone's hand, apparently reflecting a figure-ground reversal so that the image looks more like Figure 2.1.

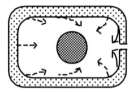

Figure 2.1. An enclosed TR.

It turns out though that ENTRY events and ENCLOSING events are experienced together with remarkable frequency. We might imagine a prototypical containment experience to be putting a cookie into a mouth, so that the mouth actively encloses the cookie after its entry. In other words both the TR and the LM move, and the enclosing motion by the LM succeeds and converges with the entry path by the TR. The image schema could look roughly like Figure 3.

Figure 3. CONTAINMENT as ENTRY-ENCLOSING.

According to this approach even canonical stationary LMs such as cookie jars and houses could be construed to enclose their contents actively after entry. Their closure might reflect objective events such as putting the lid back on or closing a door after entry, but eventually an imagined virtual closure could suffice to invoke a schema like Figure 3.[9] By the same token, a grasped TR such as a stationary cookie that does not really move relative to a grasping hand could have the ENTRY aspect of the construal imposed on it (at least in a stative configuration where nothing objectively contradicts that construal).

2.4. Schematic CONTAINMENT

In its maximally schematic form, stative CONTAINMENT could look something like Figure 3.1, which is the righthand side of Figure 3 set within a conceptual frame. Figure 3.1 is schematic in all the ways that Figure 1 is, including dimensionality and angle of scanning approach.[10] The conceptual motion indicated by the arrows corresponds to the objective entry path of the TR, or to the reaching path of a hand seeking to insert or retrieve the TR, or

---

9. Permanently open-sided containers such as drinking glasses and cribs could thus undergo idealized virtual closure based on the image of closing a door or adding a lid. An alternative way to motivate virtual closure of an open-top container would be to include the downward force of gravity to complete the enclosure from all sides. Another potential analysis would make open-top containers a special case of ENCLOSING in which the surface curves only in two salient dimensions to form a band around the TR that leaves the TR free to extend in the third dimension. This transformational variant accounts for the extension of flowers in a vase beyond its virtual top boundary, and it is needed anyway to account for uses such as an arm in a cast.

10. The schema not only allows scanning from any angle; it also allows scanning from a variety of angles simultaneously, thus constricting the search area cumulatively until the TR has been located. Compare the highly general multiple-TR transformation (Dewell 1994), which allows a path image with a single moving TR to be replicated into a multiple-path image with plural TRs each of which moves – either in unison or in sequence – in conformity with the single path image. Thus several children can all reach 'into' a cookie jar simultaneously from all sides, or walk through the same door (cf. the sets of weighted vectors posited in many current representations of spatial regions.).

to the direction of gaze searching for the TR, or to the enclosing effects of the LM, or to any practical combination of these.

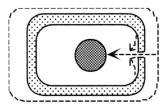

Figure 3.1. Schematic CONTAINMENT.

2.5. Functional implications

Vandeloise (1991) and others have observed a range of factors that complicate the analysis of CONTAINMENT into a single schematic image such as topological inclusion. Some of these factors, such as partial inclusion (flowers in a vase) and virtual closure (the top of the glass of milk), result to a great extent from the kinds of image-schema transformations we have already encountered. Other factors however are unquestionably functional and force-dynamic in nature, such as restrictions on the TR's movement (what Garrod et al. (1999) call "location control"). In fact the presence of force can be a defining factor, as indicated by Vandeloise's (1991: 228) example *l'aiguille/ *l'allumette est dans le champ de l'aimant* ('the needle/ *matchstick is in the field of the magnet').

Functional implications such as these could only be arbitrarily related to a static image schema. If we analyze CONTAINMENT in terms of conceptual motion on the other hand, and ground that motion in the construal of objective paths, then functional implications can be naturally motivated. A schematic pattern such as that depicted in Figure 3.1 was originally abstracted from complex experiences that typically involve not only objective motion but also force-dynamic effects and subjective impressions and functional purposes. Activating the schematic pattern naturally tends to call those richer images to mind when they are appropriate to a dynamic construal in a particular context.

Given the ENCLOSING vectors emanating from the LM toward the TR, it is a natural implication that a force of some kind will typically be exerted in the direction of the vectors, thus counteracting any potential motion by the

TR out of the LM. The TR is held in by the LM. For similar reasons, if the container moves then anything found inside it will also move contingently.[11]

Another related aspect of CONTAINMENT experiences that might be retrieved in appropriate contexts is the subjective sensation of identifying with the TR. Thus we might connect the image schema of Figure 3.1 to feeling a container such as a mother's arms or clothing or water touching our body, or sensing the restricted maneuver space of a container such as a crib.

In other words, the analysis links a variety of actual experienced situations into a remarkably tightly woven and schematic set of cognitive patterns. The result is basically CONTAINMENT as described by Vandeloise (1991), including all of its functional implications and family resemblances. CONTAINMENT can be reduced to a basic image-schematic pattern that is in turn linked to a range of more general transformational patterns, and all of these dynamic patterns are thoroughly grounded in basic experience.[12]

3.   The role of language

3.1.   The influence of particular languages

The discussion of CONTAINMENT thus far has not really mentioned language. In fact, one of the reasons that CONTAINMENT has been such a popular example in the image-schema literature is that it seems like a "conceptual universal" (Johnson and Lakoff 2002: 251). This claim can easily mislead though, if we think of image schemas as static things.

Although the schemas for ENTRY, ENCLOSING and CONTAINMENT are all grounded in essentially universal experiences, it is easy to imagine them developing differently in the semantic systems of different languages. There is good evidence that they in fact do. The work of Melissa Bowerman and her colleagues (e.g. Bowerman 1996a, Choi et al. 1999) for example shows that nothing in the Korean language corresponds exactly to ENCLOSING, and

---

11. As always we are talking of dynamic transformational patterns as appropriate to a particular context. A sense of restricting the TR's motion will not normally be evoked when the LM is a piece of clothing (although strait-jackets would certainly qualify).

12. This analysis also accounts for extended variants such as the use of *in* as a verb particle in reflexive-TR variants such as *cave in*, which are natural in terms of the dynamic scanning patterns of Figure 3.1 but would seem unmotivated if we presumed a static inclusion schema.

there is no general category in Korean corresponding to ENTRY either – at least none that can be applied to causal insertion. Tzeltal similarly lacks a semantic category corresponding precisely to CONTAINMENT, preferring more particular schematic patterns that differentiate manners of insertion and of relations between the TR and the LM (Brown 1994).

Such observations have made Bowerman (1996a: 145) justifiably suspicious of any view that portrays children as "acquiring morphemes to express spatial concepts they already have, rather than creating spatial meanings in response to language." Similarly, Slobin (2001: 421) maintains that "there is no set of prelinguistic categories that can be directly mapped onto the meanings of linguistic elements", and Levinson (2003: 297-298) is skeptical of the notion that lexemes "map one-to-one onto unitary simplex conceptual representations" and that linguistic diversity is "merely a matter of complex packaging at a higher level, of universal conceptual primes at a lower level".

The problem in this whole discussion is the presumption that any image schema (or preverbal concept) is an explicitly defined and static thing that a child either does or does not "have", rather than a dynamic pattern that recurs as part of a larger organization of patterned cognitive processes that are not necessarily clearly distinct from each other. Semantic meanings are *grounded* in prelinguistic cognition that is real and patterned and largely universal; but we need to avoid the implication that the meaning of language constructions can be *reduced* to pre-existing universal representations.

3.2. The universalizing influence of language

There has been a tendency in the literature to frame the issue of conceptual universals mainly in terms of a competition between prelinguistic universals on the one hand and linguistic variation on the other. That is, the similarity of CONTAINMENT schemas across languages is attributed to their grounding in universally common, basic and objectively similar experiences that are independent of language, while semantic differences are attributed to the way that individual languages encode those prelinguistic schemas – as if language forms were simply being assigned to some of the pre-existing structures (or to combinations of those structures). Once we think of image schemas as complex schematic patterns though, rather than as discrete static things with a fixed structure, then language might influence the further development and organization of those patterns in any number of subtle ways. Moreover, those linguistic influences would not necessarily all be peculiar to a particular language. Given similar pressures to insure successful communication, languages generally might favor the development of certain kinds of concepts rather than others. In other words, some of the universally similar characteristics of a schematic adult concept like CONTAINMENT might reflect the influence of language as well as the influence of nonverbal experience.[13]

3.2.1. Objective, viewpoint-neutral images

One of the more striking characteristics of the schemas represented in Figures 1.3, 2.1 and 3.1 is that they give priority to the objective and visual pattern of observing an event from a detached vantage, rather than to the more subjective sensations of actually participating in the event. The schemas do not directly include things like the motor movements involved in insertion, or the sensation of sensing contact with a mother's cradling arms, or of being restricted in maneuver space, or of feeling warm and secure, cf. Mandler's (*this volume*) comments about our conception of causal force. These aspects of containment are retrievable by general image-schema transformations that allow the conceptualizer to imagine being one of the entities in the scene, thus recalling aspects of the grounding experiences from which the schema was abstracted. But the adult cognitive patterns are organized so that the objective image is primary and the subjective implications are secondary – not the other way around. Even if a child begins by attaching such subjective meanings directly to a word like *in*, learning the language will eventually guide the child to form a more objective image as the primary public one that is constrained by the construction. To the extent that they are called to mind by language rather than by more immediate experience, the more subjective images will gradually be relegated to the optional further

---

13. Another nonlinguistic factor in the universal development of CONTAINMENT that is worth mentioning is the very basic nature of the cognitive processes involved. The overall scanning pattern for CONTAINMENT corresponds to a progressive zooming sequence from the periphery of the conceptual frame inward toward the focal center, and that overall scanning pattern is very similar to the ones involved in the recognition of focal shaped objects – an ability that develops by the age of 3 to 4 months (Mandler 1992: 589). Compare the scanning patterns of CONTAINMENT with the general discussion of "field scans" and "peripheral scans" in Langacker (1987: 209-211).

interpretation that comes after first establishing a viewpoint-neutral image that is publicly accessible from any perspective.

The communicative advantages of an objective image are obvious enough. In order to imagine an objectively observed scene, the hearer does not have to adopt the speaker's or any other particular perspective in order to understand. An image-schematic concept such as that in Figure 3.1 can be imagined from any angle and distance without affecting the objective content of the scene. That flexibility is important for language development, especially since judgments from a particular imagined perspective do not emerge until the fourth year (Johnston 1985: 970). Visually based images with a flexible perspective also make it much easier to integrate a particular image into a larger composite scene involving other entities and relations.

3.2.2. Shape bias

Another, related aspect of an adult CONTAINMENT image like the one illustrated in Figure 3.1 is that it relies primarily on linear scanning processes. That is true of the profiled CONTAINMENT relation (the arrows in the diagrams) and for the LM boundary where the TR enters, and when the TR and the LM are elaborated they will also usually be conceived primarily as recognizable shapes. (Contrast potential nonlinear conceptions such as texture, size or emotional reactions.) The role of language in this preference for linear scanning is reflected in studies of the so-called "shape bias". When asked if one object is like another, children will base their judgments on whatever properties seem most obviously different, including size and texture as well as shape; but when they are asked to generalize a novel name for the object children attend exclusively to shape, ignoring quite large differences on the other dimensions. Moreover, the shape bias becomes more robust with development – it is stronger for adults than for children – and it gradually becomes specific to count nouns. As summarized by Jones and Smith (1993: 125):

> In all the experiments on novel word interpretations, there is a dramatic contrast between the perceptual properties of objects that children attend to when *naming* objects versus when making other kinds of judgments (e.g. similarity).

For obvious communicative reasons, language encourages us to give priority to images that can literally delineate and define separate entities that are recognizably distinct from each other, and which can be located relative to each other and relative to a domain. These principles apply to relations such as CONTAINMENT just as they do to objects such as cookie jars. For example, the main ENTRY arrow of Figure 3.1 can be contrasted clearly with pathways that extend only to the defined outer boundary of the LM (cf *on*), and with pathways that extend to a second crossing of the LM boundary (cf *through*), and with pathways that reverse the ENTRY direction and proceed *out of* the LM. Although the shape of the basic ENTRY pathway is unmarked (i.e. schematically straight), summarily scanned pathways can potentially be differentiated from each other by shape as well. Think for example of *around* (as opposed to *past*) or of the distinction between *over* and *across* as analyzed in Dewell (1994). Other, vaguer kinds of images – those that do not involve linear scans that can define distinct entities – are of course not eliminated from our minds; but they are not constantly reinforced as the ones most commonly and directly linked to conventional language constructions.

All things considered then, a schema like that in Figure 3.1 is not nearly as purely preverbal as one might think from reading most accounts of image schemas. It not only reflects the semantic organization of a particular language system. It reflects the influence of language generally toward maximally precise and differentiated linear shapes that can be explicitly profiled and publicly accessed from a flexible perspective.

4.   Challenging the "standard view of cognition"

If we think of image schemas as dynamic patterns rather than static structures, the ramifications go beyond altering the detailed analysis of a particular image-schematic concept such as CONTAINMENT, and even beyond suggesting a much more basic role for language in the development of image schemas. It also undermines what Jones and Smith (1993:129) call the "standard view of cognition", which rests on the core assumption that concepts are "static and thing-like" units. As Smith and Jones (1993: 182) put it, the standard view reflects a traditional "partition of cognition into structure (stability) and process (variability)", with "static, unchanging representations that are repeatedly activated in different contexts".

One problematic implication of the standard view is the fairly straightforward mapping of concepts onto language that was mentioned in section 3.1. It suggests what Zlatev (1997: 139-141) has called the "atomist assumption" that word meanings are largely context-independent units, which is in turn related to the "reificational assumption" that word meanings can be viewed as mental objects. The standard view rests on the notion of prelinguistic, explicitly defined, static mental representations.

In theory of course, image schemas could inhabit a separate level of cognition distinct from conceptual structure (like Jackendoff's (2002) "spatial structure"), so that concepts could be static and thing-like units without entailing that image schemas are as well. In practice though, it is very difficult to draw a clear line between image schemas and concepts. Moreover, if image schemas structure concepts it is difficult to imagine precisely how static and thing-like concepts would develop prelinguistically out of dynamic patterns that do not differentiate structure and process. The assumptions of the standard view of cognition make it difficult not to think of image schemas as static structures.[14]

By the same token, if we recognize that image schemas are truly dynamic patterns that do not distinguish structure and process, then it becomes difficult to hold onto the standard view of cognition. If CONTAINMENT and other image schemas are intrinsically and fundamentally nonpropositional patterns, then what reason is there to assume that the concepts that develop out of them should be explicitly defined, static mental representations that can be manipulated as context-independent propositional units?

In effect then, the notion of image schemas that has been developed in this chapter supports the proposal by Jones and Smith (1993:136) that concepts generally are dynamic cognitive patterns rather than "represented entities that exist as a unit". Concepts are "the emergent products of multiple knowledge sources in specific task contexts", and cognition could be "all process" and emerge from "dynamic and changing patterns of activity" (Smith and Jones 1993:187).

What is called "the meaning" of a language construction such as the English word *in* is a conventionally learned and constrained pattern that channels the flow of thought in certain ways. Invoking a schema like that in Figure 3.1 is not a perfective act of linking a language form to a static structure that is then inserted into a context. Invoking the schema is the beginning of channeling the further flow, an opening pathway of dynamic cognitive processes and transformations that always leads somewhere else in combination with

---

14. The language we use to talk about them contributes to this vague impression as well. The most convenient terms we have to refer to mental phenomena – *image schemas, concepts, structures, thoughts, representations, meanings* – are all count nouns. It is thus part of their usual meaning that they are discrete units that can be moved around intact.

all of the other cognitive events that form the context. The effect of a language construction is somewhat like a chess opening, providing a conventionally patterned sequence that becomes progressively less constrained as it gets further from its starting point. Some aspects of the pattern will be very entrenched and automatic (such as the scanning pattern from the periphery toward the center of the LM). Other aspects will be subject to weaker conventional constraints and to a variety of contextual factors (such as the more specific nature and dimensionality of the LM, the functional implications of limited mobility or access, the subjective sensation of being in the location). The conventional semantic constraints become weaker as the interpretative flow progresses in an ultimately open-ended and underdetermined process.

References

Bowerman, Melissa
  1989   Learning a semantic system: What role do cognitive predispositions
            play? In *The Teachability of Language*, Mabel Rice, and Richard L.
            Schiefelbusch (eds.), 133-169. Baltimore: Paul H. Brookes.
  1996a   Learning how to structure space for language: A crosslinguistic
            perspective. In *Language and Space*, Paul Bloom, Mary A. Peter-
            son, Lynn Nadel, and Merrill F. Garrett (eds.), 385-436. Cam-
            bridge, Mass.: MIT Press.
  1996b   The origins of children's spatial semantic categories: cognitive vs
            linguistic determinants. In *Rethinking Linguistic Relativity*, John J.
            Gumperz and Steven C. Levinson (eds.), 145-176. Cambridge:
            Cambridge University Press.
Brown, Penelope
  1994   The INs and OUTs of Tzeltal locative expressions: The semantics
            of static descriptions of location. *Linguistics* 32: 743-790.
Choi, Soonja and Melissa Bowerman
  1991   Learning to express motion events in English and Korean: The
            influence of language-specific lexicalization patterns. *Cognition* 41:
            83-121.
Choi, Soonja, Laraine McDonough, Melissa Bowerman, and Jean M. Mandler
  1999   Early sensitivity to language-specific spatial categories in English
            and Korean. *Cognitive Development* 14: 241-268.
Cienki, Alan
  1997   Some properties and groupings of image schemas. In *Lexical and
            Syntactical Constructions and the Construction of Meaning*, Mar-

jolijn Verspoor, Kee Dong Lee, and Eve Sweetser (eds.), 3-15. Amsterdam/Philadephia: John Benjamins.

Dewell, Robert B.

1994   *Over* again: Image-schema transformations in semantic analysis. *Cognitive Linguistics* 5: 351-80.

1997   Construal transformations: Internal and external viewpoints in interpreting containment. In *Lexical and Syntactical Constructions and the Construction of Meaning*, Marjolijn Verspoor, Kee Dong Lee, and Eve Sweetser (eds.), 17-32. Amsterdam/Philadelphia: John Benjamins.

2000   Case meaning and sequence of attention: Source landmarks as accusative and dative objects of the verb. In *Constructions in Cognitive Linguistics*, Ad Foolen and Frederike van der Leek (eds.), 47-65. Amsterdam/Philadelphia: John Benjamins.

Garrod, Simon, Gillian Ferrier, and Siobhan Campbell

1999   *In* and *on*: investigating the functional geometry of spatial prepositions. *Cognition* 72: 167-189.

Hespos, Susan J., and Renée Baillargeon

2001   Reasoning about containment events in very young infants. *Cognition* 78: 207-245.

Jackendoff, Ray

2002   *Foundations of Language: Brain, Meaning, Grammar, Evolution.* Oxford: Oxford University Press.

Johnson, Mark

1987   *The Body in the Mind: The Bodily Basis of Meaning, Imagination, and Reason.* Chicago: Chicago University Press.

Johnson, Mark, and George Lakoff

2002   Why cognitive linguistics requires embodied realism. *Cognitive Linguistics* 13: 245-263.

Johnston, Judith R.

1985   Cognitive prerequisites: The evidence from children learning English. In *The Crosslinguistic Study of Language Acquisition. Vol. 2: Theoretical Issues*, Dan Isaac Slobin (ed.), 961-1004. Hilldale, NJ: Lawrence Erlbaum.

Jones, Susan S. and Smith, Linda B.

1993   The place of perception in children's concepts. *Cognitive Development* 8: 113-139.

Lakoff, George

1987   *Women, Fire and Dangerous Things: What Categories Reveal about the Mind.* Chicago: Chicago University Press.

Lakoff, George and Mark Johnson

1980   *Metaphors We Live By.* Chicago: Chicago University Press.

Langacker, Ronald L.
    1987   *Foundations of Cognitive Grammar I: Theoretical Prerequisites.*
            Stanford: Stanford University Press.
Levinson, Stephen C.
    2003   *Space in Language and Cognition: Explorations in Cognitive Diversity.* Cambridge: Cambridge University Press.
Mandler, Jean M.
    1988   The development of spatial cognition: on topological and Euclidean representation. In *Spatial Cognition: Brain Bases and Development*, Joan Stiles-Davis, Mark Kritchevsky, and Ursula Bellugi (eds.), 423-32. Hillsdale, NJ: Erlbaum.
    1992   How to build a baby: II. Conceptual primitives. *Psychological Review* 99, 4: 587-604.
    1996   Preverbal representation and language. In *Language and Space*, Paul Bloom, Mary A. Peterson, Lynn Nadel, and Merrill F. Garrett (eds.), 365-384. Cambridge, Mass.: MIT Press.
    2000   Perceptual and conceptual processes in infancy. *Journal of Cognition and Development* 1: 3-36.
Slobin, Dan I.
    2001   Form-function relations: How do children find out what they are? In *Language Acquisition and Conceptual Development*, Melissa Bowerman, and Stephen Levinson (eds.), 406-449. Cambridge: Cambridge University Press.
Smith, Linda B. and Susan S. Jones
    1993   Cognition without concepts. *Cognitive Development* 8: 181-188.
Talmy, Leonard
    2000   *Toward a Cognitive Semantics I: Concept Structuring Systems.* Cambridge/London: MIT Press.
Thiel, Thomas
    1985   Räumliches Denken und Verständnis von Lokativen beim Spracherwerb. In *Sprache und Raum: Psychologische und linguistische Aspekte der Aneignung von Räumlichkeit*, Harro Schweizer (ed.), 184-208. Stuttgart: Metzler.
Tomasello, Michael
    1987   Learning to use prepositions: A case study. *Journal of Child Language* 14: 79-98.
Vandeloise, Claude
    1991   *Spatial Prepositions: A Case Study from French.* Translated by Anna R.K. Bosch. Chicago: Chicago University Press.
Zlatev, Jordan
    1997   *Situated Embodiment: Studies in the Emergence of Spatial Meaning.* Stockholm: Gotab.

2003   Polysemy or generality? Mu. In *Cognitive Approaches to Lexical Semantics*, Hubert Cuyckens, René Dirven and John Taylor (eds.), 447-494. Berlin/New York: Mouton de Gruyter.

Image schemas and verbal synaesthesia

Yanna Popova[*]

Abstract

This chapter seeks to address the largely neglected issue of the cross-modal nature of image schemas. It examines the SCALE schema in relation to the lower perceptual modalities (touch and taste) and argues that the latter provide the experiential grounding for scalarity in our construal of perceptual properties. The phenomenon of verbal synaesthesia with its well-established patterns of metaphoric mappings from lower to higher modalities is then used as a linguistic case study for illustrating the relevance of the lower modalities to the SCALE image schema. In the conceptualization of perceptual properties the move from lower to higher modalities is shown to be in general a move from locational (SCALE) to cofigurational (CONTAINMENT) concepts. Given the current interest in issues relating to the possible correlations between perceptual knowledge and conceptual structure, this chapter also aims to further attention to the role of non-visual experience in structuring the semantic system.

Keywords: adjective/noun pairs, synaesthetic metaphor, tactile perception, BOUNDEDNESS, GRADABILITY, SCALE.

1. Introduction: Image schemas and the lower perceptual modalities

Introducing the notion of image schemas, both Johnson (1987) and Lakoff (1987) highlight the fact that they are not limited to visual properties but derive from all kinds of perceptual experience. A lot of subsequent work in cognitive linguistics has nevertheless concentrated on the visual and (to some extent) kinaesthetic dimension in the conceptualization of that experience. Some researchers emphasize the dominant role of visual information in the re-analysis of perceptual data resulting in image schemas (cf. Mandler, *this volume*). Spatial and topological aspects of experience, however, are not

---

* I would like to thank the two anonymous reviewers and, in particular, the editor of this volume for their helpful comments on earlier versions of this chapter.

extracted exclusively through vision, but also through touch, particularly through haptics and kinaesthesia.[1] A lot of the image schemas proposed by Johnson (1987: 126) can be taken to derive both from vision and touch, the latter understood as inclusive of somaesthesia, kinaesthesia and haptics. Examples would include the image schemas CONTAINER, COUNTERFORCE, SUPERIMPOSITION, SURFACE, BLOCKAGE, BALANCE, OBJECT, COMPULSION, SCALE, FULL-EMPTY, CONTACT, PATH, ATTRACTION, PROCESS, all of which emerge from perceptual data provided by both touch and vision.

I believe that the cross-modal nature of image schemas has not been given enough emphasis in the literature and this chapter offers a consideration of the SCALE schema in relation to the lower modalities. I assume that the tactile sense makes its own independent contribution to spatial cognition and argue that touch and the lower modalities are particularly suited to provide the experiential grounding for SCALARITY in our construal of perceptual properties. The phenomenon of verbal synaesthesia, which reflects linguistically some of the cross-modal transfers of properties characteristic of perceptual synaesthesia, provides the case study material for testing this claim. An examination of this verbal phenomenon reveals the dominance of touch as a source domain in synaesthetic mappings, a fact that despite being widely documented and studied remains unexplained. By relating the linguistic analysis of synaesthetic adjective-noun pairs to what is known about perceptual synaesthesia and tactile perception, this chapter aims (i) to elucidate the prevalent patterns of transfer to be found in verbal synaesthesia, and (ii) to establish the relevance of tactile experience to the SCALE image schema. It will thus also (iii) contribute to the debate about the abstract (modality-independent) versus perceptual nature of image schemas.

2. Synaesthesia in perception and language

Synaesthesia (from the Greek *syn* 'together' and *aisthesia* 'perception') is the involuntary perceptual experience of a cross-modal association. In psychological and neuro-psychological terms this means that the stimulation of one sensory modality reliably and invariably (for a particular person) causes a perception in one or more different senses. This "joined sensation" manifests

---

1. Cienki (1998) is an exception in that he discusses the specific contribution of haptics (understood as manipulation of objects) for the experiential grounding of another image schema that he proposes, namely STRAIGHT.

itself as the capacity in some people to hear colours (the most common type), taste shapes, feel sounds or experience other, equally startling sensory blendings. The condition is rare, idiosyncratic and permanent: people's particular connections between the senses are unique to them and remain unchanged throughout their lives (cf. Cytowic 1989, 1994).

While true synaesthetic perception is rare, there is a common and more general phenomenon of systematic cross-modal association, provided by the regular correlation between, for example, loudness and brightness, pitch and brightness, and size and pitch in both non-synaesthetic children and adults (Marks 1982a,b; Marks et al. 1987). Marks and colleagues propose that the ability to perceive cross-modal correlations is systematic, universal and already present in early childhood. Detecting intensity across modalities is thus an innate property of perception. However, this does not mean that the SCALE schema is necessarily innate as it results from "perceptual meaning analysis", i.e., an attentive examination of stimuli and is, therefore, a redescribed form of sensorimotor information (cf. Mandler, *this volume*).

Verbal synaesthesia is the linguistic realization of the cross-modal associations in synaesthesia. It is a metaphoric transfer reflecting some of the extraordinary perceptions of people with synaesthesia proper, who really experience one sensory modality in terms of another. In synaesthetic metaphors it is as if we experience the same, based on some form of conceptual mapping. Linguistically, there is thus very little difference between a synaesthete describing the taste of mint as "cool glass columns" and the poet Arthur Symons writing about "the scented billows of soft thunder". Even in everyday language, the use of synaesthetic metaphors is common: we speak of *sharp tastes*, *smells* and *sounds*, of *soft colours* and *voices*, and of *mellow music*.

Linguists and linguistically-minded literary scholars have been interested in the phenomenon of verbal synaesthesia for a long time. More than fifty years ago Ullmann (1951) raised the question whether there is any system in the multiple transfers of meaning between linguistic expressions, pertaining to the different senses. Ullmann's data, a large corpus of 19th century English and Hungarian poetry, indicated that transfers in synaesthesia are almost invariably from the lower sensory modalities (touch and taste) to the higher ones (sound and vision). One exception is the transfer between the two highest modalities: vision and sound, where each is equally likely to serve as either the target or the source. It is also important to note that for Ullmann synaesthesia does not include the transfers of physical sensations to mental states (e.g., *sweet temper*, *warm person*, *sharp mind* are not examples of synaesthesia). My own definition of verbal synaesthesia, however, includes these abstract senses as a special type of synaesthetic metaphors (see section 5.3).

Williams' (1976) historical study examined regularities in diachronic semantic change of English adjectives referring to sensory experience. He included in his corpus all existing adjectives of sensory experience, examined from their first citation in the OED or the MED onwards, which have provided a metaphorical transfer from one sensory modality to another. Sensory words that have not provided metaphors are omitted (e.g., *damp*, *wet*, *short*, *long*); excluded are also morphologically complex and derived words (e.g., *muddy*, *noisy*, *lemony*, *burning*). Williams' study confirms Ullmann's finding that the movement of synaesthetic metaphors is not random, but conforms to a basic pattern: in the metaphoric transfer *touch* is the largest single source, and *sound* is the largest single recipient. Moreover, Williams claims the semantic change observed in English and Japanese to be so regular and so inclusive that it qualifies to be considered a universal law of semantic change: 83 per cent of his data agree with the pattern (cf. Williams 1976: 464). Transfers against the predicted pattern, like TOUCH TO DIMENSION: **crisp* (1398) or SOUND TO TASTE: **shrill* (1567), tend to become obsolete and are not part of Standard English. Counting out such non-predicted transfers, Williams's prediction is true in 97 per cent of all instances. The only two instances of violations of the pattern, still existing in the language, are SMELL TO TASTE: *pungent* and DIMENSION TO TASTE: *thin*.

Most recently, psychological experiments conducted by Shen (1997) and Shen and Cohen (1998), which are also based on a large corpus of poetic synaesthetic expressions – this time collected from English and Hebrew poetry, have confirmed the established findings about the directionality of mappings and its universal character. In addition, they have also demonstrated that this directionality directly influences comprehensibility and recall of novel synaesthetic expressions in on-line comprehension tasks.

However, the "cognitive" explanation of the higher frequency of the low-to-high mappings offered by Shen and Cohen (1998: 128-130) is rather limited and merely states that "low to high structure is more natural" than the reverse. What they mean by that is that lower senses like touch and taste are more "accessible" than higher ones like sound and vision because they involve "less mediated experience of perception" (Shen and Cohen 1998: 128). Mediation is here understood as the availability of specific perceptual organs for the respective modalities, with touch being the only sense lacking such a special organ. The lower modalities are also characterized by direct sensory contact with what is perceived. Although suggestive, I don't believe their speculative explanation provides a thorough answer to the question what exactly the less differentiated and less mediated modalities contribute to our understanding of the more mediated ones.

Most recently, Rakova (2003) has devoted a book-length study to defending her claim that synaesthetic expressions are not metaphorical but describe literally the same concept, for example SOFT, in various modalities, although the physical properties depicted in the specific modalities are not the same. Hence, she allows no perceptual or conceptual priority to any one sense and argues:

> ... the concept BRIGHT ... that one entertains in connection with bright music and bright lights is one and the same psychologically primitive concept. (Rakova 2003: 68)

Due to limitations of space, I cannot engage here in any attempt to refute her views which go a lot further in their aim to discredit the theory of conceptual metaphor as a whole. Crucial to our concerns, however, is that her views throw no further light on directionality in verbal synaesthesia thus leaving unanswered the question why certain combinations of synaesthetic adjective-noun pairs are judged easier to comprehend and recall in experimental tasks. Despite the fact that she dismisses etymological explanations as being of "no help to cognitive semantics" (Rakova 2003: 189), it still remains pertinent to explain why of the 70 or so words describing sensory experience in Williams' corpus (1976: 475-476) an overwhelming amount of 48 describe tactile experience (inclusive of dimension) and 9 describe gustatory experience. If we accept that the concept SHARP in *sharp edge* and *sharp sound* or the concept COLD in *cold surface* and *cold colour* are the same psychologically primitive concepts, it becomes difficult to explain why the tactile meanings of these expressions preceded the respective auditory and visual ones by a minimum of 550-600 years.

3.   A brief outline of the psychology and phenomenology of touch

Firstly, it is important to clarify that the sense of touch is traditionally divided in psychology into the skin senses (pressure, temperature, pain) – also known as somaesthesia; haptics (the seeking and obtaining of information by hand); and a body sense or kinaesthesia, which is the deep pressure sense felt

through nerve fibres in muscles, tendons and joints. All three distinctions will
be included in the subsequent discussion of touch.[2]

3.1. Touch as a space-constituting and active sense

While philosophers (Aristotle, Berkeley, Diderot) have long maintained the
prominence of touch among the senses, David Katz sought to restore its importance within experimental psychology.[3] For Katz ([1925]1989), touch is
fundamental in developing our belief in the reality of the external world:

> What has been touched is the true reality that leads to perception; no reality
> pertains to the mirrored image, the mirage that applies itself to the eye.
> (Katz 1989: 240)

There are certain attributes like thickness, hardness, or the presence of vibra-
tion, the perception of which we owe exclusively to our sense of touch.
Touch also surpasses vision in judgements of texture. Revesz (1950) maintains that the tactile sense equals vision in its importance as a *space perceiving* and *space constituting* sense. It may not develop fully in the sighted due
to the influence of vision, but it is nevertheless autonomous because the con-
genitally blind have a spatial understanding very similar to that of the
sighted. More recently, in her extensive studies of very young infants, Streri
(1993) has shown that the discrimination of perceptual properties (e.g., shape
and size of objects) by two-months-old babies is achieved equally well by
manipulation only, as it is by sight only.

Touch is furthermore the only modality in which there is a distinct differentiation between *active* and *passive* perception. Touch is passive in the subjective sensation of pain or when we feel warmth and cold, but the most
common mode of touch is the intentional movement of the hand. Katz particularly emphasized the role of the human hand as the organ of touch. He

---

2. There is no single theory of the sense of touch, and many issues remain unresolved. The aim of the present discussion is to give an outline of those qualities
   of touch that can be construed as relevant in explaining its prominence for conceptualizing SCALARITY and, hence, its dominance as a source domain in the
   mappings of verbal synaesthesia. For further details, see Katz (1989); Revesz
   (1950); Heller and Schiff (1991); Schiff and Foulke (1982); Streri (1993).
3. For a brief summary of Katz's work, see Krueger (1982). For Katz's own views
   on the primacy of touch and a convincing argument for the strong causal
   connection between object and percept in touch, see Katz (1989: 238-245).

argued that with our hands we "produce" such properties as roughness and smoothness, hardness and softness:

> Touching means to bring to life a particular class of physical properties through our own activity. (Katz 1989: 242)

Because of the hand's function in active touch, the tactile sense is a unique modality in which stimulation is *obtained* rather than imposed by the stimulus.[4] Another quality specific to the tactile sense is its phenomenological uniqueness in providing first person experiences. The inner experience of my fingertip touching my lips produces a sensation both on my lips and fingertip. Standing in front of the mirror, however, I can only see myself as another person would see me, i.e., from a third person perspective. Hence, while I can feel myself touching, I cannot see myself seeing. Similarly, I can hear my own voice, but not myself hearing. Touch thus incorporates self-awareness uniquely and distinctly from the other senses. Crucially, such first-person knowledge of the world originates in one's own (hand or body) movements.

Finally, the potential capacity of touch for structuring meaning can also be traced to the possible relation between tactile sensation and memory. The very fact that manual tactile recognition takes place in two-month-old babies speaks in favour of a link between touch and (a system) memory at that age (Streri 1993: 104). In this regard touch is similar to vision and audition, because we are better at remembering and interpreting sensations we can reproduce. We can imitate a sound, draw a shape we have seen (but note the crucial involvement of the hand here), and we can reproduce virtually all tactile sensations through our own or another person's body.[5]

---

4. The role of the human hand in the development of cognitive abilities should be emphasized in this context. The adaptive properties of hand control involving tactile, visual and proprioceptive feedback in one action system (i.e., hand movement) are claimed to be the true origins of intelligent behaviour (Wilson 1998). In a similar vein, Corballis (1991, 2002) has linked language evolution to manual gestures. His theoretical claims appear to be substantiated by the discovery of the so-called "mirror neurons" (Rizzolatti et al. 1996), which get activated when particular grasping movements are either made, or observed/imagined, thus providing a correlation (a mirror) between perception and action.

5. This is observed by Eco (1999: 406, note). I believe that the ability to reproduce or intentionally produce virtually all tactile sensations may have significance for the way we conceptualize perceptual properties. The intermodal relations between vision and touch facilitate this ability (we can draw a shape we have

3.2. Touch versus vision: intermodality relations

To what extent can information provided by the two spatial senses: touch and vision, be regarded as equivalent? And in what respect is tactile perception also distinct from vision? There is evidence to suggest that, regarding the perception of distinct kinds of events, the sensory modalities of adults vary in their precision and appropriateness. Experientially we tend to rely mainly on that modality which is best and most appropriate for a specific event: touch for texture, both vision and touch for dimension, vision for shape and spatial location, audition for temporal rate.[6]

One distinct feature of touch is that it examines objects slowly and sequentially, not globally and simultaneously, as does vision. Touch constructs its content in a temporal sequence of sensations. One particularly apt description of tactile perception is provided by the psychologist Erwin Straus. I will quote from it at some length because it provides the justification for my proposal that tactile perception supplies the experiential grounding for SCALAR-ITY:

> In touching, I grasp only one piece, but as such, as a piece. In touching the edge of the back of a chair, I successively feel it piece by piece, moment by moment, by moving along the back. The momentary is part of every tactile impression, "moment" in the sense of both time and motion. Each moment is but one moment; it is experienced in the transition of what is not yet to that which is no longer. In the world of touch, there is no closed, realised horizon; there are only moments – and thus the urge to move from one moment to the next (Straus 1963: 341)

3.3. Developmental issues: haptic perception in early infancy

Haptic perception is essentially object perception with the hands. Its developmental course in infancy is constrained by both the ability and inclination

---

    seen, for example), but do not exhaust it (we cannot reproduce colour by simply moving our hand).

6. See Warren and Rosano (1991) for a review of key studies on the intermodality relations between vision and touch. For a behavioural study of the neuronal processes underlying cross-modal integration see Stein and Meredith (1993), which is primarily concerned, however, with the associations between the visual and the auditory systems.

to perform various movements with the hands (motor prerequisites) and the development of attention to object properties (cognitive considerations). Bushnell and Boudreau (1991) provide a convincing model for the development of haptic perception in the first year of life, which also is largely in agreement with the general outline of infant cognitive development described by Piaget (1952). Piaget distinguishes between four stages of infant behaviour in the first year of life, the second, third and fourth of which are of particular interest in this context. The second stage of sensorimotor development (1 to 4 months) is characterized by activities involving the infants' own bodies: sucking of fingers and toes; playing with the hands. The third stage (4 to 8 months) involves activities with external objects, but, importantly, such that are pleasing and provide interesting sensory feedback: stroking stuffed animals, shaking rattles. The fourth sensorimotor stage (8 to 12 months) is already characterized by functional behaviours, i.e., by actions on objects that are used to achieve particular ends: using buckets as containers, reaching with one toy to get to another (Bushnell and Boudreau 1991: 153).

Bushnell's and Boudreau's model for the development of haptic perception matches very nicely with the evidence in the empirical literature about the order in which particular sensitivities are predicted to emerge. Thus, temperature and size are perceivable very early, perhaps from birth, because they require only static contact. Texture and hardness, on the other hand, require simple repetitive finger movements and are aesthetically pleasing. So, they become perceivable at about 5 or 6 months of age. At that stage of development infants are actively seeking an interesting feedback, and that is exactly what they get when they feel, poke and squeeze objects. Finally, weight and configurational shape are not intrinsically pleasing or interesting, but rather, pertain to an object's function: only light things can be carried easily, only certain shapes can fit into a particular opening of the same shape, etc. Accordingly, haptic sensitivity to weight is not recorded before the ninth month, and perception of configurational shape begins between 12 and 15 months of age.

3.4. Summary: Image schemas and touch

With respect to image schemas, the following conclusions can be drawn from this brief outline of tactile perception. First, touch is as important as vision for the way most spatial properties are conceptualized, and for some it is even dominant. Second, the generally active nature of tactile perception and its phenomenological uniqueness in obtaining stimuli contribute to its often subjective, evaluative content. Third, the successive, moment by moment, nature of exploration in haptic perception can serve as a basis for conceptualizing SCALARITY as an aspect of perceptual properties (see section 5). Fourth, in development touch provides an "aesthetic" versus functional distinction of object properties thus serving as a basis for normativity in the SCALE schema.

4. Image schemas and the semantics of adjectives

There has been relatively little attention given to adjectives in cognitive linguistics. Both traditional and more recent accounts have identified gradability as their fundamental characteristic. Adjectives code qualities of experience and properties of objects, both of which are typically conceptualized as possessing inherent degrees of intensity. Gradability in adjectives reflects directly one of the most pervasive aspects of experience, namely SCALARITY. According to Johnson (1987: 121-124), the SCALE schema has the following properties: it has a more or less fixed directionality; it is cumulative; it is normative; it can be either closed or open.

The traditional semantic distinction of gradability is closely linked with antonymy: there cannot be a conceptualization of an attribute without some implicit comparison with its opposite. There is no notion of smoothness without a notion of roughness or notion of noise without a notion of silence. Mettinger (1999) even proposes a view of contrastivity in terms of SCALARITY. Thus, antonyms (*large* and *small*, *hot* and *cold*) are seen as points on a scale, which, combined with an appropriate noun, represents a particular attribute. In accordance with one of the properties of the SCALE schema, normativity, these values are measured with respect to a norm, which is specified by the noun. Non-gradable adjectives, on the other hand, seen previously in terms of complementarity (Lyons 1977: 270-276) are regarded by Mettinger as linguistic manifestations of the CONTAINER schema: *true/false*; *dead/alive*; *male/female*. These adjectives divide a particular domain into two complementary subsets; they are also non-gradable. The distinction between the CONTAINER and the SCALE schemas in structuring adjectival meaning corresponds to the more traditional division between "absolute" and "relative" adjectives (Katz 1972: 254).[7]

---

7. Colour terms are somewhat different in that they cannot be fully subsumed

Mettinger distinguishes among three types of gradable antonyms. Adjective pairs like *long/short, high/low* presuppose a scale that is bounded at one end by a zero point. These are very few because, as Lyons (1977: 276) pointed out, the notion of a limit is relevant only to a small subset of gradable pairs of adjectives and most obviously to attributes pertaining to spatial and temporal extension. The most common type of attribute is conceptualized via a scale that is bidirectional and unbounded at both ends: *hot/cold, smooth/rough*. Finally, a very small number of adjectives, such as *silent/noisy, dry/wet*, are graded on a scale that is bounded at one end by one member of the pair, which in these cases coincides with the norm: *silent* and *dry*, respectively. So, while *silent* and *dry* are not gradable because they coincide with the zero value, *noisy* and *wet* are.

Paradis (2001) suggests that boundedness,[8] as a characteristic of gradability, is as fundamental to the cognitive representation of adjectival meanings as countability is for nouns and as aspectuality is for verbs. Boundedness tells us how a particular quality is predicated of a given noun. The way a property is construed is very often evident from the degree modifier that the adjective can combine with:

> Scalar modifiers, such as *very, terribly*, and *fairly*, indicate a range on a scale of the gradable property expressed by the adjective they modify and are in that respect unbounded. (Paradis 2001: 50)

Totality modifiers, such as *totally, completely, absolutely*, on the other hand, "relate to a definite and precise value of the property expressed by the adjective and are bounded." (ibid.) Thus, the expressions in (1a) are common, while those in (1b) are unacceptable:[9]

(1) a.   very sharp, fairly coarse, rather cool
     b.   ?totally smooth, ?completely sweet, ?absolutely loud

On the other hand, different kinds of attributes (2a) demand a bounded construal; while others do not (2b):

---

under either of the two schemas: they are both absolute (chromatic versus achromatic) and non-binary (there are many varied and distinct instances of being coloured).

8. "conceptualization according to the presence or absence of boundaries" (Paradis 2001: 47)

9. Question marks are used here to indicate unacceptable expressions thereby avoiding the use of asterisks and the making of decisions about borderline cases.

(2)   a.   absolutely silent, completely dry, utterly empty
      b.   ?fairly silent, ?very identical, ?very circular

Two more existing attempts to link image schematic constraints to the construal of qualities need mentioning. Clausner and Croft (1999) argue that image schemas are in fact subtypes of domains, which possess both a locational and a configurational aspect:

> ... gradability and quantity can be analysed as locational and configurational concepts, respectively, profiled in a single image schematic domain of SCALE. (Clausner and Croft 1999: 19)

Such a proposal does not take into account that SCALARITY works differently for adjectives than it does for nouns and verbs (cf. Paradis 2001: 56). The former are inherently scalar: a property is most commonly construed as locational. As will be argued below, particular sensory modalities (and content domains) allow configurational concepts (3a), but even these configurationally construed attributes may be graded in certain circumstances (3b):

(3)   a.   three-sided object, red ball, round table
      b.   very black day, quite circular argument.

As Paradis notes, quantification of nouns and verbs requires overlaying of a SCALE schema on a content domain (*How much did you eat?, I put a lot of effort into it*), while SCALARITY is inherent in the construals of properties: *rough aftertaste, rough sea, rough day* are all understood as already having a degree of roughness.[10] Clausner and Croft are right that locationality and configurationality are properties of concepts. The important question to ask here, however, is what kinds of concepts are construed as bounded or unbounded. In the following discussion of synaesthetic adjective-noun pairs it will be shown how and why particular types of properties favour certain construals rather than others.

Finally, Croft and Cruse (2004: 164-192) argue for a dynamic construal approach to the semantics of adjectives which is largely in agreement with what is being proposed in this discussion. They introduce not three but four types of antonymy (Croft and Cruse 2004: 169-170). What is of interest here is the fact that despite their claim that particular antonymic pairs are linked non-arbitrarily to particular antonymic types, they do not seek to explain

---

10. This is confirmed experimentally by Marks et al. (1987), who found that adjectives translate better across modalities than nouns or verbs; e.g. *high-pitched* is readily judged to be brighter than *low-pitched*, but this is not the case with *sunlight* versus *moonlight* when judged with respect to pitch highness.

fully the motivation behind that link. In other words, they raise, but do not sufficiently address, the issue about the nature of the association of particular properties (content domains) with particular antonymic types.[11] They rely frequently on examples of adjectives describing perceptual properties as representatives of their antonymic types, yet do not attempt to seek experiential motivation between the properties themselves and the image-schematic construals that they favour. If they did, the question why *completely cold, completely dark* are acceptable but *completely light,* is not, could be answered, as will be shown below.

To conclude this section, different perceptual modes are experienced in specific ways, and the phenomenology of that embodied experience is reflected in the construal of the attributes that code them linguistically. SCALARITY and BOUNDEDNESS constitute the two fundamental aspects of that construal.

5. Scalarity, boundedness and synaesthetic adjectives

All the adjectives that concern us here are of physical sensations arising from one of the five sensory modalities. They encompass three of the seven semantic types of adjectives, introduced by Dixon (1982: 16): *dimension, physical property* and *colour*. In the remainder of this paper I will subsume Dixon's three types under just one: properties relating to physical sensations, which can also be mapped to abstract domains. As already pointed out, a fundamental assumption of my analysis is that embodied experience is constitutive of the ways we construe meaning; more specifically, the experiential content of the sense data provided by the lower modalities (touch, and to a lesser extent, taste) will be seen as constitutive of the ways we generally construe quality.[12]

---

11. They give only one example (Croft and Cruse 2004: 172) of such a motivated link: *hot/cold,* because according to them the biscalar disjunct type of scale, which the pair represents, correlates with our experiential knowledge of temperature (nothing can give us simultaneously a sensation of *hot* and *cold*).

12. It should not be forgotten that despite its physiological distinctness taste is a kind of touch performed by the tongue. Aristotle classifies touch and taste together, because they are the two senses requiring contact, while the remaining three perceive over a distance. It should also be noted that, in accordance with Williams's suggested law, the majority of words describing gustatory perception, originate as concepts describing touch, even though their contemporary

5.1. Presence and absence of boundaries

Perceptual experience provides us with particular sensations in the five modalities (hot, sweet, fragrant, bright, loud). Each sensation, in turn, can be analysed according to its quality, intensity, extension and duration (cf. Miller and Johnson-Laird 1976: 15). Of particular relevance in the context of this discussion are the first two attributes and their interaction. It is important to note that only the modalities of vision and sound have specific lexical items coding intensity. These are *bright/dull* and *loud/quiet*, respectively. In the remaining modalities of touch, taste and smell, intensity is rendered by a modifier of degree such as *very, fairly*, etc. The quality of a sensation in vision is hue; in sound it is pitch; in touch it is warmth, texture, pressure, pain, and movement; in taste it is sweet, sour, bitter, salty; and in smell it is putrid, ethereal, fragrant, burned, resinous and spicy (cf. Miller and Johnson-Laird 1976: 15).

The properties perceivable mainly through touch are multiple and varied, provided by sensations of pain, pressure, temperature, texture. They are construed along a scale whose two directions are equal and completely symmetrical. More importantly, the qualities of sensation activated through touch (and taste) are not absolute, but relative: they require unbounded construal. This becomes obvious when we add a degree modifier to the particular quality that is being described by the adjective, as discussed in section 4. Both novel and established synaesthetic adjective-noun pairs, most commonly combine with scalar modifiers. Hence the examples in (4):[13]

(4)   very sweet silence, very smooth redness, very crisp whiteness, very cold stillness, very coarse blackness, [very] dry sound (Homer), very heavy darkness

Very few properties of physical perception (and none from the modalities of touch and taste) can be construed as bounded. In fact, I will claim that only *silent, dry, dark (having no light)* and, possibly, the various colour terms allow bounded (absolute) construal. Of the dimensional terms, only *flat* and *empty* can be construed in absolute terms. To put it differently, we tend to

---

meanings are associated with taste only or, in some instances, have been mapped onto higher domains.

13. Unless otherwise specified in the text, all examples of synaesthetic adjective-noun pairs in this article are from the *British National Corpus* (100 mill. words), World Edition, December 2000.

construe properties as unbounded a lot more than as bounded. With respect to attributes, CONTAINER is not as pervasive in experience as SCALE.[14]

It is worth noting that being construed simply in terms of degree (i.e., a result of relative or unbounded construal), the qualities of perceptual experience provided by touch are different from those given by vision or sound. As already pointed out in section 3, tactile experience provides us with sensations that are continuous, sequential and non-discrete. Vision is different: it construes its objects not sequentially but discretely; it experiences not by degree but by totality. Hence, perceptual psychology's claim that it dominates the perception of shape. What can be added here is that shape is a configurational concept usually construed in absolute terms. In other words, apart from the concept of intensity, which is lexicalized for both vision and sound, the two latter domains favour configurational concepts. Touch (and taste), on the other hand, provide sensations that cannot be described as absolute; they are always relative, a matter of more or less, hence construed as locational. They are also unbounded: unlike in vision or sound, there are no gradable complementaries analogous to *silent/noisy, dark/light*. Because obtained by the movement of our own bodies, tactile sensations are not as constrained by the outside world as those originating in vision or hearing. Silence is the absence of the perception of sound, darkness makes vision weak or impossible, yet the absence of smoothness will be construed as a certain degree of roughness.

While a locational concept can qualify a configurational one, as in synaesthetic metaphors that are formed in accordance with the pattern from lower to higher modalities, the reverse is not the case. Synaesthetic adjective-noun pairs formed against the pattern either do not exist in language or, when artificially constructed, fail in tests of comprehensibility and recall (cf. section 2). The inverted pairs of the regular synaesthetic combinations given in (4) above look like the ones presented in (5a). They provide bounded (absolute) descriptions of a property and require a construal of the attribute as absolute (5b).

(5)   a.   ?silent sweetness, ?red smoothness, ?white crispiness, ?still coldness, ?black coarseness, ?dark heaviness
      b.   completely silent sweetness, completely still coldness, totally black coarseness

---

14. Without the qualification about attributes, this is a claim made by Clausner and Croft (1999: 22).

However, the entity that is claimed to be silent, red, etc. in these combinations is a derived noun coding a perceptual quality understood only in terms of degree. This type of combination calls for an impossible construal: a configurational concept cannot qualify a locational one.

In arguing for the existence of schematic constraints in interpreting novel and established synaesthetic combinations of the type discussed in this chapter, I do not wish to claim that these exhaust the meaning of the expressions. What is also being mapped in verbal synaesthesia is some kind of irreducible sensory content.[15] Yet, it may be that the reason touch (and to a lesser extent, taste) are such rich source domains for synaesthetic mappings is that they provide both new image content and the possibilities for unbounded construal for the higher modalities, which are ordinarily profiled as configurational. Because intensity is lexicalized only in the two highest modalities: vision and sound, it is possible to speculate how intensities of experience correlate with qualities of experience in the lower modalities. For example, the experiential quality of tactile smoothness or roughness is already associated with some degree of intensity. This unbounded gradedness remains operational throughout all subsequent synaesthetic mappings originating in tactile perception:

(6)   a.   very rough surface, ~ aftertaste, ~ countryside, ~embrace
      b.   very smooth edges, ~ taste, ~ shine, ~ country-and-western crooning, ~ transition to Chinese rule, ~ progress

If in touch (and taste) degree and quality are to some extent experientially fused, *smoothness* and *roughness* become not only new qualitative descriptions of, for example, sound, but qualitative descriptions which arrive, as it were, with their own gradable intensity. A *harsh voice* is not simply a *loud voice*, and a *soft sound* is not simply a *quiet sound:* the meanings of the synaesthetic expressions are not exhausted by a description of intensity in pitch. They combine the experiential content of the tactile *harsh* or *soft* with an implicit degree of intensity.

Attributes pertaining to colour are construed somewhat differently from attributes originating in the lower modalities. Each hue constitutes a separate gradable dimension, but these individual dimensions do not form complemen-

---

15. Within a cognitive linguistic framework, this is best described by Grady's (1997) notion of primary metaphor and, more particularly, his notion of "primary source concepts" and their "image content". Irreducible aspects of sensory experience also characterize Langacker's (1987: 149) notion of "basic domains", which include, among others, colour and two- and three-dimensional space for vision; pitch for sound; and temperature, pressure and pain for touch.

taries. Hence, *X is redder than Y* contrasts with *X is smoother than Y* in that the latter also means that *Y is rougher than X*, while the former does not imply *Y is greener than X*. All it means is that both X and Y are to be construed within the confines of redness, and differ only in terms of intensity: *X is a brighter or duller red than Y.*[16]

5.2. The SCALE schema and normativity

In his discussion of the SCALE schema Johnson observes that scales are typically given a normative character (Johnson 1987: 123). This amounts to saying that SCALARITY involves an evaluation of the property that is being graded. This is indeed the case with synaesthetic metaphors having touch or taste as a source domain. Warmth, hardness, smoothness, sharpness, sweetness, bitterness, etc. are construed as possessing a certain value which then gets mapped to other domains. This point is proved by the oddness of the expressions in (7):

(7)   ?sweet but unpleasant silence, ?bitter but exciting jealousy, ?sharp but
        nice reply, ?cold but pleasing reception, ?warm but unpleasant light,
        ?smooth but difficult transition, ?smooth but unsophisticated character

My claim is that tactile (and also gustatory) perception is always construed as normative, i.e., as good or bad, pleasant or unpleasant. This is not to say that vision or sound cannot be normative. Locational concepts construed through SCALE, however, evoke normativity in a way that configurational ones do not. The reasons for this can be traced back to some of the features of tactile perception, discussed in 3. Firstly, touch is the only sense in which the surface or the interior of the body can serve as both an object and an act of perception. Secondly and consequently, because exclusively bound up with a specific bodily location, touch is most phenomenologically real, and hence most expressive of subjective evaluation. Thirdly, in development, sensitivities to texture and warmth precede the perception of configurational shape because of their aesthetic and pleasing qualities. All these features of tactile perception speak in favour of an understanding of the sense of touch as a modality which includes value as one of its dimensions of meaning. To ad-

---

16. For that reason I hesitate to describe colour as a locational concept, though it is
    viewed as locational by both Langacker (1987: 152-154) and Clausner and
    Croft (1999). I consider it locational only with respect to individual dimensions
    of hue: the domain as a whole is configurational.

dress the question raised by Mark Johnson (*this volume*), whether "feeling merely accompanies image-schematic structures", I believe there are grounds for claiming that the normative aspect of the SCALE schema is constitutive of the ways we construe attributive meaning. Gradability involves evaluation, and while it is certainly not exclusive to the domains of touch and taste,[17] the two provide prototypically gradable properties, one of the meaning dimensions of which is invariably value.

5.3. The SCALE schema: synaesthesia and beyond

In this final section I will seek to extend some of the claims about gradability and boundedness beyond synaesthesia narrowly understood. As noted earlier, my position differs from that of some other authors (cf. Ullmann 1951) in that I consider abstract senses of sensory words, where sensory qualities are mapped to abstract domains (8a), to be subsumable under synaesthesia.[18] While (8a) presents common expressions that comply with the common pattern of mappings, (8b) does not:

(8)   a.   harsh indifference, bitter jealousy, cold assertion, smooth sophistication

      b.   ?indifferent harshness, ?jealous bitterness, ?assertive coldness, ?sophisticated smoothness

My claim is that even in these abstract senses the synaesthetic adjectives are conceptualized through the SCALE schema and part of their meaning is "a degree of the attribute described". They act as intensifiers for the quality described by human propensity nouns like *jealousy, sophistication*, etc. This also explains the common usage in initial modifying position of their adverbial derivatives. Thus, we find expressions as in (9a), but not those in (9b).

(9)   a.   harshly indifferent, bitterly jealous, coldly assertive
      b.   ?indifferently harsh, ?jealously bitter, ?assertively cold.

---

17. Consider the negative evaluation in *loud colours*, or the unacceptability of *?loud but tasteful decoration.*

18. My position also differs from that of Grady (1997) in that I take the mappings from sensory to abstract domains, which define his "primary metaphors", to be the very last step in a series of synaesthetic mappings from lower to higher modalities. Thus, e.g., his primary PLEASING IS TASTY metaphor (*sweet person*) is only the end point of a series of mappings from TASTE through SMELL and SOUND to ABSTRACT.

The question can be raised whether synaesthetic adverbs, in their function as modifiers, retain some of the perceptual content of the corresponding synaesthetic adjectives, or are simply emptied of it. The least that can be said is that positive or negative evaluation is retained in both adjectives and derived adverbs of synaesthetic origin – a fact that is evident from the selectional possibilities of the respective adjectives or adverbs. Thus, *bitterly* collocates with the adjectives in block (10), intensifying an already negative experience of some kind:

(10) jealous, disputed, hostile, attacked, disappointed, indignant, ashamed, resentful, resented, divided, opposed, criticized, critical, regretted, contested, upset, etc.

The meaning of *smoothly (*derived from *smooth)* is *continuous and effortless movement.* To the extent that the movement is effortless, this meaning incurs positive evaluation. Interestingly, *smoothly* is almost exclusively found to collocate with various verbs of (generally effortless) motion (ex 11):

(11) run, glide, slide, proceed, travel, ride, move, flow, go, fly, etc.

Colour adjectives and their derived adverbs are used very rarely as intensifiers. *Redly, whitely* still describe only a particular colour perception (12a). Only *black(ly)* can be construed as an intensifier of a negative kind (12b):[19]

(12) a. His eyes gleamed redly. Her teeth flashed whitely.
     b. black and negative mood, blackly venomous, ~ depressed, ~ angry, ~ satirical.

It has been claimed throughout this paper that SCALARITY is a much more salient way of construing certain types of properties than boundedness is. I've also linked that salience to particular properties of tactile perception. As has been known among linguists of different persuasions (cf. Lyons 1977: 270; Paradis 2001: 57), it is a fact of normal language behaviour that ungradable antonyms can be and sometimes are explicitly graded. What is of particular interest here is the fact that gradable complementaries (such as *raw/cooked,* in which one member of the pair, *raw,* requires bounded while

---

19. That *blackly, whitely, redly* can be used at all is due to the perceptual primacy of the properties they describe. Berlin and Kay (1969) place them as the first three in their order of colour terms. Developmentally, newly-born babies perceive only achromatic colours, and the first chromatic colour to be perceived is red. It is also claimed that the first colour term to be acquired by children is *red* (Johnson 1977).

the other, *cooked*, unbounded construal) change their gradability as they become metaphorical. Thus, (13a) are construed as bounded, but (13b) are graded. This is the case for dimension terms also (14a, b):

(13) a.   (totally) *raw food*, ~ *diet*
      b.   very raw nerve, ~ deal, ~ talent, ~ vulnerability

(14) a.   (completely) *empty glass,*
      b.   (very) empty threat, ~ relationship, ~ life

Curiously, the same phenomenon is observed in adjectives describing colour: gradability in this domain, although rare, is also associated with metaphorical meanings (15a, b).[20]

(15) a.   ?very black wall, ?very red dress
      b.   very red university; very black frown, ~ humour

5.4. Summary

This case study of synaesthetic adjective-noun pairs has brought to light the ubiquity of the SCALE schema in conceptualizing properties. Why is it the case that the tactile perception of warmth or smoothness, the somatic experience of pain, or the gustatory sensation of sweetness are construed in terms of grades of perceptual content, while colour is much less susceptible to grading, and shape hardly at all? It has been argued that, although the perception of intensity is innate, SCALARITY dominates perceptual experience in the lower modalities. Touch allows an experience of qualities as unbounded and graded. These are the locational concepts of SMOOTHNESS, SHARPNESS, and WARMTH. The move from touch to vision is already a move toward further differentiation and abstraction, in other words, toward configurational concepts like shape. In novel and established synaesthetic adjective-noun pairs, the move from lower to higher modalities requires construals in which locational concepts qualify configurational ones. Reversed synaesthetic patterns constitute impossible construals and, hence, fail in comprehension tasks. In my investigation I have sought and established a relation between particular sensory qualities and their construal in language. I have proposed that tactile perception provides the experiential grounding for SCALARITY and

---

20. Idiomatic expressions, like *black market, white magic, red alert*, which contain a colour word and are formed by adjective-noun pairs, cannot be graded for obvious reasons.

linked its phenomenology as a unique channel of subjective evaluation to the intrinsic normativity of the SCALE schema in synaesthetic adjective-noun pairs. Finally, I have argued that the move from concrete to abstract in synaesthetic adjectives is also a move towards GRADABILITY. When used metaphorically, even concepts normally construed as bounded become gradable.

6. Conclusions and directions for future work

A correlation between perceptual knowledge and conceptual structure manifests itself in various linguistic categories – adjectives relating to sensory experience are one obvious example, but similar considerations affect how we describe the meaning of verbs of motion or non-abstract nouns. In the distinction between perceptual and functional aspects of the semantic representation of, for example, non-abstract nouns, perception has tended to be reduced to exclusively visual information.[21] The phenomenon of verbal synaesthesia, where the world of touch brings its experiential content to vision and to other, more abstract realms, proves such treatment incomplete. Crossmodal experiences in synaesthesia motivate image schemas, and patterns in verbal synaesthesia reflect that motivation. This paper has studied only one form of verbal synaesthesia, adjective-noun pairs – a form that seems to be dominant in everyday discourse. It is both more common and less specific than other forms of synaesthesia: e.g., *sharp words* is less vivid and specific than "words which cut the air like a dagger" (Wilde). It may prove profitable to study other synaesthetic forms with respect to image schematic construal. A main conclusion to be drawn at present is that if the role of perceptual experience in structuring the semantic system is to be further elaborated, an account of the perceptual properties of the lower modalities and their realisation in language is necessary. On the basis of the discussion of the SCALE schema, I suggest that the normative aspect is a crucial component of image-

---

21. Psycholinguistic studies have shown that the semantic properties of common nouns denoting real objects can be separated into perceptually based and abstract (functional) components. The activation procedures during recognition tasks are different for each component: perceptually based semantic information is available earlier and faster than information based on functional properties (Flores d'Arcais, Schreuder and Glazenborg 1985; Flores d'Arcais and Schreuder 1987). This coincides with empirical evidence that perceptual attributes that are part of a word's meaning are the earliest to be acquired (Anglin 1983; Tomikawa and Dodd 1980).

schematic meaning. Maybe future experiments could test the axiological dimension of image-schematic concepts originating in specific modalities: I would expect the meaning of *shrill sound* and *harsh sound* to be rated as different, and *soft outline* and *circular outline* to code affectively (as well as perceptually) different content. If SCALARITY originates with and dominates the tactile, as I have suggested, its ubiquity is nothing else but a recurrent manifestation of the felt-fact of human embodiment realised, at its strongest, in touch.

References

Anglin, Jeremy M.
   1983   Extensional aspects of the preschool child's word concepts. In *Concept Development and the Development of Word Meaning*, Thomas B. Seiler and Wolfgang Wannenmacher (eds.), 247-266. Berlin: Springer Verlag.
Berlin, Brent and Paul Kay
   1969   *Basic Colour Terms: Their Universality and Evolution.* Berkeley: University of California Press.
Bushnell, Emily W. and J. Paul Boudreau
   1991   The development of haptic perception during infancy. In *The Psychology of Touch*, Morton A. Heller, and William Schiff (eds.), 139-161. Hillsdale, N.J: Lawrence Erlbaum Associates.
Cienki, Alan
   1998   STRAIGHT: An image schema and its metaphorical extensions. *Cognitive Linguistics* 9: 107-149.
Clausner, Timothy C. and William Croft
   1999   Domains and image schemas. *Cognitive Linguistics* 10: 1-31.
Corballis, Michael C.
   1991   *The Lopsided Ape.* Oxford/New York: Oxford University Press.
   2002   *From Hand to Mouth.* Princeton: Princeton University Press.
Croft, William and D. Alan Cruse
   2004   *Cognitive Linguistics.* Cambridge: Cambridge University Press.
Cytowic, Richard E.
   1989   *Synaesthesia: A Union of the Senses.* New York: Springer-Verlag.
   1994   *The Man Who Tasted Shapes.* London: Abacus.
Dixon, Robert M.W.
   1982   *Where Have All the Adjectives Gone? And Other Essays in Semantics and Syntax.* Berlin: Mouton.

Eco, Umberto
1999   *Kant and the Platypus: Essays on Language and Cognition.* Translated by Alistair McEwan. London: Vintage.

Flores d'Arcais, G.B., R. Schreuder and G. Glazenborg
1985   Semantic activation during recognition of referential words. *Psychological Research* 47: 39-49.

Flores d'Arcais, G.B. and R. Schreuder
1987   Semantic activation during object naming. *Psychological Research* 49: 153-159.

Grady, Joseph E.
1997   Foundations of Meaning: Primary Metaphors and Primary Scenes. Ph.D. Dissertation at the University of California, Berkeley.

Heller, Morton A. and William Schiff (eds.)
1991   *The Psychology of Touch.* Hillsdale, N.J.: Lawrence Erlbaum Associates.

Johnson, E. G.
1977   The development of colour knowledge in preschool children. *Child Development* 48: 308-311.

Johnson, Mark
1987   *The Body in the Mind: The Bodily Basis of Meaning, Imagination and Reason.* Chicago/London: University of Chicago Press.

Katz, David
1989   *The World of Touch.* Edited and translated by Lester E. Krueger. Hillsdale, N.J.: Lawrence Erlbaum Associates [German original 1925].

Katz, Jerrold J.
1972   *Semantic Theory.* New York: Harper and Row.

Krueger, Lester E.
1982   Tactual perception in historical perspective: David Katz's world of touch. In *Tactual Perception: A Sourcebook*, William Schiff, and Emerson Foulke (eds.), 1-54. Cambridge: Cambridge University Press.

Lakoff, George
1987   *Women, Fire and Dangerous Things: What Categories Reveal About the Mind.* Chicago/London: University of Chicago Press.

Langacker, Ronald W.
1987   *Foundations of Cognitive Grammar. Volume 1: Theoretical Prerequisites.* Stanford: Stanford University Press.

Lyons, John
1977   *Semantics. Volume 1.* Cambridge: Cambridge University Press.

418   *Yanna Popova*

Marks, Lawrence E.
   1982a   Bright sneezes and dark coughs, loud sunlight and soft moonlight. *Journal of Experimental Psychology: Human Perception and Performance* 8: 177-193.
   1982b   Synesthetic perception and poetic metaphor. *Journal of Experimental Psychology: Human Perception and Performance* 8: 15-23.
Marks, Lawrence E., Robin J. Hammeal and Marc H. Bornstein
   1987   *Perceiving Similarity and Comprehending Metaphor.* Chicago: University of Chicago Press.
Mettinger, Arthur
   1999   Contrast and schemas: Antonymous adjectives. In *Issues in Cognitive Linguistics*, Leon de Stadler and Christoph Eyrich (eds.), 97-112. Berlin/New York: Mouton de Gruyter.
Miller, George A. and Philip Johnson-Laird
   1976   *Language and Perception.* Cambridge: Cambridge University Press.
Paradis, Carita
   2001   Adjectives and boundedness. *Cognitive Linguistics* 12: 47-65.
Piaget, Jean
   1952   *The Origins of Intelligence in Children.* New York: Norton.
Rakova, Marina
   2003   *The Extent of the Literal: Metaphor, Polysemy and Theories of Concepts.* London: Palgrave Macmillan.
Revesz, Geza
   1950   *Psychology and Art of the Blind.* Translated by H.A. Wolff. London: Longmans, Green and Co.
Rizzolatti, Giacomo, Luciano Fadiga, Vittorio Gallese and Leonardo Fogassi
   1996   Premotor cortex and the recognition of motor actions. *Cognitive Brain Research* 3: 131-141.
Schiff, William, and Emerson Foulke (eds.)
   1982   *Tactual Perception: A Sourcebook.* Cambridge: Cambridge University Press.
Shen, Yeshayahu
   1997   Cognitive constraints on poetic figures. *Cognitive Linguistics* 8: 33-71.
Shen, Yeshayahu and Michael Cohen
   1998   How come silence is sweet but sweetness is not silent: A cognitive account of directionality in poetic synaesthesia. *Language and Literature* 7: 123-140.
Stein, Barry E. and M. Alex Meredith
   1993   *The Merging of the Senses.* Cambridge, Mass.: MIT Press.

Straus, Erwin
    1963   *The Primary World of Senses: a Vindication of Sensory Experience.* Translated by Jacob Needleman. London: Free Press of Glencoe.
Streri, Arlette
    1993   *Seeing, Reaching, Touching: The Relations Between Vision and Touch in Infancy.* Translated by Tim Pownall, and Susan Kingerlee. New York: Harvester Wheatsheaf.
Tomikawa, Sandra A. and David H. Dodd
    1980   Early word meanings: perceptually or functionally based? *Child Development* 51: 1103-1109.
Ullmann, Stephen
    1951   *The Principles of Semantics.* Glasgow: Jackson, Son & Co.
Warren, David H. and Matt J. Rosano
    1991   Intermodality relations: vision and touch. In *The Psychology of Touch*, Morton A. Heller and William Schiff (eds.), 119-137. Hillsdale, N.J: Lawrence Erlbaum Associates.
Williams, Joseph M.
    1976   Synaesthetic adjectives: a possible law of semantic change. *Language* 52: 461-478.
Wilson, Frank R.
    1998   *The Hand: How Its Use Shapes the Brain, Language, and Human Culture.* New York: Vintage Books.

Image schemas and gesture

Alan Cienki[*]

Abstract

An experiment was conducted to assess whether image schemas could be used reliably to characterize spontaneous gestures that co-occur with speech. Two types of gestures were selected from a set of videorecorded conversations: a group which were used in reference to abstract ideas (A gestures) and a group of others (O gestures) which had either a discourse-structuring or performative function. Four conditions were tested: two in which the gestures were viewed (either without sound or with the accompanying speech), and two to assess the role of the accompanying speech without viewing the gestures (either the audio of the utterances and written transcriptions of them, or just written transcriptions of the uttered phrases). In each condition the same six image schemas and the word "other" were given as possible descriptors. The results were that image schemas were used as descriptors with reliable agreement in all four conditions. However, different image schemas were often chosen to characterize the gestures versus their respective accompanying phrases, indicating that gestures can make additional information available to discourse participants. Furthermore, there was more agreement in the use of image schemas to categorize A gestures than O gestures, suggesting that these referential gestures are more readily imageable in form than gestures serving a discourse structuring or performative function. The findings are related to research on the role of gestures in thinking for speaking.

Keywords: abstract reference, conversation, gesture, image schema, thinking for speaking

* I am grateful to Laura Namy for her input at various stages of this project, including the design and analysis, and to Liz Milewicz for research assistance. The paper benefitted from conversations with Cornelia Müller; comments from Beate Hampe, Larry Barsalou, and two anonymous referees as well as from feedback from the audience at the 2004 conference on "Conceptual Structure, Discourse, and Language" (Edmonton, Canada), where I presented my preliminary results.

1.   Introduction

Beginning with Johnson (1987) and Lakoff (1987), the vast majority of research on image schemas has involved the analysis of linguistic data. Semantic analyses in terms of image schemas have received particular attention, especially as they relate to metaphoric use of language that is argued to map from image schemas as source domains. However, if we consider Johnson's characterization of image schemas in the Preface to his 1987 work, it was broadly comprehensive:

> An image schema is a recurring, dynamic pattern of our perceptual interactions and motor programs that gives coherence and structure to our experience. (Johnson 1987: xiv)

How do image schemas relate to other aspects of our experience? The question is enormous, and with the present study, I propose to move modestly in scope by looking not only at linguistic utterances, but also at co-verbal behavior, namely manual gesture with speech. Though the study of gesture dates back at least to classical antiquity, in the twentieth century in particular it underwent a "recession and return" (Kendon 2004: 62-83).[1] Gesture studies, as a field of inquiry, has now become the subject of regular international conferences, a journal entitled *Gesture,* and the basis for the formation of the International Society for Gesture Studies. Yet the bodies of research on image schemas and gesture studies have barely made any connection with each other.[2]

Though language and gesture have been argued to constitute aspects of a larger conceptual/communicative system (McNeill 1985, 1992), there are important differences in how the two modalities are capable of expressing ideas. Language (in terms of sound or written symbolic form) is a "linear" code that is digital in its ontology, while gesture, with its multi-dimensional forms, is analog in nature (McNeill 1992: 11). Given that image schemas, too, are proposed to exist "in a continuous, analog fashion in our understanding" (Johnson 1987: 23), it seems natural that gestures might embody image schemas. Speech and gesture also play different roles in the development of our thoughts in real time. Gesture, it has been argued, can both reflect and influence the imagery content of an idea unit as it is being "unpacked" during speech (Kita 2000; McNeill and Duncan 2000). This

1. See Müller (1998) and Kendon (2004) for historical overviews.
2. For some initial work bridging this gap, see Cienki (1997, 2002) and Calbris (2003).

also suggests a potential connection between gestures and the imagery inherent in image schemas.

A number of other factors suggest that gesture should provide fertile ground for research on image schemas. One concerns the multifaceted character of gestures and the gestalt nature of image schemas. For example, image schemas constitute patterns which can be thought of in either a static or dynamic fashion, realized as an entity or a process (Cienki 1997: 6-7). PATH can be understood as the linear motion of something or the static trace of that motion (or a potential trajectory); CONTAINER, though normally experienced as an entity, can be construed through the continued motion of an object in a cyclical path; and similar options hold for most other image schemas. Manual gestures also consist of physical form and motion: a form of the hand and forearm, and a motion in the main gesture stroke phase, optionally followed by a hold in a static position. The motion of the gesture may itself be intended to describe or outline a static form in the air. As Müller (1998: 114-126) explains, in gesturing, the hand can act (as it would in carrying out an activity with an object), it can model or sculpt something in the air, it can draw an outline (trace), or it can itself represent a form as if a sculpture. We know from sign language research (Taub 2001) that the hands can be used to express concepts in a richly iconic way, far more than is possible with the oral means by which spoken language is produced. One hypothesis, then, is that image schemas may not only serve as structuring elements of the semantics of verbal expressions; they may also constitute structuring elements of gestures, informing the iconic potential of manual expression.

An alternative approach, however, would be to focus on the fact that gesturing varies considerably across individuals, even within a given cultural group. McNeill (1992: 1), for example, argues that co-speech gestures are "free and reveal the idiosyncratic imagery of thought." He adds that they are shaped by the individual speaker's own meaning rather than by any shared conventions: "in no sense are they elements of a fixed repertoire" (McNeill 1992: 1). Even though "[the] gestures of different speakers can present the same meanings[, they] do so in quite different forms" (McNeill 1992: 22). On this logic, an alternative hypothesis is that gestures may be too variable in form to allow them to be related to patterns such as image schemas.

Below I present the findings of an experiment which assesses the degree to which gestures can be interpreted as image-schematic in form. The first part describes how the gesture stimuli for the experiment were selected and prepared. Then the experiment itself involves four different conditions. Participants in each were given a set of image schemas as descriptors and asked to use one of them or the word "other" to characterize either (a) a series of gestures without sound, (b) the same gestures with the accompanying speech, (c) the accompanying speech (phrases) only, in audio and written transcript form, or (d) the phrases in written transcript form only. The intent was to find out whether image schemas could reliably be used as descriptors for the gestures, and to assess what role the accompanying speech plays in trying to interpret the gestures in terms of image schemas. A secondary factor considered is whether gestures of different functional types, and the utterances that accompany them, are characterized differently in terms of image-schema descriptors or not.

2.   Experiment

2.1. Preparation of the material

The source of the video-recorded gestures for the experiment was a set of six dyadic conversations, which are part of a larger cross-linguistic study on metaphors for 'honesty.' The conversations for that study were elicited between pairs of friends, all speakers of American English, who were undergraduates at an American university. At the beginning of each session, the student dyad was given a set of four large cards (three with questions and one with a very short story) that prompted them to discuss how they take exams at their university. Each conversation lasted approximately 20 minutes.

Gestures occurring in the same two-minute segment of each of the six videos were analyzed (thus 12 minutes of video material in total). In each case minutes 3 to 5 were used. This provided comparable content across the tapes as the speakers were all engaged at a similar point in the procedure. Since the time period is a few minutes into the procedure, the participants had gotten warmed up and were more involved in the task, and so one could expect more natural gestural behavior.

2.1.1. Preparation step 1

The first step involved selecting which movements would be considered gestures. Gestures were coded by the author and a second trained analyst to test reliability. Our baseline was identifiably distinct effortful movements of the hands and forearms, that is, gesture strokes. We ignored "self-adjustors," such as scratching oneself. The stroke phase of a gesture may be preceded by a preparation movement to get the hand into a ready position, and/or it may be followed by a retraction movement (Kendon 2004: 112; McNeill 1992: 25). If so, the preparation/retraction was included with the stroke phase that it led up to or returned from, and was not counted as a separate gesture. Dividing points between gestures were determined by several criteria for judging the release of a distinct effortful movement, including return of the hand to a rest position, and/or relaxation of the hand between tense hand shapes. Previously prepared written transcripts of the speech in the videos were marked for gesture strokes by bracketing the speech which accompanied them (or pauses, which were also noted on the transcripts).

Of the 212 movements identified by at least one coder as a gesture stroke in the 12 minutes of video, we agreed on 156 as gestures, or 74%. Through subsequent discussion of individual cases, we were able to bring our agreement to 100%, resulting in a set of 189 gestures, which provided the starting point for Step 2.

2.2.2. Preparation step 2

The second part involved coding the gestures according to function. For this step, an adaptation of Müller's (1998) functional classification was used. This system was preferred because of its consistent focus on functional criteria, as opposed to some other systems which mix formal and functional criteria.[3] Müller draws on Bühler's ([1936] 1982) "Organon"

---

3. Müller (1998: 91-103) provides a critique of the most widely used classification systems. For example, with Eckman and Friesen's (1969) classification, the category of "illustrators" includes gestures based on form (deictics), function ("batons," which mark emphasis and can take various forms), and referent ("pictographs" and others, which depict entities and movements). McNeill's (1992) four categories of gestures – beats, deictics, iconics, and metaphorics – conflate formal, functional, and semantic criteria. Thus the formally determined

model of language, which describes three functions of a linguistic sign in every speech situation, namely: representation (*Darstellung*), expression (*Ausdruck*), and appeal (*Appell*). That is, according to Bühler, every use of language (a) represents entities, relations, etc.; (b) expresses the inner, subjective perspective (*Innerlichkeit*) of the speaker; and (c) is directed to (appeals to) a particular addressee. One function is normally highlighted more than the others in a given use of language, but the others remain in the background. Müller elaborates on the application of the three functions to gesture, noting that gestures can also be representational (e.g., depicting the shape of a picture frame), expressive (showing elation by clapping one's hands), and appeal to (be directed toward) an addressee (as with a gesture giving a blessing). Like linguistic signs, gestures serve multiple functions at once, although normally one is highlighted. For example, the manner in which one performs a primarily representational gesture can show more or less saliently "expressive" and "appeal" functions, e.g., one's affective stance toward the subject under discussion, and towards the addressee.

From this starting point, Müller (1998: 110-113) focusses on the representational use of gestures, and proposes a classification of three basic functional types: *referential* gestures (depicting concrete and abstract entities or ideas, relations, actions, etc.), *discursive* gestures (which structure the accompanying verbal utterance, for example by marking emphasis), and *performative* gestures (which enact a speech act, such as dismissing an idea). As indicated above, the first category, referential gestures, encompasses two subcategories: *concrete* referential gestures (iconically depicting something physical being talked about), and *abstract* referential gestures (depicting an abstract idea with a physical form, and in this sense being metaphoric). The basic types of the classification system are shown in Table 1.

The multifunctionality of gestures is also relevant across the categories of Müller's classification. Therefore, to use it as a basis for coding, one must focus on interpreting each gesture's primary function. For example, a gesture in which the speaker counts off the logical points in an argument on consecutive fingers on one hand would be classified as a discursive type of gesture here, as the primary function is to assist in structuring the argument. Even though the gesture also entails abstract reference as ideas are being

---

category of deictic gestures can be referential or discourse-structuring in function. The iconic nature of metaphoric gestures cannot be accounted for because of the distinction between iconic and metaphoric gestures, and the two categories are also based on different criteria – formal versus semantic.

rendered as entities (the different fingers), in the context of sequential counting, this function is subservient to the more salient function of distinguishing different ideas presented in the discourse. However, the primary function could shift to abstract reference with an appropriate change in context. For example, the speaker could change tactic from counting, and instead dwell on one particular point by saliently moving one finger out and possibly holding it out for a longer period of time. Such a gesture highlighting reference to the idea (an abstract entity) as an object (the finger) would be categorized as abstract referential. The speech context of the gesture is therefore essential for assessing its primary function.

Table 1. Main categories in Müller's (1998) classification of gestures by function

Referential gestures		Discursive gestures	Performative gestures
/	\		
Concrete reference	Abstract reference		

An earlier attempt to use the four-way classification as a coding scheme for gestures proved problematic. In a previous study (Cienki 2003) in which it was applied, Cohen's Kappa for identification of function between two coders for 105 gestures was low at .25. One important problem concerned the coding of some gestures as primarily performative or discursive in function: for example, there was difficulty in discriminating between presenting an idea (performative) or emphasizing an idea (discursive) as the primary function of some gestures. Consequently, an adaptation of Müller's classification has been used here which distinguishes concrete referential (C) and abstract referential (A) from "other" (O) gestures, the last category encompassing the two non-referential types (performative and discursive gestures). See Table 2 for details.

After training with the coding system, the author and a research assistant independently coded the set of 189 gestures identified in Step 1. Cohen's Kappa for our identification of gesture function was moderate at .59. Discrepancies were resolved through subsequent discussion, resulting in agreement in categorizing 28 gestures as C, 32 as A, and 129 as O.

For the experiment to follow, the stimuli were restricted to the A and O gestures (and/or the accompanying phrases, as described below). There were several reasons for this. One is that many of the C gestures in the data set were deictic (pointing) gestures. As is clear from Kita (2003), pointing gestures have unique properties and so deserve special treatment.

Therefore, concrete referential gestures have been studied separately (Cienki 2005) for comparison with the experiment reported below. Indeed, while something is already known about such gestures ("iconic" as per McNeill's terminology), in relation to their communicative ability (cf. Beattie and Shovelton 1999, 2001), abstract referential gestures have (arguably) received less attention in the recent gesture literature. This is due, in part, to the research tradition of studying the gestures of speakers retelling the story of a cartoon or film they have just viewed. Such studies are necessarily biased toward concrete referential uses of gesture. A third, practical reason is that, due to logistical and time limitations, it was only feasible to compare a substantive number (20) of two different types of gestures (so, 40 in total) and their accompanying phrases in this experiment.

Table 2. The classification of gestures used, adapted from Müller (1998: 113)

Concrete reference [C]	Abstract reference [A]	Other [O]
• Objects (e.g., a picture frame)	• Entities (e.g., the frame-work of a theory)	• Actions (e.g., dismissing, requesting, swearing, hand clapping)
• Properties (e.g., the straight edge of a ruler)	• Properties (e.g., honesty as straight and solid)	• Emphasis (e.g., through beats)
• Behaviors and Actions (e.g., the rolling of a tire)	• Behaviors and Actions (e.g., the "rolling" de-velopment of a process)	• Structuring (e.g., with counting gestures)
• Relative location (e.g., the space behind oneself)	• Relative location and relative time (e.g., the past as behind oneself)	• Presenting (an idea or argument)

2.3 Materials and experimental conditions

Twenty of the A gestures and 20 of the O gestures were randomly selected for use in the experiment. The videos, which were in QuickTime format, were edited to produce individual clips of the gestures selected, each clip lasting only one to two seconds. The written transcription of the speech accompanying each gesture was also noted for each clip. The relevant transcribed utterances will be referred to as "phrases" below; most were noun phrases or verb phrases, but a few consisted of only one word.

There were four experimental conditions, as follows.

Condition 1: viewing 40 gesture clips (no sound and no transcript).
Condition 2: viewing 40 gesture clips with sound and reading transcription of the accompanying speech.
Condition 3: hearing the 40 phrases uttered on the clips and reading transcription of them (no video).
Condition 4: reading transcription of the 40 phrases uttered (no video and no sound).

The different conditions were used to distinguish differences in the interpretation of the visual cues of gesture, aural cues of prosodic features of speech, and semantic cues of the utterances themselves. Specifically, conditions 3 and 4 were used as controls to establish what was being interpreted based on gesture, and what based on the verbal utterances.[4] In each condition the "A" and "O" stimuli, be they gestures or verbal phrases, were mixed in random order, and multiple orders were used within each condition to counterbalance.

2.4 Participants

Eighty Emory University undergraduate students, 20 for each condition, participated for introductory psychology course credit. All were native speakers of American English.

2.5 Procedure

For conditions 1 and 2, the video clips of the gestures were projected from a laptop computer onto a screen with a data projector. For conditions 2 and 3 (with sound), the audio of the spoken phrases was amplified with

4. In condition 2, the written transcription of the utterances was provided because the sound was not of high enough quality on all of the clips to discern what was being said.

speakers. Each clip was played approximately four times. The stimuli were presented to participants in small groups, but each participant completed his/her own score sheet independently without consultation with the others.

The scoring sheet for conditions 1 and 2 began with the following instructions:

> You will view a series of 40 video clips, each 1-2 second long. Each clip shows a person making a hand gesture. You will view each clip four times, after which you should circle one word from those given which you think best characterizes the form of the gesture. You may think some examples could be characterized by more than one of the choices given, but just pick the one that fits the best.

The instructions for condition 3 were altered appropriately to say "You will hear a series of phrases recorded from conversations," and in condition 4: "You will read a series of phrases transcribed from conversations." In both conditions 3 and 4, the task given was to circle the word which "best characterizes the phrase." In conditions 1, 2, and 3, the presentation of the video and/or audio stimuli controlled the pace of the procedure. Since condition 4 did not involve the presentation of video or audio stimuli, each stimulus phrase was written on a separate slip of paper followed by the seven descriptors, and the 40 slips of paper were stapled together as a packet. This was designed to focus the participants' attention on the individual phrases, just as participants' attention was focussed on the individual stimulus clips in the other conditions by being exposed to each one several times.

Finally, the instructions included a listing and brief explanation of the descriptors which would be provided (the names of the image schemas plus "other"). Six image schemas were used from the list of 27 presented in Johnson (1987). Since the image schemas in Johnson's list vary greatly in character – ranging from the very general level, such as PROCESS, to the very detailed, such as RESTRAINT REMOVAL – the ones chosen were at an intermediate level of specificity. The logic here is that this would lessen the attention to degree of specificity as a factor for selecting one image schema over another, and instead leave the focus on the form/nature of the image schema itself. Also for this reason, the various kinds of forces which Johnson discusses were represented here simply as FORCE because, as he notes, they share so many properties separate from their directionality, and thus FORCE constitutes a gestalt structure (Johnson 1987: 44).

The descriptors were introduced with the wording: "Here are ways to think about the words which will be used," and each was explained and exemplified in non-technical terms, as shown in Table 3.

Table 3. Description of image schemas used in the experiment

container	A container has a boundary that separates an inside from an outside. It can hold things. We can be contained (for example, in a room), and our own bodies are containers.
cycle	A cycle begins, proceeds through a sequence of connected events, and returns to the original state to start anew. We experience cycles through time in nature and in our lives.
force	Force usually implies the exertion of physical strength in one or more directions. We can experience force in terms of compulsion, attraction, blockage, or enablement.
object	An object is a material thing which we can see and feel. We may think of an object as a discrete item.
path	A path is a route for moving from a starting point to an end point. We can follow an existing path, or make a path with our own movement.
other	If none of the words above seems appropriate, circle "other" and write in a word of your own choosing which you think best describes the gesture.

The word "other" was accompanied by a blank to give participants the option of writing in their own choice of a descriptor, independent of the image-schema options provided. The descriptors were listed in random order for each clip/phrase. After going through the procedure, participants filled out a brief background questionnaire, and then were debriefed about the experiment.

2.6 Results

The responses were tallied and analyzed in the following ways. The frequency of use of the "other" category was first assessed as a measure of how strongly or weakly a given gesture clip or transcribed phrase evoked a schema. Then I examined the consistency with which the favored image schema was used as a descriptor for each gesture or phrase across participants. The amount of agreement in the choice of descriptor was then compared within and across the categories of stimulus medium (gesture versus transcribed phrase). Finally, the results from the A versus O stimuli were compared across conditions for any significant differences according to several different measures.

First, the response category labelled "other" was seldom used in any of the conditions. It was never the descriptor which received the most responses for any stimulus, and in fact the mean response for this category was consistently below 1 (Mean = .93, Standard Deviation = 1.07 for condition 1; M = .55, SD = 0.75 for condition 2; M = .76, SD = 0.70 for condition 3; M = .13, SD = 0.33 for condition 4). Given that for each gesture viewed or phrase heard/ read there were seven choices (six image schemas and an "other" category), the probability of selecting any individual descriptor given random responding would be 14% (1/7 choices). But this descriptor was consistently chosen at below chance rates, t scores (39) = 11.40 for condition 1, 19.47 for condition 2, 18.88 for condition 3, and 51.59 for condition 4, p-values < .001. This is an initial indication that the participants were receptive to using image schemas as possible descriptors for the gestures and phrases.

The data were then examined to ascertain how much agreement there was among participants in classifying the gestures without and with sound (conditions 1 and 2), and the phrases with and without sound (conditions 3 and 4), using image schemas as descriptors. In each condition, I calculated the number of individuals who classified the gesture or phrase into its most frequent image schema category for each item in each condition. Beginning with the gesture analyses (conditions 1 and 2): while almost all of the stimuli elicited some variable responding, the data revealed that participants selected image schemas as descriptors with more consistency than would be predicted by chance in both conditions, without and with sound (M = 9.5, SD = 3.23 for video alone, in condition 1; M = 9.3, SD = 2.69 for video with sound and transcript, in condition 2). Considering the categorization of the transcribed phrases, here too participants chose image schemas as descriptors more consistently than would be predicted by chance, both with and without sound (M = 8.6, SD = 2.49 for transcript and sound, in condition 3; Mean = 8.7, SD = 2.47 for transcript alone, in condition 4). The four types of stimuli elicited consistent responding at above chance rates, t-scores (39) = 13.02 for condition 1, 15.19 for condition 2, 14.52 for condition 3, and 14.86 for condition 4, p-values < .001. On the whole, there is reliable agreement about what schema each gesture or phrase is evoking, at least within any given condition of presentation.

The results for conditions 3 and 4 may appear problematic, given that these conditions were meant to serve as controls. However, the question arises: was the same schema being chosen to characterize a gesture as was used to characterize the phrase that accompanied it? A closer look at the responses reveals that this is often not the case. For example, in one clip one of the speakers says "you can learn more that way sometimes." In conditions 3 and 4, where just the phrase was given, 11 out of 20 participants in each condition selected PATH as the descriptor. However, in each of conditions 1 and 2, in which participants viewed the gesture, 17 out of 20 chose CYCLE. This is because the speaker makes a gesture with his two index fingers extended towards each other and revolving around each other as his hands move toward himself, as if depicting a rolling ball. While this was salient to participants in conditions 1 and 2, those in conditions 3 and 4 only had the accompanying phrase to rely on, and perhaps were influenced by the use of the word "way," or the notion of learning process as metaphorical motion along a path. To compare the amount of agreement versus disagreement on the image schema chosen most frequently as the descriptor, a series of Fisher's exact tests were performed across pairs of the conditions. Given the variable factors of medium (gesture versus transcribed phrase), sound (with or without), and video (viewing the gesture or not), the only comparison yielding a significant result was between conditions 1 and 2 as a group and conditions 3 and 4 as a group: this revealed higher agreement within media (gesture versus transcript) than between media (Fisher's p=.02).

Finally, we will consider the factor of gesture function. Was one group of gestures (A or O) easier to characterize in terms of image schemas than the other? Did the same hold true for the phrases affiliated with them? If we look at the results in condition 1, divided according to A and O gestures, and compare the mean number of most frequent responses for each group, a two-sample t-test shows significantly more agreement in categorizing the A gestures without sound than the O gestures: M = 10.5, SD = 3.28 for A gestures; M = 8.5, SD = 2.91 for O gestures, t (38) = 2.04, p = .05. A comparison of the gestures shown with sound (condition 2) shows only marginally more agreement for the A gestures than for the O gestures: M = 10.0, SD = 2.74 for A gestures; M = 8.7, SD = 2.56 for O gestures, t (38) = 1.49, p = .07. Comparisons of the mean most frequent responses for the phrases that accompanied the A and O gestures (conditions 3 and 4) do not reveal any significant differences (p's > .05).

Another way to examine the consistency of image-schema classifications was to determine how many image schemas were used at least once by the 20 participants per stimulus within each of the two groupings (A versus O) in each condition. A significantly lower number of image schemas used for one group would indicate more reliable agreement about image schemas as descriptors for that group. T-tests comparing the responses for the two groups in each condition only showed a significant difference in condition 2, where for the gestures with sound a significantly higher number of schemas was used for O gestures then A gestures, indicating more agreement on the characterization of the A gestures: M = 5.0, SD = 1.05 for A gestures; Mean = 5.7, SD = 0.81 for O gestures at this threshold of use at least once, t (38) = 2.36, p = .02.

An additional test considered the number of stimuli in each group for which all seven categories were selected as descriptors at least once. A lower number of such clips in a group would point to greater agreement about the image-schema descriptors for those gestures/phrases, since participants would have settled on a smaller number of appropriate image schemas for each of them. Significant differences were found only in conditions 1 and 3. Whereas seven of the O gestures without sound (condition 1) elicited responses for all seven descriptors, only one of the A gestures did so. This difference was found to be significant, p=.02, using Fisher's exact test, again indicating greater agreement in characterizing A gestures. With three of the O gestures and two of the A gestures with sound in condition 2 eliciting responses for all seven descriptors, the difference was not significant. Surprisingly, in a pattern comparable to condition 1, ten of the phrases with sound (condition 3) that had co-occurred with O gestures garnered responses for all seven descriptors, while only three of the phrases from A gestures did. This difference was also significant at Fisher's p =.02, showing greater agreement in characterizing phrases with sound that accompanied A gestures than O gestures. However, only one A phrase and one O phrase without sound were characterized using all seven categories in condition 4. In no condition were the O gestures or affiliated phrases characterized with greater agreement than the As in any of the conditions, according to this measure. The results of the three tests comparing A and O stimuli, described above, are summarized in Table 4:

Table 4. Type of stimuli (A, O, or neither —) in conditions 1 to 4 categorized
more reliably by means of image schemas
(A* = marginally more reliable than O)

Conditions	1 (gesture)	2 (gesture + sound)	3 (phrase + sound)	4 (phrase)
Mean # of image schemas chosen	A	A*	—	—
Fewer image schemas used at least once	—	A	—	—
All 7 descriptors used with fewer stimuli	A	—	A	—

Finally, a 3 x 2 analysis of variance (ANOVA: Medium [*gesture* versus *transcript*] x Sound [*on* versus *off*] x Condition [*Abstract* versus *Other*]) was performed with Condition as the between-subjects factor (with the individual clips serving as the subjects) and Medium and Sound as within-subjects variables. While there were no overall main effects, there was a marginally significant three-way interaction of Medium by Sound by Condition, $F (1, 38) = 4.04$, $p = .052$. A post-hoc analysis using Tukey's honestly significant difference (HSD) found that there was a higher consensus for characterizing the A gestures without sound (from condition 1) than the A phrases (transcripts) without sound (condition 4). This was not true for the A gestures versus A phrases with sound, or for any comparisons between the O gestures and phrases.

3.   Discussion

3.1   Interpreting the present results

One general conclusion we can draw from these findings is that gestures provide easily accessible manifestations of image schemas. As commonly recurring dynamic patterns of our perceptual experience and motor programs (Johnson 1987), image schemas are readily available, indeed "on hand," for recruitment as gestural forms. The ease with which many image schemas can be represented in gesture, either as static entities or dynamic processes, reinforces the motivation for the connection. For example, PATH can be indicated with one's forearm and hand outstretched, or by moving one's hand in a line and tracing a path; SURFACE can be gestured with a flat hand, held in position, open and tense, or by sweeping a flat hand through space, tracing a surface.

A second basic finding is that gestures can depict, or invoke, different schemas than speech alone can. This suggests one way in which they can make more information manifest and available to discourse participants. One case in point discussed earlier concerned the different characterizations of a gesture (index fingers rotating as if showing a rolling ball) and the co-occuring speech ("you can learn more that way sometimes") as CYCLE and PATH, respectively. In this instance there was majority agreement among respondents (over 50%) in characterizing both types of stimuli with the respective different image schemas. However, in some cases, there was high agreement in characterizing the gesture, but not the phrase uttered, or vice versa. So in one clip the speaker said, "So in general on a regular test," and the highest number of responses in the transcript-only condition was 5 out of 20, and this occurred for two image schemas, CONTAINER and OBJECT. Similarly, in the transcript plus audio condition, the highest number of responses was five, and again two image schemas were selected this often this time, CONTAINER and CYCLE. In the gesture which accompanied this phrase, the speaker put both of her hands out in front of her, flat and palms down, and moved them simultaneously outwards laterally. The majority of participants in both of the gesture-viewing conditions chose SURFACE as the best characterization (16 in the gesture-only condition, and 12 in the gesture plus sound condition). The reverse pattern was sometimes found as well. In a clip in which the speaker said "to put in," there was high agreement in the transcript conditions (14 responses for CONTAINER in both conditions 3 and 4). The accompanying gesture involved a simple movement of both the speaker's loosely opened hands, beginning with her palms facing her torso and moving outward to a palm-up orientation. In the gesture plus speech condition, only six participants characterized this with CONTAINER, and in the gesture-only condition, five chose CONTAINER and five chose FORCE. These findings for A and O gestures show that gestures can convey additional information to what is said, at least some of the time, and so they complement Beattie and Shovelton's (1999) conclusions from research based on the study of concrete referential gestures.

Each condition tested for the present paper showed significant results in the use of image schemas as descriptors, but the latter analyses in the

Results section revealed more agreement in the categorization of A gestures than O gestures, both without and with sound. The data suggest that the A gestures may have a more easily imageable schematic form than the O gestures. The question is whether *abstract* referential gestures constitute a special category, or whether it is simply the referential nature of the gestures that allows them to be more readily characterized in terms of image schemas. Findings from a follow-up study (Cienki 2005) indicate that concrete referential gestures from the same set of conversations were also reliably categorized using the same set of image schemas as descriptors. This suggests that referential gestures overall (both abstract and concrete) are more specifically imageable in their form than the other types of gestures ("O" gestures).

The fact that participants were able to reliably interpret the gestures in terms of image schemas may have implications for the research on thinking for speaking. McNeill and Duncan (2000) incorporate Slobin's (1987) idea of thinking-for-speaking in terms of a growth-point model, which characterizes the development and verbal expression of an idea as the "unpacking" of a unit which combines both imagery and linguistic content. While the present experiment looked at how gestures and language could be *interpreted* in terms of image schemas, the findings suggest the potential relevance of image schemas (or at least these kinds of schematic patterns) in the *formulation* of concepts for speech. For example, I would suggest that using the schematic structures provided by image schemas in thinking-for-speaking should involve less conscious effort and attention than using more complex, detailed spatial images. Therefore, the gestural production of image-schematic forms would have to involve less conscious attention than the production of more elaborate hand shapes and movements. The kinds of gestures studied here – spontaneously produced co-verbal gestures – are what McNeill (1992: 72) has characterized as "unwitting accompaniments of speech." Therefore, there is a natural motivation for why the majority of the gestures studied in these conversations (A and O types) could, on the whole, be reliably characterized in terms of image schemas.[5] Furthermore, the fact that gestures display patterns like these – ones that are widely shared in human experience – can help explain their communicative potential. If language provides prompts for an addressee to

---

5. On image schemas and mental imagery, see Gibbs and Berg (2002); Cienki (2002); and the other contributions in that issue of the *Journal of Mental Imagery*.

construct mental simulations of the speaker's intended meaning (Barsalou 1999), then some findings from research in neuroscience suggest a potential role for gesture in this process. Research on mirror neurons has shown that the same neurons are activated when a monkey observes an action and when the monkey performs the same action (Rizzolatti and Arbib 1998). Research with humans has shown that frontal motor cortex areas are activated not only when participants move their hands, but also when they observe other persons moving their own hands (DiPellgrino et al. 1992; Rizzolatti 1994). In other studies, it has been found that during hand action observation, but not in control conditions, there was an increase of amplitude of motor-evoked potentials recorded from hand muscles which are normally used when actually performing an action (Fadiga et al. 1995). Further research has confirmed these findings and also found that the motor-evoked potentials of the muscles were modulated in a fashion strictly resembling the time-course of the observed action (Gangitano, Mottaghy and Pascual-Leone 2001). These and related findings lend support to the argument that observation of hand movements, such as gestures, can provide a richer context for constructing the simulations prompted by the co-occurring speech. The evidence in the present study shows one way in which gestures can provide other information than the speech alone – that is, by invoking additional or other schemas in terms of which to interpret the entity, action, or relation being talked about.

3.2 Future directions

How do we reconcile the findings of these studies with what we know of the idiosyncratic nature of gesturing, namely that it is so variable across individuals, as noted by McNeill (1992)? While idiosyncratic in their execution, we can argue that (many or most) gestures have a basis in common patterns in our experience, and image schemas serve as prime examples of such patterns. Image schemas might provide common skeletal structures which underlie individuals' seemingly idiosyncratic gestures. For example, a given image schema can be manifested gesturally at different levels of complexity. Gestures thus not only reflect schematic patterns, abstracted from various domains of experience, they also instantiate them anew. Further research is needed on how commonly these patterns are shared cross-culturally; quantitative research in particular could shed light on whether some image schemas are interpreted as predominating more than others as the foundations of gesturing, within a given culture or across cultures.

Finally, let us consider the results of conditions 3 and 4, which were meant to be control conditions. How do we make sense out of why the phrases without gestures were also reliably characterized with image schemas? As scholars researching image schemas have long maintained, the semantics of various kinds of words and constructions can be analyzed in terms of image schemas, so perhaps this finding should not be surprising. Other research points to a relation between the cognitive processing of gesture and speech. For example, it has been found that the hand motor cortex is activated while simply listening to speech (Flöel et al. 2003). A question remains for the present experiment, however, as to whether there was a relation between the fact that the words/phrases could reliably be characterized with image schemas and the fact that the utterances were originally produced with gestures. This is particularly relevant for the phrases accompanying the A gestures, which, at least according to one measure reported in the Results, were categorized with greater agreement than the phrases accompanying O gestures. In future research it would be worth comparing whether phrases which were not accompanied by gestures could also be characterized reliably in terms of image schemas.

References

Barsalou, Lawrence W.
  1999   Perceptual symbol systems. *Behavioral and Brain Sciences* 22: 577-609.
Beattie, Geoffrey, and Heather Shovelton
  1999   Do iconic hand gestures really contribute anything to the semantic information conveyed by speech? An experimental investigation. *Semiotica* 123: 1-30.
  2001   An experimental investigation of the role of different types of iconic gesture in communication: A semantic feature approach. *Gesture* 1: 129-149.
Bühler, Karl
  1982   Reprint. *Sprachtheorie: Die Darstellungsfunktion der Sprache.* Stuttgart: Fischer [original publication Jena 1936]

Calbris, Geneviève
2003   From cutting an object to a clear cut analysis: Gesture as the
        representation of a preconceptual schema linking concrete actions to
        abstract notions. *Gesture* 3: 19-46.
Cienki, Alan
1997   Some properties and groupings of image schemas. In *Lexical and
        Syntactical Constructions and the Construction of Meaning*,
        Marjolijn Verspoor, Kee Dong Lee, and Eve Sweetser (eds.), 3-15.
        Amsterdam/Philadephia: John Benjamins.
2002   Questions about mental imagery, gesture, and image schemas.
        Journal of Mental Imagery 26: 43-46.
2003   Ontological metaphors prevail in gesture with speech. Presentation
        at the "8th International Cognitive Linguistics Conference," La
        Rioja, Spain, July 2003.
2005   Concrete versus abstract reference and the schematicity of gesture.
        Presentation at the "2nd International Society for Gesture Studies
        Conference," Lyon (France), June 2005.
Cienki, Alan and Cornelia Müller
In prep. Metaphor, Gesture, and Thought. In *The Cambridge Handbook of
        Metaphor and Thought*, Raymond W. Gibbs, Jr. (ed.). Cambridge:
        Cambridge University Press.
Di Pellegrino, Giacomo, Luciano Fadiga, Leonardo Foggassi, Vittorio Gallese, and
        Giacomo Rizzolatti
1992   Understanding motor events. *Experimental Brain Research* 91: 176-
        180.
Eckman, Paul and Wallace V. Friesen
1969   The repertoire of nonverbal behavior: Categories, origins, usage and
        coding. *Semiotica* 1: 49-98.
Fadiga, Luciano, Leonardo Fogassi, Giovanni Pavesi, and Giacomo Rizzolatti
1995   Motor facilitation during action observation: A magnetic stimulation
        study. *Journal of Neurophysiology* 73: 2608-2611.
Flöel, Agnes, Tanja Ellger, Caterina Breitenstein, and Stefan Knecht
2003   Language perception activates the hand motor cortex: implications
        for motor theories of speech perception. *European Journal of
        Neuroscience* 18: 704-708.
Gangitano, Massimo, Felix M. Mottaghy, and Alvaro Pascual-Leone
2001   Phase-specific modulation of cortical motor output during
        movement observation. *Neuroreport* 12: 1489-1492.
Gibbs, Raymond W., Jr., and Eric A. Berg
2002   Mental imagery and embodied activity. *Journal of Mental Imagery*
        26: 1-30.

Johnson, Mark
  1987   *The Body in the Mind: The Bodily Basis of Meaning, Imagination, and Reason.* Chicago: University of Chicago Press.
Kendon, Adam
  2004   *Gesture: Visible Action as Utterance.* Cambridge: Cambridge University Press.
Kita, Sotaro
  2000   How representational gestures help speaking. In *Language and Gesture*, David McNeill (ed.), 162-185. Cambridge: Cambridge University Press.
Kita, Sotaro (ed.)
  2003   *Pointing: Where Language, Culture, and Cognition Meet.* Mahwah: Lawrence Erlbaum Associates.
Lakoff, George
  1987   *Women, Fire, and Dangerous Things: What Categories Reveal about the Mind.* Chicago: University of Chicago Press.
McNeill, David
  1985   So you think gestures are nonverbal? *Psychological Review* 92: 350-371.
  1992   *Hand and Mind: What Gestures Reveal about Thought.* Chicago: University of Chicago Press.
McNeill, David, and Susan Duncan
  2000   Growth points in thinking-for-speaking. In *Language and Gesture*, David McNeill (ed.), 141-161. Cambridge: Cambridge University Press.
Müller, Cornelia
  1998   *Redebegleitende Gesten: Kulturgeschichte – Theorie – Sprachvergleich.* Berlin: Berlin Verlag Arno Spitz.
Rizzolatti, Giacomo
  1994   Nonconscious motor images. *Behavioral and Brain Sciences* 17: 220.
Rizzolatti, Giacomo, and Michael Arbib
  1998   Language within our grasp. *Trends in Neurosciences* 21: 188-194.
Slobin, Dan I.
  1987   Thinking for speaking. *Berkeley Linguistics Society* 13: 435-445.
Taub, Sarah F.
  2001   *Language from the Body: Iconicity and Metaphor in American Sign Language.* Cambridge: Cambridge University Press.

Force-dynamic dimensions of rhetorical effect

*Todd Oakley**

Abstract

This essay in Applied Cognitive Rhetoric seeks to establish a renewed connection between Cognitive Semantics and rhetorical theory at the level of textual analysis. Despite Turner's (1991) famous early initiative, sustained cognitive rhetorical analysis of canonical rhetorical texts has been rare in Cognitive Linguistics. In this essay, Talmy's (2000) system of Force Dynamics and Event Frames is applied to two paragon rhetorical texts: the Preamble to President Bush's *National Security Report* and Abraham Lincoln's *Second Innaugural Address*, the first an example of the deliberative genre, the second an example of the epideictic one. Besides a brief discussion of the rhetorical situations to which these two texts were responding, and an overview of Talmy's relevant work, the essay offers a detailed analysis of the force-dynamic patterns and supporting event frames inherent in each text in order to reveal how these image-schematic patterns shape the logic and emotion of each argument.

Keywords: force dynamics, event frames, Cognitive Semantics, Cognitive Rhetoric, inaugural addresses, National Security Strategy Report

1. Introduction

Nearly a year after the attacks on the World Trade Center in New York, the Bush administration released the *National Security Strategy of the United States of America*. Since passage of the Goldwater-Nichols Act in 1986, presidents are required to submit to Congress and the public a National Strategy Report outlining the sitting administration's mid- and long-term national security strategy. These texts are usually ignored by the public and press, but the Bush administration's policy paper enjoyed unprecedented scrutiny not only because of its temporal proximity to September 11, 2001, but because it was the first official word on what has become known as the

* I would like to thank Greta Dishong, Beate Hampe and the two anonymous reviewers for their valuable insights and advice.

"Bush Doctrine" of pre-emptive warfare. Such papers constitute what Aristotle termed *Deliberative Rhetoric*, speeches or addresses contemplating future action based on ethical principles of the greater good – such as happiness, virtues of the soul and body, wealth, friendship, and honor – and principles of expediency in finance, war and peace, national defense, trade, and law. Shortly thereafter, on October 11, 2002, the Senate authorized President Bush, Commander-in-Chief, to wage war against Iraq.

Nearly 137 years earlier on March 4, 1865, Abraham Lincoln delivered his Second Inaugural Address in Washington, D.C., the text of which was printed and commented upon in newspapers throughout the Union and then Confederacy. At the time of his second address, Lincoln was presiding over the bloodiest and most costly war in American history, with some 623,000 casualties (White 2002: 23). With General Sherman's march on Atlanta all but assuring the Union's victory over the Confederacy, Lincoln won a second term in office. Presidential inaugural addresses are peculiar manifestations of *Epideictic Rhetoric*, speeches or addresses delivered on ceremonial occasions (in this case, the investiture of political power). In the words of Campbell and Jamieson, inaugural addresses

> ... fuse past and future in present contemplation, affirm or praise shared principles ... and employ elegant, literary language ... reaffirming what is already known and believed. (Campbell and Jamieson 1986: 204)

One of the most important rhetorical tasks of an inaugural address is to "reconstitute" the citizens recently divided over its national political contest into "We, the People" through a rehearsal of shared values and political principles. Perhaps no other time in American history had the need for reconstituting the public been more apparent, for the people of the North were feeling triumphant and vengeful, and the people of the South were feeling defeated and vengeful. Lincoln's address is the shortest inaugural, only four paragraphs long, but now regarded by many political historians as the greatest speech delivered by the United States' greatest president. Forty days later, on April 14, 1865, Lincoln was assassinated.

These two texts, so starkly different, comprise the objects of analysis in the present essay. Although many contemporary discourse theorists (including myself) consider any text "rhetorical" and thus under the purview of rhetorical theories and methods, I have decided to focus on prototypical examples of "persuasive discourse" for two reasons. First, to avoid needless controversy about the scope of rhetoric, as no reader here would fail to see both texts as rhetorical. Second, and more importantly, each text makes the world conform to its words; that is, each speaker orchestrates modes of reasoning and argument, exercises stylistic options and employs modes of amplification in order to make things happen or not happen in the future. Sustained analysis of high-stakes rhetorical discourse from an image-schematic perspective is a worthy starting point for developing a closer correspondence between Cognitive Semantics (as exemplified by the work of Ronald Langacker and Leonard Talmy), which seeks to understand how we conceptualize, imagine, and reason, and rhetorical theory, which seeks to understand how we conceptualize, imagine, and reason in particular situations.

Rhetoric, to quote the modern-day heirs of Aristotle, Chaïm Perelman and Lucie Olbrechts-Tyteca ([1958] 1969: 4), "is the study of the discursive techniques allowing us to *induce or to increase the mind's adherence to the theses presented for its assent*". For these authors its seems, rhetoric is a conceptual enterprise in which speakers and writers construe a past, present, future, or otherwise imagined situation in the hope that other minds (i.e., audiences) will construe them in a sufficiently similar way, such that discourse participants come to share a common perspective, and even a common mode of action.

Perelman and Olbrechts-Tyteca's treatise presents an exhaustive description of the modes of practical reasoning that serves as an indispensable guide for contemporary rhetorical theorists. However, their theory assumes that we are capable of conceptualization and reasoning without ever trying to account for how we are so capable. Cognitive Semantics offers a useful framework for rhetorical theory and analysis. Turner's (1991: 99-120) discussion of "the poetry of argument" comprises perhaps the first instance of a Cognitive Semantics understanding of rhetorical engagement. He shows how Western mental models of persuasion depend on the notion of image schemas. Turner, however, presents a broad-brush argument that image schemas inhere in the very "logic of situations" we call "rhetorical", but illustrates his points through isolated examples rather than with sustained rhetorical analysis. This essay complements Turner's initial project by offering a sustained analysis of two texts.

Cognitive Semanticists presume that language structure, acquisition, and use emerge from general conceptual systems grounded in our everyday bodily experience. Such systems include, according to Talmy (2000: 1-18), static and dynamic cognitive processes associated with event structures, spatial orientation, motion, foregrounding and backgrounding, as well as force and causation. More specifically, the analytic perspective adopted here is that rhetoric is a tradition of thinking about human reasoning consistent with Johnson's (1987, *this volume*) view that reasoning itself depends on a basic set of image schemas, "patterned, embodied interactions that are at once structural, qualitative, and dynamic". Mandler (2004: 81) provides another useful definition of image schema as "a representation one is left with when one has forgotten most of the details of an event".

Since Cognitive Semanticists have posited many different image schemas, it is useful to narrow the field somewhat. For the purposes of this essay, I am going to focus on two classes of image-schematic structure, both described in detail in Talmy (2000: 257-309/409-470, *this volume*): *event frames* and, more prominently, *force dynamics*. Talmy never uses the term "image schema", but (in his study of closed-class items) treats force dynamics as schematic systems that emerge from the structure and shape of sensory-motor experiences. He further regards these schematic systems as topological, a view consistent with the definitions of image schema stated above. What is more, Johnson (1987: 41-64) explicitly identifies "preconceptual gestalts for force" as image schemas.

Turner's (1991) account of the image-schematic structure of the rhetorical enterprise particularly relies on force dynamics. Basic notions of oppositional force, equilibrium and balance, and the consequences of strengthening or weakening "one-side" of an argument against another are fundamental concepts elaborated on by Classical rhetorical theorists and showing up most explicitly in the concept of *stasis*, as first articulated in Hellenistic and Roman handbook traditions. Following Dieter (1950), Turner argues that the origins of stasis theory is directly traceable to Aristotle's physics, which, in turn, is based on intuitive notions of our sentient bodies interacting with other bodies in a world of forces and counterforces. Such a condition produces what Turner (1991: 120) calls "the rhetoric of everyday life". The notion that the very concept of argument is force-dynamically structured receives tacit support from Cicero and Quintilian, each of whom specifies one function of rhetoric as "to move" (*movere*) and "to bend" (*flectere*).

My purpose in this essay is to develop further a cognitive semantic mode of sustained rhetorical analysis with an emphasis on force dynamics and event frames as a necessary (but not sufficient) means of persuasion. This essay is only a modest starting point for a cognitive theory of rhetoric yet to be developed, and takes its place alongside Dishong (2004) as one of the first applications of force-dynamic image schemas in rhetorical analysis and criticism. It seeks to account only for the local force-dynamic dimensions of lexical and grammatical structures as they appear in well-established deliberative and epideictic contexts. The stable genre conventions of government policy papers and inaugural addresses occasion reasonable speculation about the global rhetorical effects of these force-dynamic modes of expression. Missing from this analysis is the critical "middle layers" of analysis linking the schematic systems with rich conceptual structure (e.g., metaphors, metonymies, nonce categories, etc.).[1] Modest though the scope of the present essay may be, a "topology-of-argument" account should nevertheless be of interest to those interested in cognitive rhetorical analysis.

Following two brief overviews of force dynamics and event frames as schematic structuring systems, and of rhetorical theory and its relation to Cognitive Semantics, respectively, I examine in detail the Preamble to the Bush administration's *National Security Strategy* report and Lincoln's *Second Inaugural Address* to show how the force-dynamic schematic system guides meaning construction.

2.   Event frames and force dynamics in Cognitive Semantics

Providing arrangements of conceptual elements and their interrelationships, event frames are central to language comprehension and use, thus allowing language users to evoke elements together that are relevant while conceiving of other evoked elements as incidental or irrelevant. Talmy (2000: 259-262) identifies five generic event frames: *Interrelationship*, *Cycle*, *Participant Interaction*, *Causal Chain* and *Object's Path*. All five, but especially the final two, comprise conceptual material for structuring the expression of force-dynamic relationships, and, incidentally, at least two of the five (Cycle and Object's Path) bear close resemblance to items appearing on Johnson's list of image schemas (1987: 126).

With the event frame for *objects' path*, which always plays a structuring role in encoding force-dynamic relations, we have a conceived path on which an object moves. This path can be demarcated in terms of periods of stasis followed by periods of motion or by "path singularities," such as abrupt directional shifts or continuous changes in the setting or surroundings. With the event frame for *Causal Chain*, the conceived entity of a causal chain can be demarcated to include the agent's initiating act as well as the final goal or

---

1. Within the allotted space of one chapter, these intermediate "layers" cannot be accounted for, as this would require the importation of a variety of theoretical entities, such as mental spaces (Fauconnier and Turner 2002), perceptual symbols and simulators (Barsalou 1999), semantic domains (Brandt 2003) and specific argumentative techniques (Perelman and Olbrechts-Tyteca 1969).

result so initiated. In such cases, the act or and goal represent the entirety of the agent's "scope of intention" (Johnson 1987: 260). With the event frame for *Participant Interaction*, we conceive of two distinct events as occurring against a situation within a demarcated temporal expanse. With the event frame for *Cycle* (also an image schema in Johnson 1987), an entity is demarcated spatially by two points and temporally by two congruent occurrences. Each point is conceptualized as a spatially and temporally distinct phase. With the event frame for *Interrelationship*, two or more component elements entail each other, conceived as a complementary relationship (in the case of only two) or conceived as juxtaposed alternative conceptualizations (in cases of more than two).

Cognitive Semantics (cf. Talmy 2000: 265-299) holds that these event frames structure language comprehension and use by profiling particular entities and relations within those frames.[2] Thus, constructions can entail a cyclical event frame that profiles a departure phase (1a), or profiles the return phase (1b), or both (1c):

(1) a.   I kept dropping my fork on the floor during dinner.
     b.   I kept having to pick up my fork during dinner.
     c.   I kept dropping and picking up my fork during dinner.

Constructions can entail a participant interaction event frame that profiles an interaction referred to but gaps the speaker's present interaction frame (2a), or profiles both the present and displaced interactions (2b):[3]

(2) a.   A friend made me talk with a woman at the party last week. Her name was Candice.
     b.   A friend made me talk with a woman at the party last week. Her name is Candice.

Constructions can entail a causal chain event frame that profiles the agent's full intentionality (3a) or profiles only the intermediary sub-events in favor of the final result (3b)

---

2. I will use Langacker's (1987: 118) term "profiling" instead of Talmy's equivalent term "windowing", but keep Talmy's counterpoint term "gapping" when referring to acts of suppressing or de-emphasizing specific elements.
3. Talmy's participant interaction frame has much in common with Langacker's "grounding", insofar as tense marking grounds a clause relative to a speech event (1999: 218-222).

(3)   a.   Distraught over the accidental death of his daughter by a drunk driver, John took a rock and smashed every window of the offender's new car.

        b.   John smashed the windows of the offender's new car.

Constructions can entail an interrelationship event frame that profiles the entire figure-ground relationship (4a), or only the figure (4b), or only the ground (4c):[4]

(4)   a.   The paper is peeling off the wall
        b.   The paper is peeling
        c.   The wall is peeling

Finally, constructions can entail an object's path event frame that profiles the entire region demarcated by the path (5a). Alternatively, constructions can profile only a small portion of an object's path, such as an endpoint (5b):

(5)   a.   I hit a ground ball past the pitcher's mound, through the hands of the short stop and into center-left field, stopping at the wall
        b.   The ball continued rolling until it hit the wall

At a slightly higher level of complexity is the schematic system of force-dynamic relations, to which I now turn. Image-schematic patterns of force and counterforce comprise a basic conceptual system of language. Without it, human beings would not be able to express complex relationships and reason about relations and events. According to Talmy (2000: 209), the *Force-dynamic System* is a fundamental semantic category that allows us to think and talk about events and relations in the physical domain as well as in the epistemic and social domains. In short, force-dynamic patterns constitute an important part of human ontology, both individual and social.

Talmy's Force-dynamic System has the virtue of offering precise analytic procedures for getting at the closed- and open-class semantics of linguistic constructions. His system, therefore, offers a method of understanding the lexical and grammatical aspects of meaning construction. At the same time, its intuitive ontological status connects the microdynamic aspects that concern linguists, with the discursive acts that concern rhetoricians.

The basic elements and patterns of force dynamics are as follows: Two opposing entities comprise focal actors in an event frame configuration. One

---

4. Example (4c) exemplifies Langacker's "reference-point reasoning" (1999: 171-202), with the explicit reference point gaining salience as the trajector, as opposed to remaining covert in (4b) and overt as part of the landmark in (4a).

entity is singled out for focal attention and is the *Agonist* (AGO). The central issue is whether the AGO is able to manifest its intrinsic force tendency – either toward motion or stasis, action or inaction – or is overcome, blocked, or compelled by a second force entity, called the *Antagonist* (ANT). This entity comes into play for the effect it has on the first, thus evoking mental scenarios of causing, hindering, and letting, as the most prevalent steady-state patterns. The force exhibited by the AGO may be constant or momentary, but in either case, the force characteristic is intrinsic not extrinsic, a point that has deep implications for rhetorical analysis. Force-dynamic patterns draw attention to the interrelational or interactional nature of AGO versus ANT, such that one entity entails the presence of the other and is always comparatively construed, overtly or covertly, as weaker or stronger.

Talmy (2000: 413-417) identifies four steady-state patterns. First is the *Causative* pattern, with a weaker AGO manifesting a tendency toward rest but is compelled by a stronger ANT, resulting in motion or action (6a,b). Second is the *Weak Despite* pattern, with the stronger AGO manifesting a tendency toward stasis or inaction. The weaker ANT exerts force against the AGO to no avail, resulting in stasis or inaction (7a,b). Third is the *Strong Despite* pattern, with the stronger AGO manifesting a tendency toward motion as set against the weaker resistance of the ANT, resulting in motion or action. In this pattern, the ANT fails to block AGO (8a,b). Fourth is the *Causative Hindrance* pattern, with the weaker AGO manifesting a tendency toward motion as set against a stronger ANT, resulting in stasis or inaction (9a,b):

(6) a. Tiger's putt made the ball roll past the hole.
     b. Poor nations keep growing their economies with the help of free trade.

(7) a. The shed kept standing despite the gale-force winds.
     b. Baghdad keeps standing despite the US bombing it.

(8) a. The ball kept rolling despite the wet grass on the 17th green.
     b. International terrorists always find ways to evade Homeland Security Officials.

(9) a. The ball stayed on the slop because of the stiff grass.
     b. International terrorists continue to be stopped at our borders.

In addition to the four steady state patterns, Talmy (2000: 417-420) identifies shifting patterns and secondary steady-state patterns, profiling change through time or duration. The first pattern is *Shifting Impingement*, with the AGO made to change from stasis or inaction to motion or action, thus profiling onset causation (10a,b). The second pattern is *Balance of Strength*, with the AGO and ANT engaging in mutual impingement, but with the balance of forces shifting as one entity weakens or strengthens. For each impingement shift there is a corresponding balance shift (11a,b).

(10) a. The putter's hitting it made the ball roll passed the hole.
  b. The Confederate's attack on Fort Sumter made the Union declare war on the Southern States.

(11) a. The twenty-five foot high waves of Lake Superior overwhelmed the Edmund Fitzgerald.
  b. US Special Forces eventually overcame Iraqi resistance to the occupation.

Secondary steady-state patterns construe a force-dynamic situation in which a stronger ANT continues to be disengaged from a weaker AGO, thus allowing the AGO to manifest its intrinsic force tendency, only this time over an extended period of time. Talmy calls this pattern *Extended Letting*. Causing involves positive impingement, whereas letting involves non-impingement. *Onset Letting* correlates with the cessation of impingement (12a,b) and extended letting with its non-occurrence (13a,b)

(12) a. The plug's coming loose let the water drain from the tank.
  b. Terrorist attacks on 9/11 permitted the President to deploy troops in Afghanistan.

(13) a. The plug's staying loose let the water drain from the tank.
  b. Americans being fearful let the President deploy troops in Afghanistan and Iraq.

As these and other examples should make clear, force-dynamic patterns extend from the domain of physical reference to social reference. They also extend to the domain of psychological reference, as one can speak of a self divided (14)[5].

(14) Lincoln could not bring himself to accept the extension of American Slavery into the western territories.

Talmy (2000: 64-67) also identifies patterns of introjection and extrajection. Introjection entails dividing a single referent into separate AGO and ANT subparts, a common tactic for dramatizing internal conflict (15a). Extrajection entails integrating separate scenes into a single AGO/ANT relationship and is

---

5. See Lakoff (1996) for an in-depth discussion of divided self metaphors as they pertain to force and counterforce.

typically used for structuring abstract events not intrinsically understood in terms of force-dynamic resistance (15b).

(15)   a.   The young Confederate soldier could not bring himself to fire on his Union brother.

     b.   Lincoln took the oath of office on March 4, 1865.

The five generic event patterns are important structuring principles of force dynamics, as they provide frames in which we construe force-dynamic representations. For instance, the *object's path* event frame inheres in all force-dynamic patterns that exploit conceived patterns of mobility or stasis along a path. *Interrelationship* may come into play when we wish to construe otherwise static entities in terms of dynamic motions, as in (16a). The *causal chain* event frame is involved in any *Shift of Impingement* pattern, as it profiles the initial causal event before the force-dynamic change. The *cycle* event frame is active when construing extended patterns like *Shifting Balance of Strength* patterns, as in (16b). The *Participant Interaction* frame is active particularly in instances of social reference, as in (16c).

(16)   a.   The paint kept peeling itself all the way down the wall.

     b.   Terrorists will keep trying to bomb the building until they succeed.

     c.   The professor pushed his political agenda on his students.

Together, event frames and force-dynamic patterns comprise two very important conceptual structuring systems of language offering a useful method and perspective for interpreting the modes of reasoning in these two texts. For expository reasons, analysis will focus primarily on the realization of force-dynamic patterns and will only mention event frames when it appears important to the analysis.

3.   Rhetoric, argumentation, and construal

Talmy himself (2000: 452-455) anticipates the general application of force dynamics to the study of rhetoric and argumentation in the domain of discourse, when he suggests that languages possess a specific range of closed-class expressions and constructions for construing "argument space". As pointed out by Turner (1991: 99-120), the very notion of an argument is a force-dynamic concept, which comes conspicuously into view when we analyze the range of ARGUMENT IS WAR metaphors. According to Talmy (2000: 452), languages such as English possess force-dynamic "logic gaters" whose functions are to "limn out the rhetorical framework, to direct illocutionary flow, and to specify the logical tissue". Relevant expressions in English include *yes but, nevertheless, granted, on the contrary*, all of which can function as means of concession and refutation in discourse. Questions of the role logic-gaters play in the two object texts will be folded into the analysis as need arises rather than treated separately.

Talmy claims that force dynamics "limns out" argument space relates semantics to the rhetorical tradition. For Cognitive Semanticists, *construal* is a principal function of language, and grammars provide resources for mentally construing situations in alternative ways (cf. Langacker 1987:183-141). Rhetorical theorists, such as Perelman and Olbrechts-Tyteca, likewise focus on construal, as they place equal if not greater weight on how a speaker or writer expresses an idea or argument.

Specifically, they invoke the notion of *presence* (Perelman and Olbrechts-Tyteca 1969: 142) as a term for the effects of construal, and define it as the display of certain elements on which the speaker wishes to center attention in order that these elements may occupy the foreground of the hearer's consciousness. The idea of rhetorical presence is that isolated modes of presentation, such as individual arguments, the arrangement of discourse elements, a stylistic flourish, an apt expression, produce specific kinds of intellectual and emotional effects and evoke different rhetorical framings. Rhetorical theory has a long history of naming linguistic patterns that produce local effects.[6] Cognitive Semantics, in turn, provides a range of analytic routines for exploring the rhetorical dimensions of lexical and grammatical items with a depth and explanatory force that remains radically underdeveloped within the rhetorical tradition.[7]

3.1. Force-dynamic analysis of the Preamble to Bush's National Security Strategy

At least fifteen of the 66 sentences that comprise the Preamble signed by President Bush appear to rely on facets of the force-dynamic system for their meaning. Taken individually, each sentence analyzed below foregrounds a

---

6. Particularly through the cataloging of rhetorical figures, such a *antimetabole, climax, metaphor, metonymy, polyptoton,* etc.
7. Rhetorical theorists may note, for instance, that the auxiliary verb *keep* is doing considerable conceptual work in a given piece of discourse, but remain unable to specify its precise nature.

force-dynamic pattern operating in the physical, social, or psychological domains of reference. These effects are instrumental in presenting the current global situation in terms of good-versus-evil, with the United States government and citizenry as agents of 'the good'. The goal is to articulate a foreign policy and stance mirroring this situation.

The argument in the preamble follows an seven step trajectory: First, Bush argues for the emergence of a victorious single model for national success; second, he claims the United States' preeminent position and purpose in the world; third, he names global terrorists as the current threat to the United States and other "freedom loving" peoples; fourth, Bush discusses the means by which terrorists seek to do harm and calls on the great powers to stand united against "enemies of freedom"; fifth, he argues that the United States should "extend" the benefits of freedom across the globe; sixth, he calls on all nations as accountable and responsible for stopping terrorists and weapons proliferation; seventh, he embraces international alliance by tapping "freedom" as the ultimate defining and necessary value.[8]

An exhaustive sentence-by-sentence analysis of every force-dynamic pattern would take up too much space. Therefore, I will limit the analysis to seven instances that correlate with the seven parts of the argument just outlined. I assume the object's path event frame is at play in both literal and figurative instances of force-dynamic sentences, but that other event frames, especially participant interaction and interrelationship, are also operating behind the scenes. Assuming as much, the analysis will examine event frames other than object's path.

With the opening sentence, Bush makes this good-versus-evil axiomatic system present with reference to the recent "great struggles".[9]

[1]   The *great struggles* of the twentieth century *between liberty and totalitarianism* ended with the decisive victory for *the forces of freedom* – and a single sustainable model for national success: freedom, democracy, and free enterprise.

---

8. I will refer to Bush as the "agent of persuasion". This is licensed by the fact that "Bush" functions as Goffman's (1974: 516-524) "principal", the person responsible for the content of an utterance or text, even though he is probably not its "author".
9. Italicized type in the example blocks highlights force-dynamic properties and sentences in square brackets are numbered according to the order of appearance in the original. See Appendix.

As an opening salvo, Bush sets the stage by using the schematic struggle between the United States and its principal enemies in the previous centuries' wars: Nazism, Fascism, and Soviet expansionism. The results of these struggles become a conceptual template for subsequent articulations of present-day foreign relations. Several things are worth noting. First, the complex subject noun phrase, *The great struggles of the twentieth century between liberty and totalitarianism*, acquires its meaning in part from an event frame of a (displaced) participant interaction demarcated by a series of punctual events involving two opposed entities. Covertly, one of the participants maybe identified as the present "speaker" and "victor." More specific to the force-dynamic analysis, the composite nature of this event frame highlights a secondary steady-state pattern of Shifting Balance of Strength, with the plural *great struggles* implying many instances of contest between AGO and ANT which ends with one gaining enough strength to overcome the other. The principal question for analysis is which entities are semantically profiled as AGO and ANT, respectively? Are these designations arbitrary labels, or are they semantically motivated?

The semantic structure of "struggles" entails two entities exerting force on each other. Hence, imputing a force-dynamic relation of some kind is warranted; however, there is no clear grammatical clue for determining which entity is to be so assigned. We therefore need to look closer at the semantic structures of *totalitarianism*, *liberty*, and *forces of freedom*. Second, we need to examine their relationships within the entire clause. The meaning of *totalitarianism* entails an entity or set of entities whose purpose is to acquire-the-whole of some other entity or set of entities. Geopolitically, the instantiated meaning implies that one sovereign power intends to acquire-the-whole, namely other sovereign powers. Add to this the fact that *totalitarianism* was specifically used to refer to 'Soviet expansionism' during the Cold War.[10] These profiles provide semantic and pragmatic motivation for assigning *totalitarianism* the AGO role. It manifests an intrinsic force tendency to move. In contrast, the schematic meaning of *liberty*, entails that (sets of) entities manifest a desire to be 'free from external control'. Politically, the instantiated meaning implies that governments intend to 'refrain' from controlling its citizenry. What is more, this term is often used as the

---

10. *Totalitarianism* was often (but not exclusively) used in reference to the Soviet Union, especially during the Reagan administration. While it may be logically possible to use it to refer to the Axis Powers of Italy, Germany, and Japan, the terms *Nazism* and *Fascism* are far more prevalent referents for these regimes.

name for the underlying principle of government. These profiles provide semantic and pragmatic motivation for assigning *liberty* the ANT role. Its intrinsic tendency is to 'block'. The phrasal subject construes the agonistic forces of *totalitarianism* being perpetually counteracted by the antagonistic forces of *liberty*, in effect foregrounding the ANT as a protective barrier.

This role assignment switches when we consider the noun phrase *forces of freedom* in the postmodification of *victory*,[11] with the first element, profiling a schematic AGO and the second element specifying the nature of the force. Now, the United States, as *forces of freedom*, are assigned the AGO role, manifesting an intrinsic tendency toward action, the nature of which seems to be to promote the *single sustainable model of national success*. This switching of roles adds an additional dimension to the flow of energy in the Shifting Balance of Strength pattern: the antagonist gains strength and subsequently realizes its own intrinsic force tendency. It does not merely continue to block the AGO; it becomes the AGO.

The opening sentence evidences a force-dynamic microcosm within the macrocosmic structure of argumentative space. The initial role assignment of totalitarianism as AGO and United States as ANT fits with the traditional *defensive* ideology, hence also fitting with the rhetorical expectation that the United States construes itself as a peaceful nation, willing to defend itself and its allies. The second role assignment of the United States as AGO (leaving the ANT role unspecified and open to interpretation) prepares the way for justifying a policy shift that is prima facie *offensive* in nature, namely that the United States should act as a force for 'the good' (i.e., freedom, democracy and free enterprise). And it is imperative for Bush's purpose that readers first conceptualize the defensive (antagonistic) posture before conceptualizing any offensive posture, as 'liberty' (i.e., governments that refrain from control) is being construed as an end. An offensive (agonistic) posture of United States foreign policy can only be justified as means to this end. The altruistic end, however, is the subject of the very next sentence.

Sentence [2] exhibits a different force-dynamic pattern, the opposite of the Causative Hindrance pattern, in which a stronger ANT permits a weaker AGO to realize its intrinsic force tendency. Such a pattern is particularly useful for construing an idealized relationship between governors and governed.

---

11. Notice that Bush did not use *defenders* or *preservers of freedom*, both of which would have maintained the initial role configuration of the subject.

[2]   In the twenty first century, only nations that share a commitment to *pro-tecting* basic human rights and guaranteeing political and economic free-dom will be able to *unleash the potential of their people* and assure their future prosperity.

In Bush's *National Security Strategy* Report, international terrorism is con-strued alternatively in terms of Onset Causation (individual events) or Ex-tended Causation (permanent condition). Bush construes *nations* as protec-tors. In analytic terms, the ANT blocks (Hindrance) an unspecified AGO who wishes to destroy human rights, political, and economic freedom. Bush ends this sentence by construing *nations* as ideally those that allow their citizens to engage in free enterprise. In analytic terms, *nations* is being construed as an ANT that engages in extended letting which does not impinge upon the second AGO, *their people*. Thus, good nations protect their people against external harm but do not do anything to hinder industry. The event frame is another Participant Interaction with an extended disengagement of the force-dynamic entities.

Bush begins the second paragraph of the Preamble touting the United States' preeminent position in the world, but immediately after claiming such power in sentence [5], claims an inherent disposition against using it. The analysis suggests that a force-dynamic pattern of internal restraint to project an altruistic intention governing the exercise of power, as becomes evident in sentence [6].

[5]   Today, the United States enjoys a position of unparalleled military strength and great economic and political influence.

[6]   In *keeping* with our heritage and principles, we do not use our strength *to press* for unilateral advantage.

Here a single referent, the United States, divides into two entities: the AGO possessing the desire and power to get what it wants and the ANT possessing the necessary strength to restrain the weaker AGO from wielding that power. The ANT side, identified with *our heritage and principles*, keeps the US from using its power inappropriately. They block unjust action. It makes sense that Bush wishes to connect and explain any exercise of power as a manifestation of our heritage to do so for reasons unrelated to selfish inter-ests. Bush construes the United States as the most powerful nation among lawful nations, thereby exploiting an Interrelationship event frame, with the benevolent United States figuring against the rest of the world, allies or ene-mies.

The next sentence is probably one of the most noteworthy and controversial, as the italicized phrase is used again in the preamble and repeated throughout the entire document, and as it is also seized on by one of its critics. It reads:

[7]   We seek instead *to create a balance of power that favors* human freedom: conditions in which all nations and all societies can choose for themselves the rewards and challenges of political and economic liberty.

Bush argues for a foreign policy situation of *balance*, a steady state opposition of forces signaling stasis. The notion of 'balance' in this social-political context typically entails the United States and its allies keeping in constant check the agonistic forces of its enemies. It is this vigilant opposition to these *challenges* that guarantees *political and economic liberty*. At least, this appears to be the intended reading. Bush seems to be arguing that nations need to establish a *balance of power* as a precondition for human liberty. The reasoning in [7], then, is similar to that of the "protecting" and "unleashing" force-dynamic pattern, only that the two event frames of blocking and letting are construed as co-extensive and durational, not as subsequent and punctual, for there is no tense shift from present to future. Instead of a punctual temporal event, a steady state balance is construed as a condition necessary for and coexisting with the activities falling under the heading of human freedom. Should the balance of power shift to the enemies, human freedom will cease to exist.

Recall that Bush began his Preamble by identifying our past enemy, totalitarian regimes that does not characterize the present-day enemy. Sentences 13-15 provide such a characterization, and the principal point is to redefine the nature of the enemy in contrast to enemies of the past.

[13]   Enemies of the past needed great armies and great industrial capabilities to endanger America.
[14]   Now, shadowy networks of individuals can bring great chaos and suffering to our shores for less than it costs to purchase a single tank.
[15]   Terrorists are organized to penetrate open societies and to turn the power of modern technologies against us.

With the events of September 11, 2001, firmly planted in the audience's mind (later to be explicitly invoked), readers have little trouble inferring the plausibility of this kind of threat. The first part of the non-finite clausal adverbial of purpose in sentence [15], *to penetrate open societies*, however, presents readers with a semantic anomaly when coupling *open societies* as the object noun phrase with the verb *to penetrate*, as penetration implies the force-dynamic resistance of its object, which the adjectival noun modifier *open* negates. It may seem odd for terrorists to have to do anything special to penetrate something that is open. The essential feature of the United States is to be open, not to erect barriers for the free movement of individuals within and without. Read this way, the Bush administration wants to argue for a new situation in which an essential characteristic of the United States (its 'openness') leaves its citizens vulnerable. On analysis, the AGO meet no resistance from the ANT. The second part of the adverbial of purpose at the end of the sentence, *to turn the power of modern technology against us*, introduces once again the Shifting Balance of Strength pattern, in which the weaker AGO gains strength directly from the ANT and uses that strength to overcome it. Bush stresses from the beginning that the United States is the world leader in modern technology – especially in matters military – but in this case technological advancement is predicated as an essential property of open societies generally. Bush is safe in assuming that most readers would assent to the factual accuracy of this notion; hence, it is a powerful starting point for establishing this new condition where the weak can become strong by virtue of shifting the balance of power from the strong to the weak. This sentence cluster prepares readers for the explicit argument advanced in [45].

[45]   The events of September 11, 2001 taught us that *weak states*, like Afghanistan, can pose as great a danger to our national interests as *strong states*.
[46]   *Poverty does not make* poor people into terrorists and murderers.
[47]   Yet poverty, weak institutions, and corruption *can make* weak states vulnerable to terrorist networks and drug cartels within their borders.

The warrant for the claim in [45] derives directly from the force-dynamic logic of [13]-[15] in which "shadowy individuals" from weak states penetrate open societies and uses their technological superiority against them. Notice, however, that Bush does not want readers to assign too great a causal role to poverty. Thus, he explicitly denies any direct causal link between poverty and terrorism. However, Bush is also aware that it would seem unreasonable to deny the connection altogether. The relation between sentences [45] and [46] exhibits the kind of meta-discursive move outlined by Talmy (2000: 452-455), with *yet* performing the logic-gater function of conceding-the-point. Therefore, the denial can be glossed force-dynamically as 'I want to deny a direct link between X and Y, but the force of reason dictates that an indirect causal connection exists between X and Y.'

Bush then construes the indirect link between the effects of poverty of the state with sentence [46]. Here our force-dynamic analysis begins with the verb phrase *can make*. The combination of modal auxiliary with causal verb profiles both an AGO and ANT. The auxiliary *can* profiles an AGO with an intrinsic tendency toward motion or action, while the main verb *make* profiles a causative ANT. A "nested" force-dynamic pattern emerges, whereby the state is divided into warring AGO and ANT entities, with *poverty*, *weak institutions*, and *corruption* collectively specifying the AGO pitted against a weakening ANT, *states*. Once weakened, a separate AGO, identified as *terrorist networks* and *drug cartels* overcome the resistance exerted by the ANT. The state is first divided into two opposing forces and second a reintegrated state comes under the influence of forces external to it. Introjection becomes extrajection. The adjective *vulnerable* epitomizes this possible condition. Sentence [47] presents us with an idiosyncratic meaning of *weak*. It simultaneously characterizes (through introjection) an intrinsic quality of certain states (e.g., Afghanistan) and (through a subsequent extrajection), a resultant state of vulnerable (formerly strong) nations. This scenario may serve to contradict readers' typical notions of sovereignty. A sovereignty fits the profile of a strong ANT capable of hindering the efforts of smaller non-sovereign groups. They should easily block these destabilizing forces. The focus of attention shifts to nations who are unable to meet these expectations, and seemingly cannot *govern themselves* [55]. Afghanistan notwithstanding, Bush leaves it to the reader to infer the identity of the so-called *weak states*.

The final objects of analysis focus on Bush's admonishments to free nations. They read:

[52]   In building a balance of power that favors freedom, the United States is guided by the conviction that all nations have important responsibilities.
[53]   Nations that enjoy freedom *must* actively fight terror.
[54]   Nations that depend on international stability *must* help prevent the spread of weapons of mass destruction.
[55]   Nations that seek international aid *must* govern themselves wisely, so that aid is well spent.
[56]   For freedom to thrive, accountability *must be expected and required*.

In the fronted non-finite adverbial clause of [52], Bush recapitulates his conception of the balance of power. It recapitulates the present and future conditions for peace. In this group of sentences, a single reference, *(all) nations*, is divided, through introjection, into AGO and ANT sub-parts in four mini-dramas of national security – enjoying freedom, deterring nuclear proliferation, maintaining international stability, and in seeking foreign aid. All manifest a force-dynamic tendency toward stasis and stability, but the repeated use of the modal verb *must* suggests an inner ANT force that applies pressure toward motion and instability. The antagonistic forces are preventive in nature. Bush is arguing that if a nation, say Saudi Arabia, does not *actively fight terror*, that nation is not a *responsible* nation and thus, at best, is not an ally and, at worst, is an enemy. This move seems designed to align nations along a stability axis, with stable nations able to prevent terrorism and weapons proliferation, and with unstable nations unable to prevent such activities. The rhetorical implication of [56] is that nations may be held *accountable* by several means, military intervention by *the forces of freedom* being one of them.

We have seen that specific force-dynamic patterns, some of which entail onset, punctual, steady state events, while others entail extended causal or letting events over great "expanses" of time. These force-dynamic patterns create local effects of struggles between *forces of freedom* and their enemies to generate the desired inferences about past National Security policies.

3.2. Force-dynamic analysis of Lincoln's second Inaugural Address

Especially when juxtaposed next to Bush's Preamble, Lincoln's *Second Inaugural* seems quietist in pursuit of its ultimate rhetorical goals. This may be a function of the person, but it is also a function of the historical occasion. Lincoln had a task very different from Bush's: it was not to prepare a nation for war, but to prepare a nation for peaceful resumption of state business after a long and bloody internal war. If preparing a nation for war is hard, how difficult must it be to prepare the citizenry to forgive, forget, and forge a new beginning with those who killed a son or brother, or, from a Southerner's perspective, those who took away their heritage and livelihood? Force dynamics has something to add to our understanding of such antithetical rhetorical situations.

The rhetorical trajectory of this brief address is as follows: Lincoln begins by revealing to his audience the behind-the-scenes machinations that brought the nation to war and then acknowledges the common opinion that the North will win the war. In the second paragraph, he explains how the United States found itself at war with itself. Lincoln then elaborates on the causes of war, openly speculating on its providential nature. Expressing hope for a quick resolution to the war, he finishes his speech with a call for reconciliation, shunning sentiments of triumph and victimization alike. Consider first sentence [3].

[3]   Now, at the expiration of four years, during which public declarations have been constantly called forth on every point and phase of the great contest which still absorbs the attention and engrosses the energies of the nation, little that is new *could be presented.*

Much can and has been said about Lincoln's word choice (cf. White 2002), such as his decision to use the noun *expiration* in relation to a quantum of time in the context of war, but what captures my attention is the verb phrase of the main clause in final position, in particular the past tense of the modal verb *can.* As Talmy (2000:440-452) points out, the meaning of *can* contrasts with *may* or *let* precisely along a force-dynamic dimension in that the former profiles the AGO's inherent ability to move or act, whereas the latter two profile the ANT's ability or inclination to hinder or permit such motion or action.

In this case, the implicit AGO refers to the speaker's ability or tendency to say something new. A participant interaction event frame profiles attention on the present speaking situation and a counterfactual alternative situation. In that counterfactual situation, Lincoln talks extensively about the events of the last four years about the *great contest* that endures up to the present time. In the actual situation, Lincoln wishes not to talk about such things. Why? Everybody already knows about such matters. Sentence three achieves the rhetorical effect drawing attention to something at the same time that one denies its importance or relevance. Lincoln calculates that these issues are already present in the minds of his audience. The facts of the case are all too familiar to the audience. Lincoln very cleverly elevates these matters to the status of unassailable facts known to everyone. Expressing new and interesting facts to the audience is simply not possible at this point. In force-dynamic terms, the speaker's impulse (AGO) to find something new to say about the events of the last four years pales in comparison to the weight of recent events (ANT), where everything has been pondered. The AGO is not strong enough to present anything new, a sentiment prompted metaphorically by the past participle, *presented,* because to present something involves bringing something into view. Lincoln sets the stage by using a force-dynamic pattern prompted by the modal verb *can* to shift the attention of the crowd from the present fixation on the bare facts of the recent war to the deeper causes thereof. In that respect, Lincoln has something new to present.

The most contentious sentence of the address appears at the end of the second paragraph. Lincoln says of the North and South:

[9]   Both parties deprecated war, but one of them would *make* war rather than
        let the nation survive, and the other would *accept* war rather than let it
        perish, and the war came. [italics in original]

This sentence exhibits four distinct force-dynamic patterns that advance a
causal argument, with war being construed as a volitional agent moving
along a path toward an end. The first force-dynamic pattern cast the South
(*one*) as the causative ANT and War as and the AGO whose tendency is not to
move or act. The stronger ANT causes war to move into the picture, thus
relying on profiling attention on a participant interaction event frame in
which one entity causes another entity to appear in a particular place. The
second pattern casts the South as the ANT in a negative instance of onset
letting scenario in which *nation* is an AGO whose tendency is to act, where
acting is understood as surviving, but the ANT blocks the AGO from realizing
its intrinsic force tendency. The third pattern casts the North (*the other*) as
the stronger ANT in a similar onset letting scenario, where the AGO's tendency is for action and the ANT "accepts" the manifestation of that action.
The fourth pattern is another instance of onset letting but one that is diamet-
rically opposed to the second. The North is the ANT that blocks the AGO, the
nation, from realizing its intrinsic force tendency, understood as going out of
existence. It keeps the nation from disappearing, and thus has the noble purpose of preventing the dissolution of the nation. In argumentative terms,
these force-dynamic patterns help set up a pattern of mean/ends arguments
in relation to an agreement that the War is undesirable, based on the prior
argument of direction (*both parties deprecated war*) that is no one is arguing about the qualities or definitions of war. The North's end was to keep the
nation together by any means possible; the South's end was to dissolve the
nation by any means possible. Each side was willing to do anything to satisfy pursuit of opposite ends.

   The third and longest paragraph both elaborates on the causes of this
great contest and ponders the God's will and purpose. The clausal subject in
[13] elaborates on the cause of war.

[13]   *To strengthen, perpetuate, and extend* this interest was the object for
        which the insurgents *would rend* the Union even by war, while the Gov-
        ernment claimed no right to do more than *to restrict the territorial
        enlargement of it.*

In this sentence, slavery is construed as an AGO with a tendency to stay put
if not for the causal forces applied to it by the ANT (the South); thus, American Slavery extends into new territory. The second force-dynamic pattern

appears in the relative clause, with the *insurgents* acting as causal ANT exerting force against the Union, cast as an AGO manifesting a tendency toward stasis and inaction. The sentence ends with a hindrance pattern in which the Government, cast as the ANT, blocks slavery, presented as the AGO, from realizing its intrinsic force tendency to move. Lincoln construes the situation in which Southern interests were more destructive than the government by casting the South in the role of causal ANT and profiling them as the primary force setting the nation down the path to war. Lincoln construes the government in terms of a hindrance ANT whose primary duty is to act in the whole nation's interests rather than narrower state interests. While Lincoln acknowledges the culpability of the two sides responsible for the war and its horrific outcome, Lincoln also wants to intimate that this responsibility is not shared equally. Causing or instigating war is worse than failing to stop it, and the fact of war may have been unavoidable and interminable, as Lincoln ponders in sentences [23]-[25].

[23]   If we shall suppose that American slavery is one of those offenses which, in the providence of God, *must needs come*, but which, *having continued through His appointed time, He now wills to remove*, and that He gives to both North and South this terrible war as the woe due to those by whom the offense came, shall we discern therein any departure from those divine attributes which the believers in a living God always ascribe to Him?

[24]   Fondly do we hope, fervently do we pray, that this mighty scourge of war may speedily pass away.

[25]   Yet, if *God wills that it continue* until all the wealth piled by the bondsman's two hundred and fifty years of unrequited toil shall be sunk, and until every drop of blood drawn with the lash shall be paid by another drawn with the sword, as was said three thousand years ago, *so still it must be said* "the judgments of the Lord are true and righteous altogether."

In [23] slavery is construed as the AGO whose tendency is toward stasis. However, a stronger ANT, *God*, causes it to move. Slavery, then, is an entity that moves along a path and the portion of the path profiled references the United States as a sovereign nation. The United States is a stationary point on the path to which the offense of Slavery comes, but whose arrival comes about not of its own volition, rather it *must* come by providential force. The causative force-dynamic pattern thereby calls attention to Slavery as something afflicting the United States. Lincoln concedes that the Southerners' contention that slavery is willed by God may be right – he does not think so, but the fact that the same Scripture can be used to support antithetical positions leaves him less than certain that his reading is the proper one. He then counters that position with the claim that God now wills it gone, thus setting up a second force-dynamic pattern in which Slavery, as a stationary AGO, has to be removed by a stronger ANT. We have a complex mini-narrative of the Slavery issue played out by two force-dynamic events. First, God and His agents, Southerners and plantation owners, drag slavery into this nation. Second, God and his agents, Northerners and abolitionists, remove by force slavery from this nation. In short, if God was on the Southerners' side when slavery began, He is surely now on the Union's side as slavery ends.

Sentence [24] presents another meditation on God's will and this war, interpreted as a *mighty scourge*. We commonly understand afflictions as something that comes enters, stays, and leaves the body. In similar fashion, the object's path event frame profiles the middle portion of the path corresponding to our body. As we can see, the analogy to the corporate body of a nation (i.e., body politic) is evoked easily in such rhetorical situations. Since this sentence seems to be directed toward God, we can interpret Him as the implicit ANT who causes the AGO war to move at a greater pace than it would otherwise. In this case, the force-dynamic AGO is not construed as manifesting a tendency toward stasis so much as manifesting a tendency for slow movement. A greater ANT force will make a stasis-prone AGO move faster through this nation.

Notice also that since the phrase *and war came*, war has been construed as an object moving along a path, either of its own volition or through the forces of the ANT. The speedily passing away of war, for Lincoln, signals that God has chosen to help the nation heal itself quickly. The very next sentence, on analysis, presents the opposite situation in which God, the ANT, *wills it to continue*, meaning that ANT permits the AGO to realize its own force-dynamic tendency toward stasis, or to continue moving at its own pace. Here, as we saw elsewhere in Bush's Preamble, appears an instance of meta-argumentation and expectation, as signaled by the logic-gaters, *Yet* and *so still it must be said*, where the adverbs advance an antagonistic position to the one previously held. The latter phrase functions as a despite force-dynamic pattern such that the contradictory situation signaled by *yet* is not strong enough to overcome Lincoln's faith that God has acted justly, even though the facts on the ground may shake one's faith in a just and benevolent God.

The third paragraph relies most heavily on the metaphors of the nation as a body, of war as a moving entity along a path, and of the nation as a point along a path. Lincoln extends these metaphoric notions with his concluding statement.

[26]   With malice toward none, with charity for all, with firmness in the right as God gives us to see the right, *let us strive on* to finish the work we are in, *to bind up the nation's wounds*, to care for him who shall have borne the battle and for his widow and his orphan, to do all which may achieve and cherish a just and lasting peace among ourselves and with all nations

The ANT, God, permits the AGO, *us*, to *strive on*. Construed this way, the statement creates the impression that the continued existence of the nation depends on divine permission. Mapped onto the implicit history of the United States, the path's starting point begins in 1776 with the *Declaration of Independence*, but comes to a halt in 1860 when the South succeeds and the Civil War begins. With his address, Lincoln wishes to mark the point on the path where *finishing the work* means reuniting the nation and resuming its (metaphoric) journey. Resumption of the nation's journey, however, is God's will. Subsuming national sovereignty under divine right marks the principal moral sentiment of the address. This final sentiment uses a different force-dynamic pattern associated with the verb-particle construction *bind up*. Now appears a situation where the *wounded* nation is both AGO and ANT, another example of semantic introjection. The AGO part would correspond metaphorically to 'its blood and guts', which manifest a tendency to move out of the body, while the ANT part is 'the skin and bandages' that keep everything together and inside. The NATION AS A BODY is a common conceptual metaphor, and a rhetorically powerful and resonating one. This pattern works because people and nation relate both via metonymy and synecdoche: emotional resonance usually reserved for the former can easily migrate to the latter.

3.3. Summary: Force dynamics and the rhetoric of argument

The two texts display similar force-dynamic tactics in the service of complementary strategies: Bush's Preamble uses them to generate the strong impression that the United States will not only defend itself against attack, but will forcibly engage so-called weak states before they can amount any attack. What is more, the motivation for such action stems from a desire to promote democracy and free enterprise. Force-dynamic patterns help the administration profile the Unites States variously as a benevolent causative antagonist, determined preventive antagonist, and, perhaps most controversially, a good intentioned agonist. Lincoln's address, on the other hand, manifests many of the same force-dynamic patterns, particularly the notion of the government as a preventative antagonist and uses it to explain a past (or passing) conflict rather than to argue for a particular position in a future one. Consistent with the more contemplative and theological tone of Lincoln's address, distinct force-dynamic patterns appear, such as the presentation of God as both a preventative and permissive antagonist, and of war as a stationary agonist, with the latter providing the means of expressing great uncertainty and ambiguity about the ultimate responsibility for the Civil War. Such uncertainty and ambiguity does not emerge from Bush's Preamble.

4. Conclusion: The rhetorical functions of force-dynamic patterns

As demonstrated in the above analyses, force-dynamic patterns and the event frames on which they rely perform important rhetorical functions. They are crucial in understanding how the local discourse evokes specific imagery for specific rhetorical purposes, such as terrorists as entities with an inherent disposition to act, or the government as entities charged with preventing certain actions and enabling others. Force dynamics is a schematic imaging system for *construing* discourse actors in relation to one another, and therefore offers a useful perspective and method of understanding how specific linguistic features can satisfy tactical aims. At the same time, the same schematic imaging system is useful for understanding how specific patterns can be used in combination to satisfy different strategic goals, as suggested by the two analyses presented above.

Force-dynamic patterns play a critical role in structuring concepts at the local lexical, phrasal, and clausal levels, which in turn produce strategic effects at the global rhetorical level. To the extent that such image-schematic notions are fundamental to human imagination and reasoning, their use in an analysis of an important document of obvious historical importance is an important first step in understanding the conceptual nature of rhetorical effect.

References

Barsalou, Lawrence
   1999   Perceptual symbol systems. *Behavioral and Brain Sciences* 22: 577-
            660.

Brandt, Per Aage
   2004   *Spaces, Domains, and Meaning: Essays in Cognitive Semiotics.*
           Bern: Peter Lang.
Bush, George, W.
   2002   *National Security Strategy of the United States of America.* The
           White House, Washington D.C., available from <www.whitehouse.
           gov/nsc/nss.html>.
Fauconnier, Gilles, and Mark Turner
   2002   *The Way We Think: Conceptual Blending and the Mind's Hidden*
           Capacities. New York: Basic Books.
Campbell, Karlyn Kohrs, and Kathleen Hall Jamieson
   1986   Inaugurating the presidency. In *Form, Genre, and the Study of Po-*
           litical Discourse, Herbert W. Simons, and Aram A. Aghazarian
           (eds.), 203-225. Columbia: University of South Carolina Press.
Dieter, Otto Alvin Loeb
   1950   Stasis. *Speech Monographs* 17: 345-369.
Dishong, Greta
   2004   Force-dynamic aspects of the genetically modified food debate.
           M.A. Thesis, Case Western Reserve University.
Goffman, Erving
   1974   *Frame Analysis.* Boston: Northeastern University Press.
Johnson, Mark
   1987   *The Body in the Mind: The Bodily Basis of Meaning, Imagination,*
           and Reading. Chicago: University of Chicago Press.
Lakoff, George
   1996   Sorry I'm not myself today: The metaphor system of conceptualiz-
           ing the self. In *Spaces, Worlds, and Grammar*, Gilles Fauconnier,
           and Eve Sweetser (eds.), 91-123. Chicago: University of Chicago
           Press.
Langacker, Ronald W.
   1987   *Foundations of Cognitive Grammar*, Volume 1: *Theoretical*
           Prerequisites. Stanford: Stanford University Press.
   1999   *Grammar and Conceptualization.* Berlin/New York: Mouton de
           Gruyter.
Lincoln, Abraham
   1994   Second inaugural address. In *The Presidents Speak: The Inaugural*
           Addresses of the American Presidents, from Washington to Clinton,
           Davis Lott (ed.), 81-83. New York: H. Holt and Co.
Mandler, Jean M.
   2004   *The Foundations of Mind: Origins of Conceptual Thought.* Oxford:
           Oxford University Press.

Perelman, Chaïm, and Lucie Olbrechts-Tyteca
  1969   Reprint. *The New Rhetoric: A Treatise on Argumentation*, Trans-
          lated by John Wilkinson and Purcell Weaver. South Bend: Univer-
          sity of Notre Dame Press [original 1958].
Talmy, Leonard
  2000   *Toward a Cognitive Semantics.* Vol. 1. *Concept Structuring Sys-
          tems.* Cambridge, Mass.: MIT Press.
Turner, Mark
  1991   *Reading Minds: The Study of English in the Age of Cognitive Sci-
          ence.* Princeton: Princeton University Press.
White, Ronald C.
  2002   *Lincoln's Greatest Speech: The Second Inaugural.* New York:
          Simon and Schuster.

Appendix

Preamble to National Security Strategy of the United States of America

[1] The great struggles of the twentieth century between liberty and totalitarianism ended with a decisive victory for the forces of freedom – and a single sustainable model for national success: freedom, democracy, and free enterprise. [2] In the twenty-first century, only nations that share a commitment to protecting basic human rights and guaranteeing political and economic freedom will be able to unleash the potential of their people and assure their future prosperity. [3] People everywhere want to be able to speak freely; choose who will govern them; worship as they please; educate their children – male and female; own property; and enjoy the benefits of their labor. [4] These values of freedom are right and true for every person, in every society – and the duty of protecting these values against their enemies is the common calling of freedom-loving people across the globe and across the ages.

[5] Today, the United States enjoys a position of unparalleled military strength and great economic and political influence. [6] In keeping with our heritage and principles, we do not use our strength to press for unilateral advantage. [7] We seek instead to create a balance of power that favors human freedom: conditions in which all nations and all societies can choose for themselves the rewards and challenges of political and economic liberty. [8] In a world that is safe, people will be able to make their own lives better. We will defend the peace by fighting terrorists and tyrants. [9] We will preserve the peace by building good relations among the great powers. [10] We will extend the peace by encouraging free and open societies on every continent.

[11] Defending our Nation against its enemies is the first and fundamental commitment of the Federal Government. [12] Today, that task has changed dramatically. [13] Enemies in the past needed great armies and great industrial capabilities to endanger America. [14] Now, shadowy networks of individuals can bring great chaos and suffering to our shores for less than it costs to purchase a single tank. [15] Terrorists are organized to penetrate open societies and to turn the power of modern technologies against us.

[16] To defeat this threat we must make use of every tool in our arsenal – military power, better homeland defenses, law enforcement, intelligence, and vigorous efforts to cut off terrorist financing. [17] The war against terrorists of global reach is a global enterprise of uncertain duration. [18] America will help nations that need our assistance in combating terror. [19] And America will hold to account nations that are compromised by terror, including those who harbor terrorists – because the allies of terror are the enemies of civilization. [20] The United States and countries cooperating with us must not allow the terrorists to develop new home bases. [21] Together, we will seek to deny them sanctuary at every turn.

[22] The gravest danger our Nation faces lies at the crossroads of radicalism and technology. [23] Our enemies have openly declared that they are seeking weapons of mass destruction, and evidence indicates that they are doing so with determination. [24] The United States will not allow these efforts to succeed. [25] We will build defenses against ballistic missiles and other means of delivery. [26] We will cooperate with other nations to deny, contain, and curtail our enemies' efforts to acquire dangerous technologies. [27] And, as a matter of common sense and self-defense, America will act against such emerging threats before they are fully formed. [28] We cannot defend America and our friends by hoping for the best. [29] So we must be prepared to defeat our enemies' plans, using the best intelligence and proceeding with deliberation. [30] History will judge harshly those who saw this coming danger but failed to act. [31] In the new world we have entered, the only path to peace and security is the path of action.

[32] As we defend the peace, we will also take advantage of an historic opportunity to preserve the peace. [33] Today, the international community has the best chance since the rise of the nation-state in the seventeenth century to build a world where great powers compete in peace instead of continually prepare for war. [34] Today, the world's great powers find ourselves on the same side – united by common dangers of terrorist violence and chaos. [36] The United States will build on these common interests to promote global security. [37] We are also increasingly united by common values. [38] Russia is in the midst of a hopeful transition, reaching for its democratic future and a partner in the war on terror. [39] Chinese leaders are discovering that economic freedom is the only source of national wealth. [40] In time, they will find that social and political freedom is the only source of national greatness. [41] America will encourage the advancement of democracy and economic openness in both nations, because these are the best

foundations for domestic stability and international order. [42] We will strongly resist aggression from other great powers – even as we welcome their peaceful pursuit of prosperity, trade, and cultural advancement.

[43] Finally, the United States will use this moment of opportunity to extend the benefits of freedom across the globe. [44] We will actively work to bring the hope of democracy, development, free markets, and free trade to every corner of the world. [45] The events of September 11, 2001, taught us that weak states, like Afghanistan, can pose as great a danger to our national interests as strong states. [46] Poverty does not make poor people into terrorists and murderers. [47] Yet poverty, weak institutions, and corruption can make weak states vulnerable to terrorist networks and drug cartels within their borders.

[48] The United States will stand beside any nation determined to build a better future by seeking the rewards of liberty for its people. [49] Free trade and free markets have proven their ability to lift whole societies out of poverty – so the United States will work with individual nations, entire regions, and the entire global trading community to build a world that trades in freedom and therefore grows in prosperity. [50] The United States will deliver greater development assistance through the New Millennium Challenge Account to nations that govern justly, invest in their people, and encourage economic freedom. [51] We will also continue to lead the world in efforts to reduce the terrible toll of HIV/AIDS and other infectious diseases.

[52] In building a balance of power that favors freedom, the United States is guided by the conviction that all nations have important responsibilities. [53] Nations that enjoy freedom must actively fight terror. [54] Nations that depend on international stability must help prevent the spread of weapons of mass destruction. [55] Nations that seek international aid must govern themselves wisely, so that aid is well spent. [56] For freedom to thrive, accountability must be expected and required.

[57] We are also guided by the conviction that no nation can build a safer, better world alone. [58] Alliances and multilateral institutions can multiply the strength of freedom-loving nations. [59] The United States is committed to lasting institutions like the United Nations, the World Trade Organization, the Organization of American States, and NATO as well as other long-standing alliances. [60] Coalitions of the willing can augment these permanent institutions. [61] In all cases, international obligations are to be taken seriously. [62] They are not to be undertaken symbolically to rally support for an ideal without furthering its attainment.

[63] Freedom is the non-negotiable demand of human dignity; the birthright of every person – in every civilization. [64] Throughout history, freedom has been threatened by war and terror; it has been challenged by the clashing wills of powerful states and the evil designs of tyrants; and it has been tested by widespread poverty and disease. [65] Today, humanity holds in its hands the opportunity to

further freedom's triumph over all these foes. [66] The United States welcomes our responsibility to lead in this great mission.

George Bush
The White House, Washington, D.C., September 17, 2002

Lincoln's Second Inaugural Address

Fellow-Countrymen:

[1] At this second appearing to take the oath of the Presidential office there is less occasion for an extended address than there was at the first. [2] Then a statement somewhat in detail of a course to be pursued seemed fitting and proper. [3] Now, at the expiration of four years, during which public declarations have been constantly called forth on every point and phase of the great contest which still absorbs the attention and engrosses the energies of the nation, little that is new could be presented. [4] The progress of our arms, upon which all else chiefly depends, is as well known to the public as to myself, and it is, I trust, reasonably satisfactory and encouraging to all. [5] With high hope for the future, no prediction in regard to it is ventured.

[6] On the occasion corresponding to this four years ago all thoughts were anxiously directed to an impending civil war. [7] All dreaded it, all sought to avert it. [8] While the inaugural address was being delivered from this place, devoted altogether to *saving* the Union without war, urgent agents were in the city seeking to *destroy* it without war – seeking to dissolve the Union and divide effects by negotiation. [9] Both parties deprecated war, but one of them would *make* war rather than let the nation survive, and the other would *accept* war rather than let it perish, and the war came.

[10] One-eighth of the whole population were colored slaves, not distributed generally over the Union, but localized in the southern part of it. [11] These slaves constituted a peculiar and powerful interest. [12] All knew that this interest was somehow the cause of the war. [13] To strengthen, perpetuate, and extend this interest was the object for which the insurgents would rend the Union even by war, while the Government claimed no right to do more than to restrict the territorial enlargement of it. [14] Neither party expected for the war the magnitude or the duration which it has already attained. [15] Neither anticipated that the *cause* of the conflict might cease with or even before the conflict itself should cease. [16] Each looked for an easier triumph, and a result less fundamental and astounding. [17] Both read the same Bible and pray to the same God, and each invokes His aid against the other. [18] It may seem strange that any men should dare to ask a just God's assistance in wringing their bread from the sweat of other men's faces, but let us judge not, that we be not judged. [19] The prayers of both could not be an-

swered. [20] That of neither has been answered fully. [21] The Almighty has His own purposes. [22] "Woe unto the world because of offenses; for it must needs be that offenses come, but woe to that man by whom the offense cometh." [23] If we shall suppose that American slavery is one of those offenses which, in the providence of God, must needs come, but which, having continued through His appointed time, He now wills to remove, and that He gives to both North and South this terrible war as the woe due to those by whom the offense came, shall we discern therein any departure from those divine attributes which the believers in a living God always ascribe to Him? [24] Fondly do we hope, fervently do we pray, that this mighty scourge of war may speedily pass away. [25] Yet, if God wills that it continue until all the wealth piled by the bondsman's two hundred and fifty years of unrequited toil shall be sunk, and until every drop of blood drawn with the lash shall be paid by another drawn with the sword, as was said three thousand years ago, so still it must be said "the judgments of the Lord are true and righteous altogether."

[26] With malice toward none, with charity for all, with firmness in the right as God gives us to see the right, let us strive on to finish the work we are in, to bind up the nation's wounds, to care for him who shall have borne the battle and for his widow and his orphan, to do all which may achieve and cherish a just and lasting peace among ourselves and with all nations.

Abraham Lincoln,
Capitol, Washington, D.C., March 4, 1865

Author index

Subject index

Cognitive Linguistics Research

Edited by René Dirven, Ronald W. Langacker and
John R. Taylor

Mouton de Gruyter · Berlin · New York

---

1   Ronald W. Langacker, *Concept, Image, and Symbol. The Cognitive Basis of Grammar.* 1990.

2   Paul D. Deane, *Grammar in Mind and Brain. Explorations in Cognitive Syntax.* 1992.

3   *Conceptualizations and Mental Processing in Language.* Edited by Richard A. Geiger and Brygida Rudzka-Ostyn. 1993.

4   Laura A. Janda, *A Geography of Case Semantics. The Czech Dative and the Russian Instrumental.* 1993.

5   Dirk Geeraerts, Stefan Grondelaers and Peter Bakema, *The Structure of Lexical Variation. Meaning, Naming, and Context.* 1994.

6   *Cognitive Linguistics in the Redwoods. The Expansion of a New Paradigm in Linguistics.* Edited by Eugene H. Casad. 1996.

7   John Newman, *Give. A Cognitive Linguistic Study.* 1996.

8   *The Construal of Space in Language and Thought.* Edited by Martin Pütz and René Dirven. 1996.

9   Ewa Dąbrowska, *Cognitive Semantics and the Polish Dative.* 1997.

10 *Speaking of Emotions: Conceptualisation and Expression.* Edited by Angeliki Athanasiadou and Elżbieta Tabakowska. 1998.

11 Michel Achard, *Representation of Cognitive Structures.* 1998.

12 *Issues in Cognitive Linguistics. 1993 Proceedings of the International Cognitive Linguistics Conference.* Edited by Leon de Stadler and Christoph Eyrich. 1999.

13 *Historical Semantics and Cognition.* Edited by Andreas Blank and Peter Koch. 1999.

14 Ronald W. Langacker, *Grammar and Conceptualization.* 1999.

15 *Cognitive Linguistics: Foundations, Scope, and Methodology.* Edited by Theo Janssen and Gisela Redeker. 1999.

16 *A Cognitive Approach to the Verb. Morphological and Constructional Perspectives.* Edited by Hanne Gram Simonsen and Rolf Theil Endresen. 2001.

17   *Emotions in Crosslinguistic Perspective.* Edited by Jean Harkins and Anna Wierzbicka. 2001.

18   *Cognitive Linguistics and Non-Indo-European Languages.* Edited by Eugene Casad and Gary B. Palmer. 2003.

19.1 *Applied Cognitive Linguistics I: Theory and Language Acquisition.* Edited by Martin Pütz, Susanne Niemeier and René Dirven. 2001.

19.2 *Applied Cognitive Linguistics II: Language Pedagogy.* Edited by Martin Pütz, Susanne Niemeier and René Dirven. 2001.

20   *Metaphor and Metonymy in Comparison and Contrast.* Edited by René Dirven and Ralf Pörings. 2002.

21   *Grounding. The Epistemic Footing of Deixis and Reference.* Edited by Frank Brisard. 2002.

22   Cristiano Broccias, *The English Change Network.* 2003.

23   *Cognitive Approaches to Lexical Semantics.* Edited by Hubert Cuyckens, René Dirven and John Taylor. 2003.

24   *Cognitive Models in Language and Thought. Ideology, Metaphors, and Meanings.* Edited by René Dirven, Roslyn Frank and Martin Pütz. 2003.

25   Rong Chen, *English Inversion. A Ground-before-Figure Construction.* 2003.

26   Liesbet Heyvaert, *A Cognitive-Functional Approach to Nominalization in English.* 2003.

27   Catherine E. Travis, *Discourse Markers in Colombian Spanish. A Study in Polysemy.* 2005.

28   *Studies in Linguistic Motivation.* Edited by Günter Radden and Klaus-Uwe Panther. 2004.

29   *From Perception to Meaning. Image Schemas in Cognitive Linguistics.* Edited by Beate Hampe, in cooperation with Joseph E. Grady. 2005.

30   Nick Riemer, *The Semantics of Polysemy. Reading Meaning in English and Warlpiri.* 2005.